SMOLDERING CITY

HISTORICAL STUDIES OF URBAN AMERICA
A series edited by James R. Grossman and Kathleen N. Conzen

SMOLDERING CITY

CHICAGOANS AND THE GREAT FIRE, 1871–1874

KAREN SAWISLAK

THE UNIVERSITY OF CHICAGO PRESS
CHICAGO AND LONDON

The University of Chicago Press, Chicago 60637
The University of Chicago Press, Ltd., London

Printed in the United States of America
16 15 14 13 12 11 10 09 08 07   2 3 4 5 6

ISBN-13: 978-0-226-73548-1 (paper)
ISBN-10: 0-226-73548-6 (paper)

Library of Congress Cataloging-in-Publication Data
Sawislak, Karen.
Smoldering city : Chicagoans and the Great Fire, 1871–1874 / Karen Sawislak.
p. cm. — (Historical studies of urban America)
Includes bibliographical references (p.) and index.
1. Fires—Illinois—Chicago—History—19th century. 2. Chicago (Ill.)—History—To 1875. I. Title. II. Series.
F548.42.S29 1995
977.3′11—dc20 95-4677
CIP

♾ The paper used in this publication meets the minimum requirements of the American National Standard for Information Sciences—Permanence of Paper for Printed Library Materials, ANSI Z39.48-1992.

For my parents

CONTENTS

ACKNOWLEDGMENTS

In the course of researching and writing this book, I received fellowship support from Yale University and Stanford University. A visiting fellowship at the Newberry Library in 1989 permitted me to spend three extremely valuable months in Chicago. Finally, a year at the Stanford Humanities Center in 1993–94 gave me the space, time, and support to complete the manuscript.

I am grateful to the librarians and staff at the Newberry and at Yale's Sterling and Seeley Mudd Libraries for all of their assistance and wise counsel. My thanks as well to the many people who make the Chicago Historical Society such a wonderful place to work, especially Archie Motley, Janice McNeill, and Russell Lewis.

I have been very lucky in my teachers. First and foremost, it is hard to overstate the debt that I owe to David Montgomery. In my undergraduate years, his lecture courses on American labor first got me to thinking that I might someday like to work as a historian. Later, as I hunted for a seminar paper topic in my first semester of graduate school, he suggested that I might investigate the working-class response to the Chicago Fire—a suggestion that eventually grew into this book. He has been an unfailingly generous mentor. My work as a scholar has been deeply informed by his insight and imagination, and I have learned an enormous amount from his advice and his example. Over many years, William Cronon has taught me a great deal about the craft of research and writing. I thank him for his rigorous readings of earlier versions of this manuscript, and for all of his encouragement and support. Deepest thanks as well to Jean-Christophe Agnew, another longtime teacher and friend. For their examples and encouragement, I am also grateful to Howard R. Lamar and Edmund S. Morgan.

On research trips to Chicago, Carl Smith has been a source of especially generous and enthusiastic support. I have also profited greatly from conversations with Toni Gilpin, John B. Jentz, and Rima Lunin Schultz. Peter Eckstrom graciously shared his unpublished work, and Terry Fife kindly took the time to investigate the availability of certain materials. As I wrote the dissertation that became this book, another set of Chicagoans arranged part-time jobs, donated computer services, and generally eased my way: my thanks to Gary Isaac, Jacqueline Stanley Lustig, Laurie Merel, Cindy Pogrund, and Lenore Wineberg.

In the latter stages of revisions, David Goldberger, Martha Ophir, and Maureen Harp all came to my aid as research assistants. At a crucial moment, Sebastian Simsch graciously helped with translations.

At the University of Chicago Press, Doug Mitchell has been a model of patience and compassionate support, as have Lila Weinberg and Matt Howard. It has been a great pleasure to work with James Grossman and Kathleen Neils Conzen, whose mix of steady encouragement and incisive criticism much improved this book.

Numerous friends and colleagues have taken the time to comment on all or part of this manuscript. Robin Einhorn and Philip Ethington were kind enough to read an early draft; both offered searching comments that helped to guide my process of revision. For debts accrued over the many stages of life of this manuscript, I also owe thanks to Eric Arnesen, Cecelia Bucki, Kathleen Canning, Tony Fels, Susan Gilman, David Godshalk, Michael Goldberg, Katherine Hermes, Margo Horn, Yvette Huginnie, Reeve Huston, Susan Johnson, Cathy Kudlick, Steve Lassonde, Barbara Lassonde, Chris Lowe, Glenna Matthews, Katherine Morrissey, John Mason, Kathryn Oberdeck, Kim Phillips, Priscilla Wald, Glenn Wallach, and Glennys Young. I especially want to thank Jacqueline Dirks and Paul Longmore for their constant support and friendship.

At Stanford, I have benefited from the camaraderie and insights offered by Philippe Buc, Albert Camarillo, Gordon Chang, George Fredrickson, Estelle Freedman, Steve Haber, Ellen Neskar, Jack Rakove, Richard Roberts, Aron Rodrigue, Debra Satz, and Laura Smoller. David Kennedy kindly read a draft of the manuscript as it neared its completion, and offered much astute advice. Over the course of hour upon hour of close readings and untold numbers of conversations, Mary Louise Roberts brought her many gifts to this book. I am most grateful for her generosity and for her sustaining friendship.

Finally, I wish to acknowledge my parents, Toby and Richard Sawislak. It is a great joy to dedicate this book to them, with deepest thanks for all that they have given to me.

INTRODUCTION

As in our national life the old regime is divided from the new by the Civil War of 1861, so in the mind of Chicagoans the city's past is demarcated from the present by the great fire of 1871.

Frederick Francis Cook
Bygone Days in Chicago, 1910.

At approximately 9 o'clock on the evening of Sunday, October 8, 1871, a company of firefighters rushed to respond to an alarm called in from the Southwest Side of Chicago. Fires were no rarity in the city: apart from its stone and brick downtown, the owners of property had most often chosen to build with wood—creating an urban landscape, like those of most nineteenth-century American cities, that stood at constant risk of devastation by flames. By mid-October, after long months of drought, Chicagoans had already endured a rash of blazes. The previous evening, a substantial crowd of spectators indeed had witnessed what seemed a major calamity when five square blocks burned clean near Patrick and Catherine O'Leary's cow barn, the site of this new alarm. Again hearing the bells that warned of fires, one immigrant peddler—a habitual "firebug" who had entertained himself the night before by looking on as the firemen did battle—asked his two fellow lodgers to go out to investigate the new blaze. But his friends were not interested. "Why should I care as long as our house is not on fire?" asked one. "There is a fire every Monday and Thursday in Chicago!"[1] Persuaded by such logic, quite sure that he was missing nothing he would not soon see again, the man went to bed.

But the fire of October 8, of course, proved most extraordinary. Driven by a gale-force southwest wind, and feeding on the parched timbers that had seen no rain for many weeks, it rapidly grew far out of control. The sleeping peddler and his friends awoke to a nightmare, as the flames cast an eerie glow on the masses of people who struggled to escape through stifling clouds of dust, smoke, and cinders. Over twenty-four hours later, lacking fresh fuel and further tamed by a lucky rainstorm, the conflagration would finally die. But in that time the heart of Chicago had burned away. Few even knew how to begin to account for the magnitude of loss; one report eventually concluded that "the seeds of permanent or temporary disease sown, the bodily suffering and mental anguish endured can never have statistical computation or adequate description."[2] Still, some important numbers are worth noting, figures that offer an immediate measure of the scope of destruction. Almost 300 lives were lost to the Great Fire, and, among the survivors, over 100,000 of the city's approximately 300,000 residents were left homeless. The blaze, moreover, leveled more than 18,000 buildings, completely destroying the downtown business district and many thousands of homes and small businesses.

Thanks to a host of witnesses, reporters, and other commentators, the massive fire in Chicago on October 8 and 9, 1871, was quickly and forever transformed into the Great Chicago Fire. For many, the scale of the conflagration perfectly befit the burgeoning reputation of Chicago—an urban wonder that had seemingly grown in an instant, only to be laid low in a matter of hours. Even before the disaster, those who sought to promote the city had steadily boasted of a collective urban character marked by grit, determination, and achievement despite any hardship. Now, facing this great trial, city boosters accordingly stepped back, took a deep breath, and went about transforming these devastating losses into "our greatest blessing."[3] As the narrative went, an extraordinary city, one that had mushroomed from a tiny, swamp-ridden outpost to a great metropolis in just a few decades, now faced an extraordinary challenge—and would, inevitably, rise triumphant. "The miracle of Chicago's growth," as one anonymous writer proclaimed, "has been equalled only by the magnitude of her downfall. But both will be surpassed by the miracle of her resurrection."[4] The lesson was clear: as past history had shown, the future of this urban place could only be equally marvelous.

Similarly, such commentaries left no doubt that the people of Chicago would join together to rebuild: in the face of a great test, a clear unity of purpose and the highest forms of human strength, kindness, and self-sacrifice seemed certain to emerge. A trade monthly editorial thus offered its statement of faith that every Chicagoan would join in this great common cause: "For all our energies are aroused, all our faculties at work, all our brains alive, and when a community is thus awoke to a determined and united purpose—only the angels can transcend their power."[5] Businessman James Milner, writing six days after the fire, proudly noted the tenor of "general sentiment" among his fellow citizens, making the claim that this was a people that embodied the best qualities of the nation: "[T]here is no whining, no 'Black Friday' hair tearing and insanity, but a grand manliness of feeling that shows American character of the highest type."[6] Disaster, Milner argued, had brought out the finest in an already "superior" populace, a display of energy and enterprise certain to be recorded as a shining example of the highest "types of human nature developed in modern civilization." To the minds of those who maintained a steadfast faith in their city, the common will that met the ravages of the Great Fire would prove yet another mark of distinction for the metropolis and its people.

James Milner capped his impassioned homily with the following aside: "I am getting prophetic." And in fact he was. For historians of Chicago have long written about the Great Fire with a tone of awe and deference that in many ways does not far depart from Milner's own heroic vision. Often talked about and celebrated in interpretations that closely mirror those originally put forth by such boosters, the disaster and its legacy have received scant analysis. Recent scholarship does include more critical evaluations of the Great Fire: Christine M. Rosen has studied its effect upon infrastructure and spatial relations, Ross Miller has analyzed the impact of the disaster upon representations of the history of the city and its architectural aesthetics, and Carl Smith has treated this episode as a case study of "urban disorder."[7] Still, the traditional historiography of the Great

Fire generally falls into one of two categories: dramatic recountings of the Fire as event, narratives that are largely commemorative of the disaster as a sensational ordeal, or treatments that instead view the Fire as a watershed in the growth of Chicago and further posit a story of community consensus in the face of devastation as a paradigm for reconstruction—and a stepping stone to future development.[8]

It is hardly incorrect, of course, to think of the Great Fire as both a momentous event and an important turning point in the history of Chicago. The destructive force of the disaster without question had enormous significance, leading to critical shifts in land use, new forms of investment, and innovations in technology and architecture that all hastened the transformation of the city into its modern form.[9] Nor is it incorrect to speak of the Great Fire and of the amazingly swift process of reconstruction that followed in language that might otherwise seem hyperbolic: this was an ordeal so apart from ordinary realms of experience that survivors seldom felt themselves able to find the words to describe what they had endured. Chicagoans, moreover, did manage to bring about a resurrection of their city that can be quite properly deemed heroic: contemporary observers and historians alike have convincingly documented the remarkable mobilization of capital and labor power that erased most visible traces of destruction within a year—and even allowed the city to expand and improve as it was rebuilt. Perhaps because its allegory of devastation and regeneration is indeed rooted in so many exceptional achievements, the Great Fire over time has taken on a benign symbolic stature quite apart from the actual horror, disruptions, and hardship that it brought to the people of the city.

But such a seamless record of achievement (and the societal consensus it tacitly assumes) has long concealed the many sharp conflicts that emerged out of this great civic trauma. Late January of 1872, for example—the cruel midst of the winter that followed hard upon the conflagration—brought a telling dispute to light. Two soup kitchens set up to aid fire victims, facilities funded by donations collected in the city of Cincinnati, were angrily censured by the executive secretary of the Relief and Aid Society: a private, elite-led charity that had received the mayor's charge to supervise municipal relief. Wirt Dexter, a respected attorney and long-time activist in the work of urban charity, demanded that the Cincinnatians immediately cease to provide a free bowl of soup to all—a practice and policy that assumed the "legitimate" need of any person who appeared at their doors. A champion of the emerging methods of "scientific charity," Dexter could not countenance the labors of the soup kitchen. In his view, all proper agents of relief had to conduct rigorous investigations meant to determine the "worthiness" of potential clients, and maintain close records of their dispensations: two basic precepts of "scientific" charity that the Cincinnati operation had opted to ignore.

Small and self-contained as a dispute over soup kitchens may seem, this conflict in fact encompassed warring understandings of fundamental social values and problems. Those who worked to deliver aid to tens of thousands of victims here struggled with issues such as the meaning of humanitarianism, the nature of poverty, and the very foundations of urban order. What truly irked Dexter was his belief that the soup kitchen possibly rewarded the idle, that a person who might otherwise be induced to earn his or her keep here could receive a meal—no questions asked. Such outright, unregulated handouts, he thought, would very likely corrode the good character of those who ate in these kitchens, instilling the habit of "dependence." For Dexter, the bowls of soups dispensed at the Cincinnati kitchens could be best described as the "bread of idleness"; a free lunch or dinner, he argued, posed an intolerable threat to "the highest welfare of the community."[10] Yet for those who ran the Cincinnati Relief Committee, a soup kitchen did not loom as a menace to future order. To the contrary, such a facility to them seemed the most direct and efficient way to deliver assistance to the largest number of suffering Chicagoans. Despite the vehemence of Dexter's complaints, secure in their own sense of their "good" works, they refused to shutter their facilities.[11]

As this episode suggests, there is another way to understand the historical meaning and importance of the urban event known as the Great Chicago Fire. Precisely because the conflagration worked its ravages in a great and growing metropolis, it is especially problematic to allow a more simple story of recovery and progress to stand alone. For cities are places that by definition are varied in their population and segregated in their physical forms, two basic conditions of "urbanism" that immediately caution against any assumption of some sort of equality of experience for all Chicagoans.[12] A new generation of urban history, moreover, has paid close attention to how cities encompass a diverse array of social groups, groups arranged into hierarchies of means, status, and authority. All of these relationships (and the forms of power they in turn bestowed) were obviously at play in the course of the January argument over the social value of the soup kitchen—and many other postdisaster points of contention.

This study, therefore, looks at the event known as the Great Chicago Fire through a close examination of the wide-ranging debates it set in motion. It explores what such an extraordinary crisis can reveal about the "ordinary" social, cultural, economic, and political relations of a nineteenth-century American city.[13] In the days and months that followed the disaster, many sorts of people living in one spatial area, under a common system of governance, and within the structural confines of the urban economy met up with a massive disruption of the regular patterns of their daily lives. During this period, they faced sweeping questions involving the meanings of charity and social welfare, work and labor relations, definitions of morality, and the limits and nature of political authority and state power. Individual Chicagoans—people divided by categories of identity such as class, ethnicity, and religion—understood and negotiated these problems in very different ways.

An episode that has long and largely remained the property of "boosters" thus can be reread as a key chapter in the social and political history of a city rapidly growing into its modern form. Further, an examination of the Great Fire in this way presents a case study of the interworkings of identity and power in an urban community. When Chicagoans struggled to cope with the ravages of the conflagration, an emergency forced them to deal quite explicitly with problems basic to their shared civic identity and fate. Their debates, in turn, exposed the array of values and perspectives that different individuals brought to these public discussions. For even as the disaster added to the mythos of their community, vesting this urban place with a particular history and common identity relating

Ruins of the Court House and City Hall.
Courtesy of Chicago Historical Society, ICHi-02722.

to the Great Fire, it at the same time required that a diverse urban polity come to terms with its true multiplicity of social identities and interests. How these many interests and identities both reflected and defined the shape of what was understood to be an acceptable civic order is the subject of this book.

It is probably impossible to portray the multiple parts of any city in their full complexity—but any understanding of the debates and contests set in motion by the Great Fire must be grounded in at least a brief sketch of the predisaster history and reputation of this particular urban place, and an outline of the economic systems and hierarchies, spatial divisions, cultural differences, and political institutions that together composed the metropolis around the time of its disaster. In 1871, as the Great Fire made its indelible mark, what shaped the fabric of life in Chicago? Who were the people who made their homes in its neighborhoods, went to work in its fast-moving economic world, and participated in its social life and politics? What sorts of structures and rules were shared by its many kinds of people?

From their city's earliest days, Chicagoans had seldom shied away from a chance to trumpet their own potential and achievement. This vigorous self-image involved more than local pride: in the latter half of the nineteenth century, no American city seemed a better symbol of national industry and progress. The story of the explosive growth of Chicago joined together the apparently boundless promises of western expansion, commercial opportunity, and individual gain, shining with the appeal and luster of all things new and vital. "There are no old men here, or old houses," wrote the *Land Owner* in 1869. "What has been is of little moment in Chicago; what is and will be, are the only care."[14] Even the *New York Tribune*, a jealous defender of the greatness of its own city, could not deny the stunning evolution of its rival. "Throughout the North, and especially the West and Northwest, there has been a steady, sound, and healthy growth," wrote the paper in 1868. "The growth of Chicago, however, must be conceded to be its magnificent and truly unprecedented culmination."[15] The archetypical "City of the West" by the time of the Great Fire, this was a place that both realized and symbolized the linear notion of progress so closely linked to visions of national potential in the nineteenth century.[16] Steeped in this set of images, many saw Chicago as the ideal place to pursue their own dreams.

To be sure, nineteenth-century Americans had ample reason to marvel (or shudder) at the story of this particular city: Chicago was most certainly a place that had earned its reputation.[17] Insisting that their town could become the grand central metropolis, local boosters built and secured the canals and railroads that transformed a once-obscure trading post into the nation's premier entrepôt.[18] A midpoint between the more densely settled East and the rapidly developing West, the trade of an expanding nation converged in Chicago.[19] Rail and steamship lines brought lumber, grain, and meat to the city, feeding the massive natural resource-processing industries that initially anchored the urban economy. The same transport networks carried finished consumer goods both to and from the city, sparking the development of a wide array of manufacture. Well on the way to commercial preeminence by the 1860s, the Civil War gave Chicago another crucial boost: far enough from the war fronts to be safe from invasion, the city profited enormously from its central role in supplying the Union forces.[20] A varied and expanding economy, moreover, attracted a growing citizenry. Between 1837, the date of official incorporation, and 1870 the population shot from 5000 to over 300,000.[21]

No other urban place was quite like what the *Land Owner* immodestly and frequently described as "Chicago the Magnificent." In terms of the sheer growth and pace of change that marked its extremely rapid development, this city plainly had no American equal. Yet, it is important to recognize that Chicago was not entirely unique: by the time of the Great Fire, the metropolis was marked by many of the characteristics typical of nineteenth-century urban society.[22] Common patterns of spatial segregation had emerged: a distinct downtown served as the center of commerce, specific districts housed industrial activities, and the inhabitants of the city had arranged themselves into neighborhoods that in large part reflected the class and ethnic identities of their residents.[23] Following the lead of eastern urbanites, Chicagoans (with the approval of the Illinois legislature) had constituted themselves as citizens of a municipality formally governed by a "weak" mayor, popularly elected commissions that controlled services such as public works and police and fire protection, and a Common Council made up of aldermen elected by ward.[24] Finally, though its remarkable expansion had indeed set Chicago apart as a site of opportunity and entrepreneurship (and far more frequently than in most American cities, people of all social classes were owners of property), the urban economy was taking a decided turn toward wage labor in the realm of industrial production.[25] Moreover, as in all large commercial centers in the nation, an increasing number were employed by increasingly larger businesses in the salaried labor coming to be known as "white-collar" work.[26] Leaders of business, industry and finance; practitioners of the increasingly regularized professions such as law, medicine, or engineering; salesmen and clerks; skilled artisans and shopkeepers; factory workers and day laborers—all, whatever their own place in the urban economy, were still subject to the speculative busts (and spectacular booms) of nineteenth-century capitalism. Despite its boosters' claims to a most singular destiny, Chicago in many ways exemplified the mass of forces that fueled the process of "urbanization" in the latter half of the nineteenth century.[27]

In terms of the identity of its people and the web of relationships that they in turn formed, Chicago was similarly both a representative and distinctive American city. Like the older cities of the East, Chicago by 1871 was marked by a high degree of demographic variation. This urban community was a home shared by a population divided most obviously by nativity and subsequent categories of ethnicity.[28] A tight linkage between immigration and urbanization had already been forged in the middle decades of the nineteenth century; along with sizable numbers of domestic migrants from more rural places, new arrivals from Europe continually set down roots in America's cities. Chicago followed this pattern—and, as it grew, emerged as an especially magnetic destination for the foreign-born.[29] By 1870, the city was home to a very large concentration of German, Irish, and Scandinavian immigrants and their children, a population of "foreigners" that far outnumbered that of native-born Americans.[30] What the *Northwestern Christian Advocate* wrote of Chicago in 1893 would have been equally true some twenty years earlier. "Ours," proclaimed the paper, "is a foreign city."[31]

Who were these immigrants, the families and single sojourners who formed the ethnic settlements that, in the words of one resident, gave Chicago the look of several "distinct cities"?[32] Approximately one-third of all Chicagoans at the time of the Great Fire were former residents of the states consolidated in 1871 as the German nation; the largest concentration of such people outside of their homeland primarily lived and worked in the city's North Division.[33] Chicago was far less Irish than New York or Boston, but the sons and daughters of Erin and their own offspring still comprised almost twenty percent of the city. Irish immigrants (like the notorious O'Learys) most often made their homes on the Southwest Side, near the stockyards, packinghouses, and docks where many found employment.[34] Finally, along with a still-minuscule black community, smaller groups of Canadian, British, and Southern and Eastern European–born people also had settled across the city. Given its especially high number of foreign-born residents, issues connected to ethnicity—problems of identity, religious and cultural differences, and political integration—were a live set of questions for the whole of the city.

"Yankees"—native-born men and women and their children—were thus a decided minority. The founding families of Chicago had moved West in the 1830s and 1840s but never severed their cultural and commercial ties to the East, especially New England and upstate New York.[35] By the 1870s, their proportion of the populace had dwindled to approximately twenty percent, but they had lost little of the influence and authority that they had from the first maintained: in the mold of older cities of the East, Chicago was in many ways dominated by an "urban elite" that one local journalist described as an assemblage of "the native Americans derived from English-speaking ancestry and the Protestant faith."[36] Living in their own very posh or at least comfortable neighborhoods, the native-born ran the largest businesses, amassed the greatest fortunes, controlled the wealthiest and most prominent benevolent and cultural organizations, and supplied nearly all of Chicago's mayors—a record of achievement that largely corresponds to that of the mostly American-

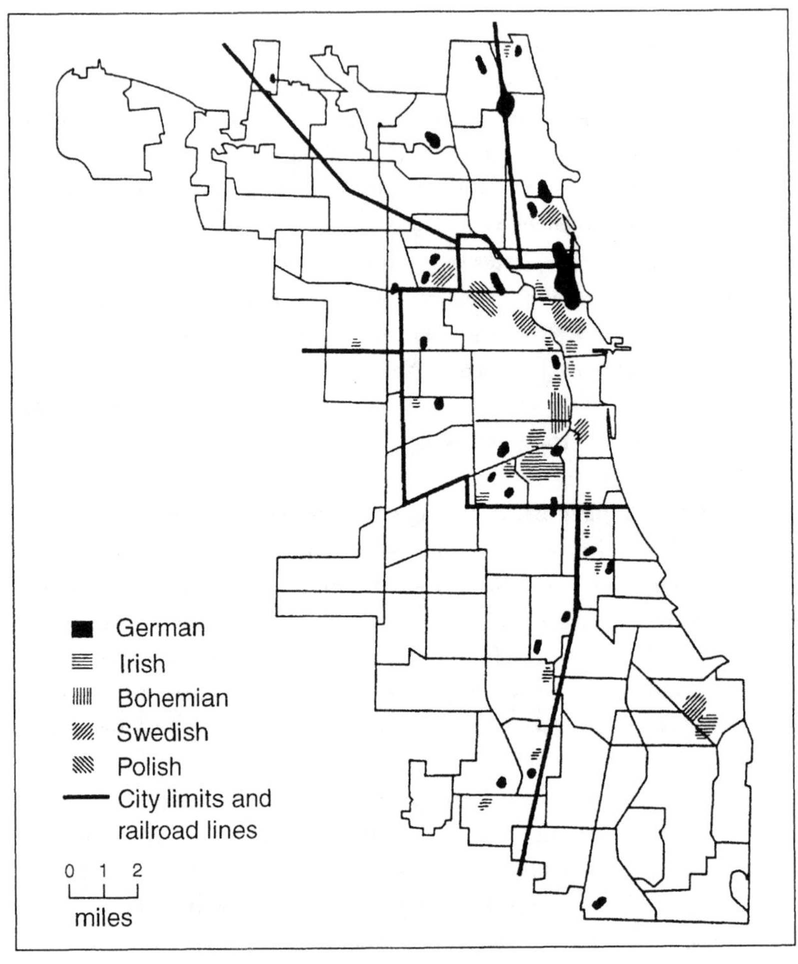

Chicago ethnic community settlement pattern, 1870. Source: Eric L. Hirsch, *Urban Revolt* (Berkeley: University of California Press, 1990), 67.

born "upper stratas" of all of the nation's cities.[37] Yet, as Frederic Jaher has noted, Chicago's rapid growth and explosive economy set apart its "urban establishment": in comparison to older cities, a noteworthy number of native-born business, professional, and civic leaders were men who themselves had earned their own sizable fortunes in their own lifetimes.[38] Along with its dearth of old men and old houses, Chicago harbored little inherited wealth. Its most prominent and influential citizens were very likely to be self-made businessmen, leaders who, from the lessons of their own lives, firmly believed in the rewards that awaited enterprising individuals—and the failures meted out to those who did not try hard enough to make their own way in the urban economy.[39]

Nativity, as in other nineteenth-century cities, had a profound (if not deterministic) impact upon economic rank, and the related and trickier designation of social class. Some immigrants of course amassed great fortunes, and certain "Yankees" struggled to survive. Still, aggregate statistics show that the twenty percent of households headed by the native-born held over two-thirds of the total wealth of the city and monopolized most nonmanual work.[40] On this abstract economic ladder, Germans tended to occupy the city's middle ranks. Skilled and semi-skilled laborers headed over half of these immigrant families; slowly but steadily profiting from the mostly favorable economic conditions of the Civil War era, a large number of German households had attained a level of median family wealth that allowed them to own their own homes.[41] Yet while this pattern held true for most Germans, their immigrant community also contained a flourishing middle class—and, conversely, many among the very poor. In the mold of other urban populations, most Irish filled the lowest ranks of the city, serving as Chicago's semi- and unskilled labor force. Overall, the Chicago of 1870 thus exhibited a highly skewed distribution of wealth, a pattern that would have seemed familiar to most urban dwellers of the day. According to the calculations of the economist Edward Bubnys, twenty percent of the richest families, mostly native-born, had accumulated ninety percent of the total assets of the city. And at the other end of the ladder, half of Chicago's households—a group composed largely of the foreign-born—held less than one percent.[42]

Such aggregate statistics and patterns raise issues that have structured many inquiries into the social order of American cities: the definition and meaning of class identity, and the question of the interrelation of class and ethnicity.[43] On the surface, it is easy in this case to discern a plain and important polarity—that the working people of the city of Chicago were overwhelmingly immigrants and that its wealthiest citizens were largely native-born Americans. It is much harder, however, to draw a more nuanced picture of class divisions with a like sense of certainty: recent scholarship cautions against any reliance upon either a blunt materialism or a simple equation of ethnicity or nativity with class.[44] Still, if hard to define with true precision, it is clear that class remained a very meaningful category of identity for Chicagoans.

Because of the diversity of people they enclosed in a bounded space and their complex economies, cities were great incubators of class formation in the nineteenth century. From their own language and activities, it is obvious that the Chicagoans of the 1870s understood such designations as "the laboring classes" and "the businessmen." They often referred to themselves in terms telling of class hierarchies and identities, employing such descriptions, for example, as "mechanic" or "capitalist." Some in the city further maintained a great concern with gender roles, the structure of families, and norms of "respectability," ostensibly "private" conduct that increasingly was seen as a sign of belonging to (or differing from) the emerging urban middle class.[45] The terminology of politics and public debate, moreover, gives frequent evidence of the import of class identity: someone fearful or disdainful of working people might collectively denigrate them as the "mob" or the "proletaire"; someone in turn angered by a man of great wealth might deem him a "monopolist" or "bloodsucker." The category of class, then, plainly was present in the ways that Chicagoans identified themselves as people distinct from one another, and conceived of the overall shape of their urban order.

According to the memoir of journalist F. F. Cook, an analysis of urban life that he penned in 1910, the Chicago of the 1860s and early 1870s was most often misunderstood. Because of its spectacular rise and the opportunities it symbolized, he wrote, many viewed the city as a place "representative of democratic equality." But to him, Chicago was in fact far better described as a community built upon "a framework of sharply accented lines traversing every sphere of life."[46] Cook's point is well-taken: as many scholars have demonstrated, American cities in the nineteenth century were theaters of class formation and places where concentrations of immigrants very visibly raised issues of ethnic difference. Chicago, the metropolis of great destiny and promise, was thus also a city like any other city: a community constructed out of a culturally diverse population arranged into social and economic hierarchies. For all of the institutions, structures, history, and even values and beliefs that Chicagoans shared, those social differences and the meanings they came to acquire were crucial to the politics of the city: the resolution of questions that confront a community of citizens.[47] Their Great Fire, with all the massive problems it raised, accordingly offered a signal moment for such a reckoning.

Historians have an increasingly clear sense of how class, ethnicity, and gender, with other categories of identity, inscribed F. F. Cook's "framework of sharply accented lines" across urban communities; recent studies of nineteenth-century American cities have added much depth and complexity to our understandings of these places and their people.[48] Throughout this book, I have sought to pay close attention to the delineation and meaning of such social boundaries and hierarchies. My own broadest conceptual framework, however, assumes that these "accented lines" were drawn in relation to a common point of reference and debate: an evolving and active contest to define the shape of civic order.

Particular communities and institutions in Chicago, as in all urban places, were and are part of a larger whole; individuals rooted in specific social identities were joined not only by the geographic space they occupied but by common ties to the urban economy and forms of municipal governance. Moreover, these people assigned diverse meanings to an identity they all shared and to varying degrees wished to claim: that of the "good" citizen or citizens—the individual or group with the authority to define a "public interest," to set a "best" course for Chicago. Taken together, the ways that Chicagoans understood such commonalities and differences added up to what I refer to as their sense of urban or civic order: an ideal that was in no way timeless or static but was constantly challenged and defended by many city residents in their efforts to impose distinct visions of just what their city should be. By concentrating on a period of crisis when central problems of urban order were suddenly opened to more obvious contest by the impact of the Great Fire, I seek to explore how people drew upon their own more specific social roles and identities to map out their understandings of their larger community. This book thus aims to reconstruct what I understand to be essential linkages between the social and political history of the city.[49]

Because post–Great Fire debates over urban order involved real policies and outcomes, I have sought to connect my analysis of the interrelations of social and civic identities with the question of authority. How do people claim to represent the "public interest"? How is authority legitimated? And how, finally, is it won and exercised? The subject is power, and, in some ways, the classic urban studies query of "who governs?"—a notion that has structured much inquiry into the political history of American cities—still pertains.[50] There are no quick answers to be found in these pages, for the resolutions to different problems did not conform to any one pattern. Accordingly, I have tried to give due weight to a variety of causal factors: individual agents were sometimes key, a broader cultural context often had an impact, the material constraints imposed by the workings of the economy cannot be dismissed, and the particularity of institutional forms at times had a determinative effect. To avoid oversimplification, it is important to back away from the metaphor of the "power game": given the complexity and variety of issues, motivations, and forms of agency at play, it is ultimately misleading, if tempting, to assign people the permanent roles of "winners" or "losers."

Still, some individuals and groups plainly exercised more influence over civic decisions than others. My argument—that native-born businessmen were the bearers of a substantial amount of power—will come as no surprise to students of urban history. But I am not interested simply in identifying incidents of "dominance"—rather, I attempt to explain how the "public interest" came to be theirs. Such men did not form an absolute block, and they did not always get what they wanted. Indeed, there are episodes in this book that might be cited as examples of how a representative democracy "works" to express the will of a broad array of voters. It seems plain, however, that the Great Fire struck at a time when the deep faith in the free market and the liberal individual held by many of these businessmen was becoming evermore tightly linked to their understandings of a true democracy and the whole of urban order. In their view, these values represented the norm; without question, they were confident that their vision was the best way for all of the people of the city. How were different people, or people who held to different ideas, thus defined as outside of (or a threat to) that order? Alternatively, how did these other people put forth claims to civic authority, to the "public interest," that rested on a form of difference? What I finally seek to explore in these pages are the ways that "universal" concepts and values such as justice, equality, or government by law are defined and understood by more particular sets of people, and how such definitions and understandings are in turn constitutive of relations of power.[51]

A word on sources. I have drawn on a diverse collection of materials: the wealth of fire histories sprung from America's first great national "media event," working papers and proceedings of the municipality, records of charity organizations, city journals and periodicals, and the memoirs and letters of individuals. Still, the sources upon which I am most heavily reliant are newspapers—journals that were invaluable for their presentation of and commentary upon an array of civic debates. Newspapers of the late nineteenth century were organs of opinion in ways that they generally are not at present; specific editors, publishers, and journalists tended to identify quite explicitly with particular partisan stances, and frequently claimed to typify the views of particular communities, such as German-Americans, or "the business class."[52] In my usage of these materials, since I often draw upon their editorial comments as representative of the thinking of specific social groups, I have tried to be precise about the editorial sympathies of newspapers and their own modes of self-identification. The new owners of the *Chicago Tribune* published this credo in 1865: "The newspaper is the great educator of the age, and if conducted in the interests of public virtue is the principle safeguard of liberty and law."[53] Such a lofty declaration says something about the *Tribune*'s own style and values, but it also speaks to my premise: that these daily and weekly journals were essential social and political documents of their time, the most regular and comprehensive sources of information of the day *and* a medium meant to persuade. Though I at many points rely upon their reportage for more "factual" descriptions, it is their partisan and social identities that makes them so critical to my analysis.

This book tells a chronological story of the Great Fire and its sequel, with each chapter revolving around a specific civic debate. My first chapter examines how Chicagoans and others made sense of the experience of the disaster and the ways that broader perceptions of urban disorder had an impact upon the first responses of city authorities. In Chapter 2, I turn to the administration of relief, and what this process in turn revealed of understandings of charity and community. Chapter 3 looks at the effort to limit wooden construction in the rebuilding city, a campaign that highlighted conflicting understandings of civic obligation and the rightful role of municipal authority. Chapter 4 considers the actual work of the "Great Rebuilding" and further centers on the problems posed and faced by unions of construction workers. Chapter 5 narrates a battle over Sabbatarian codes sprung from a post–Great Fire rise in crime, a set of events that raised questions about morality, law, and state power. An Epilogue carries through the onset of the Panic of 1873, concluding with an analysis of how the people of Chicago began to make sense of a new disaster—this one an urban crisis born of workings of the national economy.

Finally, while I have written about the Great Fire and what this episode meant for the people of Chicago, Chicagoans were of course part of a wider nation and wider world. Accordingly, this book demonstrates how a local case study can engage the very broadest questions of politics and society—and can help to reconstruct the wide range of answers offered up by nineteenth-century urbanites.

Much of what faced the people of Chicago—the dilemmas and conflicts raised by a new and increasing diversity of cultures and classes, the meanings of an industrializing economy after the end of slavery, evolving understandings of the balance between individual rights and state power—confronted all Americans. A close examination of the city in the aftermath of its unique disaster is in this sense suggestive of what went on in any other urban place in a nation that was rapidly coming to assume its modern form. Though many who lived in Chicago around the time of the Great Fire were quite sure that theirs was the most extraordinary metropolis the world had ever seen, it is clear that a study of this community offers insights into the urban history of the nation. It speaks, as well, to a process that still engages all Americans: the making and remaking of understandings of worthy citizenship, social difference, and civic order.

CHAPTER ONE

Barriers Burned

On October 8, 1871, an entire American community burned to the ground. A spark found a foothold in a landscape left bone dry by months of drought—and once the blaze had begun, nothing could be done to check the advance of what quickly became a giant conflagration. Trapped by inescapable walls of smoke and flame that closed in from every direction, over 2000 men, women, and children perished. One horrible day witnessed a level of human loss and devastation never before seen in the nation—and, indeed, never yet seen again. Such are the facts of the deadliest fire in the history of the United States: the Great Fire of Peshtigo, Wisconsin.[1]

It is surely an odd coincidence that at least two major fires ravaged the Upper Midwest on the same day, at almost the same hour.[2] It is just as surely no accident, however, that only a few Americans outside of Wisconsin know about the complete incineration of Peshtigo, a small lumbering settlement north of Green Bay encircled by the pine forests that provided so much of the wood that built (and rebuilt) Chicago.[3] For the terrible tidings of the fate of an entire rural town immediately became a mere footnote to the story of what had befallen the great and growing city. Few would even hear about the stunning toll at Peshtigo, as the fascination and drama of life, death, and struggle in Chicago took center stage in the public imagination.

Instantly carried across the nation by telegraph even as the flames marched forward, news of the Great Chicago Fire found an insatiable audience. In Boston and New York, crowds battled to catch a glimpse of the latest dispatches posted outside the offices of newspapers and telegraph agents.[4] Newspaper and magazine correspondents flooded into the burned city, and survivors eager to tell their stories streamed out; as the *Prairie Farmer*, which counted fourteen "eyewitness" speakers just one week after the flames died, would wryly comment: "[I]f the people of the United States don't know about the Chicago fire before spring it will be because they do not attend the lectures."[5] Journalists and other writers rushed to compose their book-length treatments of the inferno; Alfred Sewell, a reporter for the *Chicago Times*, scooped his competitors with a sixty-page pamphlet excitedly entitled *The Great Calamity!*[6] After that, as local historian Joseph Kirkland observed, "followed enough volumes to form a small library": publishers released no fewer than seven substantial Fire histories by the end of 1871, a mere three-and-one-half months after the disaster.[7]

Two obvious questions emerge out of a consideration of the two Great Fires. Why did the story of the tragedy at Peshtigo, a day that claimed more than six times as many lives as Chicago's inferno, fall so far from view? And why, conversely, did the Great Chicago Fire so rivet the attention of the nation? The obvious difference between the two settings of the conflagrations seems the crucial answer: Peshtigo was a modest if thriving lumber port, but Chicago was a great city. Its Great Fire was therefore a disaster uniquely urban in its character, a force that destroyed and disordered a giant built environment, hundreds of millions of dollars of property, and the lives of more than 300,000 people. What happened to the people of Peshtigo could be distilled to a painful but simple story: these were the victims of "nature."[8] But any understanding of an urban conflagration could not be so clear-cut. For many, the Fire seemed yet another symbol of an urban world that always poised on the brink of disaster, a tense and constant state inherent to the social differences and social relations that were a part of almost every city.

Cultural historians have long understood that the fantastic growth of nineteenth-century cities presented Americans with a paradox: these sites of the greatest of human achievements also seemed home to the greatest of human ills.[9] Contemporary writers frequently considered the dualisms of "the city," producing a literature that was obsessed with the apparent polarities of these new and mysterious places. Throughout the second half of the nineteenth century, an expanding middle-class readership routinely absorbed sensational novels, journalism, and works of social criticism that centered around the "good" and "evil" that supposedly held sway in every city, pieces of narrative that called alarmed attention to the specifically urban phenomenon of expanding gaps between the lives of the very rich and the very poor—the wretched and often dangerous characters who were further marked by differences of ethnicity and race.[10] Metaphors for urban life that bespoke a permanent menace, an ever-present threat to stability and order found in the very diversity of the city, commonly appeared in this discourse: one of the most famous formulations of such a vision placed New Yorkers atop a seething "volcano," and another warned all Americans that their great "nerve centers" were also "storm centers."[11]

The "true" melodramas of the Great Chicago Fire thus in a sense retold what was already entrenched as a familiar story: despite its most unusual scope, the disaster and its sequel in many ways conformed to what a wide audience already expected of an urban event. In representations of the Great Fire, the facts and fictions of life in the city indeed seemed to run together; as one eyewitness observed, "[T]here have certainly occurred more hair breadth escapes and thrilling incidents than would fill a large volume, and these too of such a nature as would vie with the wildest fancies of a sensationalist."[12] The endangering of lives, the shattering of the ordinary protections of the state and the family, the devastation of the spatial and social boundaries that structured the limits of ordinary urban life—the ever-present disorder of the city long-expressed by its contemporary chroniclers here found a concrete reality.

In the face of an urban catastrophe, the fears of urban dwellers were raised to the fore, anxieties that were to some degree structured by the notion of the city as a place that always verged on some sort of disruption. The Great Chicago Fire of course visited the sort of serious traumas that are a part of every major disaster; it makes perfect sense that the survivors would constantly express their lingering worry and longings for a renewal of stability. But it is important to recognize that the experience of conflagration not only brought the people of Chicago face-to-face with the elemental force of fire. It also, to a most unusual degree, brought them face-to-face with each other, offering a blunt reminder of the social differences that were a part of every great city. Living through such a massive urban disaster thus involved more than a common experience of chaos and struggle. It produced particular perceptions of the shape of disorder and, as a consequence, particular ideas about what should reign as the "norms" of civic order. The ways that the Great Fire was experienced, the ways in which it was remembered and retold, and the ways that authorities moved to restore calm and secure people and property in the first days and weeks of the aftermath of course impart a great deal about what it was like to survive a horrifying trauma. But these narratives and sets of decisions are also revealing of prevailing understandings of urban social relations —and particular visions of just what was required to reconstruct a sense of "order" in a great city that some viewed as essentially and eternally under siege.

RETELLING THE FIRE

"Where shall I begin? How shall I tell the story that I have been living during these dreadful days?"[13] These words of an unidentified woman express a sentiment frequently echoed in accounts of the Great Fire. For many who wrote about the disaster, the unimaginable reality they had endured led them to lament the descriptive limits of ordinary words. "All concur," declared Reverend E. J. Goodspeed, "in declaring that language fails to do justice to the rush and roar of the elemental forces."[14] Bewildered by the drama and perils of the blaze, survivors again and again disclaimed their own ability to provide a "true" account of what they had witnessed. "It is not possible for those who saw the city burn," H. W. Thomas, a local historian, declared, " . . . to describe the scene so as to make it appear real to others. Indeed, they cannot make it real for themselves."[15] Journalist Alfred Sewell offered a similar caution: "[Y]ou may read descriptions of it, but these at best are tame, lame, and indefinite to one who has beheld the reality."[16] Yet, for all the apparent unrealities they mean to communicate, accounts of the

Great Fire are grounded in the actualities of the event: a daylong holocaust that destroyed, displaced, and killed.

How did the people of Chicago perceive and endure the dangers and bedlam of this night and day? An overwhelming disorder plainly ruled: those who lived through these hours describe a total transformation of their physical world. In the glare of flames and clouds of smoke, dust, and cinders, little of a once-familiar landscape could be recognized. To a large degree, the social and spatial boundaries that characterized urban life also fell before the inferno. Crowds that hurried to escape the flames shared an experience of mass confusion and horror; all Chicagoans were linked by a human will and instinct to survive an unstoppable and devastating force of nature. Still, what seemed a universal sense of chaos and disorder was at the same time experienced and negotiated by individuals on more particular terms. As the Great Fire made its march through the city, just where and who a person happened to be without question played a central role in constructing certain parts of the awful story that survivors felt themselves unable to retell with true adequacy.

Intensely dry conditions, a 20-m.p.h. southwest wind, and an unfortunate spark at approximately 10 o'clock on the night of October 8 all combined to turn Chicago into what two historians of the Great Fire would describe as "a vast ocean of flame."[17] The chronically undermanned fire department, already exhausted by the effort required to subdue the major blaze that had raged on the West Side only the previous evening, rushed at the first alarm to the soon-to-be infamous O'Leary barn. But the strong, steady wind fanned the flames, blowing showers of burning shingles and charcoal sparks northeast toward an industrial district of lumberyards, wooden warehouses and sheds, and coal heaps—"everything," as one commentator later noted, "that would make a good fire."[18] When the flames reached the sixteen acres desolated the night before, the firemen hoped that the blaze might die for lack of fuel. This newly bare patch did act as a buffer zone, sparing the West Side from any further damage. But the driving force of the wind proved unstoppable; easily breaching the natural barrier posed by the south branch of the Chicago River, the Great Fire began to feed on the equally flammable structures of the Southwest Side.

Within four hours of its humble genesis, the Great Fire became so large, so hot, and moved so quickly that firefighters and fire engines could not stand fast before it. Proceeding north, the fire descended upon Conley's Patch, an Irish immigrant shantytown typical of this poor neighborhood, with little warning.[19] Flames, heat, and smoke roared through the flimsy and densely packed structures, in minutes claiming many of the victims of the disaster. Fire next engulfed the municipal gasworks; the explosion of a massive holding tank added an enormous amount of especially volatile fuel to the already raging blaze. Street lights all across the city flickered and died, plunging the streets into a darkness broken only by the ever-brighter glow of flames.

By the time the Great Fire reached the central business district, it no longer needed the south wind or contact with fresh fuel to continue to move north. For the mile-wide holocaust at this point began to exhibit what firefighters call a convection effect, the physics and chemistry of a giant conflagration that produce a concentrated thermal updraft—a phenomenon that allows a massive blaze to generate its own forward motion. Chicago's fire, in more simple terms, had now become a firestorm. Thomas Mosher, Jr., the official weatherman of the city, described how the wind at ground level blew straight toward the center of the fire from all directions, resulting in "a decided whirling motion in the column of flame and smoke, which was contrary to the hands of a watch."[20] Smoldering beams and rafters, blazing asphalt roofs, and clouds of smaller sparks and cinders were all propelled far into the sky. "The very air," one survivor recalled, "was full of flame."[21] Carried north by the prevailing winds in the upper atmosphere, the flaming chunks of debris started new fires wherever they fell. The tremendous heat, moreover, often resulted in spontaneous combustions far in advance of any actual flames. In the face of such an intense blaze, mercantile buildings that had been touted as "fireproof"—the downtown built mostly of brick and stone that was the pride and joy of city boosters—offered little more resistance than the wooden rookeries of Conley's Patch. Bricks withstood the heat, but mortar dissolved, collapsing masonry walls. Throughout the center of the city, marble crumbled and iron melted.

Those who were awake on the North Side could hear the alarms and look south to see the red glare. But most residents remained in their beds, trusting that the barrier posed by the main branch of the Chicago River would protect their division—until they rudely awakened to the fact that this particular fire would not stop until there was no more to burn. Around 3:30 A.M., the Great Fire gained its first purchase on the North Side. Flaming debris borne aloft by convection currents ignited a blaze that disabled the machinery at the municipal waterworks, and the main body of fire leaped the river soon after. Since Chicago had just one pumping station and that facility was now incapacitated, firefighters could do nothing more: for almost twenty hours the fire marched north, as writer Frank Luzerne observed, "without enemy to oppose it."[22] In the North Division, where tens of thousands of German and Scandinavian immigrants resided, fewer lives were lost than in the poorer districts of the South Division, but nearly every building was incinerated. Among the structures of any size, only the mansion of real estate millionaire Mahlon D. Ogden miraculously remained intact, the beneficiary of a lucky shift in the wind.[23] At the northern limits of the city, four-and-one-half miles distant from its origins in Mrs. O'Leary's barn, the Great Fire was finally extinguished near midnight. With only prairie grass and dried sod left for fuel, the holocaust could consume nothing more.[24]

"There has never been a fire," wrote a *New York Tribune* correspondent, "which so completely attended to its business."[25] Photographs of the devastated downtown indeed show nothing more than enormous heaps of rubble and remnants of walls.[26] Areas built of wood were swept entirely clean—left, in the words of one observer, "a bare, treeless, vacant plain."[27] Charred hulks of ships burned at anchor, and the skeletal remains of bridges clogged the river. When people returned to their homes and businesses, they found little to salvage; the concentrated heat did more than damage—by any reckoning, it destroyed. As the wholesaler A. C. Stinson wrote to a business associate in Boston, "I have christened this barren region

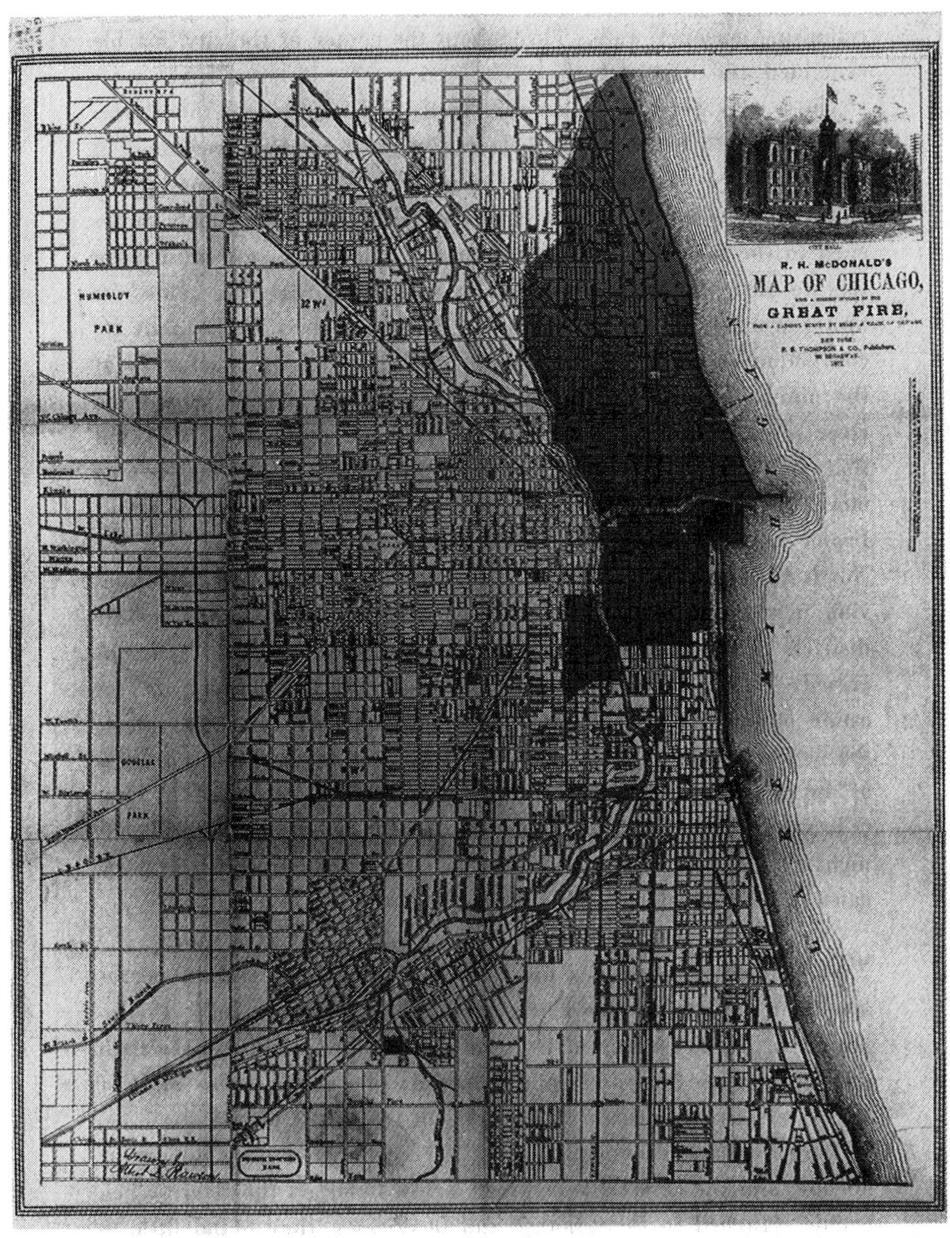

Chicago in 1871. Shaded portion of the map is the area burned by the Great Fire. Courtesy of Chicago Historical Society.

of our fair city as Debrisville; another good name would be, not the Burnt District, but the *District of Desolation.*"[28]

The Great Fire, in sum, burned over 2100 acres, a swath equal to almost three-and-one-half square miles. According to journalists Elias Colbert and Everett Chamberlin, two local reporters who authored the most comprehensive account of the disaster, 17,420 buildings were destroyed, and nearly 100,000 city residents lost their homes. The West Division, where the fire began, suffered by far the least damage: 500 modest residences and businesses were lost, with 2250 left homeless. In the South Division, site of the business center, the fire consumed all of the most expensive and valuable buildings in Chicago. Wholesale stores, hotels, banks, insurance, law, and newspaper offices, the Post Office, Customs House, and Court House were leveled; a total of 3650 buildings fell, including 1600 stores and 60 factories. Over 21,000—mostly the working-class inhabitants of the near South Side and the waterfront vice district—lost their homes. As substantial as they are, these figures pale in comparison to the virtually complete demolition of the North Side. Of the 13,800 prefire structures in this division—expensive lakeside homes and a great mass of worker cottages, storefronts, small manufactories, churches, schools, and saloons—only 500 remained intact. An astonishing 74,450 people, one-fourth of the city's population, were left without shelter.[29]

Such a statistical summary offers a vivid sense of the magnitude of the material devastation. Yet these numbers and totals do not begin to account for the emotional terrors and sense of dislocation endured by the thousands of Chicagoans who, quite literally, ran for their lives. The straight, broad, and level streets of the city speeded evacuation, a circumstance that doubtless saved many. But the tens of thousands who were forced to flee found themselves caught up in a pandemonium, scenes of intense tumult and confusion where every ordinary fact of life seemed to have gone awry. The crowd itself was frighteningly anonymous; friends, as Aurelia King remembered, were almost unrecognizable, "we were all so blackened with smoke."[30] Panic-stricken people, many clad only in nightclothes, tried to carry away whatever they could save. Businessman Thomas Foster was especially struck by a reversal of the capacities seemingly dictated

An Affecting Scene. A Sick Girl is rescued by her heroic Sister at the Peril of her Life.

Eine ergreifende Scene. Ein krankes Mädchen wird von ihrer heldenmüthigen Schwester mit Riskirung des eigenen Lebens gerettet.

Illustration from a German-language "instant" history published in Philadelpha in 1871: *Das Grosse Feuer im Chicago.* Courtesy of Chicago Historical Society, ICHi-15762.

by gender and age: he reported that "old women were carrying trunks too heavy for men, and young women were dragging trunks heavy enough for a donkey to pull."[31] The crowd jostled for space with domestic animals, the carriages of the well-to-do, and teamsters' wagons, a mix of beings seldom if ever seen before. When their loads grew too heavy, many abandoned their property to save themselves; according to Mary Fales, the "sidewalks were covered with furniture and bundles of every description." Fales remembered a night that had become day: "[T]he whole earth, or all we saw of it, was a lurid yellowish-red."[32] The exceptionally graphic words of an anonymous survivor finally conjure a complete chaos, a relentless assault upon all of the senses: "Everywhere dust, smoke, flames, heat, thunder of falling walls, crackle of fire, hissing of water, panting of engines, shouts, braying of trumpets, roar of wind, tumult, confusion and uproar."[33]

In the first hours of the disaster, residents of the West and South Divisions were able to evade the flames by traveling in nearly any direction. As the fire grew, however, escape became increasingly difficult. On the North Side, those wise enough to leave before the flames drew near could cross the north branch of the river to the safety of the West Division. Others with an early start pushed north of Fullerton Avenue, which marked the city limits. But many, frantically working to pack bags, bury their most prized possessions, or load up a wagon, stayed too long. Faced with multiple fronts of flame and winds that seemed to blow in every direction—conditions that made the course of the fire impossible to predict—throngs of North Siders pushed east toward the closest apparent safe harbor: the beaches and parks that lined Lake Michigan. A fortunate few of the thousands who rushed to the waterfront were rescued by boat. But most, hemmed in by walls of flame and unable to remain on the scorching sand, withstood the heat and smoke by immersing themselves in the frigid lake water for long hours.[34]

In a way that a list of statistics cannot show, these descriptions of the horrors visited by the Great Fire edge far closer to depicting the experiences of the survivors. The powerful image of the crowd running before the conflagration was not recorded photographically, but it has been reproduced again and again from memory: in the images

An engraving typical of the many and widely circulated images that recorded the panicked flight of Chicagoans from the Great Fire. Source: *Leslie's Illustrated Newspaper,* October 28, 1871. Courtesy of Chicago Historical Society, ICHi-02909.

and words of contemporary engravings and reportage, and in subsequent histories, panoramas, and films.[35] Depictions of the wild flight, the Darwinian stampede to a safe haven, came to function as an emblem of universal ordeal in the course of the disaster. Constructed around the compelling and sensational force of mass terror, this representation unquestionably offers an accurate portrait of a catalogue of horrors, of a common experience of a great civic trauma.

Still, such images operate on a certain level of abstraction. This interpretation of disaster conflates the details of particular and unique ordeals into a single story: the famous flight before the very famous Great Chicago Fire. Yet cities, as the fire historian Reverend E. J. Goodspeed aptly observed in one of his own accounts of the disaster, "are but an aggregation of individuals."[36] And during the Great Fire, different people obviously had different experiences. While hundreds of thousands of the stories of individuals will never be known, the extant collection of personal narratives, letters and short essays, and later reminiscences left behind by close to 100 men and women supply some of the pieces of evidence necessary to begin a more nuanced analysis of how particular Chicagoans made it through the disorders and danger of the Great Fire. And from these individual accounts, it is possible to reconstruct certain larger patterns of experience that are tied to issues of social class.

Such sources come almost entirely from the more elite ranks of the city—and most readily indicate that upper-class Chicagoans could rely on their wealth and networks of kin and friendship to mediate many of the immediate dangers posed by the Great Fire.[37] These people of course endured great traumas, but their hardship was also in part born by those they could afford to hire. Colbert and Chamberlin chose to reprint the personal narrative of *Tribune* editor Horace White, deeming the story of his family to be "perhaps the average one of the wealthier classes of the South Division."[38] Alerted to the growing magnitude of the fire, White hastened from his Michigan Avenue residence to the *Tribune* building, where he quickly penned an editorial that urged all owners of property to guard against future blazes by investing in fine brick and stone edifices such as the office of his newspaper—an ostensibly "fireproof" building that was soon incinerated. (The opinion piece was never published.) Realizing his own home was endangered, the editor rushed back to Michigan Avenue, where his wife had already packed up the family valuables. A passing teamster agreed to transport the household belongings—including their beloved pet, a "talented parrot"—for $20. The Whites drove south in their own carriage, finding shelter in the home of a friend who resided in the exclusive (and untouched) Prairie Avenue district.

On the North Side, prosperous families often endured greater personal danger than their counterparts to the south, but still could rely on the advantages of wealth to abate some of the burdens of disaster. John LeMoyne, an attorney, described how he and all of his immediate neighbors—railroad executive William Larrabee, lumberman William Houghtelling, commission merchant Julian Rumsey, and wholesaler Thomas Phillips—worked together to save themselves and some of their possessions. All of these households employed at least two domestic servants. Working with their hired help, the men loaded their families and goods into their personal carriages and wagons and fled north, often just a few hundred yards ahead of the fast-moving flames. At the end of a harrowing ride, LeMoyne was able to offer shelter to his neighbors in his second home, a summer cottage in north suburban Lakeview.[39] Harriet Rosa, a young North Side mother of a newborn infant, became separated from her husband, a salesman, in the whirl of the crowd. She spent a terrifying day and night on the beach in Lincoln Park, but was at least buoyed by the support of her milk-nurse and maid. Rosa plainly endured a full roster of the worst horrors that the Great Fire had to offer. Still, once the conflagration died, she was quickly reunited with her husband at the comfortable home of a friend in the northern suburbs.[40] All of these people had an awful story to tell—yet they are ones that ultimately ended in the happy circumstance of some salvaged property, a secure and well-appointed place of shelter, and no injury or loss of life. Able to rely on the unnamed maids, valets, and drivers in domestic service, the temporary paid labor of independent teamsters, and the helping hands of well-off friends, these men and women simply could draw upon a wide range of resources to protect and sustain themselves and their families.

By contrast, it is much more difficult to reconstruct the experiences of nonelite Chicagoans. Poorer residents of the city, like more prosperous victims, certainly relied upon ties of friendship and kin. But almost no written accounts of the Great Fire by working people are readily available.[41] In the immediate aftermath, it is probable that few in this class had the time or the means to record their own stories. Moreover, newspapers and other popular publications in general did not seek out such voices; their more prosperous audiences wanted to hear about their own, and the "plot" of the wellborn made to face the dangers of the city fit comfortably within their vision of urban melodrama. At least in the English language, the recording of an individual or personal story seemed a privilege granted only to men, women, and children of the upper classes: the question of the fate of the "mass" of people was nearly always subsumed into accounts of the massive suffering that seemed to afflict all of the city.

Some texts, however, do offer rare mentions of working people. The historian Frank Luzerne, for example, told the story of a woman he tellingly characterized as "A Real Sufferer." This Scandinavian immigrant and her family were financially devastated by the disaster, losing their North Side cottage and all of their possessions. As the flames drew nearer, they fled over the river to the West Division, where they found protection under a railroad viaduct. Three days later, weakened by cold and hunger, the family still had no other place to go and remained huddled beneath this meager shelter.[42] It seems likely that many people of lesser means faced similarly difficult trials, but the very existence of such a written account is quite atypical. Colbert and Chamberlin, who researched and wrote their text just two months after the Great Fire, themselves noted this silence, commenting that the tales told by the wealthy and comfortable were the only apparent yardsticks by which to measure the plight of "the fifty times more numerous" poor families: the people "who had no twenty dollars to give to a cartman" and "no sympathizing friends down the avenue to give them shelter and other comforts."[43] In the end, as they suggested, perhaps the only way to appreciate the trials endured by the "mass" of those in Chicago is to recognize the many stories that remained unrecorded.

One piece of hard evidence—the question of exactly who fell prey to the flames—does give a concrete picture of the much magnified personal dangers endured by certain unfortunate members of the lower classes. It is most frequently estimated that 300 people died in the Great Fire.[44] Strikingly, none of the authors of personal narratives told of losing a close friend or relative to the flames. Yet many of these writers did know the details of the deaths of a few of their more affluent peers, stories they retold with shock and horror. Colbert and Chamberlin, for example, recounted the demise of Samuel Shawcross, a wealthy man crushed by a falling wall of the Field and Leiter store as he hurried through the business district to rescue what he could from his merchant tailor establishment.[45] A most final confirmation of the "dangers" of the city, deaths such as Shawcross's, received special attention from personal narrators and reporters.[46] Still, it seems likely that these victims most often put themselves at risk, making the daring yet ultimately fatal decision to attempt to save some portion of their property.

But the great majority of those who lost their lives had no such options. Nearly all of the fatalities occurred in the shanty towns and vice districts on the South Side and north of Chicago Avenue, an area "thickly covered with the cottages of the poor."[47] To be sure, many victims lost their lives in the first hours of the Great Fire; having little or no warning of the magnitude of the fast-growing blaze, their unlucky location near the origins of the conflagration possibly meant that they never had a chance to escape. It is worth noting, however, that all of these people were rendered far more vulnerable by the particularities of their built environment. Cheap housing in the city, like that in many slums and ghettos, was poorly built and very dense; double- and even triple-built lots abounded.[48] The Great Fire blasted through such settings with enormous ferocity, its killing power further enhanced by the difficulty of escape through neighborhood thoroughfares that were often no more than narrow strips of ungraded mud.[49] Most of the victims were burned completely beyond recognition; surviving friends and relatives could not even claim the bodies of those they had lost. Quickly and anonymously interred in mass graves, a step necessary to guard against the spread of disease, these deaths would never be the subject of any formal public memorial. At least 300 victims were thus privately mourned and communally counted, becoming one more entry in the set of numbers that together describe the scope of the disaster.[50]

To come to a more complex appreciation of the destruction and disorders that the Great Fire visited upon the people of Chicago, it is thus necessary to consider these two related sets of narratives. One, by far the better known, speaks of the common horrors and aggregate losses of the whole city, of the crisis that enveloped all Chicago. The other, that of the more particular experiences of the many different sorts of people who together composed the city, is much more partial and difficult to reconstruct—but no less important. To be sure, mere humans were all joined in bowing before a terrible force of nature, and the place that was Chicago certainly endured a great trial. Such an overwhelming event was without doubt creative of a certain universality of experience. Yet in the case of an urban disaster—a horrific test of a community built out of social differences and spatial segmentations—it seems well worth adding a sense of the particular to the story of the Great Fire. For in the end, precisely because of their social differences, the many peoples of Chicago did not share an equal destiny before the flames.

BARRIERS BURNED AWAY?

Beginning in the last months of 1871, readers of *The Evangelist*, a New York City religious monthly, had their chance to imagine how the social relations of a great city were laid bare in the crucible of the Great Chicago Fire—and how those relationships might best be restored. During these months, Edward Payson Roe parceled out his fictional treatment of the disaster in serial installments. Published in mid-1872 in book form under the title of *Barriers Burned Away,* the novel became the great American bestseller of the 1870s—further proof of the enormous interest sparked nationwide by the devastation at Chicago.[51] Roe made sense of what had happened to the city by arguing that the disaster, for all of its hardships, would result in an entirely positive end: the clearing away of the entrenched "barriers" between the people of Chicago, obstacles built out of the prejudice and suspicion so often attached to social differences. A new city, he suggested, could emerge out of the ashes: a radical democracy reconstructed upon a bedrock of Christian fellowship and love. For Roe, as for other evangelical Protestants, the punishment meted out by the Great Fire thus also seemed a moment of tremendous possibility, a divinely given chance to reorder an urban community in accordance with some of their most profound beliefs.

As soon as the Great Chicago Fire ceased to burn, a wide array of observers likewise sought to explain the event and its possible consequences for the social life of the city. Had barriers indeed burned away? If so, what did this mean? In the course of their struggle to grasp how disaster would affect the shape of urban order, different Chicagoans saw different meanings in the leveling force of the conflagration. Some, in the mode of Edward Payson Roe, felt that the conflagration posed a test of faith: it was a trial, but also a moment alive with new opportunities to move Chicago toward a higher plane of spirituality. Others, however, would respond to the "leveling" of their city on a less idealistic plane, and thereby arrived at far more grim conclusions: a set of comments that again unveiled great anxieties about the social divisions that marked great cities.

Joining the conventions of romantic melodrama, the uplifting message of a Christian tract, and the historic setting of a sensational urban event, *Barriers Burned Away* was a tailor-made blockbuster.[52] The novel traces the fortunes of devout and honorable Dennis Fleet, a young college graduate from a small farming town who comes to Chicago to support his family after the death of his father. Times are hard, and Dennis can only find employment far below his station, hiring on as a porter in the gallery of Baron Ludolph, an expatriated German noblemen. Possessed of talents too obvious to ignore, Dennis quickly rises to the post of chief salesman. Yet even as his career skyrockets, Dennis is most unlucky at love: his devotion to Ludolph's daughter Christine—a beautiful and intelligent woman flawed by a cold, haughty, and irreligious character—remains persistently unrequited.

All transforms, however, in the last chapters of the novel, as Roe retells the Great Fire. Dennis rescues Christine from her burning home, and together they endure the terrors of panicked flight and entrapment on the lakeshore. (The baron is killed, entombed by debris as he—as in the true story of the ill-fated Samuel Shawcross —unwisely rushes back into his burning store to save some of his treasures.) In the climactic scene, Christine asks to revisit the place of her father's death. On the spot which represents the ruin of her former life, the ever-faithful Dennis haltingly asks a humble question: "Is there hope for me?" A new Christine, purified by her ordeal and finally ready to see Dennis as the paragon he truly is, gives an ardent response: "No *hope* for you, Dennis, but perfect *certainty*, for now EVERY BARRIER IS BURNED AWAY!"[53] She renounces her inherited wealth, European aristocratic roots, and atheism for a man who embodies American democratic virtue, the Protestant work ethic, and Christian love. With their class, ethnic, and religious differences all subsumed by the transforming power of the Great Fire, Dennis and Christine enter into matrimony as part of a new city that will make a new history.

For all its reliance on formula and cliché, Roe's novel did carry a message that had its advocates in the city of Chicago. Francis Test, a customs inspector and devout Christian, was one who thought that the Great Fire might well sweep away the social divisions of the city, and thereby spur a concrete realization of the belief that all are equal before God.[54] As he wrote to his mother three days after the Fire, "I am convinced that money will not be the main thought of any people, nor will the poor man have to take a low seat as usual." To this mind, the legacy of conflagration was plain: "We are all alike here now, or, as it is expressed, we are all on a level."[55] Like E. P. Roe, Test found comfort in the abstract notion that the devastations of the Great Fire would end in a revitalized community of Christians; both believed that disaster would in theory allow Chicagoans to recognize that the distinctions born of class and ethnic identities were far less meaningful than the common bonds of love that could be forged between all righteous people, a sensibility in keeping with the vision of social harmony held dear by many mid-nineteenth-century urban evangelicals.[56]

But such a spirit of Christian universalism was not universally shared. Unlike Francis Test, the great majority of the educated and prosperous Chicagoans who wrote personal narratives found nothing to applaud in their experience; for them, the disaster to a large degree seemed such a profoundly disruptive and discomfiting event precisely because the regular "barriers" of urban life had been destroyed. Transgressions of the normal spatial and social divisions of the metropolis were subjects that obsessed fire narrators. Like many of his fellow survivors, the attorney William Furness dwelt at length on the hardships endured by prominent bankers, merchants, judges, and their families. Driven from their comfortable homes and familiar neighborhoods, as he worriedly observed, the Great Fire exposed people unused to deprivation and danger to the elements and to a largely unknown lower class.[57] A popular fire history likewise dwelt upon the shattering of urban social divisions, conjuring a typically sensational image: "[T]hose households pampered in luxury and ease prayed for an opportunity of concealing themselves, protecting themselves, among paupers, beggars, and thieves."[58] William Gallagher, a seminary student, gave evidence of a Christian sensibility quite different from that of Francis Test when he wrote about the devastation:

> Oh! You can't begin to imagine the crushing blow that this has been to many. Wait til you have seen a man, who on Saturday was a millionaire, on Tuesday standing in line to draw blankets for himself and his family that night. Wait till you see wealthy ladies, who have lived in affluence all their lives, coming into the church to get their meals and procure a little coffee and bread, after having been caught by the fire and obliged to lie in the lake ducking their heads for hours till the flames went by, and then you can begin to comprehend how the blow has fallen.[59]

A loss of stature, an erasure of material standing and other comforts, here hardly seemed the foundational stuff of a radical Christian love. To the contrary, men like Furness and Gallagher perceived such a leveling as the worst of blows.

Personal narrators further revealed their anxiety about the disruption of usual class boundaries and hierarchies through the observations they made of working people. William Furness claimed that the disaster had predictably brought out the best in the businessmen who ran the commerce of Chicago, drawing an explicit comparison between the proper, cool-headed actions of his peers and the "only persons" who gave way to "terror and wildness": the "poorer and less educated classes."[60] Laura Rollins, a Connecticut tourist whose itinerary unhappily included a stop in Chicago on October 9, clearly expected to be menaced by those of the "rougher classes." But contrary to her preconceptions, disaster produced what she portrayed as a reversal of the norms of working-class behavior, a happy result that in itself was worthy of special note: "Very few . . . were intoxicated, and even those seemed awed into decorum."[61] While Rollins's report contradicts Furness's account, they shared a critical assumption: that the Great Fire, a definitive end to the always-tenuous stability of the city, without question would unleash disorderly conduct among the lower classes of Chicago.

The representations of a specific set of workers likewise point to the readily raised fears of more elite commentators. In a letter that anticipated debates that would later emerge over the proper shape of market relations in the rebuilding city, the seminarian William Gallagher angrily condemned the sudden good fortune of the teamsters of the city: men who enjoyed a once-in-a-lifetime demand for their services as thousands sought to engage their wagons in order to save some of their belongings from the flames. This "most inhumane set of men," according to Gallagher, commonly charged over $100 per load. Over and above such "extortion," he reported, expressmen and their "cronies" voraciously raided the wine cellars and liquor cabinets of well-born clients; had routinely taken advance payments, only to dump their loads within a few blocks; and drunkenly circled in wealthier neighborhoods to hunt for more victims of their scams.[62] Yet the *Tribune* editor Horace White, in an account written some weeks after Gallagher's letter, made a point of noting that he had not seen any such behavior on the part of teamsters, applauding what he described as their heroic efforts to keep at their labors even as the flames drew near. Well aware of the common circulation of stories about scheming teamsters, he by contrast told of drivers taking whatever a customer could afford as payment—and even working for free.[63]

It seems likely that both accounts are based on true stories: if some teamsters acted in a spirit of sympathy and fairness, there were undoubtedly others who were happy to reap whatever they could from such an extraordinary moment. Gallagher, though, had rushed to present the situation in a worst possible light, describing the scene as a "fearful state of beastliness."[64] In a move characteristic of more elite men and women who were ready to see such working people as part of "the dangerous class" (and therefore seldom able to see them as individuals), what may have been the bad behavior of some conformed to all of his expectations—and therefore, for Gallagher, seemed a valid representation of the conduct of an entire group. Most Fire histories, books written for a middle-class and elite audience, similarly created the "facts" that their readers expected to know about the lower classes of the city. Even in the face of the contrary testimony of so reputable a figure as Horace White, they in general reinforce the image of the teamster voiced by William Gallagher: that of immoral profiteer and drunken vandal.[65]

Rushing through the streets, striking a hasty contract with expressmen, crowding into the lake shallows, huddling together under makeshift shelters: the Great Fire compelled the intermingling of unlikely companions. Forced to flee their own territory, whether an ethnic neighborhood, vice district, or fashionable residence row, Chicagoans rooted in various communities met as never before on the newly common ground of a wasted city. A description of the dissolution of boundaries set forth by one narrator arrestingly communicates the fears of social difference that went hand in hand with the perils of the blaze: "The tenement families flying clothesless before the flames; the rich of a few hours before not ashamed to mix with them—as the fire of the forest and prairies make animals, commonly enemies, run together as friends."[66] As her choice of metaphor suggests, the perception of the meaning of the Great Fire held by this survivor far differed from E. P. Roe's vision of a newly Christianized and unified community. Disaster had leveled, to be sure—but social and spatial barriers, for her and for most other members of the upper classes of Chicago, would best soon be rebuilt.

Another set of stories finally underlines the problem of trying to understand the meaning of disaster in a city united by tragedy but divided in its social structure and physical form—stories that were unlikely to be told about the fire at Peshtigo, a force that leveled a small and comparatively homogenous place. Even as the Great Fire burned, a multitude of reporters scrambled to find its cause—a quest that ended in certain narratives that similarly betray an acute sense of the class and ethnic differences that for some made the city seem so perilous. It is worth noting that an urban fire stands apart from destructive events such as Peshtigo-like forest fires, hurricanes, or earthquakes in the sense that they often are not seen as simple "natural" disasters. High winds and dry conditions might speed an urban blaze, but "nature" only plays an accessory role; in the context of a built environment and in the specific case of fire—a form of destruction that in theory can be prevented—humans seem to have a far greater degree of agency and control. Or to put it another way, someone or something can be blamed. In an interpretation of disaster that again wavered between fact and fiction, the English-language press of the city immediately cast an unlikely and humble duo as the miscreants responsible for the Great Fire. So was born the legend of Mrs. O'Leary and her cow.

In point of fact, the fire did begin in the cow barn owned by Catherine and Patrick O'Leary, two Irish immigrants who made their living through a mixed bag of enterprises that were standard features of working-class family economies.[67] According to Mrs. O'Leary's testimony before the Board of Fire Commissioners, the couple lived off Patrick's wages as a day laborer, her sales of the milk produced by their five dairy cows, and the income they earned by renting half of their four-room wooden cottage to another Irish immigrant family, the O'Malleys. Accused of the careless late-night milking venture that allowed the cow to upset a kerosene lantern, the fateful bovine kick that supposedly brought doom to a city, Mrs. O'Leary denied any guilt. Like any other victim, she lamented at length her own extensive and uninsured losses.[68] The fire commissioners apparently believed her story: in their report on the cause of the Great Fire, they were ultimately content with a finding that the Fire had begun from an unattributable spark—perhaps a discarded cigar, a stray ember from a cookfire, or the sputtering of a gaslight. Their report thus declined to name any specific catalytic agent.

Instead, in a move that presaged a major post-Fire controversy over whether or not the city should ban wooden construction within designated "fire limits," the Fire Commission collectively indicted the property owners and politicians who had ignored warnings of the danger of a great fire and proceeded to build their city largely of inflammable wood.[69]

For the press corp and their public, seeking both to explain and further sensationalize the Great Fire, Mrs. O'Leary proved irresistible; as the *Chicago Journal* commented: "Even if it were an absurd rumor, forty miles wide of the truth, it would be useless to attempt to alter the verdict of history. Fame has seized her and appropriated her, name, barn, cow, and all."[70] But it is important to recognize that the tale of Mrs. O'Leary's cow, while on one level merely a picaresque invention of journalists, at the time represented a vilification fraught with specific meaning: in much of the English-language press, Mrs. O'Leary became an easy target for anti-Irish, antiworking class, and antiwoman invective.[71] The story in essence laid the blame for conflagration and chaos at the feet of a person that more elite Chicagoans would readily recognize as a member of the (in this case quite literally) "dangerous classes" of their city.[72]

In the newspapers and fire histories of the day, Mrs. O'Leary decidely was not the rather benign and comical folk figure that she has become.[73] To the contrary, she seemed a lurid example of all the worst characteristics ascribed to Irish immigrants by the native-born.[74] The *Chicago Times*, the most widely read English-language daily in the city, thus played upon commonly held middle-class stereotypes of the deceiving Irish poor in its report, falsely charging Mrs. O'Leary of applying weekly to the county agent for relief. According to the paper, an agent one day discovered her fraud and cut off her allotment of fuel and foodstuffs. The kindling of the Great Fire, the *Times* suggested, was no accident, but a premeditated act of retribution: "The old hag swore she would be revenged on a city that would deny her a bit of wood or a pound of bacon."[75] The *New York Tribune*, while stopping short of imagining a scenario so filled with class and ethnic hatred, still revealed a distinct anti-Irish bias in its lamentation of the injustice of the survival of the O'Leary home. Its correspondent bitterly described a structure "no shab-

(Copyright applied for by the Chicago Photograph Company.)

Unidentified woman pretending to be Mrs. O'Leary (a photograph widely circulated in the months after the Fire). Note that "Mrs. O'Leary's" milk cow here has longhorns and was most likely a Texas steer borrowed from the nearby Union Stockyards. Courtesy of Chicago Historical Society, ICHi-02736.

bier" than any in "Chicago nor in Tipperary": "There it stood safe, while a city had perished before it and around it. . . . And there to this hour stands that craven little house, holding on tightly to its miserable existence."[76] Though probably aware of Mrs. O'Leary's formal exoneration, Colbert and Chamberlin, perhaps equally aware of the popular appeal of these figures, refused to abandon her story. In their comments, they found fault with the industry and ability of Mrs. O'Leary—claiming that if she had milked the cow on time, she might have done without a lamp, and that if she had "plied the dugs" with proper skill, a more contented cow would not have seen fit to let fly with its portentous kick. They further censured her husband, "the lazy man who allowed her to milk"; Mr. O'Leary, a typical Irish loafer, had thus left the city at the mercy of a plainly incompetent and dangerous woman.[77] Deemed guilty on all of these manifold counts, the O'Learys seemed positive proof of the heretofore more amorphous threat posed to the city by its ever-increasing diversity of peoples.

Such fears of a dangerous "other" were even more explicitly voiced roughly two weeks after the disaster, when a new story of the origins of the Great Fire emerged. On October 23, amidst a fanfare of self-congratulations, the *Chicago Times*—a paper famed for its pioneering of what would later be termed "yellow" journalism—printed a lengthy confession allegedly penned by an exiled Paris Communard.[78] The supposed mastermind of a dozen coconspirators, the Communard claimed to have rushed straight from the barricades to set the Great Fire, a revolutionary act meant "to humble the men who had waxed rich at the expense of the poor."[79] Mrs. O'Leary, he himself proclaimed, was now old news: "No old Irish hag was milking her cow at the time, as the reporters of the city press are determined to have it." To the contrary, his incendiary band were the true villians—or, to his mind, the great heroes. Unfortunately, some of their plot had gone awry: the Communard apparently meant only to destroy the business district of the city, but the fire had grown far out of control. Conscience-stricken after the wholesale burning of the working-class and immigrant neighborhoods of the North Side, he explained that he had written to the *Times* to express his sorrow over the loss of life and property sustained by his fellow workers. But for all his remorse, the Communard did not renounce his political project, adding an ominous and explicit postscript that again played upon the idea of the ever-dangerous metropolis: "Other cities, both in this country and in Europe, have been threatened with fire."[80]

Was Chicago a casualty of class warfare? The confession and its alarming portrait of a worldwide network of revolutionary incendiaries quickly drew a host of detractors. The *Illinois Staats-Zeitung*, a Republican daily paper read by a majority of the German immigrants of the city, devoted a series of editorials to the question and deemed such a scenario to be "most ridiculous."[81] The German-born editors were doubtless far more knowledgeable about the rise of the Socialist movement in Europe than most American journalists, and scornfully dismissed insinuations of a conspiracy of working people in Chicago—a city it described as an unlikely candidate for open class insurrection, given that it was far less fraught with "opposition between capital and labor" than more established centers of industry such as Manchester, New York, or Boston.[82] The paper further noted that the governing body of organized socialism, the London-based First International, had officially disavowed the violence spawned by the Paris Commune, and finally capped its response to the *Times* with a rather sarcastic lesson in Socialist policy: "[T]he destruction of all big cities is, as far as we know, not at all on the program in the political credo of the International."[83] Remarking upon the public appetite for sensationalism—"So extraordinary an event must have an extraordinary cause"—the *Staats-Zeitung* reminded its readers that fires were of daily occurrence in Chicago and that the disaster needed no special explanation.[84] The O'Learys' critics, Colbert and Chamberlin, did not repeat the *Staats-Zeitung*'s call to demythologize the origins of the fire, but they similarly concluded that the charge of a Communist plot could not be true; the confession printed by the *Times*, they contended, was not "free from marks which betrayed its origins in the brain of a professional newspaper writer."[85]

The *Times*, long known for its general disregard for factual verification, almost certainly either perpetuated or fell victim to a hoax. But why produce or print such a transparently dubious "confession"? It again seems plain that editor Wilbur Storey and his staff were well aware of the sort of narrative that would rivet the attention of readers who expected to hear sensational and dangerous stories about the city. Moreover, the violence and disruptions of the Paris Commune, a shattering event that had ended only five months before the Great Fire, was on the minds of prominent citizens in Chicago; many wealthy families knew that city well, as they regularly traveled to the great capitols of Europe.[86] The *Tribune*, the paper read by most native-born businessmen, had provided especially intense coverage of the news from Paris, providing daily dispatches from a foreign correspondent that often appeared in the first column of the front page. Public discussions of the Commune and its meaning were not uncommon; Reverend Robert Collyer, for example, the pastor of the elite Unity Church, coincidentally sermonized about "the great woe" of Paris, the "wreck and ruin" of which he had personally witnessed on a recent voyage abroad, on the same Sunday evening that the Great Fire commenced.[87] Even before their own community was ravaged by fire, some Chicagoans were quite familiar with the story of how a great city had been torn apart by a revolution of workers.[88]

The "confession" of the Communard, then, did not appear in a vacuum. Like the tale of Mrs. O'Leary's cow, this story of the origins of the Great Fire exploited a constant social fear of an urban working class that might become dangerous, of a sinister and little-known "other" that might in fact bring down an entire city. With its portrait of the incendiary Communard, the *Times* helped to create a lasting symbolic menace: the shadowy, secret, and highly dangerous conspiracy of revolutionary workers that, real or not, would only grow in power in Chicago.[89] Hoax or not, the "Communist plot" seemed quite plausible to those more elite men and women who had absorbed the notion that any city might at any moment fall prey to its own internal differences. Even as the Fire historian Frank Luzerne expressed his own skepticism about the story of the Communard, he defended his choice to reprint the "confession" with the following comment: "That many of our prominent citizens believe in the genuineness of these revolutions is demonstrated in their daily conversation."[90]

As Horace White observed at the end of his personal narrative, "It takes all sorts of people to make a great fire."[91] To extend White's point, it also takes all sorts of people to make a great city. And when a disaster strikes an urban community, the physical experience of devastation compounds what are often social anxieties of long standing.[92] Taken together, the stories that Chicagoans and others told about the Great Fire and themselves unquestionably offer a portrait of people united by an enormous tragedy and test. According to more traditional histories of the city, a sense of common identity—of an "instant history" that now was shared by every survivor—would only pave the road toward an amazing collective recovery and a wondrous civic future.[93] But in Chicago, at the time of the Fire itself, barriers had burned away in a metropolitan space and polity that were divided in their essences—and this new "leveling" of peoples, however unusual, temporary, or superficial, for many only heightened a pervasive perception of extreme disorder. Primed to expect the worst of the majority of those with whom they shared Chicago, certain prominent citizens would move quickly to rebuild key barriers.

BARRIERS BUILT

On the morning of October 11, some thirty-six hours after the Great Fire had been extinguished, William Bross, a part-owner of the *Tribune* and a former lieutenant governor of Illinois, prepared to depart for an East Coast speaking tour that would showcase yet another of his vocations: that of eminent Chicago booster. Breakfasting in the unharmed West Side home of a friend, Bross—whose own exclusive South Division rowhouse had been incinerated—beheld a scene that dramatically reconfirmed his still-stalwart faith in the future of his stricken city: "[A]s I sat sipping my coffee over some cold ham, I saw Sheridan's boys, with knapsack and musket, march proudly by. *Never did deeper emotions of joy overcome me.*"[94] Upon orders of Lieutenant General Philip Henry Sheridan, the famous Civil War hero who himself was a fire survivor, five companies of infantry had rushed to Chicago from Omaha and Fort Leavenworth.[95] The general, with his troops and the aid of hundreds of special volunteers, would take charge of law enforcement in the city for just over two weeks.[96] For at least the portion of the unsettled, demoralized, and extremely nervous populace represented by fire narrators, the arrival of the U.S. army sent a powerful message: this most visible and effective force of order, they thought, would end the anarchic trespass of spatial and social barriers in their shattered metropolis. For some of the elite business leaders of the city, moreover, a sense of the ever-present dangers of the city heavily figured into their vision of how the powers and presence of such a military force might be mustered to rebuild a more familiar order.

In some ways, the post-Fire rule of martial law in Chicago can be understood easily as a commonsensical safeguard: an informed and experienced military commander was well-placed to take charge; soldiers could be readily transported to Chicago from their postings in the West; and, most important, a citizenry traumatized both by the disaster and the powerful rumors of new disruptions certainly welcomed the initial intervention of these troops. Like most people who endure a great disaster, survivors of the Great Fire readily imagined the trials that might yet come. While little remained to be looted in the burned district, many were concerned that professional criminals, drawn by the magnetic prospect of buried safes and vaults, would rush to Chicago.[97] Others fretted about the more immediate dangers posed by the local criminal population; as flames swept through the city jail, prisoners had been set free to spare their being burned alive. And those who had not suffered losses worried that crazed figures like the Communard might now decide to torch their still-standing homes and businesses.[98] Survivor Ebon Matthews remembered that "one who was not an eyewitness can hardly imagine the fears of incendiarism, looting, etc., which prevailed. Stories of all kinds were afoot concerning thefts, murders, and the like."[99] For many in the city, the arrival of "Sheridan's boys" seemed an immense relief; like William Bross, almost every fire narrator spoke of the comfort they drew from the presence of armed and uniformed sentries.[100]

Others, however, were more dubious about the military occupation. Though these critics understood that the army had done much to restore the confidence of survivors, they felt that such "war measures"—or, at least, their maintenance for a period of such

Cover of English-language "instant" history published in New York City, replete with an array of sensational images. Courtesy of Newberry Library Special Collections.

length—were perhaps a danger in and of themselves. For as journalists James Sheahan and George Upton commented in their Fire history, martial law in a peacetime city "endangered lives as much as it protected property."[101] A soldier, a man trained to follow orders and fight an obvious enemy, they suggested, simply could not operate with the same flexibility and knowledge of an urban populace as the local police. Moreover, Sheridan's occupation of Chicago raised a set of issues directly relevant to the key debates in the national and state-level politics of the day; as one observer asked: "[T]he question is not, can the military govern the city well? but should it interfere in the city government at all?"[102] The governor of Illinois, John M. Palmer, proved a bitter opponent of the army's usurpation of the task of peacekeeping from the Illinois militia and the Chicago police—a step he perceived as a plain federal incursion upon states' rights.[103] For Palmer and his supporters, no military officer should ever dictate policy to a democratically elected public official in a time of peace, a position that spoke to the central and sharply contested issues of state and federal authority involved in the then-ongoing process of Congressional Reconstruction.[104]

While a military presence in the aftermath of a disaster may intuitively seem rather uncontroversial, Sheridan's activities thus in fact raised some knotty problems of procedure and governance. Moreover, another complicating factor deserves consideration. For even as Mayor R. B. Mason placed Chicago under martial law and allowed such a state of affairs to continue, a host of reliable authorities agreed that the city remained remarkably tranquil. Sheridan himself, upon accepting his commission to keep "peace and good order" on October 12, reported that "no authenticated attempt at incendiarism has reached me, and the people of the city are calm, quiet, and well-disposed."[105] Illinois Adjutant General Henry Dilger, the commander of the state militia, spent three days in the city immediately after the Great Fire. He concluded that "all the rumors of incendiarism, murder, and lynching exist only in the imagination of the frightened population."[106] Police Commissioner Thomas B. Brown would later confirm both impressions: that "during the fire and the two weeks succeeding it, there were remarkably few cases of crime."[107] Popular expectations (and continuing reports) about the facts of life in the ever-dangerous metropolis were most certainly not matched by the actual conduct of its people. As James Milner, a businessman, observed four days after the Fire's end, "[F]or all the sensational accounts in the paper, there has been no disorderly gatherings, and nothing approaching a riot."[108]

The decisions for the U.S. army to take control of the city of Chicago and for martial law to remain in force for two weeks were no doubt made in haste, and to some degree doubtless involved an instinctive turn toward a visible form of authority in the face of a great upheaval. Still, it seems worth asking why the opposition of the governor and the police commission, the risk posed to civilians by military rule, and the plain fact of the overall peace of the city did not in some measure combine to bring the tenure of General Sheridan to a speedier end. The best answer to this puzzle seems to lie in the vision of urban order (and, conversely, the fears of potential disorder) held by some of the most prominent and wealthy citizens of Chicago. For even as someone like James Milner recognized that a peaceful state in fact prevailed, he at the same time heartily welcomed the bracing presence of a military force, alluding to the ever-constant danger posed by the unknown masses of the city. "With so many . . . thrown idle, with the unsettled condition that such ruin induced in their minds," he wrote, "every caution is advisable."[109] The mechanics of Sheridan's assumption of civic authority, the workings of martial rule, and the eventual justifications of his presence all reveal that an elite group of native-born business leaders were able, in an extraordinary moment of crisis, to assume control over the structures of policing and criminal justice in their city. Their desire for martial law, a step they felt necessary to secure their own lives and property, was thus translated into the system of order that Sheridan enforced over the whole of Chicago.

Thanks to the fierce opposition of John M. Palmer, the story of Sheridan's role in post-Fire Chicago is well-preserved in a host of legal and governmental documents. As soon as the general took control of the city, the governor initiated an angry correspondence with President Grant and General William Tecumseh Sherman in Washington, filed suit against Sheridan in the state supreme court, and convened a special fact-finding commission in the Illinois legislature.[110] Yet while Palmer, himself a much-lauded Civil War commander who had won the rank of brigadier general, would consistently imply that a self-aggrandizing and power-mad Sheridan had thrust himself to the fore, the evidence assembled in the several accounts of the episode suggests a rather different scenario.[111] For the declaration of martial law in Chicago was decidedly not the general's idea. From the first, calls for placing Sheridan in control of the city had come from its most prominent business leaders.[112]

According to the general, when the fire died out on October 10, he approached the mayor to suggest that it might be wise to bring additional troops into the city. A host of preliminary steps had already been taken toward the end of public safety: over 300 of the 450-strong police force had not suffered losses and were on duty, 500 volunteers from each division of the city were being recruited to serve as "special" officers under the command of district sergeants, another 500 men from nearby companies of the state militia were scheduled to arrive overnight, and 179 members of a Norwegian militia company from the largely unburned West Side already stood at their posts.[113] In addition, a force of perhaps 450 "merchant police"—the private guards and watchmen employed by railroads, hotels, and banks—remained at their places.[114] Finally, the mayor had vested the small force of soldiers then present in Chicago with police power, specifying that these men would act at the command of the police superintendent. Still, for all the forces in place or on their way to the city, Mason agreed that more army troops might be of use, and Sheridan promptly telegraphed for five companies of infantry, approximately 600 men. Further, with the blessing of the mayor, the general requisitioned tents, blankets, and food from army depots at St. Louis and Jeffersonville, Indiana, emergency provisions that were meant to aid survivors.[115]

But certain men of influence were not content with the arrangements concluded between the mayor and the general, a set of affairs that left the military subordinate to the power of municipal leaders. That same afternoon, a delegation of what General Sheridan termed "leading citizens" came to his West Side home to ask him to assume control of the city. Believing that he had no legal right to take such a step, the general refused, explaining that he felt that his forces should be restricted to a supporting role: "I felt that my duty was to assist him [the mayor] to the utmost . . . it was my earnest desire that the civil authorities should, if possible, bring the city through its troubles with such aid as the army could give." But during that evening, only the first night after the fire had finally died, wild rumors spread; though he found that stories of looting, arson, and murder were not at all true and did his best to use his personal reputation to allay the excitement, Sheridan to his dismay discovered that some of the "best citizens credited the most startling rumors." The next day, October 11, he attended a meeting of "merchants and others" at their request, where he was again urged to "assume control of affairs in the city." He again declined. But his suitors continued to implore him to lend his heroic stature and fearsome reputation to the task of resecuring Chicago. In the end, Sheridan "finally agreed."

Once persuaded, Sheridan went to work with alacrity. Hastening to the temporary City Hall, a West Side church, he announced to the mayor that he and his troops would "be responsible for peace and order in the city" provided that Mason issued an executive order to that effect. The mayor, a railroad manager who was occupying his first and only elected office, himself had strong ties to the business community; having already faced the same delegation that so doggedly lobbied Sheridan, he was quite ready to hand over the reins of power—and, as the chief executive of the city, possessed the authority to do so.[116] But two members of the popularly elected Police Board, Commissioners Thomas Brown and Mark Sheridan, were also on hand—and they did their best to force Mason to leave the problem of public safety to elected officials and civil officers.

Martial law, they suggested, was a too-drastic step for a city that was ravaged but essentially at peace. In their view, Chicagoans would be served best by a campaign for public safety supervised by the city police, the officers who were, as Brown later observed, "thoroughly acquainted with the character of the people."[117] The two therefore strongly objected to the general's request, arguing that the police, in combination with militiamen and "special" volunteers, could certainly maintain good order. The commissioners asked for some form of compromise, an agreement that might protect the city with the forces that were available but not in so doing potentially imperil the people of Chicago. According to Brown's and Philip Sheridan's separate recollections, however, the general, a man accustomed to exclusive powers of command, balked at any sharing of power. "There can be but one hand in this," he declared. "I am not willing to have anything to do with it in any other way—I'll withdraw my troops first; I am not anxious for the job."[118] After a brief but heated discussion, the two sides arrived at a course of action that reflected the unusual authority available to R. B. Mason at this moment of crisis. For the Great Fire gave a mayor with ordinarily "weak" powers of office the somewhat ironic ability to exercise substantial authority by *ceding* his right to govern. Mason thus personally made the critical choice to trust municipal safety to a party distinct from the elected officers of Chicago or Illinois, a prerogative he would again exercise in his handling of the key question of just who should oversee the city's part in the administration of relief.[119]

That same afternoon, the mayor issued an official declaration entrusting the "preservation of good order and peace in the city to Lieutenant General P. H. Sheridan, U.S. Army." Commissioners Brown and Sheridan essentially lost their fight, winning only a specific call for the police to act "in conjunction" with the military; the superintendent of police, moreover, was clearly rendered a subordinate to General Sheridan, given only a vague authority "to consult." Still, warnings of the overly harsh nature of martial law and the potential legal impropriety of allowing a military occupation in a time of peace had plainly struck a chord with Mayor Mason: he was also careful to add the rather contradictory charge that Sheridan "preserve the peace of the city . . . without interfering with the functions of city government."[120] Such a disclaimer did not alter the true impact of his decision: as a direct consequence of the lobbying of a small group of business leaders, the security of lives and property in Chicago had become the responsibility of a purely military force.

Sheridan immediately began to exercise his exclusive powers, quickly moving to establish his independence from municipal officials. He pointedly chose to work out of a South Side office far distant from the temporary City Hall; as a New York City reporter facing a long trek to win an interview would sourly observe, "[H]ere the head of the city has planted a pine table and entertains his numerous visitors."[121] In his most famous acts, the general displayed the populist streak that had made him so revered a commander among his troops: while some merchants attempted to take advantage of dire shortages of food, Sheridan took it upon himself to act as an arbiter of just prices. The day after the fire, Mayor Mason had issued an emergency order to fix the cost of bread; in an extension of such regulation, Sheridan's soldiers routinely impounded the goods of grocers and peddlers who asked prices that to them seemed exorbitant. In addition, when the owners of two South Side hotels refused to obey an order that they reduce their newly inflated rates to a more ordinary level, the general promptly seized both establishments. Such displays of authority were widely hailed (though there must have been some disgruntled food merchants and hoteliers); after hearing of the hotel incidents, the devout Francis Test proclaimed Sheridan to be "a little God."[122]

But for all the popularity and publicity of his occasional forays into the realm of moral economy, Sheridan's primary efforts were far more oriented toward the interests of the business leaders who had so desired his service. To a large degree, the occupation aimed to reestablish the social and spatial barriers that had been lost to the disordering force of disaster. In essence, the general made sure that the people of Chicago remained in their more ordinary places, or at least did not stray where they normally did not belong—essentially creating a system of policed borders that particularly aimed to protect surviving neighborhoods and valuable commercial property. With a mixed team of trained soldiers, state militiamen, police officers, and the civilian volunteers deemed "fire guards" at his disposal, the general posted hundreds of armed sentries and organized nighttime patrols for each surviving city block.[123] A strict curfew went into effect at sundown; those who wished to travel after dark had to receive special permission and learn a password that changed each day. All of Sheridan's men were authorized to fire immediately upon any person who refused to obey an order. In the first days of the occupation, Francis Test would note the rigor and strictness of those on guard and their ready willingness to point a gun. "Indiscretion" alone, he concluded, could easily prove fatal.[124] By sheer vigilance, and so drastically limiting travel and access across the city, the general thus began to reverse the stunning mixture of peoples set in motion by the Great Fire.

Moreover, Sheridan's specific placement of his various troops seems to reflect a sensitivity to the best wishes of his elite champions—and a relative disregard for the safety and comfort of the bulk of the Fire's victims, those drawn from the lower classes. The general without question devoted special attention to securing the personal safety and property of the wealthy. In one notable measure of his concern, the five companies of infantrymen, seasoned professional soldiers straight from the Indian wars, were exclusively detailed to stand guard over the rubble of the downtown business district. There, according to the *New York Tribune*, this "most vigilant and trustworthy" of the forces at hand did its best to protect what was thought to be "the wealth and treasure of the city yet in safes," troves thought to be vulnerable to the depredations of professional thieves.[125] The exclusive Prairie Avenue neighborhood, a South Side enclave of only a few square blocks, received an exceptional amount of attention; residents enjoyed the protection of two entire companies of militiamen, special brigades of primarily native-born student volunteers from the university at Champaign.

Other areas and other people, however, were not the beneficiaries of such lavish care. Militia troops from Bloomington, Springfield, Rock Falls, and Rock Island—most of whom were members of Irish, German, and black brigades—were stationed all around the rest of the city. Described by their commander as "laborers, white and black, who had shouldered the musket in their working garb," such men were apparently not deemed suitable peacekeepers for the wealthiest district of the city.[126] Finally, the demolished North Side, where thousands of displaced survivors had congregated in makeshift encampments, received minimal attention from Sheridan, a choice that suggests how the vision of order put in place by the general was so closely tied to ensuring the security of valuable property and its owners. The North Side, with almost nothing of any value left standing, seemed unthreatened to him; "In its dilapidated condition" as one reporter explained, the area "did not need much military protection."[127] Such priorities by contrast gave far less weight to the needs of propertyless people. The devastated populace of this division, the 75,000 who had resided in an area of at least three square miles, were protected by just two companies of militiamen and fire guards—the same number detailed to watch over the few hundred who made their home on Prairie Avenue.

Sheridan thus maintained control of Chicago for nearly two weeks; given that he had assumed control of an already quiet city and the serious measures of the occupation, it seems no great surprise that this period was marked by a notable calm. But support for martial law quickly unraveled after the accidental killing on October 20 of Thomas Grosvenor, a long-term resident and well-known Police Court prosecuting attorney. At 1 A.M., as Grosvenor hurried from a late meeting to his South Division home, a Sheridan "fire guard" ordered him to halt and commanded him to give the evening's countersign. Grosvenor, himself a Civil War colonel, explained that he lived nearby, and walked on without any further response. The sentry, a university student, shot him on the spot—and thereby touched off a furor.

Some supporters of martial law lionized the volunteer, arguing that Grosvenor's death was best viewed as a necessary sacrifice and a most worthy object lesson, that his loss was "in some way compensated by saving a vast amount of property from the hands of violent persons, who were held in check by this violent act."[128] The Illinois House Committee that investigated the military occupation would strongly disagree, calling the shooting an "outrage upon the civil rights of the people."[129] Whatever their own opinion, the incident led many to wonder if it was indeed best for a military force to continue to hold sway in what was by all accounts a tranquil, if devastated, community. An embarrassed Sheridan defended his man as a loyal soldier who had followed the letter, if not the spirit, of his orders, and he barely managed to stave off his own and the student's indictment for murder.[130] Police Commissioners Brown and Sheridan, who had warned from the first of the dangers of replacing the discretionary civil powers of a police officer with a soldier's rigid and inflexible application of orders, were thus sadly vindicated. On

October 23, Mayor Mason finally discharged Sheridan of his peacekeeping duties, reinstating the police force as the primary guardians of civic order.

But the story of the role of the army in post-Fire Chicago was not quite finished. "I did not believe it possible," an exasperated Governor Palmer would observe in a special message to the legislature on November 19, "that any officer of the U.S. Army could again find a pretext for intermeddling in the affairs of the State of Illinois."[131] But Palmer had not reckoned with the utter determination of some prominent Chicagoans to maintain a military presence in their city, a campaign that not only had its most immediate roots in the traumas of the Great Fire but also reflected their broader set of anxieties about the potential dangers of a largely unknown urban "mass." Five days after the occupation had ended, Sheridan received a letter from the Relief and Aid Society, the private charitable agency sponsored by leading businessmen that was, thanks to Mayor Mason's executive order, in charge of public relief. While the Society already enjoyed the protection of a special police detail, its directors still remained uncertain that stability would reign.[132] Accordingly, they urgently requested that four companies of U.S. infantry be stationed "at or near" Chicago, "until it shall appear that there is no danger of attack, by disorderly persons, upon the depots of the Relief and Aid Society, or other riotous proceedings, for which the recent appalling calamity may have paved the way."[133] Signatories included the head of the organization's Executive Committee, the railroad attorney Wirt Dexter; *Tribune* part-owner (and soon-to-be mayor) Joseph Medill; bank presidents W. F. Coolbaugh, H. K. Eames, and F. Irving Pearce; and other important merchants, businessmen, and publishers.[134] The next day, October 29, the general relayed the petition of the Relief and Aid Society to his superiors, writing to U.S. Adjutant General E. D. Townsend to ask that four infantry companies be sent to Chicago at once.

Even though his term of service had ended in controversy, it seems plain that Sheridan was quite eager to do this favor for these leading men of the city. In his letter to Townsend, Sheridan described an alarming correspondence between the presence of the lately departed federal force and a state of good order in the city:

"[T]he troops were no sooner gone than the turbulent spirit commenced to manifest itself, and seems to be increasing."[135] It is difficult to know if the general was responding to actual incidents or simply validating the worries of the Society directors; the testimony of Police Commissioner Brown, however, suggests that there had been no substantial upsurge in criminality after the lifting of martial law. Moreover, other elements of Sheridan's petition seem similarly geared to easing the way toward the return of a military force. No doubt wary of Governor Palmer and the fallout from the Grosvenor killing, Sheridan took extra care to legitimize his request by invoking the name of Joseph Medill, the *Tribune* owner and editor who was then running for mayor. Bowing to civil authority, the general made a point of noting that he was acting at the request of Medill, whom he termed the "in-coming new mayor." In an interesting and telling omission, however, he neglected to mention that Medill had signed the petition as part of a larger group of private citizens. Sheridan's careful justification of his request is further undercut to some degree by the fact that Medill, on October 29, had not yet been elected; though Medill did seem the likely victor, voting would not take place until November 4. But General Sherman was pleased to accommodate his fellow commander, turning a blind eye to any dubious claims. He instantly dispatched four companies of the Philadelphia-based Eighth Infantry to Chicago, where they remained in garrison throughout the winter just southwest of the city limits—a federal military presence that would continue to gall Governor Palmer.

In December, quizzed by William Underwood, chairman of the Illinois General Assembly Judiciary Committee, as to why the U.S. army had camped next door to the Union Stockyards, Sheridan came up with an equivocating response. "These companies," he wrote truthfully, "have never been used for police purposes . . . Nor," he continued more disingenuously, "was it ever contemplated by me that they should. They are simply in garrison for the winter; when spring comes I believe it is intended that they shall continue their march to the western frontier."[136] But the *Chicago Evening Journal*, a newspaper published by Charles Wilson, one of the signers of the Relief and Aid Society letter, had set out a much more convincing explanation for the continued presence of the army shortly after the organization had made its request. Despite Sheridan's claim to the contrary, the *Evening Journal* frankly acknowledged that the nearby encampment of infantry was meant from the start as a guarantor of good order in Chicago.[137] The newspaper fervently seconded the contention of the Relief and Aid Society that their depots needed the protection of a strong fighting force; such storehouses of wealth, the editorial argued, might seem too tempting to "crowds of the poor," the always vaguely menacing class of people now made "desperate" by disaster.

Moreover, in a scenario the *Evening Journal* found even more compelling, the paper claimed that a nearby army could also serve the end of discouraging any interference with the economy on the part of organized workers: "[T]hreatened strikes indicate that laborers willing to work might not be allowed to do so." Here the issue of the cooperation of working people, the notion that unions would combine to force wage levels above reasonable levels and prevent others from working in their stead, received an early airing—one of the first signs of a continuing post-Fire debate over whether or not such activities on the part of workers would undermine the good order of the city. Governor Palmer confirmed the power of such reasoning in his response to the Society's petition to Sheridan: an angry letter to President Grant. Again affirming the ability and right of the State of Illinois to protect its people, he expressed his disbelief that the army would see fit to honor a request made by "private citizens." For Palmer, fears of what he described as "the possible, though not probable *strikes* of laborers" should in no way become the basis of public policy—or serve as an excuse to sidestep the authority of duly elected officials.

In one of the first public manifestations of what became an ongoing crusade on the part of business leaders, an effort that would culminate with the establishment of the aptly named Fort Sheridan twenty-five miles to the north of the city in the wake of the 1886 Haymarket Affair, the *Evening Journal* argued that the federal government had every right to establish a permanent military post near Chicago.[138] It had, the paper reminded, most laudably done just so in the vicinities of New York, St. Louis, and Philadelphia, giving those cities the capacity to bring in federal troops at any hint of disorder: "That the authorities can call upon the government to assist in preventing a threatened outbreak, or putting one down has often been demonstrated." Scoffing at the protests of those "sensitive" to seeming abrogations of civil authority, the paper declared that all of the people of Chicago had "a right to the security which the presence of these troops affords them." In the view of many of Chicago's "most prominent citizens," as these arguments again suggest, the social order of their modern industrial metropolis seemed threatened everyday by its working people—whether the disorderly poor or those who saw fit to join and sustain unions. And such a dangerous city required the chastening proximity of a federal force, a military unit ready and willing to do the work of building barriers, whenever civil authorities (or those who in some way controlled civil authorities) might beckon.

In certain ways, it is difficult to evaluate the actual impact of the military occupation of Chicago upon the people of the city. Aside from expressions of relief at his arrival, little commentary concerning the general appeared in any newspapers or letters; most in the city, preoccupied with the immediate tasks of survival and assessing the work of reconstruction, perhaps had neither the time nor the inclination to indulge in what might have seemed arcane debate over states rights or the proper locus of power in municipal government. For many years, historians have most often echoed this relative silence, either uncritically lauding the general for his service, or at least making the more modern assumption that the presence of the military did not represent any unusual extension of federal powers.[139] But in trying to arrive at any conclusions about what a period of military rule meant for Chicagoans and the overall shape of civic order, it is important to recall just what the general and his forces did *not* do for the people of the city. The men who served in the occupation of Chicago did not aid the police, assist in the distribution of relief, or help in the early stages of rebuilding. To the contrary, they were put in place solely to bring about the imposition of martial law—and the according suspension of civil rule.

In the view of one of the members of the Illinois House of Representatives who served on the special committee that investigated the occupation, the whole affair seemed an egregious misreading of the primary needs of a city that was, after all, home to tens of thousands of the victims of an immense disaster. The army, Elijah Haines observed, had done much to guard against imagined disorders, of all the worst nightmares of more prosperous citizens, but far less to aid the very real and very needy mass of people in Chicago: "Had this tender been that of food or necessary supplies for the destitute, and building materials and workmen for rebuilding homes for the homeless, a proposition of thanks might be appropriate, but in place of bread we are given a stone."[140] Why, wondered the representative, had such a fighting force been dispatched to a city filled with the homeless and dispossessed survivors of a great trauma? He answered his own question with the following rhetoric: "They are men with bayonets, bringing complete military armament. For what purpose? For war?"[141] As Haines here suggested, it is worth noting that the response to this urban disaster did not necessarily have to be so militaristic.

Police Commissioner Brown, in his reply to the inquiries of the House committee, offered what might be read as another answer to the problem Haines posed: why it was that the "ministering angels" sent to Chicago "came in rigid military form."[142] The commissioner explicitly debunked what he viewed as baseless anxieties centering around class differences, the fears of elite businessmen that in his view ultimately explained the army's presence. To him, the powerful specters of criminality, riot, and strikes mirrored the sensational fictions of urban life far more closely than its realities. According to Brown, working men and women, if less prosperous than their wealthier fellow citizens, were still unlikely vandals and incendiaries; to the contrary, such people, many of whom themselves were homeowners, wished dearly to protect their own small stake in the city and were therefore "directly interested in sustaining law and order."[143] "Capitalists don't generally fight, except in defense of their property," he observed, "and men who own the house and lots where their families live are not very likely to engage in bloody riots or in destroying the property of other people."[144] Pointing to the city's only notable example of working-class protest at this point in time, a short-lived general strike in May of 1867 over the question of the legal eight-hour day, he noted that no great disruptions had occurred—and that the service of a company of state militiamen who stood on alert certainly had not been needed.[145]

In his view, the usual state of class relations in Chicago did *not* teeter on the edge of violent crisis. Such a misguided perception, Brown argued, stemmed directly from the inability of more elite citizens to appreciate what he considered to be the true "character" of the vast majority of the working people of Chicago—values of thrift and hard work that in many ways mirrored those thought to belong to any good "capitalist." To be sure, tensions did exist, and not everyone in Chicago was a saint: certain individuals, as the commissioner readily allowed, were "perhaps not as careful as they might or ought to be." Still, he concluded, anyone with any capacity to recognize the real lives and aspirations of most Chicagoans, a person who did not reflexively rush to erect barriers meant to ward off what they imagined as the entirety of a "dangerous class," would likely see they had little to fear. Brown closed with a cutting attack upon the honor and integrity of the group of business leaders who had worked so strenuously to secure martial rule, a campaign that of course undercut his own authority as an elected official. His opponents, he charged, were either unable or unwilling to look across the chasm of social difference with any degree of reason or compassion. He concluded with the following comment about the "mass of the people" in Chicago: "Any man who is afraid of them must either be very timid or very wicked."

Possibly timid, perhaps wicked—in the end, however they might be judged, those who insisted that any hope for good order in their city required the service of General Sheridan were nothing if not certain of the validity and significance of their cause. Convinced that a military force offered the best solution to the disastrous shattering of what they already felt to be a fragile urban order, these businessmen, with the aid of a sympathetic mayor, engineered an end-run around the norms of civil procedure. A group that did not share the same set of anxieties about the city, the Select Committee of the Illinois Legislature, thus drew a rather baffled conclusion after its detailed investigation of the episode: "[I]t is difficult to reconcile the conduct of those persons, who, after the excitement had subsided, were still clamorous for military rule, and so censorious of the governor." The report went on to chide the leaders who brought martial law to post–Great Fire Chicago: "After order had been restored, and the business affairs of the city has commenced to resume, as is shown to be the case very shortly after the occurrence of the calamity, people had a right to expect an observance of the laws of the State from all citizens, particularly those in positions of authority."[146] Yet those who worked to install General Sheridan plainly held to a different understanding of what constituted "order," a vision that was closely linked to specific concerns that could only grow out of the urban setting of the disaster. For in the end, the military occupation of Chicago was to a certain degree the practical result of elite worries about class difference, of their fears for and of a city that had already endured a great trauma, yet might still be undone by its own internal fissures.

In the midst of the frantic wave of early dispatches from the Fire-torn city, a reporter for the *Hartford Post* took some time to reflect on the popular frenzy that he himself was helping to create and fuel. In the process, he produced a trenchant commentary on some of the perceptions of urban order and class difference that were at play over the course of these post-Fire weeks. If he merely stuck to reports of what he had seen or verified, the reporter observed, his columns never pleased his audience: the "horrible picture" of devastation, for a readership schooled in sensational tales of the city was simply not awful enough—lacking "murder to make it complete." Without "reports of heartless killers, vigilante mobs, and miscellaneous looters, incendiaries, thieves, and extortionists," he claimed, accounts of the Great Fire could not begin to be "congruous and coherent-like" to his audience. Such readers, moreover, voracious in their appetite for extremely bad news, turned solid evidence of tranquility on its head, using such reports to justify their preconceived notions of the horrors that disaster would "truly" visit upon the city. According to the correspondent, though Sheridan himself had repeatedly stated that good order reigned in Chicago, his readers would instantly distrust the general's word. For a readership primed to expect the worst of the city, the reassurance of a man "so used to blood" did not seem believable: "This is nothing to him. . . . *Very quiet*—that's good, but as a matter of fact, they have shot incendiaries and hung them to lampposts and stoned them to death . . . for the telegraph has distinctly said so."[147] No sort of factual reportage could dissuade these readers from their readymade vision of a city gone completely awry.

With his shrewd dissection of the market for sensational stories about the city, the Hartford correspondent here outlined how expectations of disorder so powerfully conditioned the narratives that were told about the urban world of nineteenth-century America. Experiences, understandings, and memories of the Great Fire and its sequel were likewise in part formed out of such perceptions and discursive traditions: the stories of the Great Fire in the end cannot be separated from its location in a great city. For in these years of unprecedented urban growth, the "good order" of a city was often defined by the possibility of upheaval, a disorder that might spring out of a foreign and unknown "dangerous class" that seemed to pose a constant threat. At this moment, driven by such fears, a native-born elite realized its particular understanding of safety and security, one that involved an insistence upon a rigid military occupation. But such an outcome, an elite victory of a sort, was not the only possible end to a contest to define civic order. The clash over martial law was merely one of an ongoing set of debates that would take many forms and have many kinds of results, as Chicagoans struggled to reconstruct their community in accordance with their often differing notions of what best served themselves and their city.

CHAPTER TWO

Relief, Aid, and Order

As soon as it was safe to move through the ruins on the morning after the Great Fire, Alderman Charles C. P. Holden slowly picked his way through the ravaged landscape. Upon reaching the north border of the burned district, he came face-to-face with an equally surreal sight: the ramshackle encampment of thousands of homeless refugees. "Great living masses," Holden later wrote, "met our vision in every direction."[1] "On Monday, the 9th of October," as journalist Sidney Gay similarly remembered, "the city was like the resting place of a routed and fugitive army."[2] In the immediate aftermath of the disaster, the chaos of panicked escape had given way to a chaos of confusion and despair. Holden bore witness to an awful panorama of the "sick and crippled, the aged and infirm," of "women . . .hunting for their little lost ones, husbands searching for their wives." Families fortunate enough to be together huddled under shanties built of furniture, carpets, and any other goods saved from the flames.[3] "Scores of little children," the alderman further recalled, "clung to their mothers, while the mothers knew not whither to go or what to do."[4] In this anarchic remnant of community, all basic structures of order and authority had seemingly dissolved.

What, indeed, was to be done? How would the stricken city feed the hungry, attend to the sick and injured, shelter the displaced from the chill October wind and rain? A sweeping disaster demanded a similarly immense relief effort; at least 100,000 people required immediate aid. And precisely who should take charge of this enormous task?

Any assessment of how Chicagoans responded to these questions is complicated by the fact that both Fire narrators and the national media quickly elevated the "Relief of Chicago" into the realm of the mythic.[5] Just as fire narrators conveyed the fantastic scale of the disaster itself by asserting that what they had witnessed could never be accurately retold, journalists Colbert and Chamberlin employed a familiar disclaimer to introduce what they viewed as a miraculous outpouring of charity: "We cannot adequately describe the acts in which all Christendom leaned over Chicago, and poured the precious balm of sympathy into her wounds."[6] A public that had devoured news of the Great Fire instantly reacted to the crisis, flooding the city with donated goods and cash.[7] "The discordant note announcing sorrow, death, and devastation," the correspondents declared, "went forth in one hour through the civilized world." And "in another hour it flowed back, resolved into the most delicious chords of love and Christ-like relief."[8]

As the religious imagery of such language suggests, many northern presses and pulpits soon turned the "Relief of Chicago" into an object lesson in the possibilities of Christian love. Henry Ward Beecher was one of many to read a providential message into this tragic happening. "We could not do without the Chicago Fire," proclaimed the nation's most-famed minister.[9] While victims might have begged to differ, such an interpretation of disaster sought to reassure Americans that a nation in the midst of Reconstruction, and further confronted by the widening class divisions of an emerging industrial economy, could still do great deeds in service of a common humanitarian cause. "The true crown of America is her magnanimity," announced the national monthly *Galaxy*. "In what nation does charity flow more spontaneously from all ranks of its people when suffering humanity cries aloud from an Ireland, a Lancashire, a Paris, from a Savannah, New Orleans, or Chicago?" Dismayed by Washington Irving's famous 1855 description of the true American religion as worship of the "Almighty Dollar," the *Galaxy* seized upon the disaster to make a counterclaim about the moral potential of acquisitive individualism. As the magazine declared, "At least Chicago demonstrates that we sometimes use the almighty dollar as the Almighty conceivably means that the dollar should be used."[10]

Local Fire narrators echoed such themes, hailing the virtuous and community-building effects of the work of charity. In an echo of the *Galaxy* editors, South Sider Emma Hambleton drew an explicit connection between Chicago's disaster and the Union's recent trial by fire. "The fire, like the Civil War, brought reconstruction and individual adjustment to all of our lives," she wrote. "Everyone weighed themselves to see what they were worth, not only to themselves but to others . . . Relief," concluded Hambleton, "was the clarion call."[11] Martha Shorey likewise marveled at the new bonds of fellowship evident in the national giving and local administration of charity. "In the year of our Lord 1871," she proclaimed, "the grandest lesson of Christian philosophy, the lesson of human brotherhood, has been learned at last."[12] Just as boosters reacted to the Fire by extolling the city's chance for commercial regeneration, those deeply interested in the moral state of their city plainly viewed the relief effort as evidence of a spiritual regeneration born of the disaster.

There was more than a grain of truth in these claims: people across the world generously responded to the plight of the city, and many in Chicago labored hard and long to deliver aid to the victims. But despite this undeniable display of altruism (and the emotional tributes it spawned), the "Relief of Chicago" for some seemed far less than wholly humanitarian. In a letter that appeared in a city newspaper seven weeks after the disaster, a person identified only as "Sympathizer" mounted an attack upon the group that had assumed charge of public, city-sponsored relief—the elite-run charity known as the Relief and Aid Society. "The truth is," charged "Sympathizer," "that the Chicago Relief and Aid Society have failed to fill the bill, have failed to do what they agreed to do by taking care of suffering humanity in our midst." The writer concluded by drawing a bitter picture far different from the glorious accounts put forth by Colbert and Chamberlin or Martha Shorey: "Millions from all parts of the globe have sent their donations here to relieve those in distress, and not to be hoarded up and lorded over by a set of men whose sympathies are foreign to the task at hand."[13]

As this dissenting voice suggests, fire relief was anything but simple in its motivation or execution. On a practical level, all sorts of Chicagoans had suffered differing degrees of loss and had similarly differing abilities to recoup any personal toll. Moreover, the object of rebuilding shattered lives was inextricably tied to the restoration of the urban order—and both projects raised potent ideological problems. Who deserved help? What kind of aid should be offered? What was the ultimate goal of fire relief? Who should control the official efforts of the municipality, taking charge of the millions of dollars in cash and goods that were pouring into the city?

The aftermath of the Great Fire thus forced Chicagoans to reckon with the question of how they understood the very meaning of "charity." How would these people, residents of a diverse but interdependent city, handle the task of restoring tens of thousands of individuals and families to a state of economic independence? In what ways should responsible citizens deal with the fact of dependency, however extraordinary or temporary, in the context of a culture that increasingly exalted the completely self-reliant? Despite the reified ideal of benevolence long associated with this episode, the ideologies and practices of the various relief efforts that followed the Great Fire are ultimately most telling of how Chicagoans held to understandings of charity and urban community that were rooted in their own perceptions of their many differences.

THE PATCHWORK OF LOSS

Some eight months after the Great Fire, Robert Collyer, pastor of the elite Unity Church, described the effect of the disaster upon the finances of his family in a letter to a close associate. Even in the face of the complete demolition of his home and church, the clergyman could still assure his friend that everything had "turned out alright." The situation had indeed turned out surprisingly well for the minister: despite his substantial losses, Collyer in fact ended up drawing a sizable cash profit from the Great Fire. Though of course inconvenienced by the need to relocate and rebuild, he received a full insurance settlement, and his wealthy flock could easily afford to continue his regular salary. Further, he picked up a quick $2000 on the "eyewitness" lecture circuit and amassed nearly $7000 in cash and goods—gifts sent by concerned admirers for his personal use.[14]

But relatively few would share such ironic good fortune. The Great Fire brought only hardship to a man like John Linden, a Scandinavian immigrant teamster. The conflagration swept away the modest cottage he owned on the North Side. To compound this loss, a $1400 insurance policy that Linden held with a local company—a business forced into liquidation by the disaster—proved worthless. Widowered nine months before the Fire and father to three small children, the teamster did not have a regular employer and worked only sporadically.[15] He had no cash savings; all of his personal capital had been invested in his home. And though he owned his lot, the Great Fire left Linden unable to afford the materials he needed to rebuild.[16]

As these two stories suggest, the Great Fire exacted very different tolls from different people. Prosperous Chicagoans such as Collyer and his congregants obviously had the most to lose—and in fact, measured by the high value of their homes and commercial property, they indeed lost the most. But like a John Linden, those who owned little often faced the harshest consequence: an instantly vanished life-savings that could not be recouped. To assess the full spectrum of the Great Fire's impact—and thereby understand just who would come to be most dependent upon the official distribution of relief by the city—it is critical to recognize the patchwork pattern of loss that afflicted Chicagoans. Many variables, details ranging from the simple facts of just what escaped destruction to complex reckonings of access to insurance and credit, added up to define the burden of each individual or family.

The path of the Great Fire in itself determined that loss would fall unevenly across the city. Its vivid reputation often clouds what may seem an obvious point: that the conflagration decidedly did not destroy the entire metropolis. To be sure, the grand public and commercial buildings of the downtown did burn away; the wreck of these symbols of civic identity—"all," wrote one observer, "that was city-like in Chicago"—plainly struck the sort of psychological (and economic) blow that to some degree explains the durability of imagery suggesting utter devastation.[17] But as the journalist Alfred Sewell noted, "[T]hose who have supposed that the whole of Chicago, or even the greater part of its area is in ruins, make a grave mistake. . . . Much of it still lives."[18] Indeed, at the moment the flames died, seventy-five percent of all developed property remained untouched. Seventy percent of all city residents still had homes; entire neighborhoods—elite Prairie Avenue, prosperous Union Park, working-class Bridgeport, Canaryville, and Pilsen, to name a few—were completely unharmed.[19]

Further, the structural components of the transport and processing industries central to the urban economy were spared massive losses. Of seventeen large grain elevators, eleven stood away from the path of the flames; seventy-five percent of grain stocks survived. Similarly, despite the Fire's early and fatal foothold in South Side lumberyards and planing mills, seventy-five percent of lumber inventories escaped incineration. The Union Stockyards, headquarters for the meat-packing industry, stood well to the southwest of the Fire's point of origin. Finally, the railroad and steamship lines that carried commercial goods to and from the city suffered relatively little damage; most railroads maintained their terminals on the largely unburned West Side, and the Fire did not touch over twenty miles of dockage along the river. Owners and employees connected to these critical commercial ventures remained blessed by the city's status as the premier American entrepôt; still able, moreover, to rely upon links to international networks of credit and capital, the people who worked in such industries faced an immediate future that was far from completely grim.[20]

Though the Great Fire had burned a solid swath from the heart of their city, many Chicagoans were thus personally spared from a total devastation. On October 14, Daniel Ransom, a farm machinery wholesaler with offices and warehouses on the South Side, hastened to counter the notion of utter ruin, issuing a handbill headlined "Chicago Not Yet All Destroyed!" "WE ARE SAFE," he proclaimed. And business, according to Ransom, would proceed as usual—with some allowances for those who might be fire victims; the agent reminded his trading partners that "we hope to receive promptly from all who are indebted to us—AND ALL WHO ARE NOT SUFFERERS—that which is due."[21] Dr. Jared Bassett lost his office but still deemed the condition of his family to be "quite comfortable as yet our house is left, and our furniture."[22] Surveyor Samuel Greely found himself in the opposite situation: the Fire consumed his North Side home, but his business fortunes skyrocketed as he and his associates worked frantically to redraw the property lines burned away with the destruction of public plat books.[23]

Certain Chicagoans, particularly residents of the West Division, escaped loss altogether. William Furness, who found refuge in that portion of the city, took special note of an odd dichotomy sprung from the geography of the disaster; "[I]t was curious" he recalled, "to notice ladies out on the streets making calls, when we had just come from the desolation and confusion."[24] Greely's Fire narrative likewise gives a sense of the strange congruence of complete ruin and stable prosperity: three days after the Fire, upon arriving for a formal dinner at the Prairie Avenue home of railroad lawyer and Relief and Aid Society director Wirt Dexter, Greely and his wife—still clad in the costumes they had donned to flee their home—asked to retire to a private room "where we could hide our poverty-stricken appearance from the other guests."[25]

But unlike the relatively fortunate Samuel Greely, a North Sider who at least retained his business, most who lived in the district did face a particularly sweeping set of hardships. The Great Fire, of course, left this area a wasteland of ashes; Hermann Raster, editor of the *Staats-Zeitung*, thus could employ a telling shorthand to describe the scope of ruin to his daughter: "[A]ll your friends on the north side lost their homes, so it isn't necessary to name individuals."[26] In many ways, the north wards stood as a separate town within Chicago's proper limits; like the close-knit German and Scandinavian colonies in most American cities, many immigrants resided, worked, shopped, prayed, and socialized entirely within the boundaries of what native-born satirists had come to designate as the *Nord Seite*.[27] A sample from the *Staats-Zeitung* of October 13, the first issue to appear after the fire, vividly depicts the many-faceted devastation of this community:

> Mr. Gustave Drossler, who had a shop on North Clark, and his whole family died in the flames, likewise his oldest brother, and his niece, Miss Richter, who was a member of the Germania Female Choir. . . . Mrs.

> Louisa Theilemann, whose house burned down two years ago, and who only days ago started at great personal sacrifice, a German Theatre on the North Side, has lost everything. . . . The maid of Mrs. Thielemann and the maid of her neighbor, Mrs. Berthold Meyer, Ontario Street, lost their lives. Ernestine Schmidt is being sought by her husband, Christian Schmidt.[28]

On the North Side, an immigrant world had been blasted apart; Colbert and Chamberlin ultimately concluded in their reckoning of losses that "our German fellow citizens suffered the worst."[29]

While it is relatively simple to connect the magnitude of loss to the geography of physical devastation, it is much more difficult to compute the financial toll of the Great Fire with any real precision. As James Milner observed days after the disaster, "The complication of losses, affecting buildings and goods, insurance companies, importers and jobbers on the seaboard, mortgage securities, burned money, depreciation in real estate, throwing men out of employment and a hundred other things makes summing up a large amount."[30] The fire catapulted real estate, credit, insurance, and labor markets into states of flux that would wreak havoc with any attempts to fix the actual cost of damage. Though Colbert and Chamberlin valiantly calculated that Chicagoans had lost $196,000,000 in personal property, the authors at the same time disclaimed both the inclusiveness and reliability of their figure. No one, the pair argued, could account for every item "in the immense aggregate of loss."[31]

Still, a few unmistakable patterns did emerge out of this quagmire, patterns that were largely molded by the variable of social class. Put simply, more prosperous Chicagoans were far better equipped to recover from any damages. For the owners of businesses, the amount of their loss often depended to a large degree upon whether or not they could receive infusions of cash or offers of credit from lenders and investors who were unaffected by the blaze. Those with larger enterprises clearly had more valuable connections in the face of such a crisis. Investors and businesses around the country and abroad, for example, had a stake in the quick recovery of Cyrus McCormick's Reaper Works; such a firm was well-buffered by its sheer scale and ties to national and world markets.[32] Leading retailers Marshall Field and the Farwell brothers suffered respective $2.3 million and $1.9 million losses of warehoused stock and property. But both Field and the Farwells, while of course considerably handicapped by the need to relocate and reorganize, soon got back to business. "Large dealers," as Colbert and Chamberlin observed, "have great credits and great facilities for resuming."[33]

But no such safety net would secure the investments of scores of small manufacturers and shopkeepers; "[I]t is the smaller dealers," according to Colbert and Chamberlin, "who have suffered, proportionally, the worst."[34] In their estimation, for those with less than $5000 in capital and no major lines of credit at their disposal, "all that they had was swallowed up." Relief records tell the story of Frank Maiwarus, a shoemaker who lost his workroom and small retail store to the blaze. Like many who ran a small business, he had neither the business ties nor personal savings to cushion this blow, and the insurance policy he held with a local firm proved worthless. "Unable to follow any other avocation," according to the investigator who handled his case, the fifty-four-year-old German immigrant lost all he had labored to achieve in his adopted city.[35] Those who worked alone or in small partnerships often absorbed such massive blows. "With no bank account, no credit, and no location," Colbert and Chamberlin noted, petty merchants and craftsmen "were in a sorry plight, and knew not which way to turn."[36]

Insurance practices, as Frank Maiwarus must have discovered, most strikingly illustrate the class dimension of individual financial losses—both those suffered by the ruin of a business or the destruction of a home. State insurance laws at the time were very lax; according to Robert Critchell, a long-time city broker, "[A]lmost anything which was called an insurance company could do business in Chicago and throughout Illinois with impunity, whether it had cash assets, or paid up capital, or neither."[37] Good insurance practice, then as now, dictated that companies investigate the risks presented by applicants before issuing any policy. But in Chicago, opportunistic and unregulated local companies would write a policy for anyone who could afford the premium. By offering coverage so freely, the insurers ironically promoted the same slipshod building practices that made the city such a fertile field for a blaze—a gamble that cost them (and their clients) dearly when the Great Fire did strike. In the aftermath, city fire insurance companies were hit with a concentrated rash of claims that entirely overwhelmed their assets. Nearly all local firms and a substantial number of those from outside the state were driven into liquidation. As a result, the men and women who held policies with these agencies most often received little or nothing to compensate their loss.[38]

As a general rule, local companies most often serviced those with relatively little to insure: small property holders from the ranks of the middle and working classes. Since insurance defaults were not so unusual in the nineteenth century, more prosperous Chicagoans most often gave their business to established and reputable firms in the East and in Europe. Such prudence—and the ability to meet much higher premiums—would pay. Mrs. William Blair, for example, wrote to a friend about the wise decision of her hardware merchant husband to insure his business with British companies; Blair received the full amount of his policies, providing him with ample capital for rebuilding.[39] When some of Cyrus McCormick's insurers gave him the news that they could not pay the full value of his policies, McCormick promptly hired the exclusive New York law firm of Lord, Day, and Lord to pursue his claims. Shortly thereafter, McCormick joined Blair in using a full settlement to finance the reconstruction of his Reaper Works.[40] Those with substantial assets thus had access to a much more secure level of insurance protection.

Those who owned less, by contrast, were far more vulnerable not only to uninsured loss but to the very bitter fate of holding paid-up policies that ended up having no real value. Tannery worker Dietrich Voelker, for example, owned a small home and lot in the heart of the North Side German colony—an investment he had secured with a policy worth $1600. In Voelker's case, years of premium payments to his local company went for nought; he, by his own testimony, "did not get a cent."[41] Gotfried Schneitmann, a slaughterhouse worker who rented rooms, similarly failed to recover any of the $500 policy held on the contents of his home.[42] Surviving relief records indicate that of 169 applicants who held fire policies for their homes, all but five did business with local agencies—firms that on average paid less than twenty percent of the value of the policies they had written. A statistic signaling the particular fate of the German North Side further emerges from these records: nearly one-third (fifty-three) of the applicants held policies with the German Mutual Company, an enterprise run by and for members of this community that paid only eight percent on its policies.[43] A policy's payoff, in the words of Colbert and Chamberlin, often meant the difference between "utter ruin and the chance to start again." And in the end, few Chicagoans of lesser means could rely upon their insurance, as years of payments had led them to believe they could, for a decent second start.

Given all of these many complications of geography, finance, and insurance, it is probably impossible to offer any truly inclusive summary of the patchwork of loss wrought by the Great Fire. Much as every person's identity and location had a major effect upon any Chicagoan's experience of the Great Fire itself, such a range of particularities ultimately determined the sort of hardships later suffered by an individual or a family. Still, one general conclusion seems obvious: given the residential composition of most of the area that burned and the fact that those who owned less valuable property were far less likely to receive insurance settlements, it is plain that the disaster imposed an especially heavy burden upon the immigrant working people of the city. Records of municipal relief offer a stark accounting of the devastation on the North Side and in other areas that were home to the foreign-born: of the 18,478 families who received some form of aid by mid-December, only 1965 were of native birth. Eighty-nine percent of the applicants to official relief agents were thus part of the immigrant population of Chicago.[44] In its assessment of the disaster, the *Workingman's Advocate*, voice of the organized labor movement of the city, could reach the bottom line of the "complication of losses" far more directly than a businessman such as James Milner. "As might have been expected," the newspaper concluded, "the laboring classes have been the greatest losers by this calamity."[45] And this perhaps predictable fact—that those who most needed help were those who previously had the least—would have a central impact upon the theories and structures that underlay the task of municipal relief.

RELIEF AND POLITICS

On October 11, a *New York Herald* newsman wandered to the northern edge of the burned district, ending up at the same site surveyed by Alderman Holden just a day before. Ever true to the sensational expectations of his audience, the reporter composed the following account for the next day's paper of the scene he beheld: "Fifty thousand men, women, and children huddled together like so many wild animals; helpless children asking for bread; heart-broken parents, who know not which way to turn or what to say."[46] While his claim that "the greatest distress prevailed" seems beyond dispute, it seems equally likely that such a portrait of total chaos again mirrored the public taste for urban melodrama more accurately than it reflected the situation at hand. For by that afternoon, a citywide relief effort was already in full swing; if he had chosen to note their presence, the *Herald* reporter might have described the broadsides posted throughout the ruins by agents of the hastily formed General Relief Committee. Appealing "TO THE HOMELESS" in six-inch letters, the posters announced that the municipal relief effort would be headquartered in a West Side church, and further informed refugees that all surviving churches and schools were now open "for the shelter of persons who do not find other accommodations." The notice had seven signatories: Mayor Mason, and both an alderman and a private citizen from each of the three divisions of the city.[47]

At first, it seemed that city aldermen, in combination with private citizens, would assume control of the official organization and distribution of municipal relief. Even as the Great Fire burned, Charles Holden, the Common Council president, had pressed Mayor Mason to establish a system for relief.[48] The South Side alderman won Mason's quick agreement to the following plan: that a mixed body of aldermen and private citizens, with members drawn in equal numbers from each of the three city divisions, would coordinate the work of municipal relief. Such a structure would virtually ensure the presence of representatives of immigrant communities and allow the elected officers of the city to draw on the special talents of those not in public service. Within forty-eight hours, according to Holden, the labors of what was called the General Relief Committee were well launched: arrangements had been made with railroads for the free transportation of refugees, depots had been established for the receipt and distribution of donations, and "8 or 10" subcommittees were in other ways organizing to aid those in need. Housing became a special and immediate priority: public buildings were thrown open to survivors and a corp of carpenters began to erect around 200 temporary shelters.[49]

Still, despite such a seemingly promising start and Mason's official sanction, the General Relief Committee proved extremely short-lived. On October 13, four days after the fire had been extinguished, the mayor took the work of municipal relief out of the hands of elected authorities, issuing the following proclamation: "I have deemed it in the best interests of the city to turn over to the Chicago Relief and Aid Society all contributions for the suffering people of our city."[50] The Relief and Aid Society, a private charitable organization run by the commercial elite of Chicago since the late 1850s, was thus empowered to oversee the critical and wide-ranging task of administering the incoming flood of donations.[51] Just as he had entrusted municipal security to General Sheridan, R. B. Mason here again exercised an extraordinary degree of personal authority by ceding a municipal function to a noncivic body. By executive fiat, the aldermen of Chicago were barred from having any say over the finances and rules of the "official" relief effort of the city, a massive distribution of goods and supplies that would directly affect large numbers of their constituents.

In contrast to General Sheridan's well-documented assumption of control, the mechanics of the transfer of power from the General Relief Committee to the Relief and Aid Society remain somewhat obscure. The fragmentary comments of those involved in this decision indeed tell rather different stories. According to Sidney Gay, a journalist and critic who staunchly supported the decision of the mayor, the Relief and Aid Society wrested power from the aldermen of Chicago only with great difficulty: Gay dramatically declared that "the struggle was as desperate as the clutch of death."[52] Alderman

Holden's version—an elliptical reference that still pointedly managed to stress the prior efforts of his own General Relief Committee—was terse: "Thursday, the 12th, the Chicago Relief and Aid Society took charge of the great work thus fairly commenced."[53] Finally, the Society's own account excised any hint of controversy. Their story simply indicated that on October 12, Society Superintendent O. C. Gibbs and Executive Committee members Wirt Dexter and N. K. Fairbank verbally proposed to Mayor Mason that their organization take full charge of the receipt and distribution of all supplies. According to the Society, the mayor saw the irrefutable wisdom of this overture by the next morning and therefore acted to rescind his earlier, ill-conceived sanction of the General Relief Committee.[54]

To Mason, the Relief and Aid Society plainly seemed suited to the task of fire relief in ways that the city government decidedly was not. Fire relief would involve an enormous and unprecedented organizational effort—and, as Mason noted in his proclamation, this private agency had long functioned as the largest benevolent association in Chicago. The municipality, by contrast, had no experience with the work of charity; public relief of chronic indigents was a function carried out by the Cook County administration.[55] Moreover, as a former high-level manager of the Illinois Central railroad, Mason himself had long-supported the Relief and Aid Society and was consequently well aware of its practical experience and the reputations of its elite directors. Some of the premier executives in America were among the business leaders who made up the Society's Executive Board: men such as Marshall Field and George Pullman knew how to design and coordinate complex ventures. With its ardent approval of Mason's choice, a New York newspaper most likely echoed the mayor's own thoughts on the subject: "No one need fear that the relief so generously poured out will not be judiciously distributed . . . we know enough of keen, practical Chicago to confide to the hands of its businessmen all the gifts which they are to receive in trust for the whole suffering people."[56] These businessmen, for Mason, were the sort of honorable and trustworthy leaders who could best ensure the rapid and fair distribution of goods and services.

In some ways, the transfer of control to a long-established charitable agent, an organization backed by highly competent managers, thus seems quite a reasonable step. But to arrive at a more complete understanding of why the Relief and Aid Society was given charge of a public function, it is important to pose the question in other ways. Why, it also might be asked, had the mayor seen fit to exclude the aldermen of Chicago from the "official" work of relief? And why had he replaced the General Relief Committee—a body representative of people all across the city—with a private agency run solely by an appointed board drawn almost exclusively from a native-born commercial elite? From this point of view, it seems plain that more than issues of experience were at stake in Mason's decision.

Given just whom the Executive Board of the Relief and Aid Society replaced, calls for reliability, judgment, and integrity implied that the aldermen of the city possessed no such virtues. In an essay in defense of the Society, Sidney Gay—a former director—invoked the specter of a corrupt ward politics, a destructive force poised to bring an even worse state of ruin to the city. With municipal elections less than a month away, he charged, the "foul breed of city politicians"—what he deemed an aspiring "Tammany of Chicago," a potent label in the face of the prosecutions of the notorious "ring" then ongoing in New York City—planned to cement their rule "with the personal and pecuniary power which the handling of the relief fund and provisions in kind would give them."[57] In Gay's view, the aldermen of Chicago were the last people who should assume the guardianship of such a key municipal function.

Such extreme distrust of members of the Common Council can perhaps be explained as simple prudence; by 1871, municipal government was not exactly scandal-free.[58] But Gay's depiction of the aldermen as a collective force of evil does seem dubiously overwrought. While occasional problems had occurred in the council, nothing like an entrenched political machine (as Gay himself conceded) yet existed. More important, in terms of the specific question of authority at hand, Alderman Holden's General Relief Committee had in fact dispersed power between public officials and private citizens. Indeed, two prominent Relief and Aid officers—Superintendent O. C. Gibbs and Director Nathaniel K. Fairbank—held top posts on the committee. By design, the General Relief

Committee incorporated both political accountability and community oversight—checks and balances that could conceivably mediate against any gross abuses of authority on the part of aldermen. (By contrast, no one apart from the directorate of the Society oversaw the work of this entirely private organization.) In light of these circumstances, claims about the dangers posed by "corrupt" council members ring rather hollow.

Such rhetoric, however, had a plain political and ideological function. For those who made these charges were drawing out an important opposition that would appear more and more frequently in the statements of those who sought to "reform" American urban politics: that of the honest man of business, a citizen devoted to upholding the best interests of the whole of the city versus the venal and selfish politician, a man beholden to more particular—and therefore suspect—sets of "interests."[59] At the same time as this dichotomy came into play, Mayor Mason and other supporters of the Relief and Aid Society also made a critical assumption: that the commercial elite of the city stood apart from the "interests" embodied by the "corrupt" aldermen and were thus best able and entitled to decide just what steps served the "public interest," a best course for all of the citizens of Chicago. For as Sidney Gay argued, the wealthiest and most influential men of the city had no need to engage in a low scramble for personal gain; the great powers that would stem from the work of relief therefore should be entrusted to men already above any temptations.[60] With the directorate of the Society at the head of municipal relief, all could rest assured that any donation, as Gay declared, "would be used for the purpose for which it was given."[61] For the fifteen industrialists and businessmen, four lawyers, and one "society" doctor who sat on the Executive Board, the "public interest" was now theirs to define.[62]

Supposedly "disinterested" by virtue of their material success and social standing, such men of course could not be separated from the values and concerns rooted in their own personal histories and identities. From the first, then, the public service to be done by municipal relief was structured and molded by a committee that was overwhelmingly composed of native-born Protestants—eminent business leaders who were unlikely to view the mass of immigrant and working-class victims of the fire with a great deal of empathy. Indeed, as the Relief and Aid Society's central role in the effort to return a military force to the city had suggested, it seems plausible that some of the same fears of an ever-menacing working class lay beneath the eagerness of the agency to take charge of municipal relief. For if the distribution of charity were somehow mismanaged, if working people somehow became accustomed to a state of dependency—to Sidney Gay, above all the other problems brought to bear by the Great Fire, such a possibility seemed most appalling: "*the* crisis in the fate of Chicago." Whether Chicago "should ever recover from the terrible calamity that had swept over it, or whether the ruin should be utter and irrevocable," he argued, largely depended upon the "wise and economical distribution of aid."[63]

Only a business elite could properly guard against such a scenario; a representative body such as Holden's General Relief Committee, Gay implied, was too closely connected to the needs and demands of more particular communities throughout the city. Stability—the reconstruction of an urban order in which all were in "a condition for wholesome labor"—depended upon a "wise and economical" intervention by the Society. "If things had gone on as they had begun," Gay declared, "the laboring people of Chicago, instead of being cheerfully at work at good wages, would have been at this moment a starving, discontented, turbulent population."[64] Vested with the power to decide just who deserved the "world's charity" in just what measure, the "public" that the directors of the Society aimed to serve at the same time encompassed a working class that they reflexively understood as a danger to the good order of the city. In the course of all of their work, the Society would thus balance the two roles it assigned to the great majority of its Great Fire clients: that of a victim and that of a potential threat to cherished norms of economic independence.

CHARITY AND CLASS

On October 20, Frances Roberts—one of the hundreds of middle-class men and women employed by the Relief and Aid Society to carry out the daily business of relief—wrote to her mother to describe her first days on the job. Her initial experiences as a clerk had ominously suggested that she and her colleagues were only at "the beginning of a very trying work."[65] Merely getting to her job proved an ordeal: to enter the West Side depot, Roberts had to show a special pass at the head of a double file of musket-bearing soldiers dispatched by General Sheridan to maintain order among the crowd. Still, the substantial military presence failed to set Roberts at ease; "I felt all the time," she recalled, "that there was the elements of a mob." And though the true suffering of most applicants seemed only too apparent to Roberts, she and her coworkers, like all Society employees, took great care to prevent fraud—filling out forms, taking detailed statements, investigating references, and maintaining strict records of any goods disbursed.[66] Though "the slowness of red-tape" proved cumbersome, Roberts conceded that such prudence was indeed necessary. Charity based merely on sympathy, by Roberts's reckoning, would surely be abused; while the Great Fire, as she informed her mother, "has brought out the best qualities," disaster had "also developed some of the worst that exists in human nature."[67]

On the same day that Frances Roberts recorded her impressions, one man (identified only as "Burnt Out" in a letter to a city newspaper) witnessed the work of relief from a very different perspective: that of an applicant. Left homeless, and sleeping with his family in a roofed-over basement, this refugee went to Relief and Aid headquarters to ask for clothes and bedding—and quickly found himself caught up in a bureaucratic nightmare. First, "Burnt Out" stood with what Frances Roberts perceived as a mob-like mass for over an hour; upon finally reaching a Society worker, he was informed that his request had to be processed at a another depot. He headed to the second site, only to find that the man he needed to see was out for dinner. Late that afternoon, after spending four hours in lines and in transit, "Burnt Out" received an order for two blankets.

But this survivor's odyssey was far from over. The following morning, he traveled downtown to have his order countersigned; next, he went to another part of the same bureau to report the disbursement. At last free of paperwork and ready to draw his supplies, "Burnt Out" arrived at the distribution point, only to find, at 3 P.M., that this operation had closed for the day. Still determined to get his blankets, he returned early the next morning; "at 15 minutes before nine," he reported, "I got in line and staid [*sic*] there until 4 P.M. They had not served 50 persons up to that time and there were at least 300 waiting to be served." This final indignity proved to be the last straw. "I was disgusted," "Burnt Out" declared, "and have got my order and intend to keep it as a relic of the Chicago Relief and Aid Committee."[68]

The testament of Frances Roberts and the account offered by "Burnt Out" strikingly illustrate two sides of the same story. What the relief worker saw as an unruly and vaguely threatening crowd in the mind of the relief applicant seemed the inevitable by-product of an ill-designed and frustrating system. Chicago's official relief effort ultimately gave "Burnt Out" nothing; rather, in his view, he had indeed been robbed of both his time and his dignity. For her part, Frances Roberts unquestionably wanted to do exactly what the Society had failed to do for "Burnt Out": help those who had truly suffered. But despite her earnest intentions, Roberts, constrained by the dictates of the ideology of benevolence then coming to be known as "scientific charity," could hardly reach out with a free hand.

Though "Burnt Out" left unsatisfied, it cannot be denied that the Society did channel materials and services to an astonishing number of people. In a matter of days, what had been a moderately sized charitable agency was remade into a unique social welfare behemoth.[69] In its eighteen months of fire relief operations, the Society by its own count spent over $4,000,000 as it in some fashion attended to the needs of 157,000 individuals. Further, the organization remained particularly attuned to the needs of widows and deserted women and their families, and of the sick, aged, and infirm of both sexes: a community of sufferers, in keeping with common mid-nineteenth-century notions about gender and self-sufficiency, it had always considered worthy of charity.[70] But for any able-bodied working person who had fallen victim to the Great Fire—precisely the population most dependent upon the Society—receiving any portion of the "world's charity" would, as "Burnt Out's" story suggested, involve navigating the many shoals of an often hostile bureaucracy.

The Relief and Aid directors, like many nineteenth-century arbiters of charity, were deeply conscious of what they viewed as the potential dark side of the work of relief: that to aid "anyone who could help themselves," in the words of the Society director Ezra McCagg, was "in the highest degree harmful to the person aided and to society at large."[71] For one set of elite Chicagoans, then, the new "science" of charity, with its strict reliance upon systematic investigation, profound faith in the rewards of free labor, and axiomatic belief in individuals' responsibility for their own fate provided the best answer to the question of how to manage dependency—and interdependence—in their disordered city.

"Science" and Workers: The General Plan

In mid-nineteenth-century Chicago, as throughout the country, a variety of agents undertook the task of aiding those not fully or at all capable of self-support—a project, then as now, split between governmental and voluntary initiatives. The taxes levied by Cook County paid for some social services: an agent distributed food and fuel to chronic indigents, and several institutions—a hospital, an orphanage, an asylum, and a poorhouse—took in those too young, too old, too sick, or too impoverished to survive on their own. On the private side, the Relief and Aid Society, while certainly the preeminent and wealthiest benevolent association in the city, was in fact only one of many almoners. Various communities within Chicago—self-defined by gender, religion, ethnicity, and occupation—maintained their own charitable organizations. A small sampling indicates the diversity of these groups: the Ladies' Industrial Aid Association funneled support to poor young women; the Society of St. Vincent de Paul and the United Hebrew Relief Association saw to the needs of Catholics and Jews; the United Sons of Erin, the Société Française de Bienfaisance, the Germania Bruederbund, the Svea Society, and the Slovanska Lipa Benevolent Society aided their countrymen; and multiple protective benevolent associations provided a safety net for tradesmen such as plasterers, bricklayers, and steam-boilermakers.[72]

The Relief and Aid Society, by contrast, constructed itself as an independent, nonsectarian organization, asserting its "sole purpose and object" to be "the unconditional relief of the destitute of all classes, irregardless of religion or nationality."[73] With this mandate, the Society conceived of Chicago as a community in the broadest sense: the boundaries of class, ethnicity, and religion becoming evermore marked in the city were not to play any role in the agency's administration of benevolence. Instead of holding any narrow allegiance, the Relief Society aimed to substitute a "disconnected" system capable of "clear and unaffected" decisions.[74] "The whole theory of its management," one contemporary wrote of the Society, "is that charity is not a matter of feeling, but judgement."[75] But the Society's professed "independence" did not spawn policies that were somehow neutral or value-free: the vision of "unconditional relief" advanced by the organization's elite directors was a product of their deeply held belief in the power of any able-bodied person, ultimately, to help themselves.

Such ideology had its roots in antebellum America. From the late 1840s, some urban American charities began to experiment with a novel reliance upon expertise and system. In 1851, the founders of the Chicago Relief and Aid Society modeled their new institution upon New York City's pioneering Association for Improving the Condition of the Poor (AICP). The AICP, established in 1849, offered an alternative to what its managers viewed as the disorganized and overly sentimental practices of earlier charitable work in the city—benevolence fueled in large part by the sort of personal sympathy that led the charity worker to identify with the plight of his or her client. By contrast, the AICP required the rigorous collection of facts; all applicants were subjected to investigation and close supervision. Further, in a notable break from older, religiously derived beliefs that all in need deserved compassion, the AICP drew a sharp line between the worthy and unworthy poor, refusing to fund anyone thought to be willingly idle.[76] Taken by the AICP's example, Chicago's Relief and Aid Society followed this general plan of action until the end of the 1850s, when its work foundered in the wake of the 1857 depression. Resuscitated a decade later, the Society's post-Civil War activities were undoubtedly influenced by the example of the United States Sanitary Commission, the quasi-public agency that supervised the relief of Civil War soldiers and their families.[77] Applying the dictates of scientific charity on an unprecedented scale, the commission emphatically rejected "sentimental" benevolence in favor of the disinterested, "professional" examination of those in need.[78] As these terms further signal, the emergence of a "science" of charity involved questions of gender and authority, marking a transfer of the moral power attached to benevolence from the world of middle- and upper-class women to the more desexualized sphere of "experts."[79]

At the time of the Great Fire, then, the men in charge of Chicago's best-funded charitable institution held that alms-giving should never spring from mere sympathy. Indeed, in an increasingly interdependent urban world, the stakes attached to charity were very high: aid to individuals was thought to be weighted with profound import for the city as a whole. In the Society's view, indiscriminate subsidy would do far more harm than good; though any decent person would want to help those in need, such impulses had to be held in check. "Zealous and promiscuous giving," argued Ezra McCagg, "corrupts the poor"; if applicants came to expect charitable funds, a most dangerous "spirit of dependence" would sap their will to work their way up the economic ladder to productive citizenship.[80] Individuals might find a more comfortable lot for themselves —but at dire cost to the existing urban order. For the Society, the central aim of charity was to place people, as soon as possible, on the road to self-sufficiency.[81]

Internally at war between a form of humanitarianism and conservative impulses, between a commitment to aid the poor and a desire to preserve what they viewed as the proper social order of their city, the Society incorporated a seeming schizophrenia of purpose: the agency existed to give, but its directors remained ever fearful of the harm that their giving might do.[82] As a consequence, no one received aid without investigation. A professional staff sought to fit potential recipients into one of two categories within an inflexible typology: honest, hard-working, but a victim of ill-luck; or deceitful, lazy, and the architects of their own wretched state. "A discrimination must be made," according to McCagg, "between those who are helpless from their own misfortune and those whose misery arises from their own default."[83] Those deemed unworthy were remanded to the county government (considered the proper agent for the chronic poor) or simply left on their own, while those deemed virtuous received temporary assistance meant to hasten their return to independence. A profoundly individualistic ethos suffused the standards set by a largely self-made entrepreneurial elite: if applicants conformed to bourgeois ideas of respectable poverty, they would be given the chance to self-make their own fortunes.[84]

The Great Fire, then, presented the Society with a major conundrum. Ideal clients, to their minds, were the victims of ill fate: "those who are unexpectedly, and mainly through no fault of their own, brought to destitution."[85] Chicago's disaster, a world-class misfortune, therefore appeared to mark scores of thousands as worthy aidees. But even in the face of such a calamity, cool heads would prevail over warm hearts. Though the Society reported that "the pressure upon us toward irresponsible and promiscuous disbursement is strong," their commitment to "scientific charity" remained steadfast.[86] In a city now choked with innocent victims, there would be no new largesse. A key component of the Society's vision of urban order—that their city could not withstand any surfeit of dependency—thus was maintained.

In the first days of the Society's administration, its directors were forced to authorize what they viewed as a sort of anarchy. The hungry had to be fed, and the great stocks of supplies streaming into the city indeed made it possible to give food to all who asked for it. Under such circumstances, as the Society later confessed, "discrimination was impossible"; with no reliable system yet in place, "bounty fell upon the deserving and the undeserving, as certainly as the rain falls upon the just and the unjust." But as soon as these pressing needs were met, the Society unveiled a new set of policies based on time-honored institutional practice. Temporary help for the worthy coupled with extreme vigilance against fraud reemerged as the agency's credo: "To secure to the real sufferers needed aid; to detect and defeat imposition; to aid in establishing order by withholding encouragement to idleness," was, as a Society report declared, "the first object."[87]

In the space of a few days, the Relief and Aid Society transformed itself into a social welfare giant. Nearly half of Chicago's population would eventually receive some part of the $4,415,454 administered by the organization.[88] The work of receiving, distributing, and accounting for the flood of donations demanded an entirely original managerial design; as a Society report noted, "[A]lmost all other things in this world have been done one or more times; but surely the disbursement of millions of dollars among seventy five thousand persons . . . is a problem upon which experience throws but little light."[89] But the commercial magnates who ran the Society excelled at meeting precisely this type of challenge. Within a month, according to an admiring *Overland Monthly* article, the relief work in Chicago was "as thoroughly systematized as the business of any commercial house of the city."[90] In the name of expertise, order, and efficiency, a massive bureaucracy quickly emerged as Chicago's official agent of benevolence.[91]

Less than a week after the Great Fire, led by attorney Wirt Dexter and the ten other directors who constituted the powerful Executive Committee of the Relief and Aid Society, the agency began to implement a "General Plan."[92] Drawing upon then-innovative strategies, the group devised a managerial pyramid.[93] Ultimate authority rested with the Executive Committee, which (in a notable measure of the time and effort many of these men gave to this voluntary work) sat in constant session for a month. O. C. Gibbs, the organization's salaried superintendent, coordinated the sweeping task of distribution. Dividing the city into five districts and thirteen subdistricts, Gibbs employed a superintendent for each area, who in turn hired a corps of clerks and investigators; on average, each district had work for ninety staffers. In addition, independent committees handled special functions apart from the work of doling out staple supplies. These smaller task forces, each led by a member of the Executive Committee, labored to provide shelter, arrange for transportation out of the city, find employment, and offer medical services for needy survivors. Other committees managed the Society's internal work of storage, transport of stocks, auditing, and correspondence. Full reports on district and committee activities went daily to the general superintendent and Executive Committee; further, all district and subdistrict managers attended weekly performance reviews. Free-floating inspectors and an adjunct Committee on Complaints, empowered to investigate and, if need be, remedy any charges of impropriety, self-policed the organization. And, thanks to the Western Union Company, the Society enjoyed a state-of-the-art communications network: scattered depots, warehouses, and offices were all connected by telegraph lines.[94]

On one level, this corporate hierarchy must be understood as both an impressive and innovative response to an extraordinary circumstance. But the very existence of a "General Plan" also testifies to postbellum charity workers' growing sense that urban ills could indeed be managed, that benevolence, in the hands of the proper experts, had the capacity not only to reform the poor themselves but to safeguard the interests of the entire community. For the Relief and Aid directors, a stable urban order—a set of structures necessarily defined by the interdependence of diverse people—required a fundamental cultural expectation of economic independence. Individuals, to their minds, were except in rare cases responsible for their own lot in life. Moreover, a willingness to work marked any man or woman as a worthy citizen. Reverend E. J. Goodspeed, a vigorous Society supporter, thus spelled out the organization's position: "If there was ever a time when a person capable of earning his or her support should be made to do it, it is now."[95] "Work," the *Tribune* resoundingly concurred, "is a necessity. When the committees cut off all deadbeats . . . they will advance the important end of making the whole community self-sufficient."[96] As designed by the elite men (and their hired managers) who had assumed charge of municipal relief, the General Plan, basically aimed to return able-bodied victims to some form of waged work, thereby saving Chicago from the potential dangers of a dependent class.

"Any man, single woman or boy, able to work and unemployed at this time, is so from choice and not from necessity."[97] With this October 24 pronouncement, Superintendent O. C. Gibbs gave voice not only to prevailing ideologies of gender difference, family structure, and dependency but also signaled the Society's intense commitment to the promotion of working-class self-support. This set of values, joined with the truism that anyone who wanted work could in fact find a job, lay beneath all agency policy.[98] For example, in its first two weeks of operation the Transportation Committee oversaw the exodus of over 6000 victims—via free passes generously extended by city railroads.[99] Such a strategy seemed to work well for all concerned. A one-way ticket out of town granted refugees a chance to begin anew and also diminished the demand upon the Society's own resources. But free rides for those who could labor were soon deemed dangerous. One week after the disaster, the Society moved to block the departure of "undeserving persons" guilty of "imposing upon the generosity and good nature of the Railroad companies."[100] As a *New York Times* correspondent explained, "These passes are now being restricted to the aged, sick, and feeble, to women and children, and to large families, it justly being held that there is employment enough in Chicago for all who are willing to work."[101] By closing the door on a quick and cost-free exodus, the Society again affirmed the ultimate purpose of the General Plan: the construction of a self-reliant working class.[102]

The ideology of economic independence similarly informed the task of providing shelter. Within days of the blaze, most of the homeless had found some sort of indoor haven. Relying upon ethnic ties, thousands of North Side immigrant refugees packed into the homes of their West Side brethren. "The great mass still remains crowded thirty or forty in a house," observed relief volunteer Anne McClure Hitchcock. "Germans with Germans, and other foreigners with their countrymen."[103] At first, temporary barracks seemed an ideal solution to the housing crisis: 40,000–50,000 people, by the Society's count, might so be quickly and economically sheltered. But despite the apparent logic of this course, the Housing Committee calculated the eventual social cost of such a plan to be too high. Again revealing their deep fear and distrust of dependent and idle working people, the directors rejected massive shelters as potential human tinderboxes. An official report evoked the havoc that such structures might spawn: "So large a number brought into promiscuous and involuntary association, would almost certainly engender disease and promote idleness, disorder, and vice, and be dangerous to themselves and the neighborhood in which they might be placed."[104] Such disasters-in-embryo could well destroy whatever sexual, natural, and social order the Great Fire had spared.

Further, a "winter of dependence and evil communication" would wear away at the moral fiber of a set of working people of special concern to the Society: those who owned their own homes.[105] In the agency's view, this "thrifty and respectable class"—so marked by the very fact that they had accrued enough of a personal fortune to invest in their own version of domesticity—would prove critical actors in the work of physical reconstruction.[106] "Their labor and skill," as a report declared, "are indispensable in rebuilding the city."[107] And this group, to the mind of the Society, was also fated to play a key role in Chicago's social reconstruction. Eager to take advantage of what they perceived as the stabilizing effects of homeownership, the Relief and Aid directors decided to provide small, prefabricated shanties to individuals who had previously owned a residence. In these cases, charity began (and often ended) with a home.

The treatment afforded to renters further underlines the Society's faith in the transformative powers of home ownership. Very poor tenement dwellers were sent to the sort of barracks rejected as too harmful for "the better class of laboring people." Suspect for their lack of property, 1000 families eventually spent the winter in one of four such structures. There, according to the Society, "under the careful and constant care of medical and police superintendents, their moral and sanitary condition was unquestionably better than that which had heretofore obtained in that class."[108] But for those who had owned, the directors believed that the gift of a private home would instantly vest skilled workers with new incentives to industry. "To restore them to these homes," the Society argued, "would be to raise them at once from the depression and anxiety, if not despair, to hope, renewed energy, and comparative prosperity."[109] A *Tribune* editorial strenuously applauded the practice: "With this plan 30,000 people, hitherto householders, will still be in their own homes, surrounded by the sacred and conservative elements of family, of independence, of respectability, and of individual responsibility which are so immense a moral force in the community."[110] Always ready to champion the ideal social order that might be born of free labor, the newspaper thus sketched its vision of homeownership's essential part in the construction and maintenance of a republican citizenry.[111]

The burned-out North Side in late 1871, looking northeast. A few of the temporary homes provided by the Relief and Aid Society are visible, as are the wooden barracks that initially sheltered those who had not previously owned a home. Courtesy of Chicago Historical Society.

Finally, the Society explicitly devoted one branch of the General Plan to returning workers to their labors. The Employment Bureau outfitted tradesmen who had lost their tools to the blaze.[112] In addition, a small number of working-class women were directly employed by satellites of this department. Upper- and middle-class women's groups took charge of establishing small workrooms where "sewing women" were paid eighty-three cents per day to produce clothing and bedding for distribution to Fire victims.[113] To serve jobless men further, the bureau functioned as a labor exchange where "those wanting mechanics or laborers could find them, and those in need of work were provided with it."[114] The Society made sure that the bureau would serve a steady stream of clients; according to a policy put into effect within a week of the Fire, every able-bodied man or boy who applied for aid was automatically denied relief. Instead, he received a ticket and was sent downtown to the Employment Bureau. If a job was available (as, the Society stated, "was almost invariably the case"), the applicant surrendered his ticket, which then made its way back to the superintendent of the district where it had first been issued. But if the bearer failed to deliver this "certificate of character" to the Employment Bureau (and it therefore never resurfaced at the district office), the standard precept of scientific charity known as St. Paul's rule—"he who does not work, neither shall he eat"—was immediately applied.[115] Such a circumstance served as prima facie evidence of the relief applicant's willing idleness. Irregardless of any other contingency—a snafu with paperwork, perhaps, or the loss of a promised job—if a man so marked ever again dared to appear at Society offices his claim was automatically denied.[116]

In the end, working people who had suffered loses were at times doubly victimized by the Society's basic belief in the latent dangers of benevolence. Through its strict enforcement of regulations designed to thwart dependency and imposture, the General Plan bureaucracy on occasion brought additional hardships to those it existed to succor. For example, men who dutifully sought and secured jobs still often found themselves and their families in dire conditions. As a letter to the *Tribune* noted, "[T]he moment a man obtains work, his rations are cut off." But because employers never paid on a daily basis, many Chicagoans endured a period of one or two weeks when they had jobs but no cash to show for their labors—and no access to relief. "It is not uncommon," the writer declared, "to see children crying and begging for bread merely because their fathers have found work."[117] A rule designed to affirm and ensure independence here created a newly harsh state of want—one indeed beyond the pale of official action.

Further, despite the confidence of its designers, the Society bureaucracy was from the first doomed to function in a far less than "expert" or "systematic" fashion. An essential link in the General Plan's chain of command—salaried clerks and visitors—were often ill-prepared (or perhaps simply ill-inclined) to serve their clients. These foot soldiers in the work of relief, expected to assume new and largely undefined positions with minimal training, at times abused their petty yet critical powers. Most Relief and Aid employees held low-paid, high-stress jobs; it is hardly surprising that the men and women identified by the *Chicago Times* as the General Plan's "subordinate officials" rather rapidly acquired a citywide reputation for "discourtesy and neglect."[118] Along with the problem of rudeness, privileged access to a stockpile of wealth proved too tempting for some. Frances Roberts glumly described the extracurricular activities of a colleague: "Mrs. Bristol *still* continues to carry away Relief goods . . . she has had *three* wrappers and *three* dresses and other things in proportion. I hope she will be supplied after a while."[119] Adding the specter of nepotism to such reports of low-level corruption, the *Chicago Republican* acidly satirized the Society's hiring practices in a late November editorial: "Yes my son, he is an idiot, a boor, and a thief, but he is a cousin of mine, and we will make him a clerk in the Relief Society at $2 a day and all he can steal."[120] Like any bureaucracy, the dream of a flawless system could not escape the reality of the people who put it into effect.

In addition, a set of cultural barriers impeded the Plan's ability to relieve all who had suffered. The almost exclusively native-born board of the Society did not readily recognize the special difficulties faced by Chicago's massive German and Scandinavian population.[121] Here, a failure to communicate badly hampered the delivery of assistance. The Society, seemingly unaware of the fact that thousands of Fire victims spoke or read no English, neglected to hire bilingual visitors or publish official notices in either German or any Scandinavian languages. To compound the isolation of many immigrants, the Executive Committee initially failed to establish a distribution site on the North Side.[122] Aside from such practical issues, in a complaint that is as much a marker of ethnic pride as a sign of the Society's own bias, the *Illinois Staats-Zeitung* argued that the (proverbially) spotless German home invariably led Relief and Aid visitors to wrong conclusions. Culturally blinded Society workers, the paper charged, reflexively connected misery and filth—and were hence simply unable to *see* the hardships endured by many sorely pressed but still pristine Germans. "If he comes to a place where the floor is scrubbed, the children clean, and the bed neatly covered," lamented an editorial, "he writes down 'not needed.'"[123] An immediate postdisaster outcry by prominent Germans did prompt the Society to hire visitors of German descent and establish a North Side depot.[124] Still, as late as December, Germans continued to protest what they viewed as the Society's failure to take adequate steps to bridge the cultural gap between immigrant sufferers and American-born Relief and Aid executives and staff. As the *Staats-Zeitung* declared on Christmas Day, "[T]he individuals who are charged by the *Relief and Aid Society* with the distribution of supplies are largely incapable of fulfilling their tasks. Equally ignorant of both the German language and the special situation on the North Side, they behave like uneducated beadles [Armenvogte]."[125]

With their construction and administration of the General Plan, the Relief and Aid directors took on an immensely difficult task. This massive and complex work, as one contemporary rightly observed, "could not possibly please everyone."[126] Further, a deep concern for economy was both a realistic and responsible approach. At the outset of their work, Society leaders had no way of knowing just what sort or what amount of resources would be at their disposal; in late October, O. C. Gibbs was undoubtedly wise to worry that "mid-winter might find us with our treasury bare; with outdoor labor, to a large extent, necessarily suspended, and with a city full of poor looking to us for food and fuel."[127] Suspicions of fraud were likewise not entirely unfounded; investigators did uncover what seem to have been clear abuses of the Fire relief fund. Terrence Mulhern, for example, was apparently a habitual drinker who refused to find a job, preferring to rely upon the meager earnings of his washerwoman wife. Described by a Society investigator as "an idle kind of man with whom work does not agree" and the "holder of a whiskey policy," he quickly found himself stricken from Relief and Aid rolls.[128] Relief records also contain the application of Kate Moran, a homeowning widow with four adult working children, an income-producing "new milk cow," and three tenants, who had lost nothing to the Fire. Cow and all, the seeming reincarnation of Chicago's template of villainous Irish womanhood—the infamous Mrs. O'Leary—the Society visitor denounced Moran as "A Perfect Fraud."[129]

It is perhaps impossible to gauge the success or failure of the General Plan. Every Society director, every functionary, every client, or any other Chicagoan might well have had a different story to tell. What can be said with certainty is as follows: members of the Executive Committee of Chicago's Relief and Aid Society believed themselves to hold nothing but the best of intentions for the city and its suffering people. But their elite vision of stewardship, shaped by fears of working-class dependency, led them to view what were in many ways the most needy victims of disaster as possible threats to urban order. True believers in the emerging "science" of charity, the guardians of the public Fire relief fund looked out at a sea of refugees. And even as they recognized the horrors of innocent victimization, they saw a menace to their city's stability; even as they admitted that "to shirk work and live upon charity by preference was the exception and not the rule among the laboring population of Chicago," the Society constructed a set of policies that presumed the reverse to be true.[130] For its designers and administrators, the Fire relief effort that touched the lives of the greatest number of sufferers was thus conceived as the potential source of as much communal harm as individual benefit. In the city of Chicago, the "world's freely given benevolence" would not in turn be so freely given.[131]

Middle-Class Heroes: Special Relief

On March 12, 1872, Jeremiah Healey, a carpenter whose home had been lost to the Great Fire, appeared at the offices of the Committee of Special Relief to request a $50 cash grant. A separate department created shortly after the General Plan became operative, this Relief and Aid bureau was "meant exclusively to provide for those particular and delicate cases which is not possible to meet satisfactorily in the ordinary way."[132] Healey planned to use the funds to complete construction of the still uninhabitable cottage he had begun to rebuild on his North Side lot in January. On March 30, while Healey was out, a Special Relief visitor arrived at his temporary lodgings in a West Side boardinghouse. After a very short conversation with Healey's wife, the agent hastened away. "[A]s it was going to rain," according to the carpenter, "he did not stay over ten minutes." On April 13, a frustrated Healey wrote to the Society to question its failure to render any decision. "I need the money very much," he declared and, once again, made the case for his worthiness:

> I spent every dollar I had and borrowed some besides. It is three months since I started to build. I tried every way to finish it before I sent for any help, and now I am called upon for taxes and my child is nearly blind, and the doctors at North Star [free clinic] cannot do anything for her and I cannot afford to take her to an eye doctor. . . . I will be obliged to live in that cold house without a chimney or anything if you do not send me some help.

But Healey's plea failed to move the bureau. No final disposition appears in his case history, indicating that he never received the aid he sought.[133]

Back in early February, however, Mlle. A. Poncelet had easily convinced Special Relief agents of her honest need. Once the owner of a four-story residence that also housed the shop where she (as a representative of French high style) sold artificial flowers, feathers, and lace to a wealthy clientele, this prosperous businesswoman lost all her property to the Great Fire. Her insurance, like that of many small entrepreneurs, proved worthless. "Deprived of my business," she wrote, and responsible for the care of her seventy-four-year-old mother, Poncelet threw herself upon the mercy of the bureau. Only "cruel necessity" had brought her to this moment; her household, she pointedly reminded her potential benefactors, had "never before applied to any relief committee." "It seems to me," Poncelet concluded, "that you will understand my situation, and that your good hearts will prompt you to help in this way an unfortunate woman who after fourteen years' struggle finds herself reduced from a comfortable life to these distressing circumstances." And those in charge of Special Relief well understood this self-portrait of the torment of an industrious and dutiful woman suddenly robbed of her independence. The next day, Mlle. Poncelet received a $300 order for cash.[134]

Though both Healey and Poncelet suffered substantial losses, their respective treatment at the hands of the Bureau of Special Relief could not have been more different. Seen by the Society as a potentially dependent workingman, Healey was met with unexplained delays and eventual rejection. But the needs of Mlle. Poncelet, viewed as a proud, formerly independent woman of property and reputation, found immediate redress. Perhaps more than any other aspect of the Society's work, the very existence of "special relief" signals the ways that the perceptions of class difference held by a group of elite men fundamentally structured the delivery of municipal benevolence. Fears of the social consequences of indiscriminate giving shaped the General Plan bureaucracy that obstructed every working person's road to relief. In stark contrast, the comparatively few prosperous Chicagoans who looked to the city for aid became the objects of unique concern.[135] For in the eyes of the Society, those "suddenly reduced to conditions of privation and stress" were without a doubt "the keenest sufferers of all"; unaccustomed to "exposures and hardships that were easily borne by the laboring people," as an organization report explained, "the change in their condition was greater and more disastrous."[136] The story of Mlle. Poncelet's crushing fall from a bourgeois state of grace—told in a style well calculated to earn sympathy—precisely exemplified the single sort of sufferer that the Relief and Aid Society was in fact eager to aid.[137]

The preservation and reconstruction of middle-class independence lay at the ideological core of Special Relief. Bureau policy reflected this commitment: reputations, social standing, and notoriously fragile middle-class constitutions all received a sort of protected status.[138] Given the unique needs of this clientele, it was no easy task even to begin delivery of "special relief": according to the Society, most victims of means so abhorred dependence (or the very act of admitting distress) that they shrank from any exposure of their destitution. "There are many," one report declared, "who would perish rather than appear as the recipients of public bounty."[139] While a few critics such as Colbert and Chamberlain would scoff at what they deemed the "mawkish sentiment" wasted on those they viewed as the very few "too proud to beg and yet not too proud to accept bounty if it was offered them," the Society plainly presumed that some middle-class heroes would in fact be proud enough to starve.[140] Special Relief thus apotheosized economic independence to the point where those who would not ask for help were judged to deserve it most.

Even in the unlikely event that such victims did come forward, General Plan–style supplication at crowded depots did not mesh well with the Society's bourgeois sensibilities. As relief volunteer Anne McClure Hitchcock wrote to a friend in Boston, "[T]here are a multitude who have courage to starve or freeze to death, who lack courage to go to one of the Relief Depots, wait maybe an hour or two among a crowd of people hardened to charity, submit to be questioned like them, and have a pittance doled out to them."[141] The operations of the General Plan—long lines, long waits, and sparse handouts—would not, the Society claimed, "serve the needs of those whose previous condition in life unfitted them to the exposure and suffering incident to such modes of receiving relief."[142] Indeed, forcing the once-comfortable destitute to rub shoulders with the masses would have recreated the same mixing of classes that so discomfited many chroniclers of the disaster. "Delicacy of feeling," in the words of Reverend E. J. Goodspeed, did not permit well-bred survivors to stand in line with those ill-mannered enough to violate the doctrine of stoic suffering: "the hundreds of very poor, degraded, and foreign applicants who unblushingly push themselves forward into the front ranks."[143]

Privacy and deference, then, became the bureau's dual watchwords; a sentimental regard for the particular burdens thought to be shouldered by the high (or middling) brought low tempered the commitment of the Society to rigorous investigation. While General Plan employees flushed out fraud, those engaged in the task of Special Relief looked high and low for the worthy. To be sure, this work also took on the trappings of scientific charity. Clerks and visitors maintained detailed records; a Cincinnati visitor complained that "even this drawer of the bureau still contains much red-tape."[144] But the agents of Special Relief, eager to spare their clients from the public display, inconvenience, and distrust that was the lot of General Plan applicants, largely functioned to smooth the way of the formerly prosperous. Squads of female visitors walked Chicago's streets in search of those unwilling to face the indignities of the General Plan. And once a client was in the hands of the bureau, he or she needed only the recommendation of a clergyman or officer of a respectable benevolent association to secure their request. Social standing usually opened the doors to relief dollars; a "personal and confidential" relationship with someone deemed to be a trustworthy judge of character almost always substituted for the home visits undertaken to assess the character of all who asked for aid through the General Plan.[145]

The material rewards of Special Relief were likewise products of the Society's understandings of class difference. Unlike the General Plan committees, which never trusted their clients with cash, the actual aid granted by the bureau was most often a lump sum intended to restore professionals and entrepreneurs to their former stature. For a shopkeeper such as Mlle. Poncelet, Special Relief replaced lost stocks. In the case of insurance agent C. C. Phillips, the committee paid rent for a new office and supplied necessary fixtures.[146] Doctors and dentists similarly received the tools of their trades. Such professionals could be trusted to chart their own return to independence.

In addition, the lot of self-employed women particularly interested the agents of Special Relief. To a degree, gender alone marked victims as deserving of distinctive status; the organization's longstanding commitment to assisting single women and widows prompted the Society to set aside a portion of the Special Relief budget for "the aiding of women who are dependent for support upon their own exertion."[147] Cash grants allowed such fire victims to stake themselves in one of the few businesses open to women in a highly gender-segregated economy: some received up to $200 to furnish and outfit boardinghouses, cookshops, and laundries.[148] A sizable portion of the fund further went to replace sewing machines lost by "seamstresses," thereby, true to the Society credo of self-support, supposedly "putting into their hands the means of immediate and comfortable subsistence."[149] But even among a category composed of women, the Society's perceptions of class difference still held sway. Except in rare cases, sewing machines were not outright gifts; the recipient most often paid half the cost, usually $22–$25.[150] This need for upfront cash of course excluded the very poor from acquiring a discounted machine; the Society instead employed some such women and girls in its own workrooms at a set daily wage. Once again, the potentially dependent were presented with a lot far removed from that offered to the once-independent.

As the work of Special Relief continued, its predilection for middle-class clients and women responsible for their own support began to be tested. Unable to draw anything but a dwindling supply of staple goods from General Plan agencies, more and more working-class men approached the bureau to request supplemental aid. By February of 1872, surviving records indicate that most applicants, like Jeremiah Healey, asked for cash grants to repair or construct homes.[151] Further, in contrast to those who first had been led to Special Relief's door, nearly all of these later requests came from North Side tradesmen and laborers.[152] A winter of deprivation had left deep wounds; surviving records of forty-two families of an average size of six indicate that only twenty-one earned any income during these months. The observations of Frances Roberts (by this time transferred from her initial General Plan post to a job at Special Relief) suggest that these sobering figures might tell the story of any number of the Great Fire's working-class victims. "I never knew so much of the poor as I have this winter," she wrote. "Such awful destitution, as exists in every direction, cannot be imagined."[153]

Still, though the arbiters of Special Relief daily faced the bitter want left unredressed by the General Plan, they seldom wavered from the ideological and practical boundaries dictated by their particular mission. Worker applications to the bureau vividly illustrate the double standard of giving constructed out of their sense of class difference. For the Relief and Aid directors, the Great Fire's prosperous victims, traumatized by their overnight descent into destitution, required immediate and solicitous attention. By contrast, these elite men assumed that poverty and distress would to some degree be a natural (and bearable) part of the life of every worker. Sufferers from positions of comfort deserved to be freely aided. There was no need to fret about the evil influence of charity upon those already self-emancipated from the laboring classes. But for workers, the "science" of benevolence had to be applied. Enforced self-reliance, whatever its cost to individuals, was thought to serve the critical end of discouraging the potentially corrosive effects of dependency.

Such thinking, then, led Special Relief agents to reject the appeal of Nicholas Kalter, a physically incapacitated German Catholic father of seven, because he was a carpenter. A man who could not work was still considered a laborer whose skills were in demand.[154] Tbe Bureau similarly refused to assist Augusta Sansbach, a German immigrant who had arrived in the city less than a year before the blaze. Widowed within days of the Fire when a wall fell on her husband, this woman, who spoke no English and had no other family in Chicago, bore the burden of providing for four children under the age of six. To stave off penury, according to the investigator of her claim, she had been "induced to work in a brick yard and pile bricks herself"—a form of backbreaking labor the Society would never have countenanced for any woman of means.[155] The bureau was likewise unmoved by the plea of Mary Johnson, a Norwegian woman with a large family and an ill husband. The Society's visitor to the Johnson shanty found a structure "so poorly finished that the rain blows in on all sides." Still, despite the agent's assurance that the Johnsons were "quite a *refined* family," the rough equality extended to working-class applicants once again prevailed. "Rejected," wrote the Special Relief chairman, "As good as other houses of the kind."[156]

OTHER COMMUNITIES, OTHER VISIONS

In Act II, Scene II of *Relief: A Humorous Drama*—an 1872 lampoon of post-Fire charity penned by an anonymous "Chicago Lady"

—the aptly monikered Miss Pry and Mrs. Redtape, agents of a "society of ladies organized for Relief work," do their duty as "friendly visitors."[157] Knocking at the door of Mrs. O'Brien, the pair interrupt their would-be client's conversation with her neighbor, Widow Flannigan. Fictional cousins to Kate Moran and Mrs. O'Leary, the two Irishwomen (enjoying a cup of tea earlier obtained from what they term "the Relafe") have been discussing the best way to convince alms-givers of their worthiness and need. "Dooan't ye know," Mrs. O'Brien admonishes her slower-witted friend, "its the childer as does the wurrk wid the leddies' Relafe?" Herself childless, Mrs. O'Brien has already successfully deceived the relief workers by passing off a neighbor's multiple offspring as her own. This woman's cold eye views the world's sincere charity as a cornucopia begging for plunder. "It's not the days fur the likes o' us poor folks," she declares, "to be a wurrkin' an' slavin' in the seasin o' the Relafe!"

The appearance of Miss Pry and Mrs. Redtape abruptly ends this tête à tête. The two have been dispatched to investigate Mrs. O'Brien's fraudulent claim of destitution for herself and three (nonexistent) children, and her further assertion that her (alive and equally rapacious) husband had died a hero's death at Gettysburg. Though initially quite guarded, the relief workers soon fall under Mrs. O'Brien's masterful spell. In no time, she not only persuades her investigators of her claim's legitimacy but further convinces the two that she is a loyal Protestant, a lineal descendent of William of Orange, *and* the hard-working cleaning woman personally employed by Chicago's mayor.

In the eyes of Miss Pry and Mrs. Redtape, their potential aidee's gratitude seems enchantingly unbounded. "Blessin's on yez," the "Widow" O'Brien gushes, "fur yer thruble in solin' yer swate face waalkin' to me poor dwellin'!" When Mrs. Redtape protests that they are merely following society rules, Mrs. O'Brien nearly betrays herself in her rush to congratulate the two for their personal efforts on her behalf: "May the Howly Verrgin reward yez, ladies!" she exclaims in a most un-Protestant manner. But the ever-facile Mrs. O'Brien (aided and abetted by Widow Flannigan's timely reappearance with yet another borrowed baby) deftly turns her miscue to her advantage. When Miss Pry, alive to the scent of Catholicism, pointedly inquires, "What was that motion of your hands? Were you crossing yourself?" Mrs. O'Brien transforms her slip into yet another apparent act of deference. "Dade mum," she responds, "an' its wipin' the tears oot o' me eyes it wuz." At this point, having seen exactly what they wanted to see, the investigators depart, well-satisfied with their subject's worthiness.[158]

As is the case with most satire, few players in the story remain unscathed; cutting portraits of the scheming Irish keep company with hard-edged accounts of self-serving relief workers. The heroically dramatic and publicity-obsessed Mrs. Bombast ("We," she gravely informs her colleagues, "have—had—*a fire!*"), the ultra-wealthy and snobbish Mrs. Pursestrings, and the intrusive and self-righteous duo of Miss Pry and Mrs. Redtape are all targets for the "Chicago Lady's" barbs. But a few heroes do shine through. On the side of the givers, the playwright applauds the common sense and sympathy that mark the characters of Mrs. Smart, the society's chairperson, and Mrs. Warmheart, who tirelessly labors to ease the burden of victimized families. And in the ranks of the aidees, one Michael Mahoney, a teetotaling homeowner and tradesman who refuses to apply to "the Relafe," stands out as a working-class beacon of virtue. This stellar young man, in the view of the "Chicago Lady," cannot even be classed with his Irish brethren. Described "as gintale a yoong Scotchman as iver was born in Corrk!" Mahoney redeems the backsliding Katie O'Dowd (who has improperly obtained a Special Relief sewing machine) with a proposal of marriage. Won over by the prospect of a new life in "the finest new cottage in all Chicagoer," Katie renounces her ill-gotten gain, and—in a secular echo of Dennis's redemption of Christine in *Barriers Burned Away*—moves on to the moral state of homeownership and wedlock.

Relief: A Humorous Drama was undeniably informed by its author's religious, ethnic, and class identities. Her strong anti-Irish bias and at best lukewarm endorsement of Catholicism are quite plain. Further, for all its skewerings of the folly of misguided charity workers, the drama obviously supported the bourgeois ideal of self-reliance that those same workers sought to promulgate. What is unique and most remarkable about the play, however, is its forthright indictment of the narrow vision of scientific charity. Miss Pry and Mrs. Redtape, locked into a fixed ideal of what they need to see of Mrs. O'Brien, become easy prey for their client's shrewd sense of self-presentation. The double-edge of systematic inquiry thus comes clear: the hunt for the "worthy" poor ran according to a rigid criteria that effectively limited access to goods and funds but in other ways invited the very sentimentality and artifice that scientific charity was purportedly designed to defeat. In the "Chicago Lady's" view, only a Mrs. Warmheart's sympathetic eye, a gaze free of the blinders of "system," could begin to divine the true dimensions of suffering in her city.

The voice of the "Chicago Lady" makes it plain that not all Chicagoans fully agreed with the Relief and Aid Society's commitment to the science of charity. The critique leveled here came out of a nostalgia for antebellum versions of the work of benevolent women. But such middle-class women did not stand alone in their discomfort with Society practice: across Chicago, members of particular communities mobilized their own charitable works—on their own terms. At least thirty groups self-defined by gender, religion, ethnicity, and occupation channeled support to those who fell (or were placed) outside the scope of municipal relief.[159] "Were it not for other societies aiding those cut off by the stringency of general rules," observed one contemporary, "there would be heart-sickening suffering."[160] These agents had limited assets and served small numbers; compared to the Society's immense machinery of official benevolence, their works can seem inconsequential. To discount these activities, though, would be to overlook markers of a critical debate: a discussion that probed the question of what "charity," in the context of a diverse yet interdependent city, meant to both its recipients and to its givers.[161]

In their dealings with benevolence, women's groups, religious associations, ethnic societies, and trade unions served different constituencies and operated under widely varied assumptions. But all, on some level, were unable to subscribe to the Relief and Aid system. The Society's grand mechanism did take on the massive (and innovative) project of attempting, as a quasi-governmental agent, to address the wants of an entire city. But they accomplished their task by judging needy individuals according to abstract typologies constructed out of ideologies of difference; while the perceptions of class held by the elite directors of the Society figured most strongly into their understanding of what charity might do to and for their city and its citizens, the values and meanings they attached to gender, religion, and ethnicity also added into this equation. Other almsgivers, whatever the foundation of their commitment to acts of charity, by contrast conceived of the urban community in parts and in far more personalized terms: their visions of the reconstructive functions of benevolence displayed less concern for the protection of the entire urban order than for assuring the well-being of members of particular social groups. Direct markers of belonging—membership, kinship, or friendship—thus refused to yield to more abstract measures of community—citizenship or the fact of physical residence—as the baseline of determining who deserved aid, with important consequences for the forms that the delivery of charity in turn assumed.

Middle- and upper-class women did not necessarily dispute the work of Relief and Aid; like Frances Roberts, many were happy to be in its employ, and multiple ladies' societies labored as its direct adjuncts. But others, including the wives of several prominent civic and Relief and Aid leaders, were quick to buck the system. Impatient with Society regulations, Katherine Medill (wife of *Tribune* owner and mayor-elect Joseph Medill) resigned her spot on the Special Relief Committee. She instead resolved to attend to the constant in-person appeals she received at her West Side home; everyday, she claimed, "people who are in every way worthy and beyond the Society's rules" appeared at her door.[162] Aurelia R. King, wife of Society president Henry King, urged an out-of-town friend in late October that all donations be sent to her—not to the General Plan. "If you will have your contributions sent directly to me," she wrote, "I will distribute it to the needy that I know personally. I have already received money and other things from different places, which I divide and apportion exactly as I see most pressing need."[163] Scientific system was thus seemingly under assault in the private domains of some of its most notable public apostles.

But though women such as Medill and King were clearly anguished by what they viewed as the shortcomings of the Relief and Aid effort, their own charitable works were largely limited to those with whom they could most readily identify: women of (or aspiring to) their own class. Medill and her like-minded friends thus expressed a strong sense of sisterhood with impoverished educated working women.[164] Many teachers, for example, had lost their jobs; as educator Sarah Bigelow wrote to her family a few days after the fire, "I have just $1.85 in my purse, and most of the teachers are not much better off."[165] Bigelow and her colleagues fell into one of the Society's bureaucratic traps: though almost all of the city's public schools had burned, teachers were still technically considered to be employed and therefore were ineligible for aid. Further, the devastation wiped out almost all demand for the limited sector of the service economy where most educated women carved out their professional homes. As Medill's close associate Anne McClure Hitchcock wrote to a Boston relative, "[T]he number of music teachers, teachers of language, dressmakers, and young women who have been clerks and bookkeepers and ask only employment . . . that are pinched by poverty is overwhelming."[166]

While more than willing to break Society rules in their efforts to direct aid to these sufferers, it seems doubtful that the women who mobilized to help such educated working women would have desired any full-scale dismantling of the Relief and Aid system. Like the agents of Special Relief, their concern was largely restricted to the once-independent among the middle-class: women, in Hitchcock's words, who had "the courage to starve or freeze to death" but "lack courage to go to one of the Relief Depots."[167] But those men and women, again in her words, "hardened to charity" or "accustomed to poverty," simply occupied a social space outside the range of Hitchcock's sympathies. Women's call to charity here did not transcend the worldview (or even cityview) of their class.

Another set of women, however, apparently mounted a more direct challenge to the heart of the Society's philosophy of benevolence: the elevation of system over compassion. Led by Mrs. H. L. Hammond, a Protestant activist married to an official of the Chicago Theological Seminary, the ladies of the West Side First Congregational Church formed a sewing society and stockpiled household goods. Upon personal or written petition, they disbursed bedding, clothing, cookware, and crockery. Surviving records are scant but seem to reveal a moral economy of relief founded upon a more tender sense of charity: concern for those known to be in immediate distress outweighed any sort of worry over longer-term possibilities of dependency. A particular community—women who knew other women from church or as friends or kin—took each other's word as sufficient proof of an applicant's honest need. Further, unlike the Chicago women who expressly labored to aid destitute sisters of a similar status, these charity workers held fast to a style of benevolence that sometimes crossed class and ethnic boundaries. Miss Locke, a church congregant, thus recommended Mrs. Kelley—a poor Irishwomen she personally knew to be "worthy of assistance."[168] Mrs. William Dickinson "fully endorsed" the application of Mrs. Bertha Griefenhagen, a German shopkeeper and "a heavy sufferer by the fire."[169] Middle-class notions of "respectable" poverty of course informed such petitions. But personal reference and personal sympathy here allowed a tightly bonded community of women at least to begin to see beyond the prevailing perceptions of cultural and economic differences that so deeply informed the work of the Society.

Further, such a network recalled earlier, more compassionate and personalized forms of charity, the sort of antebellum benevolence rooted in ideologies of gender difference that marked middle-class women as special guardians of moral virtue.[170] By the time of the Great Fire, however, as evidenced in a bitter dispute between the Ladies' Relief and Aid Society (the subject of the "Chicago Lady's" satire) and the St. Louis Ladies' Relief Association, not all women subscribed to such a distinction for their sex. Female-staffed but ideologically equivalent to the men's Society, this group fought hard to claim a $10,000 donation from the people of St. Louis controlled by their Ladies' Relief. But Mrs. E. C. Dickinson, one of two St. Louis women on-site in Chicago, instead chose to deliver the gift to Mrs. Hammond of the First Congregational Church.[171] "Use it as you see fit," she wrote, rejecting the science of charity preached (if not always practiced) by Chicago's elite.[172] Women's instincts for care here triumphed over men's systems: "*It is sweet* to feel we have

"Ladies Distributing Clothing to the Sufferers of Both Sexes."
Source: *Frank Leslie's Illustrated Newspaper*, November 4, 1871.
Courtesy of Chicago Historical Society, ICHi-02894.

sympathy in distress or in joy," Dickinson continued. "My impulsive nature cannot disregard that most advised though not sought sentiments of the hearts!" What Dickinson and kindred spirits viewed as their very nature as women—a reflexive and kind attention to any sort of human's sufferings—led them to hold to this alternative vision of charity and community.[173]

In another relief effort, such benevolent sisterhood was matched by an ethos of "Christian Fellowship."[174] The ministers in charge of Chicago's Young Men's Christian Association were quick to set themselves apart from what they viewed as the noble and necessary, yet deeply flawed Society system. Their task—a divinely decreed labor—could not be trusted to any secular authority. "No governmental system save that of the Omniscient," according to Reverend Robert Patterson, could allay the misery that a "judicious Christian agency" might relieve through "personal observation."[175] Believers in the Golden Rule, the association desired "to do good unto all men" as a matter of course. But despite their professed belief in this tenet, the YMCA did not feel compelled to offer aid to any in want; charitable Christians, as Patterson wrote, needed to limit their alms to "the household of faith." Eager to enlarge the YMCA family, its leaders connected the delivery of relief to an evangelical project. Conscious of previous links between many sorts of disasters and upswings in communal religiosity, the association saw the Great Fire as an unparalleled opportunity for the spread of the gospel. "Men's hearts are now tender," Patterson declared. "If we now proceed, prayerfully and earnestly, to hold up Christ to our suffering brethren, we have good reason to believe that many will believe and be saved."[176] Seeking to enlarge their city's community of "saints," these evangelical Chicagoans practiced a form of charity that blended humanitarianism with proselytizing: in this case, only the saved were saved.

Along with women's groups and evangelicals, national and local trade unions adopted a sort of benevolence grounded in group solidarities. Members of these communities defined by skill sent both goods and cash to fellow craftsmen and arranged for jobs in other locales. Less than a week after the disaster, the *Tribune* reported that the National Typographical Union had already made plans to relocate over 200 printers to neighboring union cities; those who chose to stay in the city could draw upon the approximately $20,000 collected on behalf of Chicago union printers from 150 locals in the United States and Canada.[177] Similarly, as the *Tribune* reported some two weeks later, "the paper hanging fraternity" of Philadelphia sent $1253.50 "to be expended in relieving the necessities of those connected with the paper hanging trade in Chicago."[178] Grateful acknowledgments of the efforts of trade unions filled post-Fire issues of the *Workingman's Advocate*, the newspaper of the local labor movement.

Further, trades mobilized to protect their members within Chicago itself. The city's butchers, for example, formed a committee for the support of those who had lost their stores and worksites to the flames; "all Chicago butchers . . . who wish to help their burned-down business comrades" were asked to do their part to meet the "urgent need."[179] In this instance, the desire of an ethnic group to protect their own economic interests again produced a version of charity that melded philanthropy with a healthy measure of the interests of a particular community. "The retail meat business of Chicago is almost exclusively in German hands," explained the organizers of the campaign. "These people must be helped from here and from outside, because they deserve and need it. Our common interest is to keep this important business in German hands."[180] Whether a product of more remote (and perhaps more purely altruistic) trade solidarities or more complex local blends of occupational and ethnic concerns for a secure place in the rebuilt economy, these relief works again saw the personal bonds of membership in a specific community as both a badge of worthiness and a moral spur to lend a hand.

Finally, ethnic communities set out to help their own. Within the German community, for example, simply to be German was in many cases enough to merit charity. Since this enclave had lost so heavily, most Germans necessarily came to depend upon the superior financial resources of the Relief and Aid Society. Still, some of these immigrants looked both to their homeland and to their countrymen in other American cities for supplementary aid. Mindful of the steady support for victims of the Franco-Prussian War given by

Chicago's German population, the *Illinois Staats-Zeitung* rushed to call in what it viewed as the old country's debt to their city. The Great Fire, an editorial declared, was "a calamity infinitely worse for thousands of German families than the victorious war was for an equal number of families in Germany. Now is the time," concluded the paper, "that rich Germany, that is receiving 1200 millions of thalers from France, and whose capitalists own at least 600 millions of thalers of American securities, opens its hand."[181] Bolstered by the pleas of prominent businessmen who maintained commercial ties abroad, such calls across the ocean fell on receptive ears: Hamburg and Munich sent official donations exceeding those mustered by all but a few American cities.[182] German-Americans likewise tendered substantial assistance, sending cash and goods to Chicago and arranging transport for those who wished to make a new start in a new city. St. Louis Germans, for example, chartered special trains for the mass emigration of indigents. Promising safe and comfortable resettlement, the city's German population opened its arms to "all those (single and families) who want to change."[183]

Of all the varied independent agents that undertook the work of Fire relief, the United Hebrew Relief Association (UHRA)—an umbrella organization devoted to the welfare of Chicago's Jewish community—would most directly critique the Relief and Aid system. Like the Society, the UHRA believed that the city's paupers—those "never taught that any labor is honorable"—would parasitically prey upon Fire relief funds. But for the association, fear of a dependent class did not legitimate a denial of charity. To the contrary, they believed that the need to mitigate poverty's immediate toll upon individuals far outweighed the potential long-range cost to the city posed by any idle man or woman. The UHRA thus passionately argued against the practice of refusing aid to those deemed unworthy:

> You may be determined ever so firmly not to assist these cases. But you go to these hovels of misery, and see a woman broken down under the burden of her distress, in slovenly attire, dirty, surrounded by four or five children clamoring for bread. Where is your determination now? You cannot withhold assistance, you

> cannot look at antecedents. These are human beings, in bitter want. It matters not that they are the cause of their own misfortune, you must and you will help them.

The sweeping humanitarianism here expressed, though, was once again limited to a distinct community. "All barriers of distinction have been dropped within the pale of Judaism," declared the association. "We are all *B'nai Brith*, sons of the Covenant of our father Abraham, and all will be well."[184]

What was unique, however, in the Jewish response to the work of the Society involved their rejection of an approach to charity that viewed poverty as a fully individual failing. Instead, they understood this condition as a social problem: individuals were not completely exonerated from any responsibility for their lot in life, but the larger community also assumed a responsibility to effect reforms in their circumstances. For the Jewish aid association, a blind faith in the eventual rewards of self-reliance and free labor did not adequately address the issue at hand. The UHRA answer to the "dilemma" of poverty—"Assist the sufferers, but see to the proper education of their children"—thus charged both needy individuals and other members of the surrounding society to bring an end to what was understood as a *common* problem.[185] The poor had to change, but others had to offer the sort of care and training that made such change a real possibility. Like all other alternative relief efforts, Chicago Jews practiced a form of charity that highlighted the bonds within, rather than the boundaries between, a community of sufferers. Further, they set out a distinct political vision that imagined the work of urban poor relief as a project predicated upon the interdependence of all members of that community—a guiding set of principles quite distinct from those that structured the "official" efforts of the city.

In early March of 1872, some six months after his General Relief Committee had been replaced by the Relief and Aid Society, Alderman Charles Holden rose to speak on the floor of the Common Council. Two weeks earlier, the Society had taken the action that now brought Holden to his feet: on February 24, Relief and Aid administrators had stricken 800 families from its rolls. According to the Society, these people initially deserved support for losses to the Great Fire but now fell into the ranks of the "chronic poor"; since their organization did not aid such clients, the society was collectively remanding them to the care of near-bankrupt Cook County. This decision drew an outraged response from the Cook County Board, an elected body in charge of a treasury that had been ravaged by the disaster. The commissioners issued a bitter public letter, suggesting that the private administrators of the municipal Fire fund had lost sight of their mission:

> The discontinuance of relief . . . during inclement weather to 800 families, all of whom are residents of the city, and many of whom are sufferers, either directly or indirectly by the fire . . . while there is a sum exceeding a million dollars in the hands of the Relief and Aid Society, is, in the judgment of this Board, not in keeping with the object of the fund.[186]

An angry Holden, likewise convinced that the Society had here subverted what he viewed as the proper aims of Fire relief, sought to mobilize his fellow aldermen in an effort to regain control over these moneys. On March 11, he introduced a resolution that the Society be compelled to turn over the balance of the Fire relief fund to the treasury of the city, whereupon any future disbursements could be overseen by the elected officials of Chicago.[187]

But the Executive Board of the Relief and Aid Society remained unperturbed by such a challenge. As the council's Committee on Finance pondered the legal ramifications of Holden's resolution, the Society, a leisurely ten days later, made its own public response to both the condemnation of the County Board and the activities of the Common Council. First, the directors noted that only $600,000 remained in its coffers—a sizable sum but one not equal to the million dollars they had supposedly left unspent. Yet this point supposedly would soon be moot, since the Society expected to disburse all Fire funds remaining in its charge within the next six weeks, and certainly by the end of April. Far more critically, the agency claimed that it could not legally relinquish any cash to the city; they were bound by the charge of ex-Mayor Mason, they asserted, to account for the whereabouts of every last cent. The directors concluded by reiterating their attitude toward the unworthy poor: "It is never the aim of this Society," they declared, "to assume charge of such as become dependent paupers."[188] Such arguments effectively deflated Holden's resolution; his proposal died in committee, as the Common Council ultimately saw no need to take any action at this point in time.

By the end of April, however, the Relief and Aid Society had not disbursed the $600,000 at issue. Indeed, at the formal conclusion of work for Fire relief in mid-1873, the organization still had not spent these funds.[189] Their internal decision that all "honest need" born of the Great Fire had been effectively remedied ended profitably for the Society: the Fire donations they refused to relinquish to the city provided a comfortable operating fund that allowed the organization to suspend all of its own fund-raising for over ten years. Only in 1885 would the elite supporters of the work of the agency again be asked personally to contribute to the cause of relieving the want of the "worthy poor." For at the time of the Great Fire, the Relief and Aid Society had completed its mission to aid the people of Chicago to its own satisfaction—and come in well under budget.

In the days and months following the Great Fire, Chicagoans thus fought to master the practical challenge of funneling relief to a massive number of needy people. As they wrestled with this task, they further entered into contests over the role of "charity" in the definition of urban community and urban order. In so doing, various actors struggled to arrive at their own balances between ethical impulses toward altruistic philanthropy and more practical (though to their own minds no less ethical) concerns for the protection of particular groups. The structure of municipal relief, a situation where a private agency was given charge of a public function, starkly raised the problem of how one set of policy makers came to construct a "public interest," to marshall the power and claim the authority to define the "best" course for a multiplicity of peoples. In the end, the elite directors of the Relief and Aid Society created a set of rules and regulations that sought to fit the experience of diverse individuals into categories that were largely a product of their own perceptions of class and ethnic difference. Yet, for them, there was no doubt that they had acted in the interests of all Chicago.

CHAPTER THREE

Burdens and Boundaries

"How shall we rebuild our city?"[1] So went the urgent query of "Engineer," writing to the *Tribune* some six weeks after the Great Fire. A sprawl of pine cottages, frame sheds, and lumberyards had served as the first fuel for a holocaust that grew to rip through what were thought to be "fireproof" edifices built of brick and stone. The risks of wooden construction—a danger made real again and again by the disastrous blazes that regularly struck nineteenth-century American cities—would never become more clear.[2] Still, as "Engineer" worriedly observed, Chicagoans had immediately resumed their old habits of building with wood. "We find the same masses of lumber are being piled into buildings," he wrote. "Many are now starting to state that such a fire cannot occur again in *hundreds of years*."[3] What seemed an obvious "awful lesson" had apparently not been learned; such a short-sighted response, in "Engineer's" view, could easily bring another disaster to the city. As he noted, "We have the same vast unbroken plain to the west and south; we still have thousands of frame buildings, with shingles and tarred felt roofs; we may have a drouth equal to the last, and we are still open to hurricanes when natural laws work that way." Though the Great Fire both realized and came to symbolize irrevocable changes for Chicagoans, the city would never escape its weather, geography, and particular choices about the construction of an urban environment. "Pray, let us not forget these facts," warned "Engineer." And he ended with an even more significant appeal: "[L]et us provide against them to the best of our abilities."

But how to provide against such dangers? What sort of steps were necessary to safeguard the city from another Great Fire? In the months immediately after their disaster, Chicagoans had the chance to ponder such issues. Most major reconstruction could not yet begin; the short days and often severe winter cold posed substantial obstacles to standard methods of building. For the most part, the city's people turned their attention to pressing questions of relief and survival—and hunkered down to wait for a promise-filled spring. Yet, in the arena of municipal politics, the dream of a "fireproof" city injected great energy and debate into this in other ways more dormant period: Could the city, in the name of public safety, regulate a property owner's choice of building materials? Or to take the opposing point of view, in what ways was an individual property owner obligated to protect the shared space of the larger municipality?

Municipal reconstruction thus presented Chicagoans with far more than a physical and technical challenge. For even before most of the work of rebuilding began, city residents engaged in a debate that paradoxically revolved around the desirability of achieving what nearly everyone understood to be an unrealizable ideal: a city safe from fire. Rebuilding with stone or brick did nothing to address the hazards posed by Chicago's surviving wooden structures—which, for all the force of the Great Fire, remained standing over three-quarters of the city's area and were presumably just as prone to combustion as they ever were. Still, the public discussion of this in some ways moot issue raised a host of critical questions. In the course of debating just how to construct a new city, various Chicagoans found a forum for the articulation of their understandings of the rights and duties of worthy citizens. By holding to particular understandings of how individuals should foster civic welfare (and how, in turn, the municipality was bound to act toward its citizens), participants in this contest sketched out conflicting visions of the social contract drawn between owners of property and their community.

During these winter months, the struggle to erect a "fireproof" city thus again exposed how Chicagoans constructed their claims to serve a broader "public interest" or to act as "good" citizens. Like the

Lakefront shantytown, winter following the Great Fire. Detail of stereoscopic view taken from the top of the Water Tower, the tallest standing structure in the area.
Courtesy of Chicago Historical Society, ICHi-16674-D.

various understandings of charity that emerged out of relief efforts, a split again developed between the interests and aims of native-born business leaders who reflexively assumed their right to act as civic stewards, and those who argued for a vision of civic welfare that instead gave more weight to the interests and aims of particular communities within the city. This time, the contest largely occurred in the arena of municipal politics, as a newly elected mayor, the city council, and their constituents debated the wisdom of forbidding wooden construction across the whole of "New Chicago." As Chicagoans reckoned the costs and benefits of such a public policy, the class and ethnic identities of these citizens once more proved inseparable from their political process.

SECURING THE CITY

In the first weeks after the Fire, while some newspapers continued to print sensational accounts of Mrs. O'Leary, her cow, and the mysterious Communard, a more sober *Chicago Tribune* drew attention to what it deemed the ultimate cause of the calamity. The paper argued that the commercial boom that fueled Chicago's "instant" rise to metropolitan preeminence had also sown the seeds of its stunning disaster: "No city of size and wealth was ever built in such a helter-skelter manner. . . . So intent were we in spreading the city out and gathering the money in that scarcely a dozen men in the city knew how vulnerable we were."[4] Caught up in a profit-seeking rush, the editorial charged, the builders of Chicago had paid scant attention to the potential benefit of the municipal regulation of construction. A civic commitment to fire prevention did predate Chicago's conflagration: from the late 1850s, statutes had marked off fire limits that encircled the central business district. A form of fire prevention common to nineteenth-century cities, these boundaries banned wooden construction and especially flammable businesses such as lumberyards within designated "fire zones."[5] But as the *Tribune* observed, the limits had not been altered to account for the extensive growth of the city during the 1860s, and therefore encompassed only a small portion of the downtown. Even more problematic was that fact that the limits were largely unenforced—resulting in the densely packed, mostly wooden cityscape that had proven so ripe for the ravages of fire.[6]

The *Tribune* found two related causes and agents behind Chicago's tragedy: property owners who had built with an eye only toward their own profits, and the city's too-lax system of regulation. The paper accordingly called upon both individual owners and the officers of the municipality to bring about a new era of personal and civic responsibility. The reluctance of many property owners to erect more costly brick and stone structures, coupled with the failure of the city administration to secure public safety, had proven profitable for some—but hazardous for all. As an editorial declared: "We have been too good natured towards those who have, to save a few hundred dollars of their expenses, persistently kept in jeopardy the safety of the whole community by maintaining in the heart of the city great numbers of most inflammable structures."[7] The *Republican* weighed in with a similar—if more heated—denunciation of those who irresponsibly opted to build with wood: "[T]he man who so trifles with the life of the city . . . is no better than a traitor and an incendiary."[8] While grimly conceding the futility of lessons learned too late, "of locking the stable door after the horse is stolen," the *Tribune* insisted that Chicagoans now take advantage of what it viewed as a second chance to safeguard the metropolis.[9]

To accomplish this goal, the *Tribune* sanctioned a new exercise of civic authority: in the judgment of the editors, the physical safety and economic well-being of Chicago and its citizens hinged upon the expansion and enforcement of fire limits. They insisted that a wisely conceived and duly administered policy could both save the city from future devastation and aid greatly in the more immediate project of recovery. For while it was plain that rebuilding had to proceed with all due haste, the rebirth of the city must not come at the cost of solid, fireproof construction. "Not only must she rise," the editors proclaimed, "she must *rise to stand*."[10] In the name of the general welfare, the *Tribune* thus demanded that Chicago's fire limits be made coextensive with its city limits.

The logic behind such a policy rested upon a conflation of commercial and civic interests. To the editors, the prosperity of Chicago—and its very recovery from calamity—in great part hinged on the prohibition of wooden construction. Cheap wooden warehouses, workshops, and homes, they declared, posed an ever-present threat to the better-built portions of the city—especially the valuable downtown offices and mercantile establishments consumed by the flames. "To compel persons to erect brick buildings within an enclosure of wooden ones is little less than criminal," the paper charged. "It is simply devising a trap to catch valuable property, so that it can be readily burned up."[11] Hundreds of East Coast and European investors had just seen their investments go up in smoke, and no smart businessman would sink money into a site foredoomed to incineration. If Chicago hoped to reattract the outside capital historically essential to its prosperity, those with funds to lend or invest needed to know that the risk of conflagration would be diminished.[12] For the *Tribune*, the obligation of every property owner to help secure a "fireproof" city took precedence over the property rights of individuals—especially those of the men or women who for whatever reason preferred to build with wood.

But before Chicagoans could begin to consider the wisdom and practicability of using civic power to check the prerogatives of property owners in such a fashion, city voters faced a critical decision. They had to determine who would serve as the city's chief executive and officially oversee the mammoth task to come, the "Great Rebuilding." In a massive complication of the city's oft-tangled electoral scene, the Great Fire had struck less than a month before Chicagoans were due to select a mayor and half of the city council, some twenty aldermen.[13] Since Mayor Mason, a self-avowed lame duck, had expressly declined to work toward enacting any policy concerning the problems created by the Fire, it became clear that the council would postpone its consideration of fire limits until after the November 7 election. Noting the mayor's fervent wish to leave office, the *Chicago Times* offered this acid epitaph for his term of service: "[W]e know of at least one Mason who will never help to rebuild the city."[14]

It is hard to blame Mason for his eagerness to step aside. Along with all the other challenges it posed, the Great Fire brought Chicago to a crossroads in its governance that would place novel demands upon all of its politicians. The elected leaders of the city now faced a very full agenda: they needed to monitor and hasten reconstruction, cope with the loss of property and voting records, and repair a shattered mechanism for tax collection. Given such circumstances, who could take over from the unwilling Mason, and best serve in what was bound to be the difficult role of the post-Fire mayor of Chicago? As the election began to assume its ragtag shape, the daunting problems brought to the fore by the Great Fire became the key questions at issue.

In a moment of unique crisis, there would be no business as usual—an interruption of the norms of municipal elections that opened the door to what would otherwise have been a rather unlikely agenda. For many, it seemed that the times demanded a mayor who stood apart from the ordinary fray of urban politics, someone who could immediately command the respect of both city residents and the outside investors whose dollars were so crucial to the recovery. Due to what the *Illinois Staats-Zeitung* termed "the whole situation of Chicago"—plus, no doubt, the hard reality that the Great Fire had destroyed any chance for a normal election, and, consequently, any party's concrete sense of its own potential fortunes—political leaders abandoned their more regular lines.[15] "The two parties have regarded it as just and proper to conclude an armistice," observed the *Staats-Zeitung*. "The election of 1871, so to say, shall not count in the party politics of Chicago."[16]

Such was the most unusual genesis of the Union-Fireproof ticket—a body of self-described "wise, prudent, and honest" men joined under a rubric that expressed the convergence of their desires to reform the physical and electoral environments of their city.[17] A caucus of ranking Democrats and Republicans, driven by a shared desire to ensure the revival of the urban economy and a quick reconstruction, drew up a list of candidates meant to bring a new sense of honor, competency, and high civic purpose to Chicago's elected body of leaders. The ticket immediately set about distinguishing its members from those presently in power—the collection of "bums, scoundrels, and leeches" who had permitted the unregulated wooden construction that left the city vulnerable to a massive blaze, and could never take the sort of principled stand necessary to prevent another disaster.[18] Crisis, they argued, mandated a change in all the usual workings of municipal governance. As the *Chicago*

Times charged: "To allow the coming election to go by default would be a greater calamity than that which has already visited us." "Good men," the paper concluded, "must take the time to control the matter."[19]

Union-Fireproofers seized this moment to practice an antipolitico style of politics: their "good men" by definition could not come from the ranks of party regulars. Drawing a binary opposition between the honest, capable businessmen they wished to install and the incompetent, scheming politicians they wished to replace, the ticket promoters again reinforced what they portrayed as a dire need for their version of reform. Fireproofers constructed their vision of an ideal set of candidates out of what many historians have identified as a commonplace of the post–Civil War liberal political thought: to their minds, the time had come for a centralization of too-scattered social authority, for solid men of commerce to step into public office.[20] A new public interest—one to a large degree defined by capable businessmen and rational business principles—had to come to the fore in civic life.

Given their constellation of beliefs, Fireproofers found an obvious rhetorical foil in a drama then unfolding in the pages of newspapers all around the country: the fall of New York City's Tweed Ring. Fireproof invocations of the Tweed Ring had few bases in the facts of governance in their own city; Robin Einhorn's recent work suggests that the Chicago of this time had virtually no semblance of what might be understood as a Tweed-like political machine.[21] Still, pointing to New York's shameful example—which, thanks to the crusading cartoons of Thomas Nast, loomed as a potent symbol of urban corruption in the early 1870s—Union-Fireproofers made what seemed an obvious claim: that an honest and effective municipal government required the talents of men of commerce—*not* the aptitude for spoilsmanship so strongly associated with urban politics.[22] Robert Collyer, a prominent Unitarian minister who later became a major voice in the fire limits debate, cogently expressed the notion that only the supposedly disinterested and ever-rational approach of a businessman could serve the civic welfare. As he told a *Tribune* reporter, "I have for a long time now had a sure conviction that honest and able men ought to fill every place in our City

Government with no more reference to the party which with they affiliate than a great merchant would allow in the conduct of his business."[23] Those who handled public moneys and public affairs, the men who collected taxes and arranged for the delivery of services, should not bow to politics.

For Union-Fireproofers, the best of the available "best men" seemed to be the *Tribune* owner Joseph Medill.[24] A nationally recognized Republican whose rigid personal style sharply contrasted with the less formal manner of most Chicago politicians, Medill, in a few attempts had (perhaps for this very reason) never won an elected office.[25] But in the disordered post-Fire city, the past failures of the candidate became his great strength—he, for one, could not be blamed for prior mistakes. Further, his newspaper had given an ironic boost to Medill's political stock by trying to draft a leader of the city's German community, the banker Henry Greenebaum, to run for Chicago's top office. Pointing to his international standing in the world of finance, the *Tribune* had called upon Greenebaum to lend his stature and good name to Chicago.[26] Though the banker speedily declined the offer, the *Tribune*'s endorsement of a German-American candidate garnered an enormous amount of goodwill in this immigrant enclave. "Medill," the *Staats-Zeitung* declared, "is a man of honor." He merited acclaim (and election) both for his personal stature and his willingness to accept a German-American as the leader of his city: "Just as he in good faith proposed the name of the German Henry Greenebaum, so Greenebaum and all good Germans will stand by him faithfully."[27] Finally, as a renowned model of probity, Medill seemed precisely the sort of man whose election to the mayoralty would instill confidence in potential sources of capital. In a notable measure of the political consensus forged out of the economic pressures brought to bear by the disaster, even the nominee's longtime nemesis, *Chicago Times* editor Wilbur Storey, agreed that the "upright and honest" Medill would "maintain and strengthen the credit of Chicago."[28]

Not all Chicagoans fell into step with the Fireproof call for reform; despite pulling off the unprecedented coup of winning the support of every major partisan newspaper, Medill's candidacy did encounter some resistance. Several incumbent Democratic aldermen

Joseph Medill. Courtesy of Chicago Historical Society, ICHi-16828.

—exactly the sort of party regulars the Fireproofers had set out to demonize—organized a ticket known simply as "the Opposition." Council President C. C. P. Holden, fresh from his lost battle to control some aspects of municipal relief, headed their roster of nominees. In addition, one newspaper bitterly refused to back Medill. The *Republican*, a haven for ex-*Tribune* employees, lobbed repeated bombs in the direction of their former boss. If the anointed candidate "was such an exceeding popular man," John McNamara, the editor, sharply inquired, just how had he managed to lose so many previous elections?[29] "Will someone," he wrote, "please tell us when Mr. Joseph Medill displayed all those sterling qualities for the possession of which the people of Chicago are called upon to rise up as one man and make him Mayor?"[30] Moreover, the *Republican* strongly condemned the Union-Fireproof nomination process; in their view, the ticket's antiparty stance certainly did not translate into any extension of participatory democracy. A high-level, closed-door caucus had tapped Medill and his slatemates: "If it was necessary to make a Union-Fire ticket," asked the editor, "why did not the central committees of the respective parties call a convention for this purpose?"[31] These "best men" could hardly be deemed the people's choice. As the paper concluded, a "set of personal favorites," the preferences of "a few men who happened to control a few newspapers," had been foisted upon Chicago's voters.[32]

The final question raised by the *Republican* cannot be fully resolved; it is impossible to measure the degree to which support for Medill grew out of his near-sanctification in the press. Medill's stature as a civic leader certainly predated the Great Fire. Yet it seems clear that the city newspapers played an especially influential role in molding the shape of municipal politics in the weeks immediately after the disaster. In a city where most usual modes of communication had been disrupted, the press stood apart as a clear, accessible source of information.[33] There can be no doubt, however, that the *Republican*'s critique exposed the strategic irony that in great measure fueled the Fireproof campaign: within the world of city politics, the powerful here posed as the powerless. An assembly of political insiders constructed a ticket whose candidates in part distinguished themselves by emphasizing their independence from regular party structures.[34] When election day arrived, Fireproof leaders had maneuvered into a no-lose situation: riding on calls for reform, this slate could still rely upon existing party organization to muster a winning vote.

In addition, the city papers worked hard to elect the candidate they had in great part helped to create. Just prior to the election, the *Tribune, Times,* and *Staats-Zeitung* set out to smear Opposition candidate Holden, spreading unsubstantiated rumors about the council president's involvement with fire relief. During the two-day reign of his General Relief Committee, charged the papers, Holden had pocketed $15,000 of donated funds. And once expelled from the administration of municipal charity, the press further alleged, the alderman had improperly attempted to charge personal livery fees to the Relief and Aid Society.[35] Though both stories were false (and promptly retracted), this mudslinging found its mark.[36] Holden's supposed betrayal of the public trust became standard rhetorical fare for Medill backers: "Would you elect a man," asked a Fireproof orator, "who rides about the city at the expense of widows and orphans?"[37] The *Staats-Zeitung* similarly asked all Germans to support Medill and his ticket, the men "who do not use charity funds entrusted to them to ride around the city at the expense of widows and orphans."[38] The *Times* further damned the Opposition by twinning these slanders with the potent specter of Tammany Hall. As the paper proclaimed, "Let Boss Holden retire with Boss Tweed, and their respective gang of rotten thieves."[39]

With the approach of election day, the business-class interests wrapped within the Fireproof demand for a new style of politics became increasingly plain—particularly in the chosen forum of the city's Republican commercial leaders, the *Tribune.* Two days before the vote, candidate Medill's newspaper bluntly called upon businessmen to act to protect their interests. In a vivid analogy, the paper harkened back to the first days after the fire, when fears of looting had gripped the city. During that awful time, declared the editors, "anybody who had any property, or felt any devotion to the public good" had walked nocturnal patrols along with Sheridan's soldiers and state militiamen. Now, the paper charged, aldermanic "robbers under the cover of law" similarly threatened to plunder and ruin Chicago, this time through dishonesty and maladministration. But just as a strong show of unity and weaponry had deterred looters, these forces could also be bested. As the editors proclaimed: "Instead of a night's patrolling, musket in hand, so a day's faithful service at the polls is all that is required of the citizen."[40] Good government—and, by implication, Chicago's stable social and economic order—rested in the hands of the city's commercial class. "Our business men," warned the *Tribune*, "cannot afford to neglect the work which the commonwealth demands of them on this occasion."[41] "*We will win*," went an election day plea, "*if business men will only turn out and get their friends out*. Let us save what we can from the flames."[42] Just as business leaders had moved to secure their vision of social order by insisting upon Sheridan's presence and taking charge of Fire relief, the Fireproof campaign likewise became another opportunity for men of commerce to work to consolidate the influence they hoped to hold in "New Chicago."

Opposition candidate C. C. P. Holden did not enjoy November 7. Tagged as "*C*hief *C*aucus *P*acker," held up as a symbol of corruption, identified with disorder, and abandoned by others in the top ranks of the Democratic party, the alderman predictably proved a mismatch for Medill. On what must be reckoned as one of the oddest election days in Chicago's political history, the *Tribune* owner steamrolled to a 10,000-vote margin of victory, and a majority of the Fireproof aldermanic candidates scored similarly impressive victories.[43] Since voter registration records had burned, the election ran on trust and personal connections: each man had to produce two witnesses to swear to his identity.[44] If fraud (doubtless easy to accomplish under such rules) did occur, this regular feature of Chicago elections took place under unusual conditions. A mere four weeks after the Great Fire, few men had the time or inclination to engage in traditional all-day election day drinking, parades, and poll-watching.[45] According to the *Times*, voters simply arrived at their polling place—in the burned district, "rude shanties" erected for that purpose—marked their ballots, and walked away. Indeed, in a city known for high turnout, only a small percentage of eligible men turned out at all; as the *Tribune* noted, "[A] very light vote was polled."[46]

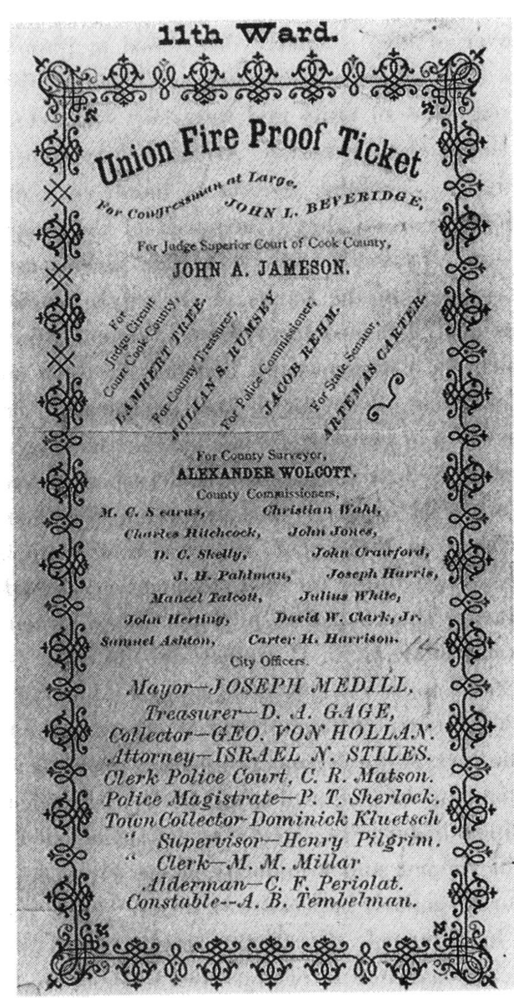

11th Ward.

Union Fire Proof Ticket

For Congressman at Large,
JOHN L. BEVERIDGE,

For Judge Superior Court of Cook County,
JOHN A. JAMESON.

For Judge Circuit Court Cook County,
LAMBERT TREE.

For County Treasurer,
JULIAN S. RUMSEY.

For Police Commissioner,
JACOB REHM.

For State Senator,
ARTEMAS CARTER.

For County Surveyor,
ALEXANDER WOLCOTT.

County Commissioners,
M. C. Stearns, Christian Wahl,
Charles Hitchcock, John Jones,
D. C. Skelly, John Crawford,
J. H. Pahlman, Joseph Harris,
Mancel Talcott, Julius White,
John Herting, David W. Clark, Jr.
Samuel Ashton, Carter H. Harrison.

City Officers.
Mayor—JOSEPH MEDILL.
Treasurer—D. A. GAGE,
Collector—GEO. VON HOLLAN.
Attorney—ISRAEL N. STILES.
Clerk Police Court, C. R. Matson.
Police Magistrate—P. T. Sherlock.
Town Collector-Dominick Kluetsch
" Supervisor—Henry Pilgrim.
" Clerk—M. M. Millar
Alderman—C. F. Periolat.
Constable--A. B. Tembelman.

Campaign broadside circulated on Election Day, 1871.
Courtesy of Chicago Historical Society, ICHi-20843.

According to the largely jubilant press, the Fireproof landslide marked a new departure in civic affairs. A mayor and a ticket pledged to pursue what they believed to be the best course for the entire city had replaced a government portrayed as fraught with corruption and greed. The *Times* proudly announced that "the party of Chicago" had vanquished "the party of the spoils."[47] The victor similarly judged that a long history of municipal administration devoted to the pursuit of narrow interests had at last reached an end. Joseph Medill believed he could do far better; his ideal of civic stewardship placed the pursuit of what he understood to be the common welfare far above any personal preference. "I shall endeavor to be governed in all my official action," promised the mayor-elect, "by an eye single to the public good."[48] Rushing even before his inauguration to fulfill his promise to reshape Chicago, Medill convened a blue-ribbon committee of property owners and politicians to study the fire limits question. To his single eye, the expansion and enforcement of municipal regulation of construction unquestionably represented a public good.

But despite Medill's apparently broad popularity, a concrete realization of the Fireproof platform was no foregone conclusion.[49] To begin with, some basic mechanics of governance posed major problems for the new titular head of the city. Chicago's chief executive held fairly limited powers; as a typical nineteenth-century "weak" mayor, Medill would need to work closely with influential, popularly elected commissions—and of course would require the concurrence of the city council on all policy decisions.[50] Further, while the Union-Fireproof ticket had won a sizable block of seats, their candidates did not hold a majority. Opposition candidates had triumphed in six contests, and twenty sitting aldermen remained unconnected to the Fireproof agenda. Given these numbers, Medill's promised transformation of Chicago's political and physical landscapes from the first faced an uphill battle. Alone among the celebrating press, the *Republican* drew attention to this skewed balance of power, and went on to charge that Medill's rigid personality made him unlikely to succeed in the arena of municipal politics—where shared authority made the ability to compromise an essential skill.[51]

Perhaps even more problematic was the fact that the ultimate meaning of the mayor-elect's "mandate" was not entirely clear. Indeed, it soon became apparent that Medill's landslide did not translate into sweeping popular support for his ticket's keystone pledge: the extension of fire limits. The consensus and goodwill created by a well-packaged, well-publicized candidacy began to break apart once the new mayor had to venture into the real, contested world of putting a proposal into effect. Only two weeks after Medill's election, the *Republican* resumed its role as naysayer, warning that any notion of wide support for the actual enforcement of a new municipal regulation for construction would prove illusory. As the paper happily observed, "Mr. Medill's plan for civic reconstruction does not seem to attract the general approbation which our Mayor-elect considered it certain to secure."[52]

For here a theory could not be reconciled with its practice. "In the abstract," wrote the *Republican*, "it is a bill worthy of all support." No one argued against the aim of better guarding the city against fire. Yet the issue was not nearly so simple as it seemed; major questions remained unsettled: Would stricter fire limits really make any difference to a city still full of wooden structures? Could such regulations ever be rigorously enforced? And on the level of principle, how could the individual rights of property owners be balanced against the public good of fire prevention? The idea of a Fireproof city, the paper damningly judged, was in the end "marked with all impracticabilities."[53] But would the mayor-elect recognize that his vision of what was right for Chicago would be rivaled by other understandings of what steps might best serve the civic welfare, or constitute the "public interest"? The *Republican* thought not. "For Mr. Medill," the paper concluded, "we predict a most ignominious career as an incumbent of the civic chair."[54]

DRAWING LINES

Joseph Medill became Chicago's twenty-first mayor on December 4, 1871. In an inaugural address notable for its earnest and detailed consideration of the state of the city—and, according to more than a few weary listeners, its extreme length—the new mayor reiterated the basic themes of the Fireproof campaign. Retrenchment, economy, and a new spirit of integrity, Medill declared, would soon wipe away any last vestiges of "knavish combinations of unscrupulous partisans."[55] Further, to ensure that Chicago's chief executive would wield the political power to bring about such change, Medill formally announced his plan to introduce a "Mayor's Bill" in the Illinois legislature. This proposed modification of the city charter would, for a temporary two-year term, radically tilt the balance of municipal authority toward the mayor, granting him unprecedented freedom in appointments, control over the city council, and veto power.[56] Finally, true to the slogan of his slate, Medill concluded with a pledge to make Chicago fireproof. "No more important questions," he admonished the council, "can engage your attention than those of the future fire limits."[57] And in this matter the choice seemed clear: "Can there be any doubt as to our duty?" The rights of private property owners had to be curtailed in the name of public safety. "Except for the most temporary uses," declared the mayor, "I am unalterably opposed, from this time forward, to the erection of a single wooden building within the limits of Chicago."[58]

At his inauguration, Medill thus renewed the urgent call he had helped to compose days after the Great Fire at a *Tribune* desk. "The fire-limits," he proclaimed, "should be made co-extensive with the boundaries of the city." In regard to existing wood structures, the mayor predicted that such buildings would eventually burn down or, more likely, be replaced by permanent edifices. Under the protective cloak of expanded fire limits, a better-built city would soon emerge, greatly appreciating the city's credit and real estate values. "It is," he argued, "the wisest financial measure that could be enacted." Any set of boundaries that sought to enclose only a portion of the city, he went on to assert, would prove untenable on both practical and ideological grounds. An "inner fire-line" would seem an arbitrary barrier to city residents—and, as bitter experience had shown, be violated with impunity. Worse, limits internal to the city enforced an inequality of property rights among Chicago's citizens, a situation that Medill, as a staunch believer in the equal treatment of all citizens before the law, found intolerable. "Special privileges," he announced, "are odious in a republican country." In his Chicago, all citizens would have to accept their civic duty of doing without wooden construction. As the mayor bluntly expressed it: "Either let us forbid the construction of these buildings which tend to jeopardize the city, or allow all citizens an equal privilege to burn down their neighbors."[59] True to the *Republican*'s word, Medill brooked no compromise: only coextensive city and fire limits could fully and fairly advance the public interest.

For in the minds of Medill and his backers, all Chicagoans were obliged to protect their city. All shared an equal interest in achieving the undisputed civic good of fire protection. And all, it therefore followed, were bound to act in conformity with whatever course was deemed to serve the end of meeting this common goal—in this case, the enactment of coextensive fire limits. Further, in applying this syllogism, Fireproofers held to a vision of citizenship that presumed an equality of membership: the liberal ideal of many individuals bound to a social contract with the state. But the real differences that marked these individuals—including those, for example, of class—were both subsumed within and devalued by this more abstract theory of political identity and responsibility.

In this way, Medill's blue-ribbon committee had the ability to recognize some of the particular values held and concerns faced by the diverse peoples who together composed the city of Chicago. Yet their conception of the duties of the abstract "good" citizen, their conflation of a theoretical political equality with all other forms of equality, made it possible for them at the same time to posit a unitary civic interest—one, by no coincidence, that they claimed the best capacity to define. As the committee reported, they appreciated the reality that their city was stratified by wealth and had therefore "weighed the interests of all parties both rich and poor." Their universalized conception of the obligation of the citizen, however, led Medill's appointed panel to conclude that the interests of all these different parties were (or should be) the same: they, in the end, found "these interests identical."[60] In the aftermath of the Great Fire, Fireproofers thus expected all property owners, regardless of their economic stature, to acknowledge and respect the necessity of extended fire limits. The higher cost of building of brick or stone, they recognized, would force some poorer Chicagoans to shoulder great burdens. Yet they agreed that long-term savings on insurance and maintenance would eventually compensate any burned-out property owner for following through on what seemed their clear civic duty.

But such an abstract vision of civic obligation and such optimistic predictions about the economics of fireproof construction soon ran head-on into the reality of class difference. For the Great Fire had devastated much of Chicago's low-cost housing—including thousands of worker-owned pine cottages.[61] Chicagoans often pointed with great pride to the fact that a substantial proportion of the working people of the city owned homes; at a time when property ownership was becoming a powerful mark of respectability, civic boosters saw Chicago workers as far more fortunate than the laboring people packed into New York or London tenements.[62] Homeownership also loomed large as a primary cultural badge of economic independence and worthy manhood, both much-valued components of "good" citizenship.[63] The *Tribune,* predictably blind to the irony of simultaneously promoting both inexpensive housing and the more costly building method mandated by the Fireproof agenda, made this declaration on December 4: "A Man needs a house . . . cheap homes for the workingman is a subject of primary importance."[64] Further, homeownership was clearly not merely an ideological and material preoccupation of the commercial class: the workingmen and women of the city themselves were eager to acquire property. As a spokesman for one of the several union-sponsored home building associations in Chicago wrote in 1867, "[A] man can have no better base of operations than that of a cheerful, comfortable home suited to his means and wants."[65]

Now, however, many of these working-class homeowners had absorbed a staggering blow. How could people of limited means who faced total loss—with troubles often compounded by insurance failures and the destruction of their workplaces—hope to do much more than nail together a temporary wooden shanty on their property? The logic of long-term benefits seemed cold consolation in an immediate crisis. Even more troubling, if the city legally barred a property holder from rebuilding with wood, and he or she could not afford brick or stone construction, this site lost all value for its owner. A lifetime of work and savings might well evaporate; only the cut-rate prices offered by speculators would seemingly be left to such unfortunates. In the minds of working-class homeowners, then, the Fireproof conception of civic duty weighed most heavily upon the population of property owners least able to bear its costs. As Alderman Michael B. Bailey, a victorious Opposition man, observed in a speech to the city council a week prior to Medill's installation, it should come as no surprise if many Chicagoans refused to accept their mayor's vision of a safe, solid Chicago. "The great difficulty," he predicted, "will be to satisfy those of moderate means that you are not oppressing them."[66]

With Bailey's speech, Fireproofers received a first clear signal that their claim to represent the public interest would not go uncontested—and that others would advance differing versions of the same claim. At a November 27 Common Council meeting, the blue-ribbon committee charged to study new municipal regulation of construction returned with their endorsement of coextensive fire and city limits. At the report's conclusion, Bailey, whose North Side ward had been destroyed by the Fire, rose to warn that his working-class constituents would insist upon their right to reconstruct with wood. Everyone of course desired a safer city, he declared, and the high-priced real estate and "elegant building blocks" of the downtown area obviously deserved to be guarded against the erection of nearby "fire-traps." But advocates of a complete ban on new wood construction had turned a blind eye to the needs (and rights) of a citizenry divided by class—particularly to those of the thousands of working people who had lost their homes in the Great Fire. In the view of the alderman, proponents of a fireproof city had wrongfully conflated civic welfare with the wishes of the owners of expensive property—and their nervous, once-burned insurers. Defining the public good differently than did Medill, Bailey went on to imply that the specific interests of the commercial elite had played no small role in shaping the understanding of civic duty held by Fireproofers. "It often happens," he observed, "that those who are most persistent in the advocacy of stringent fire ordinances have some private end in view—and care but little about the public welfare."[67]

Hardly "disinterested," Medill's plan for coextensive limits was also, in Bailey's opinion, far from equitable. The alderman did concede the prudence of an amended fire protection ordinance, proposing the extension of existing limits over a larger portion of the city center, strict municipal control over the location of lumber yards and other especially inflammable businesses, and the enforcement of various construction codes. But, Bailey argued, the too-sweeping Fireproof plan concealed an improper and (in a barb doubtless aimed straight at Medill) "unrepublican" attack on the personal freedoms of *all* property owners—large and small. "The spirit of our institutions makes us sensitive in regard to any arbitrary abridgement of our Liberty," he declared. "Our lawmakers cannot be too careful in the curtailment of any individual rights for the general welfare." Moreover, on the level of plain common sense, the alderman dismissed coextensive fire limits as unworkable, given the thousands of wooden structures that had survived the Great Fire and the pressing need for the quick construction of shelter. To Bailey, the answer could only be found through compromise. Medill and his allies, he cautioned, needed to guard against dictating what might seem in the heat of the moment to be a proper policy—and they needed to pay more attention to the needs and desires of the city's less-prosperous homeowners. As the Opposition man concluded, "The old ordinance was a dead letter, and the new one will be treated in the same way unless it accords with the views of the majority of those interested."[68] Most of the burned-out homeowners in Chicago, as Bailey suggested, thus had ample reason to contest the Fireproof plan.

Within this population, the German-American community remained particularly sensitive to the enactment of any laws that might interfere with the rebuilding of their devastated North Side neighborhoods. As soon as it had resumed publication, the *Staats-Zeitung* had alerted its readers to a bleak possibility: that the course of reconstruction might well bring the ultimate doom of their ethnic enclave. Some degree of anti-German sentiment, the paper charged, always lurked beneath the surface of social relations in their city—and the Great Fire could well allow nativists to seize their moment.[69] One grim scenario seemed especially threatening to the editors: that wealthy, native-born South Siders might quickly move to turn the fire-cleared northern wards into a much-needed centralized freight and transport district—an act that would effectively eradicate the "Germandom of Chicago." "Where up to now German businessmen, craftsmen, and workers found a pleasant home," warned the *Staats-Zeitung*, "numberless railroad trains will speed over hundreds of tracks, smoking machine shops, mills, and lumber depots will take the place of friendly flower-framed little houses."[70] Pollution, noise, and density would of course cause land values to plummet. In the face of a shattered immigrant dream of American economic security and mobility, Chicago would forever lose its special luster as a place where thrifty, independent working people could reasonably expect to own homes in pleasant neighborhoods. All city Germans, the paper dramatically concluded, would sink into the lowest orders of urban life: "Then you are condemned to become a dirty district of proletarians!"[71]

The passage of a few weeks proved that the *Staats-Zeitung*'s anxieties were unlikely to be realized; though the Great Fire did bring spatial realignment to Chicago's downtown and spur the relocation of some lakefront industry, residential areas in general retained their character.[72] Still, despite their apparent irrationality, such fears for Chicago's "Germandom" signaled a depth of sentiment that deserves attention. It seems plain that this post-Fire anxiety was nurtured in a larger cultural and political battleground: in the minds of many Chicago Germans, the project of rebuilding could not be separated from their ongoing struggle to define an ethnic identity within an American city. As the *Staats-Zeitung* declared, "[T]he preservation of Chicago as a city where the German element has the same power and social standing as one of native birth depends upon the reconstruction of the North Side."[73] For this voice of an immigrant community, full membership in the civic polity—a complete sense of citizenship, of belonging in an American community—hinged upon the resurrection of the space they had staked out within the city. Since most German-American home and business owners could ill-afford to rebuild with brick or stone, the enactment of coextensive limits might further degrade what many already felt to be a tenuous social status. The *Staats-Zeitung* thus charged its readers to be ready to protect their immigrant world within the city: "Whether Chicago shall become a Yankee nest where the 'Dutch' form a contemptible subordinate class, or if it should be resuscitated as the most cosmopolitan city in America—this is now up for decision."[74]

Throughout December and into the first weeks of 1872, elected officials faced such competing pressures as they struggled to make their own decision, to arrive at an acceptable reconciliation of civic obligation and individual freedom. Medill made his best efforts to speed a resolution: Fireproof aldermen repeatedly called for the passage of coextensive limits. Most independent and Opposition aldermen, though, were pleased to delay any final action. For if property owners built with wood before the council passed a new fire limits ordinance, their structures would in essence beat the clock—and be immune from any new regulation. Lot owners were eagerly seizing the moment; despite the hardships of winter work, a rush of wood construction was underway. "All over," according to the *Tribune,* "there are frame buildings in course of erection, by whose permission and authority no one seems to know, and no one seems to care."[75] Noting the many owners "straining every nerve" to build with wood, Medill's paper some two weeks later replayed what had become its standard cautionary refrain: "[U]nless the proposed ordinance becomes a law in a very short time, Chicago will be in as good condition as ever for a conflagration."[76]

But the council, split between Fireproofers and those determined to defeat coextensive limits, refused to agree. And in the meantime, hundreds of private citizens added their voices to the debate. From all parts of the city, property owners besieged their aldermen with a flood of petitions and remonstrances.[77] Attending neighborhood meetings, walking door-to-door to collect signatures—ordinary men and women here chose to speak in an elevated language of rights and responsibilities.[78] As individuals and as members of groups, the signers of these communications set out their understandings of their identity as citizens—and their particular claims to the definition of a common civic good.

Unsurprisingly, North Siders most frequently petitioned the council, joining together as burned-out neighbors to ask that they be allowed to rebuild with wood. One communication of "respectful protest" deemed coextensive limits to be "unjust and uncalled for," especially in the wake of "the terrible losses many of us sustained." The high cost of brick construction, coupled with the failure of so many local insurance companies, would, according to these nearly 200 signers, drive them to sell off their lots "at ruinous prices."[79] Among some twenty of their fellow Clybourn Avenue residents, Peter Weber, Edmund Carter, and William Klein—a painter, a mason, and a plumber—likewise implored the aldermen not to "ruin our interests," not to "compel us to sell our land to greedy land speculators."[80] And in late December, 122 "residents and land owners in the North Division" set out similar arguments. Further, they pushed their reasoning beyond the more material realm of unbearable costs, arguing that they had earned their status as worthy citizens with a prior collective contribution to the growth and prosperity of the city. "We built Chicago (the North Division) once whence there was nothing but wild prairie," declared the petitioners. "We the persons who built the city once before should be heard in such a great question."[81]

Such burned-out North Siders were not unique in their criticisms of coextensive limits; many of those who had not lost their property to the Fire were moved to register their disapproval. Several dozen West Side residents, fearful that increased construction costs would harm growth in *their* division, set out a definition of public good that equated their best wishes for themselves with those of all Chicagoans: "We do not believe that the interests of the city or of the West Side demand such extension."[82] Two separate petitions of South Siders made an identical claim, arguing that new limits covering their division "could not further the interests of the city."[83] Though a few luxurious neighborhoods hugged the South Side lakefront, most residents of the district lived in poorer areas not yet served by sewerage, or gas or water lines. Under what Robin Einhorn has termed Chicago's "segmented system" of government, lot owners had paid to bring "improvements" to their property through the tax mechanism known as "special assessments"; the city government to this point had never understood the provision of such services as meeting a common civic interest that deserved to be financed through general revenues.[84] So why, asked these South

Siders, should they now be forced to pay higher construction costs to secure the larger civic good of better fire prevention? It seemed a very unfair exchange. To the minds of laborers like Andrew Walsh and James Kelley, the wagonmaker Henry Kaiser, the grocer John Klebanow, and sixty-six other self-described "South Side Property Holders," the fire ordinance so valued by their new mayor could thus justly be deemed "injudicious, unreasonable, and oppressive."[85]

Unlike the Fireproofers, these antilimits petitioners held to a vision of civic responsibility that could account for the differences that marked individual Chicagoans. Men and women of moderate means—laborers, craftworkers, and small business owners—in this instance set themselves apart from wealthier Chicagoans, the property owners who could more easily afford to erect more fire-resistant buildings. Still, all of these signers imagined and presented themselves as full citizens—political beings quite capable of articulating their own notions of the public interest. And to their minds, a de jure prohibition of wood construction equaled a de facto denial of the ability of all Chicagoans to remain full citizens of their community.

While the great majority of extant petitions opposed coextensive limits, those who approved of Medill's vision also called upon the council. Nine West Side neighbors wrote to demand coextensive limits, protesting "the passage of any fire ordinance which would exclude them and their property from its benefits."[86] A liberal theory of the rights and duties of citizens undergirded their specific arguments. All citizens, they reasoned, were equal members of the civic polity. Further, all citizens who owned property paid taxes, thereby assuring the continued functioning of the urban "corporation"—and paying for city services such as fire protection. Hence, all property owners deserved to benefit in equal measure from the services they had financed. No good citizen could opt out of this social contract. "They are subject equally," claimed the petitioners, "with all other members of the corporation to the burdens imposed by corporate authorities for corporate purposes."

As citizen-members of what they viewed as the city-corporation, these West Side professionals—lawyers, bankers, and businessmen

—prevailed upon their aldermen to ensure that they would receive their services due for payments rendered, the equal protection of coextensive limits in exchange for their tax dollars: "We demand it as the duty of the official agents of the corporation, which includes all and taxes all, and which is in turn bound, upon every principle of justice, to secure to all the equal benefits of its laws." The standard Fireproof abstraction of the universalized citizen here was assigned the somewhat more specific role of the "taxpayer," an echo of the classic republican principle that only those who owned property deserved to be fully vested in the state and its governance. Further, these nine West Siders not only reflexively envisioned all Chicagoans as part of an undifferentiated social contract, but they also understood a need for the rational application of business principles, a consolidation of authority, as "disinterested"—part and parcel of a unitary civic good.

While not every Chicago professional or businessman held to this set of beliefs, these petitions again underscore the ways in which the Fireproof plan, for all its supporters' claims to represent the common civic will, grew out of a set of interests rooted in the native-born commercial class.[87] A suggestive pattern emerges out of a comparison of the occupations and ethnic origins of the signers of the fire limits petitions. The two surviving prolimits petitions were overwhelmingly endorsed by men who would have described themselves as part of the "business class": brokers, bankers, merchants, insurance agents, attorneys. Further, many in the employ of such professionals and men of commerce also signed on: nonmanual workers such as clerks, cashiers, and bookkeepers. Finally, very few had Irish, German, or Scandinavian surnames. By contrast, the anti-limits petitions represent the sentiments of a much broader range of peoples. A mix of laborers, craftworkers, small business owners, professionals, and more substantial merchants all added their names to the roles of those who opposed the Fireproof plan. Further, German, Irish, and Scandinavian surnames were common. And while most petitions arrived from all across the city, organized by groups of neighbors to articulate the desires of the residents of one particular area, one of the two extant prolimits petitions took the different, highly significant tack of organizing by *class*. In mid-January, an unidentified manager of Field, Leiter, and Company (later Marshall Field's) sent this note to Mayor Medill: "I enclose a petition signed by every mercantile businessman we could find. . . . These men pay a large amount of taxes," he added, "and are the *live elements* of our city."[88] Such men of commerce—the economic engines who fueled civic prosperity, the owners of large amounts of property—were, in the view of the Field, Leiter manager, a set of outstanding citizens whose voices especially deserved to be heard and heeded.

Did coextensive fire and city limits serve the public interest? Men like this high-level merchant and the nine West Siders were entirely confident that they did indeed. So certain were they, in fact, that they were quite prepared to mobilize civic authority to require all Chicagoans to comply with the vision of civic good that they themselves had defined. For in their view, a democratic system mandated a government empowered to enforce their understanding of the social contract. Only a rigorous adherence to an undifferentiated vision of the rights and duties of the citizen, a rejection of what they viewed as more particular (and hence less worthy) claims and interests, could properly restore social order to their Fire-shattered city. As the West Siders' petition concluded: "The only security for our property, our lives, or for the public peace and order consists in the requirement that all persons, of whatever section, class, rank, or degree, shall be equally compelled to respect and abide by the law and all lawful authorities."[89]

But as the antilimits petitions made plain, others rooted in social and economic circumstances born of what Fireproofers understood as more "particular" identities held to a contrary notion of their rights as citizens. In part equating their civic identity with some of the differences that marked all Chicagoans, men and women of moderate means, ethnic minorities, residents of specific areas—or people cobbling together a combination of any of these three identities—alternatively constructed their interests as being the same as those of the city. In this way, the debate over fire limits in Chicago was also a contest to determine just what sort of social identity carried political authority in the city—a clear test of how the liberal notions of the universal citizen held by some would or would not devalue the differences that others did not separate from their sense of what constituted a proper civic identity, or, in other words, the role that a "good" citizen had to play.

As January 15 approached, it seemed that all of these questions revolving around private property and civic responsibility might be settled. Finally bowing to Medill's repeated requests, the aldermen agreed to convene on that night in special evening session for what was meant to be their last consideration of the fire limits ordinance. It was time to decide what was best for Chicago—and who could best speak for Chicagoans.

DEFINING DEBTS

"This is no joke, to forbid sixty thousand inhabitants of the North Side to build such houses as those were in which they lived and were satisfied these last twenty-five years."[90] Anton Caspar Hesing, owner of the *Staats-Zeitung*, and the most visible political leader in Chicago's German-American community, so began his remarks to an assembly outside the home of Alderman Frank Carney on the evening of January 14.[91] The crowd that stood on the North Side with Hesing of course had scarcely forgotten the seriousness of the problem they believed they faced: the very next night, the long anticipated and much feared Fireproof Plan might actually be enacted. Though Hesing himself had not so long ago worked hard to elect Medill, his goodwill had since soured.[92] For the new mayor's unwavering call for coextensive limits seemed to him far too extreme, a policy likely to undermine the stability and prosperity he had hoped the election of Medill would bring to the city. The vision set out by the mayor—a dream of a "New Chicago" marked by an era of new executive control, the consolidation of civic authority, and the advancement of a public interest largely defined by the native-born commercial class—to Hesing spelled another disaster: this time, one brought about by the city's own hand. As his *Staats-Zeitung* argued, "[T]o forbid all wooden structures inside the whole space that in part still consists of fields, meadows, vegetable gardens, or empty prairie, but is named on the map Chicago, means to stop the further growth of the city." It was, concluded the paper, "nothing less than suicide."[93]

Even more important, aside from the more abstract question of whether or not coextensive limits would impair future metropolitan growth, Hesing and his followers—unlike the Fireproofers—were quick to focus on the immediate consequences (and costs) of coextensive limits. And the most glaring injury they could see was one that they understood as a product of class difference. On this night, then, North Side property owners of moderate means had come together to claim their rights and assert their interests in opposition to the wishes of more prosperous Chicagoans—a group the North Siders lumped together as the "capitalists" and "the money-bags."[94] Those pressing for extended fire limits, Hesing proclaimed, were driving a stake into the heart of the city—its working class. As he thundered in the classic terms of the labor theory of value, "Capitalists have not made Chicago what it is." To the contrary, "innumerable workers of every type have made certain men rich by their work."[95] Where was the justice, he asked, in depriving these essential citizens of their just reward—not even to allow them a piece of land to call their own? Carney and his fellow council members, Hesing concluded, had to ensure that catastrophe would not "make the rich richer and the poor poorer."[96] At the meeting's end, those in attendance formally condemned any plan that would extend fire limits into their North Side neighborhoods. In addition, they agreed to assemble the next night, the evening of the special council session.

At about 7 P.M. on January 15, a hundred North Side homeowners again began to congregate outside Alderman Carney's home. But the apparently all-male crowd now meant to do more than listen to a few speeches; on this night, their message would be delivered in person.[97] Led by a band and torchbearers, carrying placards emblazoned with slogans such as "Leave a Home for the Laborer" and "No Tenements," the protestors headed south to the hastily constructed City Hall—an edifice, ironically enough, built of wood. As the crowd moved south toward the river, its ranks swelled. With destroyed bridges yet to be replaced, a deafening din resounded as about a thousand marchers made their way through the Clark Street tunnel. Once in the city center, the protestors regrouped, arranging themselves into a phalanx eight-men deep. Headed by Hesing and a former alderman, Frank Conlon, the march then proceeded to City Hall, where the council was already in session.[98]

Newspaper reports of what happened next vary widely. All of these accounts do agree on the following basic facts: what had been intended as an orderly presentation of an antilimits petition turned raucous and destructive when a police guard barred the protestors from entering the council chambers; the ensuing uproar forced an abrupt adjournment. At this point a web of other tales and interpretations begin. According to the outraged *Times* and *Tribune*, hundreds of thugs had stormed the very citadel of civic order. Breaking desks and smashing windows, the "mob" utterly disrupted council business—prompting a number of aldermen, one *Tribune* headline claimed, to "Seek Shelter in the Cloak Room."[99] An equally outraged *Staats-Zeitung*, however, told a different story. While conceding that the North Siders' protest had gotten out of hand, Hesing's paper pointed the finger of blame at Chicago's police. It was true, the editors agreed, that "a few rowdy youths" had broken windows, and it was certainly a scandal that one banner had shown gallows, posing a less than subtle threat to the health and welfare of the Fireproofers. But at bottom, charged the paper, the incident turned on the nativism of the city's ostensible peacekeepers: a force the *Staats-Zeitung* described as devoted to "keeping down" and "killing the Dutch."[100] To Hesing and his editors, the protestors had acted in pure and simple self-defense; no one would have thrown bricks had not the police "driven the people like a herd of cattle, without giving them time to go on their way." Finally, the *Staats-Zeitung* attacked the sensational reports published in the major English-language dailies: "Absolutely mendacious and devoid of even an atom of truth are all descriptions which represent the City Council as pandemonium . . . , or even try to create the impression as if the aldermen had to flee for their lives."[101]

Such divergence in accounts of the incident predictably signal the even more striking divergence of opinion as to its meaning. According to the *Staats-Zeitung*, a group of voters had merely exercised their constitutional right to assembly, coming together to communicate their stance on a vital issue to their elected representatives. This informed activism, claimed the paper, could only be reckoned as an exercise in good citizenship. But Mayor Medill, for one, did not view the tumult of the evening as the benign product of earnest civic spirit. In a strongly worded message to the council, he deplored what he termed an exercise in "mob dictation." To his mind, the practice of participatory democracy had in this instance crossed well past its proper bounds: what Medill saw as a brazen effort to intimidate the lawmakers of the city was anathema to his understanding of a peaceable, republican community. No "good" citizen would ever seek to sway the votes of their elected representatives in such a disorderly and confrontational manner. The mayor thus served notice that similar disruptions of civic deliberations—or any other transgression of "good order"—would not be tolerated. "The supremacy of the laws," he pronounced "shall be maintained at all hazards." Much as Mayor Mason and Relief and Aid Society leaders had displayed their eagerness to call in the U.S. army to squelch potential threats to municipal stability in the day immediately after the Great Fire, Medill likewise indicated his willingness to suspend civil rule to maintain his vision of civic peace. "If the organized police force of the city should prove inadequate," he warned, "the military power of the State shall promptly be invoked."[102]

In a city still in the process of recovering from the extreme social and spatial disorder wrought by the Great Fire, the fire limits incident—whatever its true dimensions—summoned a specter of mob rule that drew an emotional response from the city's major English-language papers. "Is civil government in Chicago a failure?" asked the *Times*, comparing the City Hall marchers to the "riotous demonstrations" that had gripped Paris in both 1848 and during the recent past months that had witnessed the bloody rise and fall of the Commune. In a particularly dramatic declaration, even another Great Fire was made to seem a less painful fate than the possible erosion of civic order. "Better," the paper darkly concluded, "that conflagration should sweep from this earth what remains of the city than its future should be shaped and its prosperity made to be dependent on the lawless violence of a mob."[103] The *Tribune* echoed this trope of disorder but looked closer to home for its comparative example, rhetorically equating what it saw as the North Siders' disregard of law and order with the Ku Klux Klan's savage rejection of the dictates of Reconstruction—a horrifying campaign of racial violence at that moment tearing up much of the American South.

According to these commentaries, both the integrity of civic rule and stable class and ethnic relations in Chicago hinged upon a quick and forceful validation of state power. Adopting a particularly striking metaphor of immigrant conquest, the *Tribune* observed that the fire limits question was "not the only *casus belli* which is liable to bring down an army of Germans from the North, or of Irish from the West." In such a trying time any subversion of municipal authority could easily snowball. "There are plenty of pretexts for riot," the paper continued, "when the lawless feeling is aroused, and an impression created that the City Government is weak."[104] The more extreme (and more widely read) *Times* went even further, issuing a call to meet what it viewed as this assault upon civic order with deadly force. "A volley of musketry or a few charges of grape and canister fired into the crowd," the paper pronounced, "could not have made any serious mistakes."[105] Those who chose to challenge the good order of the city needed to know that their acts would not go unpunished, that strong leaders of a strong government would not hesitate to quell perceived disorder with the heaviest of hands.

Moreover, the *Tribune* and the *Times* made much of the fact that the protest had originated on the largely immigrant North Side, turning their reportage into a forum for the expression of nativist sentiment. Both papers made reference to Chicago's 1855 "Lager Beer War"—a march of German immigrants opposed to municipal temperance laws.[106] An event that occurred in the heyday of political nativism, the Lager Beer War had similarly involved an organized protest of North Siders that ended in violence. The *Times* seized upon the fire limits march as proof of what it portrayed as a shameful pattern unique to city Germans: their readiness to take their politics to the streets. Such immigrants, the paper declared, had completely failed to adopt a proper regard for American forms of government. The German presumption of "the right to intimidate Councilmen, and to endanger the city by the erection of wooden firetraps" was indeed an act of political tyranny, an attempt to impose the particular interests of one ethnic community upon all Chicagoans.[107] Could such demagogues be considered "true" Americans? Did they deserve to be citizens of this city in the Republic?

The *Times* most definitely thought not. "If they do not like our American institutions and ways," opined the paper, "let them return from whence they came."[108] Here, a definition of "good" citizenship that imagined not only a unitary civic interest but a single correct American identity held sway.

Chicago Germans, though, were not about to take the *Times'* advice. Unimpressed by this assault upon their public spirit, community leaders similarly staked a claim to the mantle of good citizenship. Their sense of civic virtue, however, grew out of their particular identities as immigrants and as people of more moderate means—two sorts of social differences that to their minds did not make them poor citizens but in fact privileged them to speak on behalf of all Chicagoans. A complex argument thus turned the tables on nativists: German immigrants, at this juncture, invoked their ethnic difference to present themselves as more truly American than any of their native-born critics. Their logic ran as follows: Fireproofers, they charged, were themselves guilty of subverting what city Germans viewed as a defining component of life in America—the ability of less prosperous people to own their homes. After the Great Fire, North Siders had fought hard to reclaim their place as full citizens of Chicago by insisting upon the preservation of their right to rebuild with wood. The enactment of coextensive limits, as they had steadily argued, would effectively rob burned-out immigrant working people of what they had sought in America: the ownership of property and the chance to achieve a degree of economic independence far beyond what they might have attained in their homeland.

Was it proper, then, to deny access to this American dream, the hope of attaining the independence granted by homeownership? Anton Hesing countered the *Times'* specter of European mob rule and open class warfare with his own apocalyptic vision of the tenements and rigid class hierarchies typical of the cities of the Old World. In a letter sent to the *Republican* two days after the City Hall march, the publisher thus bluntly questioned the patriotism of Fireproofers: "Those are *not* true Americans—no matter where born—who would consign our laboring classes to the condition of *proletaires* by depriving them of a fair chance to live under their own roofs."[109] Wilhelm Rapp, in a speech to the Chicagoer Arbeiterbund, similarly urged his audience of German-born workers to continue to press for public policies that accommodated their definition of worthy citizenship—one that corresponded to their own understandings of what their particular class and ethnic identities added to any calculation of a larger civic good. "The Germans have prevented the big money-bags from . . . bringing the worker into the same dependent position as in the big cities of Europe," Rapp proclaimed. "You, my friends, are the recognized and honored champions of freedom and of right generally, and of the freedom and right of the worker and middle classes in particular."[110] In contesting the Fireproof agenda, German immigrants consciously asserted their ethnic difference and nonelite class positions to offer an alternative claim to represent a broader public interest.

At this point, the clash between the two definitions of worthy citizenship at issue in this controversy—Fireproof universalism versus antilimits particularism—found its most vivid public expression. A discussion that began as a consideration of the rights and wrongs of municipal regulation of construction spun off into a sweeping debate about the place that immigrants could hold in the civic order. What sort of social contract marked their integration into American civic life? Just how much did newcomers "owe" to their adopted home? Within days of the City Hall incident, an exchange of letters on this precise subject drew wide attention. The Unitarian minister Robert Collyer, the pastor of one of the wealthiest churches in Chicago, and *Staats-Zeitung* publisher Hesing squared off over the question of the duties of the "good" citizen—as especially refracted through the eyes of immigrants. Nearly all the city newspapers carried full transcripts of the two letters, deemed by the *Republican* as having been penned by "representative men who have championed each side of the present controversy."[111]

Collyer, a Yorkshireman who had come to the United States at the age of twenty-six, initiated the exchange with an open letter to the *Tribune*.[112] Setting a tone of reverent patriotism, the minister reminded Hesing that they had last seen each other abroad—in Heidelberg, to be exact, on the previous Fourth of July. There, standing together under an American flag, they had spoken wistfully of their shared longing to be at home in Chicago on that Independence Day, to be "where there was a celebration, to hear something of the old story." Deeply moved by their conversation, Collyer recalled, he had even spent all the silver in his pocket to persuade a passing harper to play what had unfortunately turned out to be a barely recognizable version of "Yankee Doodle." The clergyman next reflected on his own good fortune: once "as poor a man as you would wish to see," his twenty-two years in America had gifted him with prosperity, security, and political empowerment. And such success, he believed, was in large degree the story of all Chicago immigrants: abandoning a "hopeless fight against poverty and caste" in the Old World, "all found here better wages, equal rights, a good education for our children, and thank God! many of us, before the great calamity, a home we could truly call our own."

Given the landscape of opportunity he had found in Chicago, the behavior of the fire limits protestors bewildered the clergyman. How, he wondered, could such a "gross assault . . . on our American usages" be undertaken by men "who owe nearly everything they have in the world to the generous opening America has made for us," by those "able to participate in the style of life that transforms all that will truly enter into it from a machine to a man?" Small wonder, observed Collyer, that native-born Americans—a group he viewed as the true heirs of those who fought and died in the Revolutionary War—were outraged by the seeming ingratitude of foreigners who had profited from the American way. Immigrants, he asserted, owed any gain they had won as individuals to the nation, to the great republican experiment that was America: "I say I owe my home itself to the land I live in." If a representative city government therefore decided (as Collyer believed it should and would) to regulate methods of construction, any personal costs were a small price to pay for the privileges and rewards of American citizenship. With the Fireproofers, he believed that two American equalities, that of opportunity and that of membership in a civic polity, in turn mandated that all of Chicago be joined in an equality of sacrifice. The unchecked right to build with wood had to bow before the larger "public interest" in public safety.

Even as he recognized that the fiscal burdens of such a step were highly uneven, the clergyman, like Medill's blue-ribbon committee, saw no reason to allow this fact to alter his thinking. The notion that a ban on building with wood oppressed the poor, he argued, was at best specious and at worst pernicious. He conceded that a challenge on such grounds might be valid in Europe, where, in his view, workers truly faced a lifetime of poverty. But in America, Collyer claimed, dreams of advancement did come true—if the individual was worthy. The poor of Chicago lived in a land of opportunity, where hard work and good conduct inevitably met with material reward. "I should be very careful," he therefore warned, "how I said much about 'poor men' where no man can be as poor as *we* have known poverty, except by his own misconduct."

Even if all owners of property were forbidden to build with wood, the minister confidently predicted that the opportunity so closely tied to his vision of America would yet prevail—that any worthy soul might struggle but would overcome. With diligent labor and proper budgeting, he argued, the expense of rebuilding with brick could easily be recouped: "We can save enough if we try, out of our wages, to make up the difference in a very few months." Flush with faith in his adopted country's promise of democracy and mobility, confident that the experience of every immigrant could match his own, the clergyman soundly chastised Hesing and his followers for their ingratitude. Thus holding to both a liberal vision of the undifferentiated citizen and a universalized notion of immigrant experience that glorified individual achievement, Collyer set out the following reckoning of the moral economy of civic obligation: "America has done too well by us to deserve this return at our hands."

One day later, the open reply issued by Anton Hesing more than matched the clergyman's reliance upon the stock symbols of patriotism. Yes, the publisher began, he certainly remembered his encounter with Collyer on the past Fourth of July—and the flag under which they stood, he pointedly reminded, in fact had been his. Just as he carried and proudly unfurled his American flag wherever he traveled abroad, Hesing made it plain that an inept rendering of "Yankee Doodle" could never satisfy his love for the anthems of his nation: in Naples, he had paid an orchestra five dollars for their superior rendition of "Hail, Columbia." Yet despite his eagerness (and ability) to wrap himself in the flag, the publisher argued that such gestures ultimately had little to do with worthy citizenship. Indeed, he warned, blind nationalism should never replace informed participation. True Americans, according to Hesing, remembered that theirs was a land of social and political diversity, with a republican system at root committed to a fair hearing for dissent—the sort of tolerance for differing opinions that, he observed, decidedly had not been a part of the response of the Fireproofers to those who opposed their plan.

To be sure, Hesing personally found much of resonance in Collyer's celebration of American opportunity—even as he rejected its attendant plea for gratitude. While the publisher's origins were not nearly so humble as the clergyman's, his thirty-two years in the United States had also been blessed with exceptional prosperity. But though both he and Collyer had scaled the ladder of success, their experiences, according to Hesing, had fundamentally differed. The Yorkshireman—by his own proud recollection—knew only "the kindest consideration" in his adopted country. Germans, by contrast, had not always been welcomed with open arms; nativist prejudice, the publisher observed, had long been a fact of their American life. As he declared: "There has been a time within my memory when the natives of Germany were, by native American mobs, . . . treated with as fiendish barbarity as ever Europeans have been in China, Chinese in California, or Jews in Roumania." Even to the present day, he charged, champions of a so-called "all-Americanism" constantly vilified German-Americans for any failure to live up to an assimilated norm—ridiculing accented English and sneering at ethnic traditions. Asking for a German's complete fidelity to his adopted land thus asked this immigrant to forget a legacy of hostility generated precisely by those who claimed to represent a "pure" vision of national values. "If you had seen and gone through all this," Hesing chided Collyer, "you would be less hasty in assuming that it is as easy for an American citizen of German birth to forget his nativity altogether, as it is for one born in England."

But for all these obstacles, Hesing continued, those of German birth considered themselves "as good and true Americans as any born in this country." Moving quickly to the specifics of the fire limits protest, Hesing pointed to the potential tyranny of those who would substitute a reliance upon symbols and rhetoric for a consideration of public policy that sought to balance many sorts of particular interests. As the publisher bluntly declared: "If you tell me, Mr. Collyer, that the *people* desire the fire limits to be coextensive with the city limits, you mistake an assumption for fact." By Hesing's measure, neither Joseph Medill nor any of his fellow Fireproofers spoke for all Chicagoans—much less all Americans. Respect for the social differences that marked individual citizens, he concluded, might well add a healthy ingredient to this or any other discussion of civic matters. Perhaps only an immigrant, he argued, someone constantly made to feel his foreignness, could maintain the intellectual distance to remind Chicagoans that their municipality, like the Republic itself, was built upon respect for and acceptance of political and cultural diversity. Collyer, concluded Hesing, held fast to a vision of American identity that too readily excluded those not eager to conform to Anglo-Saxon norms.[113]

Collyer and Hesing at this moment grappled with knotty and enduring questions of politics and identity: Who was a "good" citizen? How could an immigrant become a worthy American? Further, with their remarkable exchange, these "representative men" provided a succinct summary of the basic struggle wrapped within the fire limits debate: Collyer's adherence to a liberal vision of an undifferentiated citizenry and the Fireproof claim to represent a unitary "public interest" here clashed with Hesing's alternative definitions of civic good—the counterclaims raised by those pressing to legitimate interests that had emerged out of what were proudly asserted as more particular immigrant and working-class identities.

For all their eloquence, Collyer and Hesing of course did not resolve the complicated conflict they addressed, and it is impossible to assess the immediate practical impact of these letters. In a sense, their dispute perhaps can be understood as more important for what it said than for what it did. For the conflict crystallized by this exchange—whether or not interests rooted in particular identities could prevail over interests represented as more universal norms—would continually come to the forefront of public debate in the months and years following the Great Fire. The specific issue of fire limits, however, did find resolution—at least on the level of formal policy.

After a few more weeks of proposals and emendations, the council finally passed a fire protection bill on February 12.[114] Two days later, Mayor Medill affixed his signature to the ordinance, which extended the existing fire limits over both a larger portion of the downtown and wealthy residence districts immediately to the south and west of the city's center.[115] The bill further enacted more stringent controls over the location of especially inflammable businesses such as lumberyards, imposed some new construction codes, and contained the "Cincinnati Amendment"—a provision (used with great success in that city) that permitted a majority of owners on any block to vote to extend fire limits over their own property. In many ways, however, the fire limits bill was most notable for what it did not do. As Christine Meisner Rosen has observed, the legislation lacked a provision for enforcement, suggesting that adherence to these codes would continue to be quite lax.[116] On the burned-out North Side, moreover, only a small lakefront strip already given over to industrial use fell within the new "fire zone." Five northern wards with heavy immigrant concentrations were left free from municipal regulation.[117] North Siders had secured their legal right to rebuild with wood.

Competing understandings of the public good of fire prevention were to some degree reconciled in the final ordinance, which extended the "fire zone" over more expensive real estate, introduced a provision for self-determination, *and* gave property owners of limited means the right to rebuild with wood. This public policy unquestionably incorporated a more pluralistic sense of civic good; the fire limits bill indeed can be understood as building upon a definition of the "public interest" that recognized and sought to accommodate the differing claims of different people. In the end, many sorts of Chicagoans had seemingly "won."

But for Joseph Medill, such a compromise spelled defeat. With the fire limits controversy, the mayor and his fellow Fireproofers learned a practical lesson about the essentially local nature of municipal politics. A chief executive elected with what he viewed as a mandate to exercise a newly centralized form of civic control found that he could not best the opposition of aldermen who drew their power from their own ward-based constituencies, citizens who mobilized not only to defend their particular interests but to claim that the recognition of such interests was essential to the proper order of their city. On a more ideological level, the defeat of the Fireproof plan thus signaled a rejection of the liberal vision of an undifferentiated citizenry, of the notion, advocated most strenuously by men self-identified as part of the business class, that all Chicagoans who owned property were part of a set of equal members equally bound to uphold the social contract that they believed to lie at the foundation of civic order.

Doubtless due to the Council's near-total rejection of the Fireproof agenda, the passage of the new ordinance drew surprisingly little commentary in the English-language press. Medill's *Tribune* struggled to make the best of a bad situation; "short as it is," declared an editorial, the bill could still be reckoned "a great improvement."[118] But the always less-subdued *Times* responded with its usual serving of nativism and revived the rhetoric of corruption so central to the Fireproof campaign. Renewing its attacks on ward politicians who would not look beyond their own particular (and therefore illegitimate) interests, the paper again called for a new era of municipal governance, one in which "the forces of a bummer caucus, controlled by a dozen unprincipled knaves, will not be able to overcome the forces which demand public service for the public good."[119] Only native-born men of commerce, the commercial class that had made Chicago great, could define and enforce the civic interests that would properly secure the future of the city.

An elated *Staats-Zeitung*, on the other hand, devoted multiple columns and many days to its celebration of Chicago's "Germandom," reveling in what it saw as the successful immigrant defense of the rights and dreams of the "cosmopolitan working class that here feels contented."[120] The paper could not resist a last nasty swipe at the mayor and his Fireproof agenda; as one editorial declared: "Before Mr. Medill in his message published the absurd plan, . . . probably not a hundred mentally normal people in the city had thought of the possibility that somebody might recommend such a plan in sober seriousness."[121] Robert Collyer received similarly direct censure. Branding him as an "unctuous servant of God," the editors lamented the American adoption of a "European prototype" that prompted the self-proclaimed "better classes" to look to the clergy to silence the voices of those they saw as the "mob" or "rabble."[122] Stupidity compounded by presumption, the *Staats-Zeitung* concluded, lurked at the heart of the Fireproof plan—a bad policy which in itself deserved attention and redress. Still, the response of the newspaper to the defeat of coextensive limits again suggests that the gravest wrong of the whole controversy was directly connected to an ongoing process: the efforts of Chicagoans to negotiate the tension between their many social differences and the common political identity of the "good" citizen. How this identity would be claimed and controlled was of paramount importance. For as the *Staats-Zeitung* again and again reminded, the issue that fueled the entire contest could be boiled down to one basic element: what these immigrant Chicagoans understood as the Fireproof insinuation "that the Germans did not understand their duty as American citizens."[123]

"We cannot eat our cake and have it." So P. W. Gates, a respected manufacturer and supporter of the Fireproof Plan, bluntly (if in a somewhat garbled fashion) assessed the choices that faced all property owners in their quest to guard Chicago against another conflagration. In regard to the question of fire limits, he declared, citizens could not expect to "retain all natural and legal rights at the same time." Participation in a republican government mandated that individuals sacrifice certain freedoms to the public good; "[N]either in peace or war," explained Gates, "can the State exist except at the expense of the general body."[124] Any governmental regulation would exact a toll in personal liberties. And in the months after the Great Fire, given the inability of most Chicagoans of lesser means to build with anything but wood, that toll further levied real—and highly divisive—economic burdens.

As winter neared its end and Chicagoans readied themselves to commence their "Great Rebuilding," the technically moot question of fireproofing thus proved to be packed with meanings. In a city of increasing ethnic diversity and inequalities of wealth, Chicagoans in these months battled over their understandings of their obligation to protect their common municipal space—and, in the process, proposed and attempted to enforce opposing definitions of the "good" citizen and the "public interest." Fireproofers, people largely connected to the native-born commercial class, were eager to realize their vision of what was best for Chicago in the physical form of a city completely built of expensive and substantial structures supposedly safe from fire. Their theory of politics imagined a group of citizens that were made equal by their very status as citizens—and who thus were bound to assume the personal costs of any measure deemed to advance a public good, even if those costs imposed unequal burdens. In this way, Fireproofers claimed to move beyond the realm of particular interests, to speak and set the best course for a unitary "public." But many immigrants and people of more moderate means believed that a rebuilt Chicago had to accommodate (and thereby physically reflect) the reality of the ethnic diversity and stratifications of wealth that marked its residents. The service of more particular interests, they in turn claimed, could in fact be the service of the "public interest." And the social identity of the "good" citizen could to some degree reflect the different identities of the many sorts of peoples who shared the common space of the city of Chicago.

CHAPTER FOUR

The Meanings of Cooperation

On the first anniversary of the Great Fire in October of 1872, the *Land Owner* joined the chorus of voices that rose to commemorate the amazing physical rebirth of Chicago, offering an especially worshipful assessment of the work of reconstruction. "There has been but one parallel to the mighty creation recorded in Genesis," intoned the real estate monthly. "That parallel is the rebuilding of Chicago in twelve months."[1] The often heavy hand of boosterism doubtless lay beneath such a claim. Still, the construction season of 1872, a period popularly known as the "Great Rebuilding," did witness an astounding mobilization of labor, capital, material, and skill.[2] Thanks to an army of building tradesmen, laborers, contractors, engineers, and architects, the center of the renewed city rose with remarkable speed; within the year described by the *Land Owner*, the devastated downtown had been entirely replaced. According to the *Tribune*, one brick, stone, or iron building from four to six stories in height was completed for each hour of the 200 working days between April 15 and December 1—an estimate of activity that did *not* include the thousands of new wooden structures central to the debate over a "fireproof" city.[3] Some eighteen months after the disaster, few physical traces of the Fire remained evident. In addition, the city expanded as it rebuilt: construction *outside* the burned district alone equaled prefire standards for the annual pace of building. Given this record of achievement, it seems a small wonder that so many so marveled at the sheer pace of change in Chicago.

The spectacular ends of the Great Rebuilding in turn prompted a sweeping romanticization of its means. The *Land Owner,* for example, had drawn another metaphor from the Scriptures in a July account of the rebuilding downtown: "Day by day, with the click of trowel and ax, the cheerful cry of heave, ho! and the ceaseless din of laboring hands goes up our Tower of Babel—the burnt south side."[4] Since the Bible's literal lesson (that of a construction project laid low by a massive failure to communicate) would not exactly serve the journal's purpose, a clever editor instead set forth a much more optimistic version of this old story. "It is a Babel of noise and work," the magazine declared, "but without confusion. Harmony of purpose and unity of design permeate the whole."[5] Joined together in the worthy task of building a new city, the writer claimed, all Chicagoans worked in concert. Such an image of pure community, of a citizenry inured to its differences, would appear again and again in both contemporary and historical descriptions of the city's physical renaissance.

But what *had* happened in that year—in the realm of relations of employment? How did certain Chicagoans balance their identities as citizens and as workers? To consider the rebuilding of Chicago in this way is to tell a story that is at once familiar and less known. Any detailed look at the actual workings of the Great Rebuilding quickly deflates the long-standing notion of a common effort magically free of conflict and deeply complicates the abstraction of the hard human effort that rebuilt the city. For this is a story that in fact reflects many struggles. The Great Fire vaulted workers in the building trades into a unique position; never again would the fate of the city rest quite so critically upon their labor and skill. In these months, questions concerning the function and potential power of unionism thus received a particularly intense forum. Workplaces proved to be sites of contests over wages, work conditions, and the hours of labor. On a more structural level, employers and workers alike faced up to the Fire's impact upon markets for labor—a process that highlighted Chicago's close connection to national (and even international) economies of waged work. In the course of the Great Rebuilding, a major city remade itself—a heroic feat easily constructed as a collective act somehow apart from more ordinary problems. But it is critical to recall that "New Chicago" grew out of hard work and often contentious discussions about the terms of waged labor. The individual and shared negotiations of city workers were integral to this process.

Moreover, another level of contest marked the Great Rebuilding, a struggle best described as a set of debates over the social, economic, and political meaning of "cooperation." Post-Fire Chicago became a proving ground for what was emerging as one of the most potent social and political questions of the late nineteenth century: as a contemporary commentator might have phrased it: Could Labor and Capital cooperate? The intensity of the work of reconstruction dramatically raised this issue—a subject beginning to preoccupy many in a republic that had just so painfully secured its commitment to free labor. As the industrial economy founded upon waged work began its post–Civil War ascension, more and more Americans wondered about the instability and discord that such a system might foster.[6] Would it be possible to secure a harmony of interests between workers and employers? What would such a state of affairs involve or resemble?

At this moment, Chicagoans on both sides of the wage relation set out divergent visions of the road to economic prosperity and social unity. For activists in the building trades, "cooperation" functioned as a synonym for unionism, and further denoted a specific economic and social philosophy that called for more collectivized forms of enterprise. But for most of the city's contractors and business leaders, workers seemed most cooperative when they sold their labor as individuals, reaping whatever the open market would bear. Liberal individualism—a set of beliefs connected to a deep faith in the "free market"—here collided with more collectivist understandings of what best served a broader "public interest."

Finally, given its specific urban context, the debate over the meaning of cooperation involved even more than one episode in the emergent struggle to define the just workings of a free labor economy centered upon waged work. For during this period, the municipality's very ability to be rebuilt hinged upon the agreements struck between construction workers and their bosses. This set of relations accordingly assumed much-heightened social and political import.

How could (or should) the obligations of citizenship affect what was normally understood as the private realm of economic contract? In this time of crisis, based upon their shared membership in the urban community, what did workers and employers owe to their city? What would stand as truly "cooperative" behavior? What would mark a worker or employer as a "good" citizen? During the Great Rebuilding, discussions of relations of employment in the building trades thus served as yet another forum in which various Chicagoans claimed to represent a broader "public interest"—and in turn defined their particular understanding of an urban order.

The afternoon of October 10, 1872, witnessed a telling conjuncture of events. At a formal commemoration of the Fire's anniversary, Mayor Medill saluted the unity of purpose, the most admirable spirit and will of the people of the city.[7] That same afternoon, city police answered a call to disperse a crowd of union bricklayers—men on strike to protest a cut in the summer's standard wage.[8] In one year, a Great Rebuilding indeed produced a New Chicago. Yet in the space of the same year, conflicts revolving around the meaning of "cooperation" between workers, employers, and the larger collectivity of the city were both joined and revisited. Even as they remained enmeshed in the external market forces that primarily drove the wage labor economy of construction work, union men and their employers engaged in a series of ideological and practical struggles. As much as it tells a story of concrete common achievement, the year of the Great Rebuilding also involves an enduring story of oppositions: a debate over what the collective organization of workers would mean for a civic order that increasingly rested upon the idea of a free market that served—and was served by—"free" individuals.[9]

SETTING TERMS

"Go to Chicago now! Young men, hurry there! Old men, send your sons! Women, send your husbands! You will never again have such a chance to make money!"[10] In cities along the eastern seaboard, audiences hungry for word of the Great Fire also absorbed this urgent advice from William Bross. Eager to draw capital and labor to his city, the ex-Lieutenant Governor and part-owner of the *Chi-*

cago Tribune had immediately set out on a speaking tour to spread word of the individual opportunities that might be born of collective disaster. In these first critical weeks, he and other publicists drew a compelling picture of the unparalleled prospects to be found in post-Fire Chicago; in "the race for fame and fortune," Bross tantalizingly proclaimed, "all can now start even."[11] Newspaper reports added heft to such declarations, again and again noting the city's new and pressing need for workers in the building trades. As the *Tribune* enthused in late October, once again looking to the Bible for its metaphorical inspiration, "never was there such a field for employment since God said 'let there be light'!"[12]

The vivid promise of success proved magnetic. During the year of the Great Rebuilding, for at least 30,000 people—"all," in the words of the surveyor Samuel Greely, "who had skill, muscle, and material to sell"—Chicago seemed a site of enormous possibility or, at the very least, a place where they might improve their fortunes.[13] Still, some of those drawn to the city knew enough to cool their heels for a time, for given the technological constraints of mid-nineteenth-century building methods, the coming onset of cold weather would force the postponement of anything other than wood construction. Skilled tradesmen understood that more substantial work in brick and stone—the remaking of the central business district—would not commence in earnest until the arrival of spring.[14] The interim months of winter thus acted as a sort of overture to the major construction season—a time that witnessed both the physical labor that set the stage for the spring's Great Rebuilding and a preview of the ideological debates over the meanings of cooperation that would be joined more directly as the construction season began. Finally, as these winter months of relative inactivity came to a close, both older residents and a rush of new arrivals began to understand how the city's enmeshment in national and international labor migrations would affect the structure of wage relations in Chicago.

"Hannibal crossing the Alps and Napoleon retreating from Moscow were mere skirmishes in comparison to the battle waged all winter long by Chicago's builders," declared the *Lakeside Monthly*, a local magazine, in homage to its city's great cold-weather feat: the first months of reconstruction. The winter's tasks were formidable indeed. First, before any new structures could rise, the devastation itself demanded intense labor. As the *Lakeside Monthly* observed, "A fire does not simply destroy what is valuable; it leaves behind and to be cleaned away much that is worthless."[15] Sent out to survey the wreckage, a *New York Times* reporter wrote of sinking ankle-deep in rubble with every step; one survivor described the scene as an "almighty brickyard"—so chaotic a mass of burned and broken material that he "hardly knew how or where to take hold."[16] Moreover, smoldering embers and other dangerous legacies of the Great Fire's intense heat hindered initial attempts to remove debris. Twelve days after the blaze, according to Dr. Jared Bassett, the inner reaches of piled bricks and stones still remained too hot to permit bare-handed labor.[17] After two weeks, as they attempted to clear their lot to erect a Relief Society shanty, the widow of North Sider Casper Hahn recalled that only constant drenching of the remains of their small house prevented any spontaneous rekindlings.[18]

Nevertheless, displaced persons and businesses required shelter, and the work of clearing and construction swiftly commenced. Like the Hahns, thousands of homeowners on the North Side nailed together the prefabricated wooden structures made available by municipal relief. In the realm of commercial building, as soon as the ruins of the downtown cooled to a tolerable degree, thousands of pick-and-shovel-wielding men and boys and hundreds of teams and wagons—all apparently employed by private property owners—moved in to knock down crumbling walls, reclaim usable brick and scrap iron, and daily dump 5000 wagon loads of worthless rubble into Lake Michigan.[19] Arduous working conditions added to the physical demands of these tasks. Such dense and frenzied activity, in combination with steadily worsening weather, forced laborers to work through constant smoke and fog, a predicament aggravated by occasional cold rain and sleet. Worst of all were choking clouds of grit and dirt. "All is hurry and confusion in the burnt district," reported the *Republican* on October 25. "The dust and ashes in the streets, stirred up by the wheels of vehicles or the feet of pedestrians, makes locomotion, or even existence, in that region disagreeable."[20]

Once plots of ground were cleared, most owners of commercial property arranged for the erection of temporary wooden sheds and barracks. Within a week of the Great Fire, carpenters working at a wage of $3.00–$3.50 per day, a rate slightly above their pre-Fire standard, had built over 100 long and low warehouses that served as interim homes for wholesale and retail establishments.[21] In addition, some anxious owners tested the limits imposed by cold weather and immediately moved to erect permanent edifices. Some 212 brick and stone buildings were underway on the South Side by the end of November. The Central Union block, the first commercial-scale complex built of brick, was ready for occupancy on December 16, a mere ten weeks after the disaster.[22]

Yet too-quick rebuilding had its own risks, for special complications and expense accompanied out-of-season work for bricklayers, plasterers, painters, and glaziers.[23] Bricks, for example, could not be manufactured when temperatures dipped below freezing. Since local supplies were quickly exhausted and could not be replenished, stocks had to be imported, instantly tripling prices.[24] In addition, cold weather turned masonry construction into a far more intricate and risky enterprise. Without summer's hot and steady sun, it was difficult to keep bricks dry—a necessary first step in building with this material. Further, in warmer seasons, brick walls set over time, becoming increasingly stable as their mortar hardened. But in the winter, mortar often froze before bricks could set, resulting in a wall held together by little more than balance and gravity.[25] Such construction was hardly solid or safe; in December, the *Workingman's Advocate* noted that ordinary winds had knocked down several newly constructed four- and five-story buildings. As the editor wryly observed, "The rapidity with which Chicago is coming up after the fire is only as astonishing as the rapidity with which she tumbles down again."[26]

Whatever their resolve, it soon became plain that mere humans could not systematically defeat the elements. In the coldest months, most rebuilding ceased. On more ideological levels, however, debates over the meanings of cooperation began to take shape. For the winter also made it clear that the spring would bring what seemed to be unprecedented power to building tradesmen in Chicago, a remarkable chance to revitalize and expand a trades union movement that had suffered declining fortunes in the previous few years.[27] "From present indications the coming spring will be one of the best for workingmen which has ever been known," declared the *Workingman's Advocate* at the very end of 1871. "Masons, bricklayers, stonecutters, plasterers, and carpenters and joiners are sure of constant and renumerative employment."[28] In response to what they perceived as a golden moment, union leaders eagerly touted their most basic vision of cooperation, working to build strong trades organizations. By contrast, voices from the business class publicly worried that workers might take "unfair" advantage of heightened demand for their skills. Such commentators raised the twin specters of "extortion" and strikes—and in the process laid the groundwork for portraying the activities of trades unions as threats to the good order of the city.

A first telling skirmish over how free laborers should act in this unique market came to a head less than two weeks after the Fire. On October 20, the *Tribune* reported that a number of union bricklayers had walked off their job after a contractor had refused to increase their daily wage to an unspecified level—but a rate, the paper disapprovingly noted, that was substantially above their pre-Fire standard.[29] The strike, the account further observed, had been thwarted by the presence of nonunion bricklayers from another city, men willing to replace those who had left their places. The more hostile *Times* set out a report that not only criticized the supposed action of the bricklayers but explicitly condemned any organized strike for higher pay as a self-interested act that posed a dire threat to the city. "The conduct of these trades union people is that of the worst enemies of Chicago," wrote the editors. "Our people cannot afford to, and will not build at such rates of wages as these selfish people declare they will demand."[30]

A few days later, the Bricklayer's Union responded to this story (and its implications), denying that its members had acted in any such fashion. According to the union, unscrupulous contractors had planted false reports of wage increases—a scam that allowed these middlemen to pocket the difference between what they asked for a job and the rate they actually paid to the tradesmen they then hired. In this instance, argued the union, the *Tribune* and the *Times* had wrongly held workers culpable for the avarice of their employers. To avoid such slanders, the organization advised its members to contract directly with architects, the professionals in charge of most late-nineteenth-century commercial construction. Finally, the union took a step meant to reassure all in the city that it had no wish to wring undue profits from a common disaster, offering the following vow: "We, the Bricklayers of Chicago, do hereby pledge ourselves to work at ordinary wages to rebuild our city."[31] Attentive to their duties as citizens of a stricken city, these tradesmen thus promised *not* to succumb to the temptations of what appeared to be the highly favorable market for their skills. Though of course anxious to obtain good wages in order to recoup some of their own losses, "they would scorn to fatten off anyone."[32]

In the days that followed, the statements of both employers and unionists reflected a common theme: a discomfort with any overt attempts to capitalize on the immediate imbalance between the supply of and demand for skilled masons. The *Times* of October 28 sharply condemned all unionists. "These people," declared the paper, "flatter themselves that they grapple Chicago by the throat." Not even acknowledging the bricklayers' statement, the *Times* urged employers to meet such "extortion" with stern resolve: "[I]t lies with the sensible men of our city to assume a firm stand. Compromise will prove a fatal policy."[33] On October 30, however, a much more moderate *Tribune* editorial praised the bricklayers' explanation and pledge. The paper in particular lauded the fact that the union had *not* relied upon the ties of their craft to dissuade bricklayers in other cities from flocking to Chicago—a tactic that would have "unnaturally" protected the local value of their skill. Further, the *Tribune* fully approved of the bricklayers' choice to "normalize" the price they asked for their labor. "The union," the editors declared, deserved the thanks of "all Chicago" for "resisting all appeals to strike for an arbitrary rate of wages, and for their good sense in leaving wages to regulate itself by the demand"—especially in this time of crisis.[34] Finally, in its commentary, the city's labor paper likewise denounced efforts to secure immediate gains. The *Workingman's Advocate* strongly argued that an attempt to "force wages up to an unreasonable level" would be "the height of folly," for nothing good could come from bad feelings between Chicago's employers and its organized workers. The *Advocate*, for its part, simply counseled patience and trust. "Old hands," the city tradesmen long known to contractors and architects, would in its judgment certainly be hired before any job-seeking out-of-towners. In the spring, the paper confidently predicted, wages would exceed those paid in any other American city. And at that point, demand would outrun supply "such as to warrant asking an advance."[35] Forbearance would bring its own rewards.

In this early discussion about the reasonable and proper conduct of the bricklayers, both employers and unionists appeared to share a faith in the ultimate righteousness of the balance that would be struck between supply and demand. But the quality and content of that faith differed in a quite striking manner. For the *Tribune*, a key organ of Chicago's commercial leaders, the only "good sense" for wage workers—and, by implication, the only "good citizenship"—came with acceding to this principle: to leave "wages to regulate itself by the demand." Herein lay a hardening axiom of industrial capitalism, with a powerful form of moral judgment attached to the propriety of falling into step with such a set of principles. To go on strike or otherwise exercise collective power signaled a rejection of what many employers understood as "cooperation" on the part of their employees: an individual's acceptance of the wage determined by the rules of the market. For such men of commerce, the laws of supply and demand would without question advance what they understood to be the larger public good. Regardless of its outcomes, the system itself was just and proper—a key economic cornerstone of the social order.[36]

For the *Workingman's Advocate* and the Bricklayers' Union, however, any faith in the functioning of a free market was clearly more of a tactical decision than an abiding and universalized belief—a decision born of their sense that workings of supply and demand at this particular juncture would serve their interests if they bided their time. For alongside the sense of civic responsibility that led them to pledge to hold to their pre-Fire standard, union leaders worried that any premature push for higher pay scales would backfire. Such a step, they feared, would inevitably draw "foreign" workmen in search of easy money to Chicago, thereby flooding the market for construction workers and "lessening instead of increasing the rate of wages."[37] And much more sweepingly, on a level apart from strategizing for this moment, unionism in its essence rejected the economic individualism promoted by the business class. By contrast, the unionist vision of "cooperation" encouraged organization by trade, the joining of individuals, precisely in order to affect and hopefully improve upon how any one worker might fare in the marketplace.

Cooperation, as practiced by the building trades, clearly did not reject capitalism as an evil system. But in the view of unionists, the laws of supply and demand could well produce evil results. The end products of an unfettered free market, they concluded, would *not* always be just—a good example being what they understood to be the morally suspect possibility of drawing great profit from the intense demand for bricklayers created by the Great Fire's ravages. At this point, the bricklayers had called upon the power of unionism in the marketplace to stabilize wages at their pre-Fire rates—an intervention into the mechanics of supply and demand that blunted their own opportunities for gain. If the trade had simply acted upon their market advantage, they believed, their employers would have suffered unduly from the fallout of a tragedy; as the *Workingman's Advocate* counseled, "We know our workmen have been sorely stricken by the great calamity, but they must remember that they are no worse off than a number of their employers."[38] For these union leaders, then, moral judgments about the workings of supply and demand did not rest upon a reaffirmation of the rightness of these "iron laws"; rather, reckonings of what was fair and just had to be considered in light of the social effects and outcomes of the capitalist system.

As a matter of strategy, Chicago unionists thus retained a hopeful faith in how they would fare in the spring's labor market, and accordingly called for relative patience and quiescence. Yet these tradesmen at the same time believed that the best way to remedy injustice on the job or in the market was to join a union—and that the Great Rebuilding had gifted them with the chance to strengthen the labor movement of their city. All winter long, unionists readied for the spring by signing up new members. The carpenters, for example, held mass meetings throughout the city, "cordially inviting" all "qualified journeymen" to join together.[39] Their efforts yielded seven new locals, with a total membership nearing 5000.[40] By the end of March, a reorganized Plasterers' Union claimed to represent between 300 and 400 men, and the Bricklayers Union numbered 800, with every meeting bringing "new accessions."[41] On a citywide level, activists resuscitated Chicago's General Trades Assembly, a union council of some thirty trade organizations that had been largely moribund since city employers had largely evaded the dictates of a new state law mandating an eight-hour day (and weathered a series of resultant strikes) in May of 1867.[42] Flush with these successes, a late March *Advocate* exhorted its readers to ready for the historic work of the Great Rebuilding with a historic display of trade solidarity: "There was never a better opportunity presented to the mechanics of any city than is now present to the workingmen of Chicago to practically illustrate the advantage and practicability of cooperation."[43]

Such vital signs of life among Chicago unions inevitably drew an anxious response from city businessmen. Since the Eight-Hour agitations in 1867—a three-day attempt at a general strike that first alerted many Chicagoans to the power of organized worker protests—work stoppages had loomed large as a special menace to urban order. Though antebellum cities in the East had witnessed large-scale worker actions, a strike on this level was new to Chicago in 1867. It seemed, for some, to stand as a completely improper (and highly alarming) challenge to the norms of economic contract and personal freedoms.[44] In the abstract, it was not uncommon for conservative thinkers of the day to accept the workers' right to strike. But even more liberal economic and political theorists were uncomfortable with any actual exercise of worker power that impeded the full functioning of the free market; employers, for example, had to have the capacity to hire replacement workers without dealing with any obstacles that might be posed by those on strike.[45] Especially provoked in 1867 by what they perceived as the Eight-Hour strikers' illegal interference with others' "right to work," Chicago business leaders had demanded military action to check the movements of roving bands of workmen who enforced the strike at various worksites.[46] A *Tribune* editorial exemplified the deadly seriousness that the strike inspired in men of commerce, offering this proscription for any workers who refused to desist from their strike activities: "If they will not obey the written law, then perhaps they will obey powder and ball; if they resist police authority, they invite the authority of grape and canister."[47] Despite many reports that such skirmishes remained isolated at specific worksites and that the overall "peace of the city" faced no serious risk, the mayor took no chances. John B. Rice had issued a proclamation warning strikers that "the strong arm of the law would be brought at once to bear" upon any hint of strike-related disorder in city streets.[48] For the mayor, a threatened order could seemingly be resecured by the threat of force.

Some disruptions certainly had marked those spring days; the Eight-Hour strikers had without question been rowdy and forceful in articulating their demand: that a new state law creating a legal eight-hour day be recognized by all employers. Still, only a few incidents of conflict at specific worksites had marked the strike. The much-feared general strike certainly did not materialize, and the level of violent conflict on the streets and at workplaces, measured blow for blow, hardly matched that inspired by the passionate political fissures and extreme emotions of the city's Civil War years.[49] Still, an inflated image of riot, tumult, and citywide danger grew out of 1867, an image that plainly lingered in 1872. Even before the Great Rebuilding commenced, according to a February issue of the *Workingman's Advocate,* city unionists already met with "prognostications on every side that strikes and riots were going to be the order of the day."[50] Worry over the potential for labor unrest further spurred the efforts of business leaders (ongoing since Sheridan's post-Fire appearance in the city) to establish a permanent military garrison in or near Chicago. Most dramatically, the president of the Board of Police Commissioners requested in late March that the governor of Illinois assist with the rearming of the city's force. (Most of the police's stockpile of muskets and shot had been lost to the Fire.) In justifying his petition, Mancell B. Talcott explicitly argued that a lack of police firepower left Chicago vulnerable to worker protest. "If we should have any [strikes] during the present year," he warned, "it is probable that they would be of greater magnitude than any we have had to encounter heretofore."[51] By the commissioner's count, 300 muskets and 10,000 rounds were needed to ensure civic safety.

In 1867 and again in 1872, the response of Chicago's public authorities to the reality of (or apparent potential for) conflict between workers and employers conflated private disputes over terms of employment with a threat to civic order. Peace between capital and labor, by extension, seemed in and of itself to constitute a "public interest." The tactic of the strike, which sought to alter the outcome of what most civic leaders believed to be the inexorable and ultimately just laws of supply and demand, therefore appeared to subvert the "natural" economic and social order.[52] Such an order would ideally be built out of the labor of cooperative individuals—as opposed to those individuals who chose the form of cooperation otherwise known as unionism.

For a business class drawing tight connections between economic individualism and social order, strikes seemed to bring confusion and chaos to the city—even without a Great Fire to set the stage. Given the physical and psychological disorderings of the disaster (plus, far from incidentally, the great civic need for workers' labor and skill), any stoppage of work could be seen as a danger—regardless of the details of the particular disputes that might arise in private contractual negotiations between workers and employers. The *Times*, within weeks of the Fire, had warned of the possibility of a "hydra-headed rebellion of labor," unspecified but extremely dangerous actions sure to be "contrary to the interests of the public."[53] And as the *Tribune* declared in May, just as the Great Rebuilding poised at its beginning, "[T]he cessation of labor *en masse*, by any class of workmen, especially, at a critical period, is a detriment to the public interest."[54] Private relations of employment were at this moment conceived as part of an essential civic good.

Unionists were well aware of the menace that their institutions and ideals appeared to pose. As in the case of the bricklayers' pledge to stabilize wages, trade leaders consequently went to great lengths to construct a positive public image for their organizations—one that by contrast linked union membership to a model of solid and responsible citizenship that in itself advanced a broader civic good. In keeping with the ideology of the National Labor Union (NLU), the short-lived umbrella organization of trades founded in 1866 that enjoyed especially staunch support in Chicago, and the tenets of most working-class reform associations of the day, city labor leaders were devoted apostles of self-improvement.[55] The *Workingman's Advocate* continually advised its readership to adopt standards of conduct that in many ways resembled the clean living and paths to success that were increasingly idealized by more elite Americans, counseling attendance at libraries and lectures and a strict avoidance of saloons. Yet a major twist set apart this vision of self-betterment and a virtuous life: for these workers, the gains won by individuals went hand in hand with maintaining the collectivity of their trade. "Stand by one another; . . . talk cooperation whenever you have a chance," urged the *Advocate.* "Act as though the success of the movement depended upon your own exertion, and, depend upon it, you will become better men, better husbands and fathers, and better citizens."[56] Most decidedly not a force of disorder, unionism as described by unionists paved the way to higher forms of individual, familial, and civic stability.

Finally, many union leaders of the day shared a faith in a particular ideology that went by the rubric of "cooperation": a set of beliefs that dictated specific practices in the market, practices meant to lead to a more just and fair economy and society. William H. Sylvis, the Pennsylvania-born iron molder who became the first national labor leader in America, spelled out the meaning of this usage of the term in a speech in Chicago in 1865. "By cooperation", he declared, "we will become a nation of employers—the employers of our own labor. The wealth of the land will pass into the hands of those who produce it."[57] Cooperation as a specific ideology and practice thus involved the formation of both worker-owned businesses and consumer cooperatives. Through such activities, unionists maintained that working people could create a different form of life in the market—one that, unlike the relations of wage labor, returned the lion's share of profit to its producers. Sylvis offered this succinct diagnosis of the problem that cooperation sought to address and transform: "Under the system of paying wages to labor and profits to capital there never was nor never could be an identity of interests between employers and employed. Both were actuated and controlled by the same principle—to buy in the dearest and sell in the cheapest market. The result of this could be nothing but antagonism."[58] But if, through cooperative enterprise, the ever-warring parties of capital and labor under the wage system were "united in the same person"—at least in theory, such a practice could achieve a "real identity of interests."[59] For these labor leaders, the field of competitive capitalism could yet be remade into a seedbed for mutuality.[60]

As the Great Rebuilding commenced, a sharp conflict therefore loomed large: the gulf in understanding and practice between unionist and business-class visions of cooperation. As warmer weather began to arrive, however, the distress of those who viewed organized workers as anathema to civic order must have to some degree abated. For despite a unique situation that appeared to value skilled work at an unprecedented premium, the city remained enmeshed in national and international markets for labor. Structural forces—the hard realities of supply and demand—began to come into play. Even as Chicago unionists mounted a stalwart defense of their cooperative ideology and proclaimed their confidence that the reconstruction of the city would catapult the building trades to new heights of enrollment and influence, all working people found themselves in an increasingly adverse situation. By the winter's end, what had seemed a labor market tremendously advantageous to workers had decidedly swung round to the benefit of employers. Moreover, a shortage of low-cost housing exacted an additional toll.

Basically, as union leaders had feared, the opportunities that had looked so golden to Chicagoans also enticed building tradesmen and laborers from throughout the nation and across the Atlantic. With Chicago's unsurpassed (and unburned) rail network providing quick, easy, and cheap access to the city, a migration of between 30,000 and 40,000 people in the year following the Great Fire ensured a consistent oversupply of labor. Less than three months after the disaster, the *Tribune* offered what proved shrewd advice to cost-conscious employers, counseling them to postpone their hiring for perhaps a month, when "the influx of alien labor" would "doubtless duly temper and equalize the matter of wages."[61] As early as January, the Relief and Aid Society had rethought its immediate post-Fire fears of a labor shortage, aiming a nationally distributed circular at those considering a move to Chicago. "Mechanics and laborers," the Society cautioned, "are making a great mistake in coming to this city in search of work. The supply of labor of all sorts is far in excess of the demand."[62]

Late-nineteenth-century workers frequently migrated in search of more lucrative employment; still, it seems surprising that early warnings of a labor glut had so minimal an effect.[63] This particular "job rush," however, was not only the product of a nationally known event: it was also exceptionally well advertised. The *Tribune* of October 28, for example, pointedly targeted the "thousands of laborers now starving in New York and other cities" with a call for 500 stonemasons, 2000 carpenters, and any number of plumbers, gas fitters, and ironworkers who would be willing to work through the winter at $4–$5 per day. And "in March," the paper declared, "there will be employment for twice as many men of these trades." Further, city boosters such as William Bross actively recruited labor and skills for Chicago; the pack of lecturers who rushed from the city often dwelt on the new opportunities there to be found. Some property owners and contractors themselves traveled to nearby cities to recruit workers. O. Vance Brown, for example, promised months of steady work at high wages to the twenty-five bricklayers and carpenters he brought from St. Paul to rebuild his business.[64] Finally, various entrepreneurs sought to profit from the migration itself. Shipping lines and passenger agencies vigorously promoted their travel services. Seizing upon the extensive European publicity of Chicago's tragedy in Europe, these organizations ran dozens of advertisements in urban newspapers that hawked the high wages and steady work that were supposedly the lot of all who came to the city.[65] According to the *Advocate*, the invented testimonials of supposedly satisfied customers only added further illusory appeal.

Such campaigns found their marks. The efforts of unions to warn off out-of-town members and letters home telling of the real experiences of migrants could do little to counteract their luster.[66] Under the headline of "EMIGRATION BY WHOLESALE," the *Advocate* reported in early March that 400 bricklayers, direct from England, had landed in the city.[67] By April, according to the paper, batches of twenty-five or thirty foreign bricklayers, carpenters, and plasterers arrived on a daily basis.[68] European migrants were most often too late to find steady work; blessed with a geographic headstart, thousands of workers from the Midwest, East, and California had already streamed into Chicago.[69] As hiring for the spring construction season began, the *Advocate* described the grim scenario facing those who would work to rebuild the city: "The market for skilled mechanics is glutted, thousands being in our midst who cannot obtain employment at their trade."[70] The labor paper added a few weeks later that "the folly of men rushing to the city from all points of the compass, under false representations, is daily becoming more apparent."[71] A surplus of jobs at high pay, then, hardly lay in store for migrants, let alone the working people who had long resided in Chicago. To the contrary, most workers scrambled simply to find employment. Dreams of great gains in wages also vanished. For all the expectations harbored by Chicagoans and migrants, few who sold their labor had the power to increase its price.

Moreover, along with depressing wages, this influx of labor carried another costly consequence. Additional thousands now required shelter. But due to the fire, cheap housing was in extremely short supply. A letter to the *Tribune* noted in mid-May that "where one first-class dwelling was destroyed by the fire, twenty cottages of the poor shared a similar fate."[72] "It is really becoming a serious question how we are going to house all these newcomers," observed the *Land Owner* in April. The real estate journal optimistically predicted that new housing could be built by individual homeowners—a rather unrealistic expectation that stood as both a measure of the trade magazine's faith in self-making and its editors' lack of understanding of the materiality of working-class lives, given that most new arrivals (and displaced Chicagoans) had neither the time nor the means to buy a lot and erect a home.[73] The most economically

Carpenters at work on the Michigan Central Railroad Office, South Water Street. Photograph by Jex Bardwell. Courtesy of Chicago Historical Society, ICHi-20844.

vulnerable people in the city, those who had not owned property prior to the Fire and those who had not immediately been able to rebuild on their lots, now faced another harsh result of the disaster: a much-inflated rental market.

Few owners of surviving buildings followed the lead of the city's bricklayers; unlike the tradesmen who had pledged to ask for no more than their pre-Fire wages, most landlords rushed to cash in upon the heavy demand—without drawing any commentary about "extortion" or "unnatural" pricing from the *Tribune* or *Times*. D. F. Gleeson, a bricklayer, precisely noted the irony of this silence in a letter to the *Tribune* on May 5: "Why not say to the house and land owner, you must not take advantage of the calamity that has befallen our city by raising the rent on your tenants?"[74] Despite the occasional appearance of such protests, only the *Workingman's Advocate* steadily focused on the Fire's impact upon the cost of housing—and what it deemed the "oppressive injustice" of the situation—reporting in March that the average rent had risen between thirty and forty percent.[75]

Mechanic F. Grant Tulloch encountered even more staggering price hikes in his search for accommodations. Before the Fire, Tulloch wrote to the *Tribune*, he and his family paid $16 per month to reside in a four-room cottage on the North Side. Once burned out, the family was forced to spend the same amount to cram into two small rooms. On May 1, however, Tulloch's new landlord increased the rent to $25 monthly. The tradesman refused to accept these terms and set about locating yet another home. "I searched nearly every street within the limits of the city," he reported, "to see if I could do better." But he could not. Tulloch and his family unhappily resettled in a West Side flat at the same $25 rent. To add insult to injury, this flat had leased prior to the Great Fire for a mere $12.[76] And Tulloch's experience was apparently more the rule than the exception. The *Republican*, in mid-March, described rents as "fabulous"; in May, the *Advocate* lamented that "the rents have gone up in our city to an extent that it is nigh well impossible for a mechanic, no matter how frugal or industrious, to make both ends meet."[77] Such high rates, the *Times* reported in September, would prevail throughout the summer and fall.[78]

By the coming of spring and the much-heralded commencement of the Great Rebuilding, the structure of the labor and housing markets in Chicago had landed the working people of the city in a wrenching double bind. An extraordinary demand for skilled construction work did in general keep the wages of most tradesmen steady at levels equal to or even slightly above pre-Fire rates.[79] (It is much more difficult to locate information about the status of lesser-skilled men or working women; for those with less specialized expertise, it appears that real wages declined.)[80] But a plethora of jobs in construction was more than matched by an influx of "foreign" workers—a migration that completely erased any hopes for (or fears of) a major jump in the price commanded by labor and skill. At the same time, however, a sharp rise in the overall cost of living in the city ensured that most working people, no matter how steady their wages or long their hours of toil, would fall behind in their efforts to support themselves and their families, let alone accrue savings enough to recover whatever losses they themselves might have sustained. What had seemed a gold mine for those with skills to sell thus fell prey to the constraints of market forces, those both local to the city and in the national and international realm.

For unionists in particular, the structural consequences and ideological ferment of the months preceding the Great Rebuilding posed an enormous challenge. A city dependent upon skilled labor for its very regeneration seemed ripe for attaining a new level of influence for the vision of cooperation held by union leaders. Yet a potent business-class fear of strikes, deemed dangerous both for their potential hindrance to the work of reconstruction and, more sweepingly, for what many perceived as their intrinsic subversion of the "natural" laws of supply and demand, had immediately cast unionism and its practitioners as threats to civic order. What upper-class Chicagoans understood as their city's overriding interest in a "cooperative" labor force, a form of social harmony most likely to be realized by individuals making contracts to sell their labor as individuals, had revealed the skills of workers in the building trades to be a "product" like no other: one where capitalizing upon a market advantage did not follow a proper, settled logic of the free market, and in fact would lead to great disruptions in the social order.

F. Grant Tulloch, the mechanic unable to find an affordable flat for his family, well understood this double standard, a set of social practices and cultural beliefs that instructed wage workers that they had to abide by the rules of the market, that the opportunities they would find there would indeed end in proper rewards—but also condemned any working person who might somehow acquire too much, who might somehow profit in a way considered to be disruptive of normal economic hierarchies of gain. "How can you, in fair play," he wondered, "blame the laborer or mechanic for putting a higher price on his work, when there is a greater demand for it, any more than the house proprietor, who as there is now more demand, increases his rent?"[81] A landlord could profit from high demand for his real property; such an act only responded to the laws and logic of the market. But if a worker sought a similar reward for the scarcity of his "property"—the labor and skill he might sell for a wage: this choice was deemed "immoral" and "unnatural."

A self-described "Mechanic" offered an even more biting analysis in a May 8 letter to the *Tribune*. Disaster, in his view, had hardly united Chicago in the grand project of rebuilding; to the contrary, the Great Fire had only exacerbated existing class divisions, throwing the disjunction between the market system experienced by richer and poorer citizens into stark relief. "Are not those who own cottages and prate about losses by the fire grinding the very life's blood out of the class they need most to build them up by compelling them to pay out in rent more than double their former rates?" he declared. "Are not this same class of mechanics put upon in one thousand and one ways, just because they dare to speak of their labor as being of more value to themselves than formerly, if they would live a life of decency, as heretofore!"[82] For a landlord, the greater demand spawned by a common misfortune could rightly redound to their profit—without any need to worry about the hardships faced by their tenants. This was only the natural and proper consequence of a free market system. Yet for this worker and countless others, such logic at this moment offered only cold consolation. Not at all free to respond to a jump in the cost of housing by raising the price of their labor—constrained by the numbers willing to take their places, hostility to and suspicion of worker organization, and a pressing need simply to survive and move on to rebuild their own lives—Chicago workers here faced a hard lesson in the operation of supply and demand. Theoretically "free" actors, city wage earners were in fact enmeshed in economic and social hierarchies that limited their resources and opportunities.[83] Workers thus lived within a market system morally justified by its proponents for its theoretical accordance of choices that they in actuality could seldom make.

In the minds of most employers and civic leaders, however, what Tulloch and the "Mechanic" viewed as a fundamentally unjust result of the market system stood as an unquestioned norm of "fair play" and social order. And with the arrival of spring and the true and final commencement of the Great Rebuilding, Chicagoans were forced to confront the disparity between the ideals of unionists and the view of wage relations in turn promoted by business leaders. For despite their clearly defensive and weakened position, the heads of building trades unions resolved to mark the opening of the construction season with a display of worker unity, a public showcase for the size and potential strength of their organizations. The date the unions picked was May 15—a mid-week workday meant to be supplanted by a worker holiday in celebration of a "Grand Demonstration of Trades Unions."[84]

FRIENDS OR ENEMIES?

On Tuesday, May 14, the *Illinois Staats-Zeitung* alerted its readers to the "Workers' Demonstration" planned for the next day. Union leaders had widely promoted the gathering as an intended show of civic goodwill, a public relations tactic well-absorbed by the German-language daily. "It is meant," wrote the *Staats-Zeitung*, "to become a new point of departure for the future behavior of labor toward capital, in so far as the reconstruction of our city." But high hopes for a fresh start, the paper predicted, were likely to be overwhelmed by the rehearsal of older grievances. As their article noted, unionists believed that "greedy landlords" and the reserve army of workers "lured . . . even from Europe" had combined to land city workers in their double bind. Labor leaders would surely use this forum to advance the organization of workers as one answer to such troubles. On the other hand, the *Staats-Zeitung* observed, employers accused unions of "exercising a tyranny," of acting as obstacles to the spirit and mechanics of a free market. Unions, to their minds, had spawned tensions between workers and employers "which potentially could not only be unbearable, but also dangerous to the public well-being." Measuring the terms of disagreement, the *Staats-Zeitung* lamented what looked to be an "abyss": the severe gulf in understanding between "the two factors without whose unified and active combination New Chicago cannot be erected." By anyone's definition of the term, labor and capital seemed most unlikely to cooperate, thereby imperiling the progress of the Great Rebuilding. As the paper grimly concluded, "This is a serious conflict."[85]

Yet the *Staats-Zeitung*'s balanced if sober account merely occupied the moderate center in a field of much sharper condemnation and praise. Once announced, the May 15 rally became a major focal point for a weighty debate: As Chicagoans struggled to rebuild, would labor and capital cooperate? On whose terms? More specifically, could unions play a useful and proper role in a free market economy? And how should individual workers act within this labor market? Like the dispute over the idea of a "fireproof" city, the conflicts crystallized by the "Grand Demonstration" suggest how a more particular social identity can lie beneath an assertion of a more general civic authority. For here, once again, people rooted in different identities claimed to represent a broader "public interest." Citizen-workers presented the market power of their institutions, the trades unions, as part and parcel of a just and proper civic order.[86] Ironically enough, however, at the event meant to highlight their own legitimacy, unionists came face-to-face with a vividly oppositional stance set out by their own most prominent civic leader—Mayor Joseph Medill.

Eager to counter depictions of unionism as a force of disorder, rally organizers immediately made special overtures to the most visible symbols of authority in Chicago. Mayor Medill was recruited to serve alongside the president of the NLU, Richard F. Trevellick, as the event's featured speakers. A delegation headed by Andrew Cameron, the editor of the *Workingman's Advocate*, attended a May 6

Board of Police meeting. There they secured an escort of twenty-five mounted policemen but failed to win the official participation of the police commissioners.[87] In addition to such formal outreach to city leaders, the *Advocate*—ever sensitive to the ready vilification of working people in much of the English-language press—beseeched unionists to police themselves. "Workers," urged the paper, "disappoint your enemies, who expect or rather hope to see a riot. Pursue the even tenor of your ways."[88] Only a completely disciplined and temperate march could give evidence of their seriousness of purpose and "prove to the world the falsity of the libeller's charge."[89] Taking great care to present themselves as the most solid of citizens, unionists prepared to send what they viewed as a message of reason and conciliation. As one movement member proclaimed, "Let Capital be just and Labor will be content, and the grand work of rebuilding will proceed without disturbance or interruption."[90]

In their quest to claim an upright civic identity, unionists faced a sticky tactical dilemma revolving around the issue of the strike. On one hand, the choice to withhold their labor ultimately formed the bedrock of their own market power; on the other, fears of such worker actions lay at the root of their opponents' most heated invective. And at this moment, since the disaster had invested their labor with extraordinary civic meaning, any substantial break in the work of reconstruction might quite arguably imperil the recovery of their community. As a consequence, union leaders went to great lengths to refute the notion that they were merely self-interested profiteers who cared little for the future of Chicago, a label they had been battling since the union bricklayers were first tagged with charges of post-Fire "extortion." "We have no desire," declared the *Advocate*, "to stand in the way of our city's progress." Moreover, in a May 11 "Plea For the Laborer," the paper reiterated that Chicago trades unions always viewed strikes as injurious to both workers and employers, a position consistent with the platform of the NLU. If a conflict arose, a strike was a last resort—the tactic adopted only if all means of amicable negotiation had failed.

Yet at the same time that they reaffirmed their commitment to their city and disavowed any easy readiness to strike, unionists set out a staunch defense of their right to act in common—and the validity of their most specific post-Fire grievance. Did not skilled workers, they asked, deserve to reap a living wage at a time when their skills were so essential? Throwing the vocabulary of the free market back at labor's critics, the *Advocate* offered the following justification for the unions' hope to obtain higher wages: "We cannot see either the injustice or impropriety of men who live from hand to mouth, acting on the theory that has been drummed into them for years, that prices are regulated by supply and demand, asking, during the summer months—their harvest—for an increase of wages of FIFTY CENTS PER DAY."[91] For union leaders, economic and social harmony had to rest upon a set of wage relations that conceded that workers could act collectively to defend their interests as individuals. Definitions of what constituted "cooperation" between workers and their employers could not exclude or somehow look askance at the organized cooperation of unionists.

But such a defense of unionism clearly did not correspond to the civic vision maintained by the business class. Tellingly, these painstaking efforts to explain and justify the union cause were completely ignored by the city's major English-language dailies. Indeed, for the two weeks preceding the worker rally, the *Tribune* and the *Times* leveled a barrage of criticism at unionists: a series of censuring commentaries that claimed to reveal the "true" designs of the organized workforce of the city—*and* why those same designs would never be realized.

On May 1, in conjuncture with an editorial noting the fruitless failures of the 1867 Eight Hour agitation (on the event's fifth anniversary), the *Tribune* once again began to insinuate that private disputes between workers and employers could be creative of broader civic disorder. The paper quickly rechristened the "Grand Demonstration" as "the grand cooperative strike"—a usage it would never drop.[92] Further, the editors refused to allow that the planned rally might in fact only be a rally, consistently referring to its organizers as "strikers," running headlines such as "THE IMPENDING STRIKE," and dispatching reporters to provide lengthy analyses of the relative organizational strengths and weaknesses of each building trade.[93] Still, for all its overheated (and inaccurate) reportage, the *Tribune* remained convinced that the city would easily evade any danger. As one editorial argued, the inherently orderly forces of supply and demand would instantly doom any worker action: "[T]here is already a surplus of laborers here whose necessities for work are so pressing that they will not join in any strike."[94] And even if this obstacle was somehow bested, the city could rely on the powers of its press. As the May 14 *Tribune* boasted, "[T]he press of Chicago has but to say the word and in ten days there would be enough workmen here to supply the places of all those who unwisely choose to throw up the good positions they are holding."[95] The labor market, or manipulations thereof, would insure the stability of relations of employment.

All of this commotion begs a question: If the editors were in fact so confident that the rules of the market would ensure an uninterrupted Great Rebuilding, why subject unionists to such a sustained critique? Given the *Tribune*'s doubtlessly correct sense that the ample supply of construction workers would quickly derail any strikes, the paper's coverage of the labor rally seems unduly extreme. While it is plausible that the editorial staffs of the *Times* and *Tribune* were simply taking what they perceived as a wise prophylactic step, an early and stern warning against the stoppage of work that was meant to last throughout the season, their responses further suggest that the practice of unionism in itself posed problems for the reconstruction (and maintenance) of civic order. For in their view, if workers elected to act as a collectivity, the autonomy and independence of individuals might be undermined.

As a bulwark of the liberal Republican ideology of free labor, the *Tribune* did not deny that workers had the right to organize themselves into unions.[96] Yet the paper betrayed its discomfort with this form of economic collectivism by its constant elevation of the values ascribed to its opposite: those upheld by the entrepreneurial man of business. Echoing the calls it made during the debates over municipal relief and fire limits to bring the supposedly rigorous and upright methods of commerce to the world of politics, the paper once again equated the sphere of business (and the individual pursuit of economic gain) with a larger vision of what served the public good. Writing about what it termed "The Projected Strike" on the morning of the rally, the *Tribune* set forth a final plea that unmistakably celebrated such a vision of order: "Above all, let it be businesslike, each man deciding according to what will be most for his own interests. In this manner only can the aggregate decision promote the interest of all."[97] Civic peace would thus be best maintained by rejecting the very mutuality dictated by the practice of unionism.

Extending the logical "rightness" of economic individualism, the *Tribune* asked workers to recognize their status as independent actors in another critical arena of market relations: that of consumption. For once working people assessed their interests in terms of their role as consumers (and *not* as fellow members of a trade) they would quickly understand that any delay in the process of rebuilding would only compound their problems. Any work stoppage, the paper reasoned, meant that fewer homes and stores would be built. Since supplies would fall short of demand, high rents and prices would persist. "For every day the work is delayed," an editorial estimated, "the workmen engaged in it would find an extra dollar per month added to their rent next winter."[98] Wages were only worth as much as they could buy; by withholding their labor working people only harmed themselves as well as impeding the larger civic project of rebuilding. Far from portraying municipal reconstruction as a collective effort of equal benefit to all Chicagoans, the *Tribune* here offered a blunt assessment of the Great Rebuilding's meaning for a citizenry divided by class: "The poor of Chicago have a far greater interest than the rich in the rapid, prompt, and cheap rebuilding of the city."[99] Any smart citizen-consumer—a person who would always purchase housing, food, and other goods as an individual market actor—might best avoid the collectivism of unions.[100] The logic of market relations for the *Tribune* again dictated the shape of civic order.

In the week prior to the labor rally, the *Tribune*'s ceaseless talk of strikes and robust defense of supply and demand drew sharp responses from those more sympathetic to workers and their unions.[101] Many simply argued that tradesmen deserved both respect and a decent wage for their hard labor: "Mr. Editor," wrote one mason, "if you had to stoop your back at least 2000 times per day for brick and mortar, under the burning sun, you would not think that $5 was too much."[102] A real estate broker, J. Esias Warren, penned an especially incisive piece that appeared on May 11. Describing construction workers as "the great army upon which we depend for the restoration of our desolated city," Warren, like other commentators, called for a forthright recognition of the double standard that denied workers any right to profit from the great civic need for their skills, even in the context of newly risen costs of living. "Grasping landlords, . . . the builders, the architects, and the speculators generally think it is a fine thing to make rapid fortunes out of increased demand," he observed. "But these righteous individuals are horrified when the mechanics and laboring men, with better reason, ask for a little extra pay."

The broker, however, moved beyond this obvious fissure over the justice of the post-Fire market, diagnosing the conflict as to some degree a problem rooted in the blinkered vision of the upper classes: the same sort of reflexively negative perceptions of the working class that lay beneath the bureaucratic system constructed by the Relief and Aid Society and the military occupation of the city. As the "strike fever" of the English-language press had clearly demonstrated, more elite Chicagoans were quick to generalize about the supposedly bad behavior of working people—leading to judgments, Warren noted, that they never would arrive at in regard to their own actions. He allowed for the plain truth that the city was home to a certain number of "noisy, boisterous, and intemperate mechanics." But, as he reminded, "all merchants are not honest; all lawyers not true; some of our doctors are quacks; and a few of our clergy, perhaps, fall below the standard of saints." The often automatic upper-class association of laboring men and women with disorderly conduct, the construction of the entire working class as a constant threat to civic order, led him to the following conclusion: "Should a universal strike be precipitated the men responsible for such results would not be the mechanic and the workmen, but the men who have misjudged them in advance for crimes they have not committed, and for motives by which they have not been actuated."[103] Talk of a worker conspiracy, Warren suggested, willfully misread the evidence at hand, with consequences that were themselves possibly dangerous to the city. Even as they increasingly idealized the individual in the free market, more elite Chicagoans were seldom able to differentiate between individual working people.

Given the situation at hand, the gaps in vision and understandings that marked the spheres of both wage and class relations, could labor and capital ever cooperate? Despite the troubling implications of his piercing analysis, J. Esias Warren, for one, predicted that all might yet be well. The answer, however, for him could not be found in an all-out attack on workers and their unions. On a practical level, he instead proposed the creation of a citywide board of arbitration composed of "mechanics" and "builders," a body equally representative of workers and employers that would adjudicate disputes. And on the level of belief, he made a sweeping call. What was needed, he argued, was tolerance, empathy, and a broad recognition of the fact that all Chicagoans, whatever their social and economic differences, were members of the same urban community. As such, their shared identity as citizens meant that "their interests" in a quick and uninterrupted rebuilding were "identical." If "a kind and justly spirit," a deep concern for "the welfare of the city," could only prevail, "every obstacle now feared would be thoroughly and effectively removed." In Warren's ideal city, labor and capital, if not equals, were truly partners in a broader civic enterprise. But the question remained whether such an ideal ever could be realized.

On May 15, some 6000 tradesmen took a holiday from their labors, assembling downtown at 9 A.M. to commence a procession that wended through Chicago's three divisions. A driving rainstorm put a damper on the rally's first stage. Still, sizable crowds gathered streetside as contingents of stone-cutters, horseshoers, plasterers, carpenters, painters, lathers, and bricklayers—headed by a seventeen-piece band, a cordon of police, and carriages conveying the press, parade marshals, and "lady friends" of the marshals—all passed by.[104] Since much traditional union regalia had been lost to the fire, costumes and banners were rather makeshift. Yet the marchers still managed to send strong symbolic messages identifying their assembled body—skilled workers and union men—as essential citizens. All of the trades carried American flags, and some further displayed iconic representations of what Sean Wilentz has termed artisanal republicanism, a set of emblems common to such nineteenth-century processions. Five-hundred stone-cutters in part staked their claim to respectability and national tradition by marching behind a painting of men laboring under the proud gaze of George Washington.[105] Other banners joined a sense of civic belonging to the basic messages of unionism; the painters and horseshoers, for example, trailed after the same standard declaration: "United We Stand, Divided We Fall." Throughout, a solemn silence prevailed, broken only by the bands that headed each trade delegation. True to the *Workingman's Advocate*'s charge, decorum reigned supreme; as the *Staats-Zeitung* reported, "Dignified and measured was their appearance and attitude from the beginning to the end."[106]

Around noon, the marchers arrived at a vacant West Side lot not far from Mrs. O'Leary's barn. There the unions filed past a reviewing platform (hastily reerected after its collapse during the morning's storm), each in turn offering a formal salute to Mayor Medill and Police Commissioner Mark Sheridan. A crowd of over 20,000 jostled in a drizzle, as *Advocate* editor Cameron, the rally's chair, called the meeting to order. After informing the assembly of a final piece of ill luck—that NLU president Richard F. Trevellick had missed a train connection in Erie and therefore would not appear as promised—the editor turned over the rostrum to the assembly's remaining honored guest.

"It requires no figure of speech," began Mayor Joseph Medill, "to justify me in calling this vast assemblage the bone and sinew of the city."[107] Having paid metaphoric and literal tribute to the place of workers in the body politic, the mayor went on to applaud their motives for assembly. Though the "busy tongue" of rumor had led many to believe that this gathering of trades was intended to inaugurate a general strike, he trusted that its objects were in fact those he took to be shared by every good citizen: to rejoice at the end of winter and resolve to undertake the project of rebuilding with vigor and speed. Despite his conciliatory and sympathetic opening, however, Medill's listeners were soon reminded that their mayor was no ordinary politician. Never one to tell his audiences what they wanted to hear—a habit that goes far toward explaining his short career as an elected official—he proceeded to deliver his own candid assessment of the problems and prospects that faced Chicago workers.

Medill, a strong liberal Republican, cast the question of wage relations within an interpretive frame constructed by his most basic concern: the protection of individual freedoms and opportunities.[108] The mayor quickly conceded the ability of workers to organize and take other actions in defense of their interests. "You have the undoubted legal right," he told the crowd of tradesmen, "to put your own price on your services"; moreover, workers were free to "combine and strike" in pursuit of such an end. Two critical caveats, however, also had to be applied: unionists could *not* compel fellow laborers either to join their organizations or to sell their labor only at some standard price. Such "coercion," according to Medill, destroyed personal freedom and liberty of action. In addition, since "the rights of people are exactly equal," no legal obligation bound bosses "to pay any attention" to union rules and standards. Just as any worker possessed the "unquestioned privilege to demand whatever wages he pleases, and to work much or little," employers were free to determine the numbers they wished to hire, the hours of labor per day, the kind and quality of work to be done, and the wages to be paid.

The free market, for Medill, therefore rested upon contracts that were products of free will and free action. As he explained his understanding of the bond between employers and employees to Chicago's gathered union stalwarts: "It is his privilege to propose and yours to accept or decline; and yours to offer terms and his to accede or refuse." Secure in his belief that legal protections of individual freedom ensured equality of opportunity, the mayor thus portrayed the playing ground of wage relations as a completely level field—one where equal parties had the equal ability to enter into contracts or to reject agreements that they found unsuitable. But once he turned his attention to the way that this theory functioned in practice, Medill described quite a different landscape—a terrain fraught with basic obstacles for those who sold their labor.

To the mind of the mayor, capital and labor were "natural partners"; since neither could exist without the other, society's progress plainly depended upon their cooperation. Strikes and lockouts, he asserted, were indeed "a species of civil war," battles that invariably wounded both sets of combatants. Nevertheless, while Medill believed that employers and employees shared an essential interdependence, he was also quick to observe that they hardly had access to equal resources. For labor, as he noted, relied upon capital for employment, a fundamental asymmetry that meant that labor was always the far weaker—or more dependent—partner.[109] In light of this imbalance, unionists from the first faced a central disadvantage in any attempt to forward their own aims.

Medill chose to illustrate his argument through a none-too-coincidental discussion of the strike, an analysis that employed a hardnosed calculus of what he felt to be the real costs of any stoppage of work. In a strike, he observed, workers exercised power by withholding their labor, attempting "to force capital to surrender by the method of starvation." To be sure, a business deprived of its workforce would eventually decay; still, the reserves of capital would almost certainly cushion any immediate impact upon employers themselves. But workers, as he pointedly warned, were deprived of their incomes—and would almost certainly face dire personal and familial consequences: "Capital has a magazine of provisions from which to draw its rations, but Labor has an empty larder and women and children suffering and crying for bread." Medill therefore saw no good in strikes—certainly not in his own city, at the present moment. Since "the great law of supply and demand" so plainly favored employers, Medill counseled the union men to go forth with great caution: "All coercive measures," he predicted, "will come to nought."

Medill went on to dose his listeners with even more bitter medicine, echoing the *Tribune*'s argument that the poor, due to their vulnerability as consumers, would gain more than the rich from a quick rebuilding. Rent, he knew, had risen to a degree that caused great hardship. But landlords could hardly be deemed "heartless or depraved" for their simple obedience to the "irresistible law of supply and demand." Betraying his discomfort with what he saw as the disordering effects of "combination" in a free market, the mayor offered what his audience must have seen as a somewhat galling defense of landlords: "[T]hey have no Unions to force up rents or to prevent their decline." If workers wanted rents and other living costs to come down, Medill asserted, their remedy was obvious: they had to cooperate in achieving the speedy, uninterrupted replacement of burned buildings. Any collective action in pursuit of higher wages would invariably redound to the disadvantage of every individual;

only time, and tradesmen's calm acceptance of whatever wage the market would bear, could correct the imbalance of the market for housing. As the ever-blunt Medill informed a crowd devoted to worker solidarity, "[S]triking against builders is, therefore, striking against your own bread and butter, and your own interests."

With these arguments, Medill at once proved himself as fierce a defender of economic "law" as he was a champion of political rights and freedoms. Both axioms indeed interlocked to form the bedrock of his understanding of a democratic order. The mayor's theory of liberal government placed the equality of individuals before the law at the very root of a free society. Moreover, his exposition on the necessity of the freedom of individuals to act in the market pointed toward a growing moral justification of capitalism as a system that similarly enshrined the ideals of individual freedom and equality—in the form, more specifically, of equality of opportunity.[110] Out of this set of economic and social practices, individuals would earn their just rewards. The free market for him seemed an ideological mirror for political and legal freedoms of action.

Yet even as he apotheosized the rights of the individual in the market, Medill showed himself to be well aware of the fact that capital and labor, while interdependent, were by definition not equal, not at all the abstract individuals of liberal theory. Herein lay what might be read as a paradox: Could unequal parties be said to make "free" contracts?[111] Medill, though, saw no contradiction in his simultaneous elevation of the rights of individuals in the market and his recognition of structures of power that constrained the actions of the same individuals. Like most political leaders of his day, he could not imagine a vision of public good that included interventions into the economy intended to bring about a greater equality of means, a decision that the civil state might move in some degree to rectify the permanent asymmetry of wage relations, and act to close the gap between the resources and power of capital and those of labor.[112] The market, for Chicago's mayor, had to be the province of the individual.

But "how," he asked, "shall the condition of the laborer be improved?" Since strikes were so patently unwise, since he saw no need for the state to move beyond its role as the supposed guarantor of equality before the law, what forms of action were available to working people? The mayor was not entirely unsympathetic to labor's calls for arbitration and cooperation; both strategies, he thought, were in principle based in some measure upon "fair dealings." Yet he doubted that these plans ever met with much success in practice, in the face of the twin barriers of the knowledge and resources required to run a business and what he perceived as the low level of education among many workers. Medill ultimately was forced to admit that he, like everyone else, had no definitive solution; the "ablest minds in Europe and America," he noted, were still wrestling with the question. Left standing without any new answers, the mayor instead drew upon a powerful set of older beliefs distilled out of his own history.

Telling his audience he could do no better than advise them to follow the course he himself had pursued, Medill ended his address with what he viewed as a foolproof recipe for self-making, a proscription that vividly captured his abiding faith in individual achievement:

> Work steadily at the best wages offered; practice economy in personal expenditures; drink water instead of whiskey, keep out of debt, put your surplus earnings at interest until you have enough to make a payment on a lot, build a cottage on it at the earliest day possible, and thus be independent of landlords; go with your wife to church on Sunday, and send your children to school.

In the event that a young man had yet to find a spouse—and thus fall under what was then considered to be the invariably beneficial influence of marriage—the mayor instructed his unmarried listeners "to court some worthy girl and marry her." Under such a program, no one could expect quick riches. But good conduct, Medill confidently declared, would eventually bring its reward. "Push forward hopefully and perseveringly," he concluded, "and there is no fear but you can better your conditions and become independent long before old age overtakes you." Steady work, sobriety, savings, home ownership, Christianity, marriage, a family—Medill here laid out the icons of emerging middle-class understandings of stability and good citizenship.[113] Strikingly, all of these goals and achievements were predicated upon the efforts of individuals, as individuals, to bring about their own slow but sure rise through the ranks of the American economy and society.

As Medill stepped down from the podium to unsurprisingly tepid applause, Andrew Cameron rose to introduce the message of the assembled unionists: a series of resolutions that again set forth the claim of the building trades to desire nothing but civic peace and good order. Disavowing all "violence" in favor of "moral suasion," the unions continued to defend their public image, formally repudiating "the oft-imputed charges of lawless character"; upon the "honor of the workingmen of Chicago," they pledged to work tirelessly to rebuild their city. In keeping with the aims of the NLU, the rally next endorsed the principle of cooperative enterprise, encouraging tradesmen to band together to run their own businesses and thereby become their own employers. In addition, a stalwart affirmation of their cause asked all nonunion "mechanics" to join in their ranks. "In union there is strength," declared one resolve. "The object is to ask nothing but what is right—to submit to nothing that is wrong."

Finally, the assembly's resolutions contained a practical keystone, a proposal that contained within it a distinct and important vision of what cooperation between labor and capital might entail. Restating the concept previously set out by J. Esias Warren, the building trades proposed that all disputed contracts be heard before a Board of Arbitration—half of its members to be selected by workers and half by employers.[114] In the event that this panel failed to agree, a third party "agreeable to all those interested" should render a final and binding settlement. If Chicagoans honestly desired to avoid work stoppages, union leaders argued, open discussion was the surest means to secure this end. Workers and bosses could meet each other halfway, on territory permanently designated as neutral; "The 15th of May," proclaimed the *Advocate*, "will be regarded as a day in which was inaugurated a system which will substitute reason for passion, secure justice to both classes, and cause strikes to be regarded as a relic of the past."[115]

For the unionists, any genuine cooperation between labor and capital, a state of affairs that could remove the seemingly permanent problem of irresolvable conflict without resort to strikes or lockouts, required employers to share a certain amount of economic authority. With their call for a Board of Arbitration, the building trades envisioned a marketplace in which private disputes between employers and employees could be resolved in a public forum—a city-sanctioned court of appeal where the imbalance of power inherent to the wage relation would, at moments of impasse, to some degree be redressed. Through this institutionalized intervention into the mechanics of the free market, the establishment of an equally representative body, labor and capital could indeed become partners of a sort, working in tandem to arrive at "fair" resolutions to contractual disputes. For all of the civic good implied by business-class calls for "cooperation," unionists believed that such rhetorical nods to "partnerships" between capital and labor obscured a basic reality of the wage relation: that both sides maintained different (and often opposing) interests. But a place at the table for labor on a citywide Board of Arbitration—this was a step that offered a meaningful recognition of the interdependence of labor and capital, one that might indeed bring about a greater measure of economic equity.

"What did it mean, what was its object, and what will be its effect upon rebuilding Chicago?"[116] So the *Tribune*, flummoxed by the fact that their predicted strike and/or riot did not materialize, wondered about the previous day's rally. In many ways, the puzzlement of the paper is understandable. It had expected the worst sort of disorder—and aside from their call for arbitration, the organized workers of Chicago had walked away from their grand demonstration without formulating any sort of grand scheme. No plans were laid for a strike, no Boards of Arbitration were ever convened.[117] Moreover, while the march and rally had drawn an impressively large crowd, newspaper accounts suggest that at least half of those working in the building trades had chosen not to cease their labors on this Wednesday.[118] Many read the spotty attendance as proof positive that the glutted labor market would effectively bar any effective organizing, let alone strikes.[119] In the end, the gathering of unionists carried an ironic legacy: the rally planned as a showcase for the potential strength of organized labor in Chicago more plainly revealed its weakness. Moreover, the address of Medill offers stark insight into the broad set of economic, political, and cultural barriers that from the first confronted any collective action on the part of working people.

The "Grand Demonstration of the Trades Unions" marked no special turning point in Chicago's post-Fire wage relations. It did not, despite the best efforts of the *Times* and the *Tribune* to paint it as such, serve as the catalyst for a new spirit of aggression among the organized trades of the city. It did, however, lie at the center of a discussion that drew two divergent modes of thought into sharp focus, modes of thought and visions of civic order that were rooted in distinct class experiences. At issue was what would become the dominant social and political question of the last quarter of the nineteenth century in America: Could Labor and Capital cooperate?

Certainly, answered Joseph Medill, speaking both in his temporary role as mayor and out of his identity as a representative member of Chicago's native-born business class. Labor and capital could without doubt find their way to a harmony of interests. But cooperation, as he understood it, had to be governed by two inviolable sets of laws: those protecting personal freedoms and those protecting the free market. A cooperative labor force was one attuned to their own best interests as individual workers, consumers, and citizens, a state of affairs which by extension secured the best interests of the urban community. Cooperative working people accepted the rules and realities of supply and demand and sought simply to make the best of their own opportunities—ever patient and faithful that such good conduct would over time bring its rewards.

The organized building trades of the city likewise responded in the affirmative. But their understanding of cooperation differed radically from the definition offered by Medill. For these men, cooperation mandated forms of regulation of the free market; indeed, the decision of union members to act in concert reflected their belief that an economy free from any sort of collectively based interventions on the part of labor would always function in favor of capital. Further, in addition to cooperating among themselves, if workers ever expected to gain assurance that their labors would afford them a decent life, a more cooperative ethos had to be injected into the workings of competitive capitalism. A representative Board of Arbitration, for example, would recognize the "partnership" between labor and capital on more than what they viewed as rhetorical terms. Such an institution moved to in some measure correct the asymmetry of the wage relation in the "free" market, granting each side equivalent responsibilities and powers to determine just and fair contracts. Pressing for the adoption of a form of capitalism governed by a more mutualistic vision, the unionists rejected the business-class gospel of free markets and free choice. Guarantees of political equality, they believed, at best served as partial remedies to righting the wrongs of a society pervaded by economic oppressions.

PEACE AND WAR

On the day after the "Grand Demonstration," the industrialist George M. Pullman received a letter from the man hired to build his new home, a Prairie Avenue mansion later famed for its lavish appointments. Architect Henry S. Jaffray was pleased to report that "we are making more headway than I had expected," progress won despite what he deemed to be the generally "disaffected spirit which now prevails among mechanics." Jaffray's crew had not marched with their fellow tradesmen. "Although this is the day appointed for their procession," he wrote, "I have every man at work, same as yesterday." The architect went on to assure Pullman that no serious labor troubles were likely to surface for quite some time: "After this absurd display of today is over, men will probably return to work and keep quiet until October, when there will be universal concessions on the part of employers." As the construction season neared its end, he reasoned, builders' rush to complete their contracts before the onset of winter would give workers the bargaining chip they needed to gain higher wages. But for the moment—and throughout the spring and summer months of the Great Rebuilding—Jaffray expected calm.[120]

For all of their ideological disagreements, did the workers and employers of Chicago in fact cooperate? Did their combined efforts end in an actual process of reconstruction that was relatively free of conflict? For the most part, George Pullman's architect proved an accurate prophet: for all of the intense anxiety surrounding the May 15 rally, the tens of thousands of workers who labored to create "New Chicago" had few overt disputes with their bosses. Only in the waning days of September did relations of employment in the building trades visibly begin to disintegrate, as first the city's organized carpenters, and then its bricklayers, mounted significant strikes. As the Great Rebuilding drew to a close, Chicagoans thus witnessed firsthand two separate attempts at the exercise of the ultimate threat and power of unions, attempts that offered stark examples of the structural and political obstacles—along with all the cultural sanctions—that organized workers had to negotiate. And throughout the spring, summer, and early fall, even though there were no similarly obvious flashpoints, specific tensions and gaps in understanding continued to mark the sphere of wage relations. Cooperation, in its practice, proved as multileveled and contested as in its theory.

Even without major disputes over the terms of work, the summer months in certain ways were still a time of hardship for those who labored to rebuild Chicago. Though wages and hours remained steady for the approximately 50,000 employed in some facet of construction work, not everyone found a job—resulting in some migration away from the city.[121] Hundreds of contractors (some of whom were skilled tradesmen who seized upon the demand created by the Fire to begin their own business) struck verbal agreements with their workmen, who most often were nonunion men recruited on-site.[122] According to the *Workingman's Advocate*, those without a written contract sometimes lived to regret it, since bosses often had notoriously faulty memories when it came to the subject of wages owed.[123] Even for those with regular employment, high prices and rents quickly consumed their pay; "[M]oney," as one workman succinctly described the state of affairs, "is scarce here."[124] Further, in addition to financial worries, building tradesman and their unskilled helpers braved much heightened personal risks. To be sure, construction workers always faced dangers on the job. The pace and density of the work of the Great Rebuilding, however, exacted an especially heavy human toll.

The building of "New Chicago" turned most every downtown lot into a bustling swarm of materials, men, working animals, and machinery. Streets were virtually impassable; masses of wood, stone, and steel swung from hoists and derricks, crowding the skies above. Most new structures in the business district were primarily built of brick, some of which had been scavenged from the rubble of burned buildings. Still, to provide the greater portion of the estimated 1,000,000 bricks laid per day during the Great Rebuilding, brickyards in Chicago and surrounding towns ran day and night at their full capacities.[125] Masons "thick as bees"—perched on scaffolds less than three feet apart, with room just to turn—worked from the bottom up to standard heights of four to six stories, relying on legions of hod carriers (and, in some cases, brand-new horse and steam driven elevators) to keep their bricks and mortar close at hand.[126] Plasterers, carpenters, painters, and glaziers moved in to finish each story as the building progressed; in some instances, owners and tenants occupied lower floors even before, as one reporter wrote, "the sound of the mason's trowel ceases."[127] But as structures went up, walls often came down. Both the swiftness of work and the occasionally inferior quality of available brick led to buckling and "springing"—unpredictable and sudden collapses that sometimes buried workmen beneath them.[128]

Moreover, the remarkably quick resurrection of Chicago's downtown could not have been accomplished without the introduction of new technology, mechanical devices of recent invention that immensely speeded work, yet often proved quite dangerous to workers. The most critical—and risky—addition to the arsenal of builders was the derrick, a narrow crane that hoisted blocks and beams high into the air. Workers and passers-by picked their way through a forest of these devices, which, for all their utility, were still quite imperfect. Mechanical and human failures plagued these machines and all those around them; they frequently dropped their cargo, or simply became unbalanced and toppled—with deadly results. "The derrick, like the press and pulpit, is a mighty engine for good and evil," observed the *Tribune*, commenting on its mixed blessings in late June. "It serves anti-podal purposes with good effect, being a powerful aid in rendering protection for life through the creation of shelter for man and business, and in ending forever the sorrows of the unfortunate."[129]

At a time before the advent of state regulation of worksite practices or the avenue of legal recourse that would come to be known as workman's compensation, a contractor's conscience was his only guide (and economic incentive) to ensuring that his crews labored under safe conditions.[130] But given the number of accidental deaths and injuries in post-Fire Chicago—a figure, at the height of the construction season, that reportedly reached as high as a dozen per day—it seems plain that many builders were unwilling to sacrifice speed for safety.[131] Even the *Tribune*, usually a die-hard booster of the business community, was moved to chide those "so reckless to human life." The paper went on to provide a stunning count of these casualties, suggesting that the Great Rebuilding's cost in lives would actually exceed that of the Great Fire: "Before the city is rebuilt, more lives will have been sacrificed to the New Chicago than were engulfed in the fiery end of the nearly-forgotten city."[132]

Nevertheless, for all its horror at these grim numbers, the *Tribune* clearly valued what it considered to be the broader civic good of a fast reconstruction above the possibility of implementing more deliberate and therefore less hazardous methods. A somewhat ironically titled piece on "Labor Saving Machinery" ended with a suggestive remark about the use of derricks: "[T]heir immense utility to the general public counterbalances the damage to the individual, fatal though it be."[133] Though the editors doubtless were saddened by the many cases of workmen killed on the job, their calculation of just what constituted a public good speaks of the emotional abstraction born of their own distance from the world of working people. The nameless "individual" worker had to be sacrificed for the sake of civic order, a situation that seemed painful—but not painful enough to be remedied in any fashion. Working-class victims and their friends and families, on the other hand, were hardly likely to concur with this representation of their best interests. Here again, the *Tribune* reflexively equated the aims and goals of its more elite readership, a group that faced no personal risk, with those of the entire urban community.

Frequent worker deaths led to frequent worker funerals, a cir-

Reconstruction of Marine Bank Building. Note use of derricks and floor-by-floor progress of construction. Courtesy of Chicago Historical Society, ICHi-02845.

cumstance that in itself proved revealing of class differences over how the work of the Great Rebuilding might best proceed. The ritual of trade union burials, which called upon all union members to cease work and parade the coffin of their fallen brother to its grave site, offers a telling glimpse of the inability of the business class to comprehend an important ethic of the trades: that of mutualism and respect in life *and* death.[134] For workingmen, funerals were a testament to the esteem a tradesman had earned lifelong through his conduct and his skills. Yet the *Tribune* saw nothing honorable in these tributes to a lost workmate; to the contrary, they seemed to contradict the best interests of the city. Was it truly necessary, asked the paper, that a thousand carpenters, stonemasons, or bricklayers abandon their work to trail behind one man's hearse? To uphold an archaic custom, argued the paper, these men did a disservice to themselves, to nonunion workers, and to all Chicago. Not only did the unionists forego their pay of a morning or afternoon, but their absence from their jobs idled their unskilled helpers—and, worst of all, delayed the overall progress of municipal reconstruction. A far better plan, suggested the editorial, would be to delegate fifty men to any funeral, and have the rest donate perhaps a dollar out of that day's wage to any survivors. Money, the paper assumed, could adequately substitute for a massive display of sympathy and solidarity.

Such a proposal, however, did not grasp the fact that the very structure of union funerals to a large degree rejected the *Tribune*'s cherished ethos of economic individualism. The paper could not reconcile its own set of beliefs with those held by tradesmen, failing to understand that such ritual reaffirmations of the union community had an intrinsic value for its members—a value that could not be calculated in hard cash or in terms of individual profit and loss. And beyond this gap in understanding, union funerals rankled on an even deeper level. By their suspension of labor, their elevation of the collective identity of a trade above every single workman's attention to his job and the wishes of his employer, such ceremonies seemed not merely antiquated but quite subversive. The repercussions of union funerals, for the *Tribune*, echoed far beyond the private relations of employment: "They are," proclaimed the paper, "a public and private injury, from which no possible good results." A time-honored tradition of the most basic working-class form of cooperation for the *Tribune* seemed entirely uncooperative; as this offended champion of individualism and utility concluded, "[I]t is a gross and inexcusable waste."[135] A union practice was thus once again perceived by more elite Chicagoans as a potential danger to the whole of civic order.

Finally, as this season of great productivity—and great strains—neared its end, the relations of employment in Chicago suffered a first highly publicized break. In mid-September, organized carpenters began to press for a wage increase. The Carpenters and Joiners' Union, while numerically the strongest of any of the building trades, had gone through the Great Rebuilding under a cloud of internal squabbles over apprenticeship requirements and association leadership. "Their very dissensions," pronounced the *Advocate*, "make themselves an easy prey."[136] All of the other unionized building trades had maintained enough organizational strength to keep their wages at or slightly above their pre-Fire standards, with most of their members earning between $4.50 and $5.00 for a ten-hour day. But carpenters could command only $2.50 or $3.00 for the same amount of labor, a sum not far above that paid to many unskilled workers. Such diminished earning power left carpenters especially vulnerable to the increased cost of living. Further, since "drivers of the saw" were compelled to serve a longer apprenticeship and maintain a more expensive set of tools than other building tradesmen, this shortfall in earnings seemed to them even more vexing.[137] As cold weather once again drew near, carpenters felt that they could seize the moment: since buildings in the latter stages of construction particularly relied on the trade for interior finish work, contractors now had a heightened need for their skills.[138] Strategic timing, they believed, might counteract their season-long inability to maintain an effective organization.

The union decided to take action at a mass meeting on September 16, asking all employers to advance their standard wage to $4.00 per day. Contractors had one week to acquiesce; if they refused, all union carpenters would strike. Yet, for all the will behind this ultimatum, the carpenters walked an especially hard road in their attempt at organized cooperation. First of all, out-of-towners still viewed Chicago as a labor mecca. Though the wages commanded by the trade did not measure up to the city's inflated cost of living, they were still higher than rates offered elsewhere—and any pay at all, of course, looked good to someone who was unemployed.[139] Further, in comparison with other building trades, the carpenters faced a unique problem: it was difficult for them to draw boundaries of union membership based on a distinctive competence. Almost all men and boys knew something of the basics of carpentry; unlike the work of stone-cutters or masons, it took no special training to do the repetitive work of the trade—driving nails or making cuts according to the marks and measures made by a more highly skilled colleague. Thousands temporarily displaced from their regular jobs earned a living in the summer after the Great Fire by signing on as carpenters. According to the *Times*, only 2500 of the more than 8000 workmen employed in the trade had actually completed a standard apprenticeship—a count that was perhaps exaggerated by this antilabor paper, but one that still points to an important truth about the ease of entry to this particular trade.[140]

A final obstacle dogged the union. The carpenters' organization had grown enormously since the Great Fire—and the rapid expansion of any union posed its own problems. Quick surges in size gave organizations little time to groom new officers and stewards, making it difficult for unionists to enforce discipline in their own ranks. Moreover, in light of the carpenters' long-standing local reputation for discord, they seemed to have an especially poor chance at the successful coordination of a strike. Indeed, a signal lack of common resolve quickly became apparent, as many carpenters immediately exempted themselves from their association's strike order. These unionists accepted conditional terms specifying that, if they remained at work, their employer would advance their wages if the strike succeeded at other venues—agreements that kept these workers at the places but undermined both trade solidarity and the very tactic of applying pressure by staying off the job.[141]

In light of their relative failure even to secure the cooperation of their own trade, organized carpenters and their supporters were forced to rely upon appeals to the notion of civic cooperation—the ideal, like the one imagined by J. Esias Warren, of good citizens joined in a common task. Adding their own twist to some of the same language used by those, such as Mayor Medill, who liked to speak of the "partnership" between capital and labor, the carpenters set out what they viewed as a moral claim to a higher standard wage. Judge Ben Miller, a friend of the union, made the argument most clearly in a speech on the evening of September 18. Employers, he declared, could certainly continue to purchase the labor of carpenters at bargain rates. But as citizens of Chicago, he felt they were obliged to show some respect for the tradesmen he described as their equal partners in the city's astonishing resurrection. In the aftermath of a shared civic disaster, he declared, there could be no "war" between the ultimate aims of workers and their employers: "What could capital have done after the fire without labor? Labor assisted capital as capital assisted labor. All the capital in the world could not have rebuilt Chicago without skilled labor. Men worked heroically at their task, throughout a hard winter and the heat of summer, never once asking for an increase of wages. . . . Now," he concluded, it was "time that their service be properly recognized."[142] Lacking access to any market power through effective organization, the carpenters' best weapon was rhetorical—a demand that at its heart was an unlikely request that employers set aside the rules of supply and demand in deference to the contribution of skilled workmen to the public good of rebuilding, and grant a value to their work well above its market price.

In a city where imagined strikes had sparked such impassioned debate some four months earlier, the carpenters' actions occasioned only a fairly sedate response. For Chicagoans were well aware of the realities of the market for labor—a set of structures that loomed as a massive barrier to any attempt at workers' control. Contractors certainly were unimpressed; not at all moved by the union plea to recognize the trade for its civic (as opposed to its market) worth, they largely remained confident that the weakness of the trade would allow them to carry the day. "The strike," declared one employer, would "surely fizzle."[143] The *Tribune*, faithful to the logic of the free market, simply pointed to the oversupply of men able to work in the trade. "Any carpenter who desired to see in the present juncture means to enforce their demand," coolly observed an editorial, "must now plainly discover that their own brethren have by their numbers defeated the project."[144] Only the *Times* mustered the antiunion fervor of the spring, again giving evidence of the sense of threat and disorder so easily attached to worker efforts to alter the "rules" of the market. "A mob of unruly carpenters are hindering the reconstruction of the city by a strike," the paper announced on the day after approximately 1000 union men did walk off their jobs. "Like all other moves of the same stripe, it is useless and dangerous."[145] Still, even as it accurately diagnosed the strike as foredoomed to failure—nearly all union carpenters either returned to work with no raise in pay or simply were replaced within forty-eight hours—the *Times* again hammered home the message that the collective activity of workers invariably imperiled the city: such an effort, an editorial asserted, was "prejudicial to the good order of the community."[146]

The strike of the carpenters secured them little, offering a plain illustration of how the success of any worker action in these years before state intervention on the part of unions depended on something that was extremely difficult to attain: the near-complete and well-disciplined organization of a trade. Despite the legal freedom of individuals to choose to join together, worker cooperation could not easily withstand the force of wider markets for labor, the resistance of employers, or the array of negative images associated with unions and unionism. Still, the defeat did not sound a death knell for unions in the building trades, as the Great Rebuilding soon witnessed another interruption. Less than two weeks after the carpenters failed to gain any widespread increase in wages, the organized bricklayers of Chicago also called a strike over the issue of pay. Yet a crucial difference underlay their motivation: unlike the carpenters, who had sought to force their standard rate up to what they considered a fair level, the bricklayers walked off their jobs to protest a wage cut. On October 2, claiming that the price of brick had increased to an intolerable degree, boss masons had reduced bricklayers' wages from $5.00 for ten hours to $4.50 for the same amount of time. A union counteroffer of a proportionally equal wage in exchange for a shorter workday—$4.00 for eight hours—was immediately rejected. The bricklayers then voted to cease their labors on October 4. "No union man," decreed their strike order, "will be allowed to work for any contractor in the city of Chicago, until the contractor shall first sign a written agreement that he will pay $4.00 per day for eight hours' work."

Coming hard on the heels of the carpenters' disastrous walkout, the strike of the bricklayers seemed similarly ill-omened. The oversupply of labor certainly included idle masons, and any action by bricklayers was further hampered by its timing. Since masons did the first work on most structures, fewer and fewer of their trade were needed as more and more buildings approached completion—a fact that the boss masons well understood. Still, in contrast to the weak and fragmented carpenters' union, the organized bricklayers had a history of successful collectivism.[147] In addition, a strong national trade network kept strikebreakers from flocking to Chicago; the same evening the union posted their strike order, members left by train to recruit support from union lodges in other cities. Finally, the carpenters had acted aggressively to secure a higher standard rate. But even as they used this moment to again restate arguments for the eight-hour day, the bricklayers were clearly striking to protect what they had long earned: the summer's standard wage.

Unionists and their allies again and again pointed to what they portrayed as their innocent victimization. The boss masons, they maintained, eager to squeeze even greater profits out of the season of great opportunity, had caused the strike themselves. In the view of the union, the newly risen cost of brick offered little excuse for the cut in wages, since all savvy builders had long ago struck contracts for the future delivery of bricks at a fixed rate and were thus unaffected by any present surge in prices. Moreover, unionists felt that they should not be expected to absorb such a blow, given their crucial contribution to the overall task of the Great Rebuilding. Throughout the season, as German bricklayers indignantly wrote to the *Staats-Zeitung*, they had "helped diligently and without complaint . . . to rebuild Chicago."[148] Finally, in the immediate aftermath of the disaster, had they not pledged to ask no more than their pre-Fire standard—thereby, unlike virtually every contractor and landlord, foregoing their own chance to gain from much-heightened demand? Surveying the situation, the *Workingman's Advocate* again remarked on the apparent double standard concerning just who might rightly profit from Chicago's tragedy: "Had the men taken advantage of the situation in April last they would have been considered dishonorable. Are the bosses less so today?"[149] And what was the bricklayers' reward for their consistent efforts to prove their worth as citizens, to have held down wages when they could have commanded high rates, and then to have worked in concert with their employers all summer long?[150] Complete hypocrisy, the union concluded—mendacity spawned by the avarice and moral bankruptcy of their employers.

Beginning on October 4, nearly all of the 4000 organized bricklayers in Chicago left their places, returning only when the boss masons signed contracts acceding to the union demand of $4.00 for eight hours. The situation was tense: bands of between 100 and 150 strikers walked from site to site, by their presence seeking to assure that no other workers would take their jobs. Frustrated by these tactics, the boss masons organized their own meetings to call for police aid in removing union men.[151] Commanders did dispatch officers whenever they believed that crews still at work might be in danger; a detail of forty men, for instance, appeared to disperse a crowd of 125 union men at the new McCormick Reaper factory on October 9.[152] Still, for all the strains that marked these days, few clashes escalated beyond anything but heated verbal exchange. More severe incidents did occur: in one conflict, Peter Button, head contractor for a major hotel, pushed a striker off a wall that the bricklayer had climbed to speak with men still at work—leading to the arrests of Button for assault and of the union man for trespassing.

Button was not alone in maintaining such strong feelings. Deeply offended by the strike, by the challenge of the union to their right to secure their profits by imposing a cut in wages, the boss masons were willing to suspend all brick construction, if need be, to defend their prerogatives as employers. "It is better," declared the Builders' Association, "to stop all building operations until next year, rather than to submit to the dictation of the strikers."[153] According to this group of Chicagoans, the civic good done by the rebuilding did not at all outweigh their own interests in resisting the collective effort of their workmen. For the association, any form of cooperation that involved a concession on their part could not be tolerated.

Despite the staunch opposition of the master masons, the bricklayers won their battle. Unlike the hapless carpenters, the specificity of their skill and the strength of their organization held off the threat of replacement; union masons, within a few days, had essentially shut down the work of building with brick. As the *Tribune* noted one week into the strike, the absence of the approximately 3000 bricklayers who worked for bosses who had yet to settle had also idled 3000 laborers who worked as their helpers—adding up to $21,000 per day in what the paper disapprovingly described as "wages lost to the laboring classes."[154] Two days later, the *New York Times* confirmed the impact of the walkout: the bricklayers, their reporter observed, were "seriously interfering with the work of rebuilding the city."[155] Moreover, the powerful union claim to innocent victimization won over some key figures. Eager to complete work on his new Palmer House before the onset of cold weather once again made it impossible to build with brick, hotelier and businessman Potter Palmer fired his contractor, who had refused to settle. Taking the even more extraordinary step of appearing at a strike meeting, Palmer promised that he would employ only union men at the $4.00-for-eight-hours standard. Within a few days of Palmer's announcement, more and more boss masons saw the risk of alienating their clients and began to cave into the bricklayers' demands—one by one making their way to union headquarters to sign off on new contracts. Though a few determined builders held out until mid-November, the union for the most part beat back the wage cut, securing both a proportionally equal wage and a shorter workday. Cooperation in the form of unionism, for the bricklayers of Chicago, had succeeded. But in light of the fierce resistance of the Master Masons and Builders' Association, the ultimate aim of the labor movement—to work to achieve a more mutualistic form for the economy and society in general—must have begun to seem increasingly utopian.

On the afternoon of October 10, 1872, a group of Chicagoans gathered in celebration. Exactly one year had passed from the date of the Great Fire. The city held no formal commemoration, and vagu talk of a day-long holiday for wage laborers had been rejected a ill-considered. But at 2 P.M., Mayor Medill and other dignitarie assembled to dedicate the magnificent new Board of Trade building At the end of a characteristically long-winded speech, the mayo marveled at the capacity of his community to rebound from th Fire's devastation—indeed, even to reap blessings from a clear evil Chicago had grown in its population and its commerce, in the process becoming "more solid, safe, and beautiful"; further, all th world now knew of the city and its achievements. Medill set out proud tribute to the united and unbroken spirit of his citizenry "[T]he magnitude of the affliction shocked all nations, but suddenness of the recovery and the swiftness of the resurrection of th consumed city have filled them with admiration and praise of th indomitable, lion-hearted people of Chicago."[156] "It was a fearfu punishment," he concluded. But in a year's time, disaster had transformed into "a public benefit." Versions of Medill's remarks—a representation of an abstract "people's" record of progress and th notion of a "public benefit" somehow emanating from calamity— have long endured as the best-known stories about the Great Re building.

One day earlier, William O'Brien, president of the Bricklayers Union, had released an open letter that presented a far differen picture of what the city—and its many and diverse peoples—ha witnessed during this extraordinary year. In a missive directed "T an Unprejudiced Public," O'Brien sought to justify and explain th then ongoing strike of his union. Reflecting upon the results of th Great Fire, the bricklayer noted that working people had "share equally" with "the millionaire," that all Chicagoans had endure dire misfortunes. Yet despite a certain common experience of calamity and loss, he observed, the worker faced a much crueler road t recovery than those of more substantial means. The local insuranc companies that protected the homes of laboring men and women ha failed, leaving thousands with little or no assets. "No eastern o European capitalist came to his succor," declared O'Brien. "Hi mechanical skill and ten fingers remained his only friend." Still, h argued, for all of their troubles, the men of his union had retained sense of their obligations as citizens, from the first refusing to profit from the disaster-born demand with their pledge not to ask more than pre-Fire rates. A moral commitment to common interests had prevailed over market-driven individualism. But in O'Brien's view, his union's primary employers, the master builders of the city, were merely eager to protect their own earnings—and most certainly could not make the same claim. "Now mark their conduct in October with ours in May and it is a poor rule that don't work both ways," he ended. "'Don't take advantage of Chicago's misfortune' was their watchword then. 'Don't take advantage of Chicago's misfortune' is now our response to their demands."[157]

For all the validity of Medill's celebration of civic achievement, O'Brien's sharp reminder of the fundamental difference of class experience—both that of the disaster itself and in the realm of the market—also deserves close attention. While the mayor's account harbors much truth, it (and the history that followed from such a narrative) also elide another central reality: that the Great Rebuilding involved debates and conflicts over the structure and social meaning of the wage relation. These were questions and issues that would reverberate throughout the ascension of industrial capitalism in the latter years of the nineteenth century: What did workers owe to their employers? How should employers treat their workers? And how did the state of relations of employment contribute to the construction of a broader sense of what constituted social and economic order?

In post-Fire Chicago, in their separate and often opposing quests to claim to uphold a proper civic order, unionists and the foes of the collective action of workers held to distinct visions of the meaning of cooperation. Employers and men like Joseph Medill in general sought to elevate the individual in the market; only by behaving in this fashion could building tradesmen promote what more elite Chicagoans understood as the civic good of a cooperative working class. But for unionists, cooperation was instead synonymous with worker organization, and further named a larger labor movement ideology that called for the creation of market practices that moved toward a greater equalization of the resources commanded by workers and their employers. The struggle of Chicagoans to rebuild thus went hand in hand with a struggle to define how "free" individuals should best act within a market system, in the end revealing how the "natural partnership" of capital and labor did not maintain within it a true identity of interests for both sets of parties—and in fact involved permanent asymmetries of power.

CHAPTER FIVE
Laws and Order

On a Sunday, October 12, 1872, W. W. Everts, pastor of Chicago's First Baptist Church, delivered his commemoration of the first anniversary of the Great Fire. Standing firmly in the ranks of those who understood the calamity as divine vengeance—a claim made by some devout Christians from the first days that the city lay in ruins—the minister described a causal link between physical ruin and eroding standards of social conduct.[1] "It is true," he declared, "that this disaster pointed immistakably to the sins of this city."[2] Still, Everts managed to see the silver lining in what he understood as Chicago's collective punishment: in his view, such a trial might also prove the salvation of the city. Much as Joseph Medill's secular voice had emphasized the commercial and political benefits of disaster in his anniversary address at the Board of Trade, Everts described the aftermath of the Fire as a period rich in moral and religious opportunity. "The conflagration swept away the rubbish to prepare the way for a magnificent temple," he proclaimed. "It seemed a curse; but it was turned into a blessing." Given a fresh start by the hand of God, Chicagoans might recreate a purer urban world.

Yet the minister sharply broke with the celebratory tone that marked most public comment on the end of this most eventful year. Despite its similar focus on the opportunities born of crisis, this sermon was no valentine to a newly moral city. To the contrary, Everts used his pulpit to caution that any chance for spiritual gains now faced grave jeopardy. In the year since the fire, he soberly observed, a clean slate had been clouded by the quick return of old and evil habits: "[T]here has been a new departure in intemperance, profligacy, and crime." For Everts, the destruction of the city could not simply be dismissed as the product of bad planning or bad luck—and might well recur, should its divine message go unheeded. With their choice to concentrate on physical and economic rebuilding, by turning away from any substantial reconstruction of a common moral life, Chicagoans were tempting their collective fate. He ended with a blunt warning: "If we are simply growing in splendor . . . while our hearts are not right with God, we shall as truly bring upon ourselves a great curse as God reigns in the universe."

Reverend Everts worried that disaster would lead inexorably to an ever greater doom. Or might the Great Fire instead show the way to a higher plane of civic life? In raising these questions, he clearly drew upon a theological tradition laced with older strains of anti-urban and apocalyptic thought.[3] But as he spoke in October of 1872, his fears and hopes were magnified by a new controversy local to Chicago: an emerging battle over the enforcement of municipal Sabbatarian laws. Some three weeks before, a coalition of temperance activists had seized upon mounting anticrime sentiments to press for what they viewed as the key first step in a war on sins of all sort: police action in accordance with an 1845 ordinance that forbade the sale of intoxicating beverages on Sundays. While other Chicagoans, especially immigrants, would fiercely dispute the right of the city to enforce Sabbatarian laws, the way to civic order seemed plain to Everts and his followers. A Christian Sunday, according to such men and women, stood as a key foundation of the republic and the city; a day given over to peaceful reflection secured an essential elevation of "the family" and "spiritual culture and moral impulse"—indeed, of "the whole of civilization."[4] The biblical commandment to preserve a holy Sabbath thus demanded that municipal law curtail the operations of saloons and beer gardens; fidelity to the "ordinances of God" here required the subordination of what Sabbatarians described as the lesser dictates of "popular will."[5]

While disputes over temperance and a holy Sunday were certainly nothing new to "New Chicago," the aftermath of the Great Fire did witness an uncommonly vivid contest over the propriety of city regulation of the conduct of its residents. Between September of 1872 and November of 1873, the many ramifications of the fight over whether or not Chicagoans could buy liquor on Sunday largely defined the contours of organized politics.[6] These tensions obviously sprang in great part out of the conflicting social practices and moral visions of certain ethnic and religious groups—and thereby figured prominently in both the creation of ethnic identities and the forging of notions of cultural and political pluralism. Moreover, questions centering around temperance also involved far-reaching problems of the function of law and the "proper" role of the state. Like the Fireproof attempt to legislate citywide fire limits, the discussion pivoted upon differing understandings of what constituted a correct balance between the freedom of individuals and communal responsibilities. At that moment, wood construction seemed for some to pose a clear danger to all Chicago; now, for another group, Sabbath-day drinking appeared to lay at the roots of a dire threat to civic order. And much as working-class homeowners organized in the early months of 1872 to defend their capacity to rebuild, those who sought to preserve their "personal liberty" to spend Sunday however they saw fit made the argument that Sabbatarian codes were contrary to the most basic meaning of a republican society.

Public discussion consequently revolved around two major questions: whether private habits of Sabbath-day drink did or did not pose a threat to civic order, and what steps city officials should or should not take in response to such behavior. Also up for discussion were topics such as the meaning of "moral" conduct, how good citizens should spend their Sundays, and whether republican principles demanded municipal regulation of the consumption of alcohol *or* required the protection of personal freedoms. Related to all of this was a question that underlay more and more political debate in a city of growing ethnic diversity: Who could be a good "American," and on what terms? Yet, even as this new set of debates began to roil, the largest problem at issue remained the same: various Chicagoans again battled to achieve a municipal policy that served their particular understanding of civic order. Once more, a struggle to define and claim to represent a "public interest" brought a variety of positions to light—differing understandings of morality, law, and the role of the state generated by different communities within the city.

A PROPER SUNDAY

On a Sunday afternoon in mid-March of 1873, Frances Roberts "had a treat." On that day, the secretary of Robert Collyer's Unity Church and the former Relief and Aid worker finally went on an outing she had longed to take ever since her arrival in Chicago—a visit to "the great German *Halle* where they have all sorts of entertainment."[7] Her impressions of the Aurora Turner Hall describe a setting and ambience common to the many sizable saloons and halls frequented by German immigrants on their days off from work: in a "very large" room "with an immense gallery running all around," hundreds of men, women, and children had gathered to converse, drink beer, and enjoy an orchestra's performance of famous arias and "other music of the best quality."[8] Pipes and cigars, Roberts noted, were another favored pastime. "When I got home," she wrote to her mother, "I seemed to have been soaked in Tobacco smoke, and had to hang my clothes in the wind all day next day." But such an inconvenience seemed a trifling price to pay; as Roberts enthusiastically reported, "[T]he music was very fine, and the beer very good." Though most of her associates at Unity Church would have disapproved of how she spent this Sunday (even, as she confided, skipping a morning sermon by visiting dignitary Mary Livermore), Roberts personally saw nothing wrong with her alternative plans for the Sabbath day. "I enjoyed the scene," she concluded, "and shall want to go again, though other people think it very wicked to go at all."

As Frances Roberts well knew, various sorts of Chicagoans would have disagreed about the moral implications of her Sunday afternoon. For German-Americans, a family trip to a beer garden seemed a completely normal and enjoyable way to spend some of their often-scant free time with friends and neighbors.[9] For some churchgoers, the same excursion seemed a shocking disregard of religious decorum. Yet, whatever their particular feelings and beliefs, anyone would have conceded that Frances Roberts had in fact violated a municipal statute. Like other establishments that sold liquor on Sundays, the Aurora Turner Hall did its business in the face of Chapter 25, Section 4 of Chicago's City Ordinances: an 1845 regulation prohibiting the opening of any "tippling house on the Sabbath day or night."[10] While this law had gone unenforced and largely unnoticed virtually since its enactment, Roberts' venture came in the midst of the renewed post-Fire battle over the purpose, justice, and enforcement of Sabbatarian codes.

The contest began to take shape at the end of the Great Rebuilding; as the striking carpenters and bricklayers resolved their struggles over wages and hours, an anticrime movement ended up serving as a first platform for those committed to the cause of Sunday closing. Just as the seeming opportunities presented by the task of rebuilding drew thousands of workers to the city, disaster apparently attracted plenty of people looking to profit from dishonest labors. In the words of the journalist John J. Flinn, "[C]riminals of every description arrived in shoals."[11] Chicagoans began to witness a significant upsurge of thefts and muggings. "Footpads and sneak thieves are becoming very bold," reported the *Tribune* in January of 1872. "Scarcely a night passes but one or more men, detained at their work until a late hour, complain to the police about being garroted or relieved of every valuable they had in their possession."[12] The police could do little: the Great Fire had wiped away the traditional boundaries of vice districts, culprits could easily hide out in the ruins, and an entirely new company of offenders had arrived to supplement the criminal population already known to the force.[13] "The most experienced officers," observed Flinn, "had to learn their trade over again, just as if they had been assigned to duty in a new city."[14] For all the largely imaginary threats to "order" that had stirred anxieties after the Great Fire, disaster had in fact created a more crime-ridden city. "Never was there a time in the history of Chicago," asserted the *Times* in its anniversary comment, "when there was less security for persons and property than now."[15]

In early fall of 1872, when a string of murders punctuated a steady diet of less violent offenses, a coalition of leading citizens decided that enough was enough. Led by banker Henry Greenebaum, some sixty-five prominent businessmen—a coalition of both immigrants and the native-born—came together to express their dissatisfaction with the present systems of criminal justice. On September 10, Greenebaum, the German-American and Jewish community leader who had been the first choice of Joseph Medill for the post-Fire mayoralty, announced a rally in support of prompt trials and the capital punishment of murderers. Frustrated with the police—a force, they thought, that had been badly crippled by a legacy of aldermanic control—these commercial leaders proposed to create an anticrime organization run by "citizens": men who claimed to stand apart from the what they viewed as the corrupt realm of urban ward politics.[16] At this mass meeting, Greenebaum specifically hoped to establish a "Committee of Twenty Five": a task force of businessmen drawn in equal numbers from each of the city's three divisions that would be empowered to offer bounties, hire private detectives, and engage prosecuting attorneys.[17]

In interviews with the press, Greenebaum announced that his efforts had two closely related goals: to guard the security of all good citizens, *and* to maintain Chicago's all-important reputation as a safe place to do business. In a plea to his fellowmen of commerce, the banker argued that the foreign investors still essential to the process of rebuilding could quickly sour on a city where vice and danger were known to rule; everyone, he warned, might well worry that a gleaming "New Chicago" had risen from the ashes only to risk association with unsavory places such as Louisville and Baltimore—the two most notorious American cities of the day.[18] For the banker, as for so many urban boosters, a healthy and expansive economy lay at the bedrock of the public interest. Moreover, extending his appeal beyond the more specific concerns of businessmen, he called upon the "civic spirit" of all who had chosen to make Chicago their permanent home. The prevention of crime, according to Greenebaum, constituted a civic good that transcended any economic or ethnic divisions. Even in a city that he freely acknowledged to be built out of many sorts of communities, communities that at times hewed to conflicting interests, he firmly believed that the object of greater public safety would receive truly universal sanction. For who would oppose a war on crime? "The people of all classes are thoroughly aroused," he declared. "The feeling goes beyond party, nationality, and religion, and is shared alike by all good citizens."[19] In the name of the civic order to be upheld in a less dangerous city, harmony would surely rule.

At the September 12 mass meeting, however, it soon became clear that defining and seeking to act upon an anticrime mandate would prove much more troublesome than Henry Greenebaum had hoped. Sandwiched into the temporary Board of Trade building, a crowd of perhaps 2000 first heard speeches from the banker and from Charles Reed, the states' attorney. The gathering next registered their discontent with the police and the courts—resolving, with only one (anonymous) dissent, to create the Committee of Twenty Five. But the discussion then took a sudden turn toward a much more divisive subject. William Tooke, a physician, stood to offer the following resolution: "that we candidly commend to the authorities of this city the propriety of executing faithfully the Sunday liquor laws"—calling, in essence, for municipal enforcement of Sabbath day prohibition.[20] "Thereupon rose a most tremendous noise," reported the *Tribune*. "Some hissed and some applauded."[21] The raucous and split reaction to the doctor's proposal could not have come as a surprise, for it mirrored a long history of disputes over the municipal regulation of alcohol. But the assembly would not revisit these issues on this night. With some fancy parliamentary footwork, Greenebaum answered Tooke by engineering an instant adjournment—ending the meeting, as one correspondent admiringly wrote, "before the good doctor discovered he had been euchred."[22]

While Greenebaum's end-run for the moment postponed a discussion of Sunday closing, his rather dramatic reaction to a simple raising of the question suggests its extreme sensitivity. To be sure, the touchy subjects of governmental regulation of liquor and of the Sabbath day had already simmered in the city, state, and nation for decades. Sunday laws, a legacy of the colonial statutes of Puritan New England, moved West with settlers from that region. In a reflection of the then-relatively homogenous Protestant population of the Midwest, both the state of Illinois and the city of Chicago had such legislation on their books by the mid-1840s.[23] Still, though these codes were technically in force, the great majority of antebellum temperance activists had preferred to rely upon the voluntary education and rehabilitation of individuals; with the exception of the Maine Law movement of the early 1850s, few chose to press for the legal regulation of the conduct of the entire community.[24] Since persuasion, rather than coercion, operated as the watchword of most antidrink initiatives, activists in Chicago and throughout the nation seldom insisted upon the enforcement of these ordinances.[25] Efforts to apply liquor laws did lead to local flare-ups: the 1855 Lager Beer Riot, touched off by a Know-Nothing mayor's attempt to collect license fees from saloons, was the city's most notorious prewar temperance-related clash.[26] Often cited by protemperance forces in the Great Fire's aftermath as historical "proof" of the disrespect of immigrants for "American" ways, the incident involved a confrontation with the police that ended in the deaths of two marchers—a conflict notable in Chicago's antebellum history both for the deep feelings and violence it provoked and, according to Robin Einhorn, for its near-unique capacity to raise the question of what policy served a broader "public interest" at a time when city government normally steered well clear of any involvement in such determinations.[27]

During the war years, Chicago's role in the Union effort pushed the regulation of alcohol well off the center stage of city politics.[28] But by 1870, public debate over such laws had reemerged with full force. In his December "State of the City" address, Mayor R. B. Mason—a staunch antiliquor man denounced by German opponents as the worst kind of "Templerenzer"—bemoaned what he viewed as a shameful saloon-to-church ratio, proposing the creation of stricter licensing procedures.[29] And by the next April the city council faced a resolution on Sabbatarian enforcement.[30] Meanwhile, protemperance forces at the statehouse in Springfield were marshaling support for the "Ohio Law": an act that made saloon owners legally culpable for damages done to persons or property by anyone who had become intoxicated in their establishment. Over and above the bitter resistance of German-American legislators, the law passed in January 1872.[31]

By the fall of 1872, then, Chicagoans had resumed already long-standing battles over state control of alcohol—and were quickly becoming reacquainted with the deep divisiveness that such discussions engendered. At bottom, the conflict turned on the definition of just what constituted and best safeguarded "freedom" in an American city. Given the ethnic divisions brought to the fore by such competing claims, the problem in turn became conflated with a debate increasingly heard in urban politics: what it meant to be an "American" in the face of enduring "ethnic" traditions and identities. On one side, in the years after the Civil War, more and more evangelical Protestants convinced of the necessity of a uniform moral sensibility in America were turning from their prior faith in "voluntaryism" and persuasion toward a belief in the necessity of coercion. Their quest for a Christian America, a republic and a "civilization" devoted to and kept pure by an obedience to divine law, meant that the state had a duty to regulate the Sabbath-day habits of all citizens.[32] But such logic met with intense opposition. To those unconvinced of either the danger of drink or what was termed a "cosmopolitan" Sunday—and therefore unconvinced of the need for legal regulation in these arenas—liquor laws were commonly construed as assaults upon American guarantees of liberty. As one Chicago organization of German-Americans typically resolved in mid-1873, "neither the State, County, nor City have the right to impose upon one part of the population the view of another part of the population, as to how to attain happiness in this life and the hereafter."[33] The powers of government, according to such arguments, should never be used to enforce a particular moral standard.

Further, together with this fundamental rift over the proper nature of the civil state, temperance issues usually produced sharp fissures along the lines of ethnic and class identities. While some immigrant Chicagoans certainly favored liquor laws (and voluntary abstinence and moderation was supported by great numbers within the Irish and German communities), most of the foreign-born saw no inherent danger or immorality in the habit of social drinking, in passing time at a saloon or beer garden.[34] By contrast, those who readily vilified alcohol and promoted liquor laws were almost exclusively native-born men and women. Faced with such adversaries, immigrants often understood temperance initiatives as direct attacks upon the traditions of their homelands. An April 1873 letter to the *Staats-Zeitung* gives a sense of the content of this common grievance: "When we Germans believe that it benefits us after a week's work to fortify ourselves on Sunday through several glasses of beer with our friends, who has the power to forbid us to do that? Who has the power to force us to go to church, when we want to visit beer halls?"[35] Disparaging such regulatory efforts as the product of the "narrow and intolerant" minds of "Yankee Puritans," German-Americans here affirmed their own ethnic identity and simultaneously participated in the "ethnicization" of native-born Americans—making it plain through their stalwart defense of their customs that they were no longer strange interlopers in a nativistic America but one of many, if different, still legitimate groups staking a claim to recognition and power.[36]

Given the overall profile of the economic means of the groups at odds, class differences added further complications to this clash. Temperance activists were largely drawn from Chicago's more wealthy ranks; as minister David Swing wrote in 1873 of the connections between organized religion and native-born definitions of "respectable" affluence in Chicago, "The church is a stepping-stone to society as well as to heaven."[37] Their fight to close saloons on Sunday, the sole day of leisure for the mostly immigrant working people of the city, thus could be perceived and portrayed as a plain example of class tyranny. If the "rich money-bags" took away the "poor workingman's" right to relax in a tavern, music hall, or beer garden with friends and family, as *Staats-Zeitung* owner Anton Hesing declared in one formulation of this complaint, "nothing remained for him but work, work, work."[38] The chosen leisure of working people here seemed to come under attack from members of the class that already dictated most of the terms of their lives on the job and in the social hierarchy of the urban world.[39]

It seems a small wonder that temperance and Sabbatarianism, as catalysts for the public discussion of all of these intertwined questions of class, ethnicity, religion, and the role of government, stood apart as singularly volatile postbellum social issues in cities with large populations of immigrants. Small wonder as well that Henry

Greenebaum responded with such apprehension to the mere mention of the possibility of Sunday closing in Chicago; he probably recognized just how rapidly what he had understood as the "universal" appeal of his anticrime movement might break apart on this shoal. Only criminals liked crime, and no one could disavow the public good to be gained by achieving a safer city. Still, a world of differences could be exposed by debates over how best to rid Chicago of this problem. In a city that was home to established and sizable Irish and German communities, with temperance forces animated by their reading of the moral imperative of disaster, this battle to define civic order soon produced some uniquely turbulent political weather.

RIGHT VERSUS RIGHTS

On September 17, five days after its creation, the Committee of Twenty Five held its first meeting. Curiously (and none too auspiciously), only nine men managed to attend. According to a *Times* reporter, most of the evening passed in a "somewhat desultory" airing of personal opinions and grievances.[40] Greenebaum, the acting chair, once again expressed his dismay with the city's police, the lumber dealer R. P. Derrickson decried the inefficiencies of the trial system, and Public Works Commissioner Louis Wahl chastised reckless horse-car drivers, a set of men that he identified as an especially dire menace to civic safety. After holding forth for a while on the problems of pedestrianism, Wahl declared that he "had one more thing on his liver"—and he proceeded to drop what Greenebaum, his fellow German-American, must have considered to be something of a bombshell. Despite his foreign roots, announced the commissioner, he agreed entirely with those who "laid the root of our evils at the door of intemperance." Whiskey, proclaimed Wahl, was surely responsible for nine-tenths of all crime in Chicago. To sever this causal link between liquor and lawlessness, he reasoned, the city had to enforce its own law—and close all saloons on Sundays.

Predictably, this call to fight crime through Sabbatarian enforcement touched off a minor furor, drawing an immediate and combative response from Anton Hesing. How, he wondered, could Wahl allow himself to make the gross assumption that Sunday drinking inevitably led to criminal conduct? Derrickson followed Hesing into the fray, asking whether or not liquor laws needed to distinguish between the "Dutchman's beer" and the "Irishman's whiskey." "Was it right," he asked, "to hit at one and not the other?" Through their challenges, Hesing and Derrickson raised a host of knotty problems. Did Sabbatarian codes in fact retard crime? Should laws be directed against specific areas of the liquor trade? And, most sweepingly, did the city have the right to regulate the conduct of its citizens in such a manner? Greenebaum (whose hopes for police and judicial reforms doubtless were steadily receding) again attempted to settle the debate over Sunday drinking simply by refusing to hear it. Pointing to the lateness of the hour, he requested a postponement of the question—and promptly adjourned.

The disarray of the first meeting of the Committee of Twenty Five perhaps reflected the struggle of any new organization to find its ideological and structural footing. But the relatively diverse group of businessmen and civic leaders convened by Greenebaum did not have the time to iron out internal discord. Their own predictable splits over the causes of and proper responses to the complex problem of urban crime left this body vulnerable to being overwhelmed by a more unified lobby. For temperance activists stood ready to seize the mantle of crime fighting—and its lack of a clear agenda meant that the Committee of Twenty Five would not long control the discussion it had commenced. On September 25, two weeks after the banker made his first public call to action, another self-described committee of "citizens" invited all "order-loving" Chicagoans to another mass meeting: a gathering billed as an effort "to arrive at the cause of the present state of public demoralization."[41] But the ninety signers of this letter, all prominent Protestant clergymen and native-born businessmen and professionals who belonged to their congregations, had no intention of mirroring the lack of consensus displayed by the Committee of Twenty Five.[42] To the contrary, this second assembly meant to address the present problem of criminality by revivifying a long-held conclusion about the roots of lawlessness, a set of beliefs distilled out of an evangelical Protestant theory of what made for a godly life on earth. "What they will suggest as a prevention is not difficult to predict," observed the *Times*. "Most of the signers are strong advocates of prohibition."[43]

The next evening, a contingent of citizens again assembled at the Board of Trade, filling the same space as the previous meeting that had hatched the Committee of Twenty Five.[44] But this assemblage quickly staked out its own turf: the police, the courts, the effects of poverty, the presence of a great number of transients—all other possible explanations of the rise in crime were, as the *Times* had predicted, deemed secondary to the problem of drinking on the Sabbath day. Speaker after speaker railed against this root of lawlessness, making the argument that municipal control over the sale and consumption of alcohol plainly served the worthy end of securing public safety. In a comment that harkened back to the debate over wooden construction and the notion of a fireproof city, one orator, Dr. N. S. Davis, called for the elevation of civic needs over private rights, for the duty of government to protect all citizens from the contagious effects of drunkenness and criminality. "A man has to be careful when he puts up a building," he reasoned. "Was a man allowed to go ahead and make himself dangerous?" And a solution to the threat posed by individuals who menaced the city by their habits as Sabbath-day drinkers seemed within easy reach. Though long unenforced, Sabbatarian ordinances did exist—and their proper application, according to those assembled, could deliver Chicagoans from their present evils. "Put the law into practice," pronounced one confident Methodist minister, "and three-quarters of the crime would disappear in a week." The meeting did endorse anticrime measures apart from Sunday closing, nodding in particular to the good that rehabilitation and education might do. Still, what Henry Greenebaum had originally conceived as an overhaul of Chicago's police and courts, a "citizen's" movement capable of winning what he hoped would be the support of a diverse set of people, had been transformed into a Sunday closing crusade—a form of action that only one particular faction had endorsed as the way to lessening crime.

This second assemblage quickly moved to put its ideology into practice. Civic order, for the ministers and their followers, required the firm and fair administration of *all* civic rules; in their view, turning a blind eye to statutes clearly violated the public trust attached to any government office or service. Sabbatarian codes existed, they declared, and sharply questioned why they were not enforced. After engaging in some numerical one-upmanship by christening itself as the Committee of Seventy, the assembly promptly served notice that the elected officials of Chicago would no longer be allowed to shirk their duty, appointing a subcommittee to pay a visit to Mayor Medill. Finally, Reverend Abbott Kittredge closed the assembly with prayer—and a rousing reminder that the Great Fire, along with all its material consequences, had surely brought a window of spiritual opportunity to the city. "Let us look to the purity of our city no less than to the elegance of our building edifices," he proclaimed. Thusly charged, a small delegation prepared to ask the mayor to see to the citywide enforcement of their moral and civic vision.

Well aware of the storm brewing over Sunday closing, Joseph Medill had long expected these visitors. When the subcommittee appeared at City Hall on October 2, he had already prepared a characteristically thorough and lengthy statement. After an initial exchange of pleasantries, the delegation sat silently through the answer to their petition—an hour-long position paper on Sabbatarian codes.[45] Commencing with an unusual measure of tact, Medill was careful to express his sympathy for the abstract aim of promoting sobriety. "You need not waste words in trying to convince me of the evils of intemperance," he declared. "I allow it." But beyond this point, as he quickly made clear, he and his visitors shared scant common ground. Though he well understood the perils of an intemperate life, the mayor strongly disputed the precise linkage of post-Fire crime and Sunday drinking that undergirded the mission of the Committee of Seventy. For to his mind, common sense alone easily explained Chicago's crime wave. Since the Great Fire, as he noted, the city had endured a period of unprecedented disruption; to top the problem of physical dislocations, thousands of strangers—including many of the less than completely honest or noble—had streamed into Chicago. "Under these circumstances," asked Medill, "can it be wondered that crime and drunkenness have increased?"

Taking little time to fall back into his habitual bluntness, the mayor announced that Sunday closing offered no satisfactory solution to Chicago's present dangers. It was simply naive, he asserted, to think that the suppression of drink on one day of the week could bring about an overall transformation in the state of public safety and morality. He went on to argue that undertaking the task of Sabbatarian enforcement would further cripple the city's already strained ability to protect its people. Chicago could only afford 340 regular policemen, he noted, half of whom were off-duty at any given moment—and those on the job had their hands full. Thousands of saloons, beer gardens, restaurants, and retail stores sold liquor across the city; since the application of Sunday closing laws would fall to patrolmen, any such move promised to level an impossible burden upon the force.[46] Moreover, along with highlighting the impracticability of monitoring so large a number of establishments with so few men, Medill pointed to the fact that no sizable American city had ever successfully enforced its Sabbatarian codes. European immigrants, he observed, most often saw no wrong in the practice of social drinking on the Sabbath—or any other day. Given that Sunday closing crusades in Boston and Brooklyn (two renowned strongholds of Protestantism) had recently met with complete failure, how could Chicago hope to control the Sabbath-day practices of its even more largely foreign-born population? If people wanted to drink, declared Medill, they would find a way. Ever a believer in the laws of supply and demand, the mayor curtly dismissed Sunday closing as a waste of public resources. He ended with this sentiment: "Whether good or evil, on Sundays or weekdays," the appetites of individuals for their liquor would keep this market very much alive.

Medill here displayed his wide streak of secularism, a growing sensibility among post–Civil War political leaders that the civil state had no business acting in service of the moral codes dictated by traditional Christianity.[47] While he personally did not endorse Sunday drinking, Medill accepted the practice—and the tolerance for cultural pluralism that such an acceptance involved—as a fact of modern American urban life. And while the mayor therefore did not oppose the desire of Sabbatarianists to reverse what they viewed as the "demoralization" of the city, he strongly disputed their tactics. If champions of Sunday closing truly wished to improve their city, he argued, they first needed to abandon their reliance upon coercive legislation. Sunday drinking, he thought, would cease when individuals made a private decision to stay away from saloons; education and persuasion, rather than governmental regulation, would bore to the root of this social problem. As Medill informed the delegation, the city could not direct its energies toward a task that, to his mind, correctly belonged to the churches—and any other voluntary organizations pledged to combat intemperance. In an interesting reversal of his position on the issue of fire limits, Medill, the staunch advocate of a citywide ban on wood construction, employed some of the same arguments set out by his opponents in that earlier fight. "Blanket regulation" of this social practice, the mayor now declared, served no good purpose; it was erecting a too-sweeping barrier to individual freedom that only invited transgressions. In the case of a "personal" liberty that did not present any clear and immediate danger to property, he could envision no useful and appropriate role for state authority.

His visitors, however, had a clear sense of the rightfulness of that same role—and the many objections of Medill of course failed to appease his visitors. Three days later, the Committee of Seventy issued a highly aggrieved response to the mayor's missive.[48] The Sunday closing forces set out a step-by-step refutation of Medill's claims, forcefully affirming the multiple civic interests they believed to be served by a Christian Sabbath. They ended by playing their trump card, restating a simple but potent fact. The law, proclaimed the committee, was the law—and the mayor was obligated to see to its enforcement. How, asked the temperance lobby, could the civic leader of Chicago ignore its civic code? A history of nonenforcement, an undermanned police force, a series of ideological quibbles—all of these excuses, according to the committee, were quite besides the point. "He is not to stop in the performance of his duties to criticize a law, or speculate upon the probability of its complete success," insisted a team of spokesmen. "It is his sworn duty to enforce the law."

Hailed not so many months before as Chicago's savior, as the head of a Union-Fireproof slate that stood apart from the ordinary "corruption" of urban politics, Medill was now deemed a disgrace. For this group, his anticlosing stance had soured his reputation to the point where he seemed to exemplify the style of politics that his Fireproof campaign had promised to quash. Displaying a convenient ability to forget that their mayor had been chosen for office precisely because he had never mixed in local ward politics—and that all of the same native-born businessmen and professionals who made up the Committee of Seventy had rejoiced at his election—Sunday closing leaders announced that Medill (teetotaler though he might be) was in fact a slave to "liquor interests." "We have an executive officer," blasted the committee, "who has not the conscience or the moral courage to do right, and would rather violate his oath of office than offend the voting power of the saloons to which he owes his election."

Such perceived ethical shortcomings, however, paled in comparison to what the committee saw as Medill's worst sin: his betrayal of his own "American" heritage. His defense of secularism and pragmatic acceptance of the norms of German and Irish culture clashed entirely with what the committee described as "the genius of American civilization," a Protestant definition of national tradition did not have room for immigrant habits of Sunday drink. Their response to the mayor vividly confirmed the group's equation of the Sunday law, a civic order made secure by a Christian Sabbath, and a proper sense of "American" values of sobriety, piety, and respect for the Fourth Commandment: "The ordinances of the city are not to be set aside or trampled down or made a mockery in order to suit the conflicting notions and customs of foreign lands." In contesting this vision, by naming Sunday closing as a relic of a time when state enforcement of a unitary Protestant morality could be seen as a proper act of civic guardianship, by admitting a toleration of cultural difference born of the reality of the far more diverse demographics of late-nineteenth century cities—Medill, once again, displayed an unswerving (and highly impolitic) honesty. For the Committee of Seventy, their former champion had clearly fallen from grace.

A novice officeholder unused to such quick reversals of fortune and opinion and a relatively sensitive public figure, Medill was deeply stung by these assaults on his integrity. Moreover, he now confronted an impossible quandary. Though quite disinclined to risk the limited police resources and fragile cultural unity of the city to secure what he viewed as the largely pointless end of Sabbatarian enforcement, he still had to reckon with the hard fact that Sunday closing was the law of both Chicago and Illinois—and that he, as the chief executive of the city, was duty-bound to see to its enforcement. Facing a true Hobson's choice, the mayor publicly announced his decision in an October 10 communique to Chicago's police commissioners, the civic officers directly empowered to command the force.

In his message, a very unhappy mayor hit back at his critics, accusing them of forcing him to exercise an "abnormal" form of civil authority. Why, he asked, did these men and women of the church have so little confidence in their own powers of persuasion? Twenty-five years ago, he noted, the labors of voluntary societies such as the Washingtonians and Father Matthews Associations had proven object lessons in effective temperance work.[49] Relying upon "arguments, reasons, and tender appeals directed to the conscience of the people," declared the mayor, "their success was wonderful."[50] Legal coercion had no place in their project; never, Medill pointedly remarked, did the efforts of such groups "resort to the constabulary." But the Sabbatarianists who now prevailed upon his office to enforce their will were guilty, he charged, of an "odd deficiency of faith." Drawing an extremely unflattering comparison, Medill deplored what he viewed as the utter hypocrisy of the Committee of Seventy's choice to elevate compulsion over conversion, referring to what he viewed as a most evil historical precedent involving the joining of the powers of the church and the state. "The Inquisition," he proclaimed, "was based on the same lack of faith in the efficacy of moral and spiritual methods to cure heresy in men."

But while the mayor took pains to display his abhorrence of the methods of moral and social reform preferred by the evangelical Protestants of his city, he nonetheless felt compelled to do their bidding. Sunday closing, he allowed, was indeed the law. As such, it was his duty to put Sabbatarian enforcement into practice: "[A] sworn officer of the law," he wrote, "cannot refuse to enforce it." Though the obligations of his office were plainly at war with his personal judgment, Medill in the end saw no choice but to hold to the letter of the civic code. As he instructed the police commissioners, "I therefore and hereby ask your board to enforce Chapter 4 of Section 25 of the city ordinances, and all other ordinances related thereto."

Police Superintendent Elmer Washburn, himself a controversial figure who was most unpopular with the force he commanded, did not act immediately on the mayor's charge.[51] On the next Sunday, October 13, trade in liquor went forth much as usual; according to the *Tribune*, only "one or two of three hundred North Side saloons" bothered to hide their usual crowd of beer drinkers behind closed doors and dropped blinds.[52] Patrolmen stood idly by and (as was the custom of many who walked beats) even stopped in to socialize with patrons; because the force had not yet been so ordered by their commander, they took no steps toward enforcement. But on October 16, prodded by a visit from another Committee of Seventy delegation, Washburn issued General Order #6—a directive requiring officers, whenever they saw an open saloon on Sunday, to present its owners with a summons to appear before the Police Court.[53] October 20 thus took on a special significance for Chicagoans: it was to be the first truly dry Sabbath in their city.

As October 20 approached, more than a few voices spoke out to condemn this turn of events. Attorney Barney Caulfield, one of the still-functioning (but none-too-healthy) Committee of Twenty Five, lamented the Committee of Seventy's appropriation of the original mandate of his organization. "We were appointed," he reminded, "not so much to enforce morality and temperance as to fight crime."[54] Echoing Medill, Caulfield expressed his distrust of such state coercion in the name of civic order; "[N]o people," he asserted, "could be made moral by legislative enactment." At the same meeting, Henry Greenebaum worried that the temperance lobby had cast far too broad a regulatory net. Plenty of German Chicagoans, he warned, would bitterly resent Sabbatarian enforcement, a step they were sure to view as an intolerable assault upon their personal liberties to spend their Sundays however they might choose.[55] Greenebaum condemned the Committee of Seventy's conflation of crime-fighting with Sunday closing, declaring that he would be forced to resign from his own committee if the tenor of civic discussion did not change—a statement he made good on October 24.

Anton Hesing, who also soon tendered his resignation, likewise denounced those who would tamper with the Sabbath-day customs of the Germans.[56] However sincere their beliefs, the publisher argued, religious Chicagoans were not entitled to insist that the rest of the city adopt their moral standards. "As long as it is quietly and decently carried on," as he declared in a pointedly provocative comparison, "a saloon has the same right as a church."[57]

Two months of wrangling over how best to fight crime had done little to ward off thieves and murderers—but had produced a stark three-way split over the issue of how best to secure this form of civic order. As the police began to hand out summonses, the social identities of particular groups to a large degree figured into their political demands and affinities. Sabbatarianists, mostly evangelical Protestants committed to a Christian agenda for the civil state, were thoroughly convinced of their duty to end Sunday drinking. But their stalwart stance had energized an equally stalwart opposition: German-Americans and other immigrants were similarly sure of their duty to resist enforcement. They thereby sought to stake a claim to a vision of "American" freedom that in no way hinged on the enforcement of a particular religious agenda but, by contrast, had to be inclusive of cultural and moral differences. In a middle ground, more secular native-born businessmen and professionals like Joseph Medill perhaps sympathized with the aims of Sabbatarianists, but felt that a mustering of state power to serve a particular form of religiously derived moralism was wrong, that an array of traditions and social practices had to be tolerated in a modern American age. And more pragmatically, the mayor and fellow Republicans worried that a hard line on Sunday drinking might drive German-Americans out of their party, further weakening an already eroding Civil War coalition. With the issuance of Superintendent Washburn's General Order, all of these interested parties watched as the previously more abstract debate over the propriety of Sunday drink in Chicago skidded toward a concrete climax. Could the city actually enforce a dry Sabbath? What would be the consequences of such a step?

At 10:00 A.M. on October 20, as hundreds of churchgoers streamed into their morning services, 500 German-Americans stepped out to attend to a different sort of business. In a carnivalesque display that must have infuriated the Committee of Seventy, a band of saloon keepers and brewers paraded a train of beer wagons through the North Side, freely dispensing samples to all who wished to partake. The marchers thus lampooned Sunday closing by taking advantage of a legal technicality: municipal ordinances forbade the sale of intoxicating beverages, but no civil authority could interfere with such hand-outs. Other Sabbath day drinkers found different ways to indulge their habit. Some made the short trip beyond Chicago's northern limits, joining boisterous crowds that filled the beer gardens and saloons in neighboring Lakeview. Better-heeled residents visited the hotels and restaurants of the South Division; though licensed purveyors of alcohol, such establishments did not fall under the law's specific regulation of "tippling houses." Still others patronized wholesale liquor stores, which similarly remained outside of the scope of the Sunday ordinance. And many women simply resorted to the traditional suppliers of that sex: the more expensive but more discreet drugstores. "The apothecaries," observed the *Tribune*, "were simply radiant. . . . They were continually relieving distress from bottles labeled 'Laudanum' and 'Castor Oil'."[58]

In addition to exploiting all of these legal loopholes, Sunday drinkers benefitted from the simple fact that no law can be enforced if the police and the courts fail to notice and respond to its violation. Over the next few weeks, vigilant Sabbatarianists—bolstered by the work of several private investigators hired by the Committee of Seventy—swore out hundreds of complaints before the police magistrates of the city. But such efforts largely proved to be futile. The Police Courts, especially that of the North Division, dismissed the great majority of such cases on the grounds that the entry of a police officer into an offending saloon constituted an illegal search.[59] Saloon keepers, saloon customers, and the police and magistrates thus arrived at a mutual understanding: on Sundays, if taverns and beer gardens decorously lowered their blinds and had their customers enter and exit via rear doors, no patrolman would interfere. "Thanks to the insight and indulgence that the police and police court officials have shown," the *Staats-Zeitung* reported approvingly in mid-November, "the tavern keepers have so far suffered little from the Sunday law."[60]

By exploiting the gap between the law and the mechanics of its enforcement, Sunday drinkers and purveyors of drink remained virtually free from any new regulation. Still, such an accommodation neither resolved nor silenced the political debate surrounding Sabbatarianism. As the Sunday closing lobby tried in vain to secure enforcement, German Chicagoans in particular continued to voice their anger at a series of public meetings and in the press, again and again raising the banner of "personal liberty." In response to the uproar, a *Tribune* writer sought to explain this immigrant watchword to his largely native-born readership by creating a German everyman—one "Mr. Schmidt." Encountering a locked door at his neighborhood tavern, "Mr. Schmidt" enters into a telling meditation upon his (and, by extension, his community's) attitude toward state control of Sunday drink:

> He asks himself whether the results of a long civil war, of the loss of 100,000 lives, has been that he, an American freeman, is deprived of the inestimable blessing of drinking beer on Sunday. Has free government come to this? Had he left a despotism abroad, where beer drinking was allowed, to come to a republic where it was not permitted?[61]

A shuttered saloon thus could "strike at the very foundation of belief"; "Mr. Schmidt" was moved to wonder just what "freedom" meant in his new homeland. What might seem a parodic tone in fact quite accurately reflected the intensity of feeling bound up in these questions. For these German immigrants, a central vision of the meaning of American republicanism here had been betrayed.

Echoing such sentiments in a speech before an October 24 mass meeting, Frank Lackner, an attorney, further invoked the specter of years of German-American struggles with nativism. His community, he declared, had already battled for decades to receive what he felt to be their full and obvious due as American citizens: a form of respect and validation that of course included their freedom to express themselves through visibly "ethnic" traditions. Lackner did not hesitate to name the enemies of his people, lashing out at the "narrow" and unreasonable minds of evangelical Protestants. Were the temperance people, he asked, in fact so deluded as to believe that "a race that has fought for years for its rights would be swindled out of them by a handful of fanatics?"[62] The *Staats-Zeitung* ran a series of heated editorials, similarly rallying all Germans against encroachments upon what it viewed as inviolable national freedoms. A piece on the first ostensibly "dry" Sunday thus dusted off a slogan long applied to attempts to enact or enforce liquor laws: "There is only one thing to be done: determined resistance and firm union."[63] Faced with an external challenge to their identity as good Americans, German immigrants drew together on the grounds of ethnic difference to defend their proper place in their new homeland.[64]

In response to such barbed pronouncements, *Tribune* editorialists began to express their worry about the ardent sentiments fueled by the debate, and the seeming erosion of any more moderate paths. Due to its highly divisive nature, the writers declared, Sunday closing was an issue certain to polarize the city and thereby, in and of itself, presented a threat to urban order. The paper accordingly urged the exercise of tolerance and reason, arguing that the great majority of saloons and beer gardens were simply neighborhood gathering spots that posed no danger to the public. And beer itself, in the *Tribune*'s view, was likewise harmless; as an editorial explained in a comparison meant to resonate with its native-born readership: "To say to a German that his daily beverage is intoxicating in character and is flooding the community with crime is just as absurd and unjust as it would be to say to the American that his use of coffee and tea is deleterious to the public morals."[65] One group's attack on crime, the paper recognized, was another group's attack on culture, tradition, and identity—an assault sure to elicit a furious and thereby conceivably ominous response.

Moreover, apart from the particular ethnic and cultural hostilities raised by Sunday closing, the editors insisted that the true problem at hand involved a question over what constituted the correct role of government in a civil society. The most perilous danger at hand, according to the *Tribune*, plainly was not liquor or crime. Rather, the city stood at risk from potential consequences of an abuse of civic authority, of an attempt to use state power to advance what most citizens understood as the particular moral agenda of a religious minority. If advocates of Sunday closing continued to insist upon the obedience of the city to the letter of the law, the paper therefore cautioned, civic unrest would inevitably ensue—in the form of popular protest of this misguided application of municipal authority. Churchgoers could say goodbye to their quiet Sabbath days: as the events of the first "dry" Sabbath had so plainly demonstrated, enforcement would "crowd our streets on Sundays with processions, music and banners, and noisy demonstrations." Worse, argued the editors, such conduct could easily lead to more serious upheavals: "It will tend to provoke violence and perhaps bloodshed." Fearful of the disorder to be spawned by this law, unpersuaded that such a code did anything to fight crime, the *Tribune* asked all "responsible" citizens to weigh what it saw as the alarming cost of Sunday closing against its highly dubious benefits. "Is it wise," asked the paper in concluding, "to deliberately array the German population against the Americans on a question of conscience for the sake of enforcement of an obsolete law in a manner so palpably unwise and unprofitable?"[66]

Such opinions, however, brooked no sympathy in the Sabbatarian camp, whose faith remained unshaken. Intensifying their ongoing criticism of Medill and other officials, the Committee of Seventy also began to condemn the German-born residents of the city, even more explicitly turning the question of Sunday drink into an acid test of "American" civilization and values. At a West Side temperance meeting on November 1, for example, a speaker accused "the Germans" of raising only "false issues," denying that Sunday closing had any relation to the problem of "personal liberties." The annals of history, he went on to imply, entirely discredited the claims of immigrant Germans to possess any understanding of the concept of American rights. While he professed personally to hold a "kindly feeling" toward these people, everyone had to recall that "several thousand Hessians once came here to prevent Americans from gaining their liberties." How could the heirs of these hired guns—the thugs of the Revolution—ever be trusted to know the best course for the nation, let alone the city?[67] No matter that Chicago's immigrants had come from all over a country just forged out of a diverse set of principalities and states: the acts of certain Germans close to 100 years before had cast a shadow over an entire people.[68] As the *Tribune* had worried, such essentialized visions of ethnic identity seemed certain to create a polity that was not only split but at war.

In addition, the Sabbatarianists moved beyond their critique of the particularities of German history, making the argument that any immigrant who sought to retain an "ethnic" custom that somehow offended native-born Americans should automatically be marked as a bad citizen, as a person made suspect and dangerous by their difference. One week earlier, before the German-Americans of Chicago would be denounced as the Hessians of their day, another Sunday closing rally had listened to a homily from a familiar voice, a blunt claim that immigrants had no right to doubt or seek to modify what already stood as the glory of "American" civilization. On the evening of October 24, 300 supporters assembled at the North Side Unity Church. There they heard Reverend Robert Collyer—the same man who had engaged Anton Hesing on the question of fire limits—again call upon the Germans of Chicago to recognize what he viewed as the true obligations of American citizenship: a duty to accept the genius of the laws of their adopted country, and a complete conformity to what already were enshrined as its moral and cultural norms.[69]

In a virtual reprise of his comments on the subject of the Fireproof City, the minister made a claim to an authentic understanding of the problem, reminding his audience that he too was an immigrant—but one who believed in obeying any law on the books, "whether he liked it or not." The Germans, he declared, were in many ways a wonderful people; even if they did drink a great deal of beer, they were a race blessed with the "fine points of industry, frugality, and temperance." Still, according to Collyer, the German community had one glaring fault: as the events surrounding the fire limits debate had revealed, Germans were far too ready to use their newly found freedoms to challenge the rule of native-born Americans. As men and women who owed any present prosperity to the opportunities they found as immigrants, Germans were obliged to adhere to the civic codes adopted by "original" citizens; the members of this community, argued the minister, had "to begin to identify themselves with the native-born." American citizenship, he felt, required working toward assimilation, toward acceptance of a set of common and universal practices and values rooted in the traditions held dear by native-born Protestants. Since civic order required a holy Sabbath, a toleration of cultural pluralism was *not* a reasonable demand.

Along with his vigorous defense of a one true America established by true Americans, Reverend Collyer raised two potent issues that would resurface as this conflict continued: to what degree a stable order in a free society depended upon obedience to its laws, and to what degree the process of enforcement should rely upon the use of force. By disregarding or otherwise sabotaging the Sunday closing ordinance, he argued, many in Chicago (including many officers of the state) were openly flouting the codes that were meant to safeguard the city and its people. This, declared the minister, was a grave and disturbing development. For the law—and respect for it—lay at the bedrock of any higher human civilization; "Without the force of law," he asserted, society would disintegrate. Given the critical importance of the law to the basic shape of civic order, Collyer was horrified by the laxity and disrespect displayed from the mayor on down.

By contrast, he felt that every possible step should be taken to secure enforcement; the minister stood more than ready to sanction the use of coercive force to convince all citizens of what he saw as their essential duty to conform to the rule of Sunday closing. Unlike the German and Irish Americans who were, he felt, so gleefully subverting the stability of their city, this immigrant, as Collyer made clear, "was on the side of law and the maintenance of law." As he announced to a cascade of cheers, he stood on alert, if need be, "to raise a company and fight for it."[70] If obedience to the law stood as a synonym for civic order, then any resistance to the rightfulness of an existing statute—even one now apparently representative of the will of a minority—could seem so threatening that calls for force seemed necessary and proper.

Chicagoans now found themselves at loggerheads. A distinct but highly vocal minority remained convinced that dry Sabbaths would pave the way to a newly cleansed and far more stable urban order, while a clear majority, for a variety of practical and ideological reasons, saw the Sabbatarian ordinance as at best useless and at worst a despotic and possibly explosive application of state power. Was it in the best interest of the city to enforce this law? Or was it best ignored? For Committee of Seventy spokesman George Scoville, the quest for civic safety plainly required the enforcement of Sunday closing. He made his point with a simile sure to strike deep chords in the still-rebuilding city: "People get drunk in saloons and therefore become dangerous to the community. So it is proposed we stop it, as we would a match factory."[71] In its comments, the *Tribune* employed a related set of images that played upon a fear of fire—but in service of a contrary message. Chicagoans, the editors observed, already well knew just how dangerous tampering with liquor laws could be. Attempts at municipal regulation of alcohol, they argued, had and would continue to spark intense debates over issues basic to the identity of particular communities within the city. Moreover, Sunday closing raised central questions about the functions and limits of government, crystallizing a struggle that would surely next move into the realm of formal electoral politics—a prospect that the editors clearly found to be most unwelcome. Referring to the violence of the 1855 Lager Beer Riots (an incident it deemed "A Useful Bit of History"), the paper offered the following caution: "How easy it is to start a large conflagration from kindling material."[72]

WHO GOVERNS?

Back in mid-summer of 1872, in the months just prior to the early autumn crime wave that would lead to ascension of the Committee of Seventy, the Great Rebuilding continued apace. Yet for Joseph Medill, even at this relatively early point in his term, the duties of executive office had apparently worn thin. On July 15, the mayor sent a letter to the Common Council, informing the aldermen of Chicago of his wish to absent himself from the city for a period of unspecified length, but probably in the realm of two or three weeks. In order to insure the smooth functioning of the municipality in his absence, Medill asked that an "Acting Mayor" be designated to assume his powers.[73] Three days later, however, the mayor changed his mind, sending along a brief message that he had reconsidered his earlier request and would continue to be present at City Hall.[74] But by the late summer of the next year, after another thirteen months in the mayoralty, his patience and stamina were utterly spent. On August 11, 1873, Medill suddenly resigned from office.[75] Within the week he had closed his West Side home, taken a train to New York City, and was occupying a first-class cabin on a steamer bound for Europe, where he and his family would wait out the duration of his term in the comforting isolation of a Paris flat.

Though abrupt, the abdication of the mayor was not unexpected. From his first days on the job, Medill had taken poorly to the style and pace of elected office; his habitual earnestness, stiff formality, and fairly thin skin did not serve him well in a position that often demanded flexibility and compromise. In nineteen eventful months, the high hopes of a very serious man had become the butt of a biting and widely circulated joke: "Yes, he has changed from Fireproof to waterproof!"[76] While Medill had managed to swallow his failure to secure citywide fire limits, accepting the solution hammered out by the Common Council, the problem of Sunday closing presented him with a truly no-win situation. His resistance to sabbatarian enforcement estranged him from the Committee of Seventy and their followers, a group of citizens who had rejoiced at his election. And once Medill gave into the demand that he hold the city to the letter of its law, he drew the scorn and animosity of German-Americans, former allies who had once stood at the heart of the mayor's greatest political achievement, the Civil War–era Republican party of Illinois.[77] His unusual elevation to his office within a month of the Great Fire thus ended in a singular legacy for his term: as the *Staats-Zeitung* trenchantly commented in May of 1873, "Mr. Medill will have the distinction to have been esteemed as highly, and later to have been esteemed as little, as no one else has previously."[78] With his life-long dream of officeholding turned to ashes by the realpolitik of his city, the inability of Medill to complete his term seems almost a foregone conclusion.[79]

Yet along with this toxic mix of personality and circumstance, it is important to note that Joseph Medill held to a set of ideals that did not mesh well with the reality of democratic process in an increasingly diverse city. An exemplar of prevailing notions of liberal reformism, the mayor believed in a vision of urban order that rested upon the definition of a unitary civic interest. His ambition, as the *Tribune* reported it, was "to be Mayor of all Chicago—not of a clique, party or faction."[80] He was certain that an educated, enlightened, and fair-minded leader (or set of leaders) could, through rational deliberation, in fact speak for and act in the best interests of an entire polity.[81] Like the Progressive urban reformers that he to some degree anticipated, Medill believed that a city in some sense could be "managed" by its "best men"—the "disinterested" experts of his day.[82] These people, he felt, could rightly identify the civic interest and therefore determine the course of municipal policy. For all its claims to universalism, such thinking was of course in itself rooted in a particular identity. But Medill, like the rising class of businessmen and professionals that he in many ways represented, reflexively made the assumption that a stance emanating from his own social position should function as a norm, as a way to measure the shape of civic order as a whole.

A ward-based system of representation, however, presented a liberal like Medill with an intractable institutional form.[83] Even with the aid of the extraordinary powers granted by the "Mayor's Bill" passed immediately after the Great Fire by the Illinois legislature, the ability of the mayor to act remained sharply constrained by the Common Council—a set of alderman who were ultimately beholden to the individual voters who resided in their wards. As the debate over citywide fire limits had proven, a mobilized majority of immigrants and working people could effectively thwart the agenda advanced by Medill on behalf of a relatively wealthy and native-born group of citizens. In a time of growing class, ethnic, and cultural differences, it thus had became more and more plain only a die-hard idealist could aim to serve as "the Mayor of all Chicago." For politics and policy making in the city had by this time moved into the realm of the competing interests that were often a product of differing social identities, the sorts of groupings and coalitions that the *Tribune* mocked as mere "cliques" and "factions."[84] Yet more and more people saw nothing wrong with what might be deemed a form of pluralism, with staking a claim to a civic interest that was rooted in a particular identity—an identity that indeed was often and bluntly so named as a way to claim political authority.

As 1873 began and municipal elections drew nearer, as the question of Sunday closing became firmly intertwined with electoral politics, the mayor must have seen that unless he resigned he stood to become a key player in the sort of struggle that he could not accept or tolerate, let alone manage or win. For as soon as the seriousness of a Sabbatarian crusade became evident, German-American leaders had begun to organize a practical defense of their community at the ballot box. An immigrant vote counted just as much as one cast by an advocate of a dry Sabbath, they reminded—urging Chicago Germans, just as they had in response to earlier temperance initiatives, that they should support only those candidates who had pledged to resist Sunday closing.[85] Thanks to the timing of the next municipal elections, the Committee of Seventy (and all other citizens of Chicago) now faced an unanticipated result of the push to fight crime through Sunday closing. By spring, it was clear that the upcoming race for civic office in early November—the selection of a mayor, other executive officers, and half of the Common Council—would largely unfold as a referendum on a single issue: the propriety of state-enforced Sabbatarianism.

In Chicago, as never before, what men like Medill would deride as a politics of "interests" therefore came to shape the contours of a citywide election. Others, of course, saw this same moment as a happy flowering of pluralism, as an opportunity for immigrant and working-class Chicagoans to name their interests as those of their city—and for their chosen (and to some degree, self-appointed) political leaders to assume control of municipal governance.[86] By election day, the communities at odds over Sunday closing had organized themselves into distinct partisan groupings, organizations named to reflect their most basic ideals and identities. On November 4, an unprecedented coalition of German and Irish immigrants known as the "People's party" squared off against the Law and Order ticket, a creation of the native-born clergy, businessmen, and professionals who stood in the ranks of those who understood a holy Sabbath to be essential to the maintenance of urban order. A competition for ballots throughout the city would once and for all reveal just what the voting polity of Chicago saw as the sort of Sunday, the sort of government, and the sort of linkages between identity and citizenship that upheld what they understood to be in their own best interests. It now remained, as a Committee of Seventy spokesman pronounced, "for the people themselves to chose for themselves."[87]

As the fall of 1872 gave way to the winter of 1873, drinking on the Sabbath (or any other day) moved indoors—and few champions of Sunday closing had the fortitude to walk the streets in search of offenders. During the rigors of cold weather, the subject of Sabbatarianism accordingly lost a great deal of its urgency. But in April, Police Superintendent Washburn was suddenly no longer willing to allow his officers to turn a blind eye to violations, and he took the step that roused the controversy from its hibernation.[88] With the apparent sanction of Medill, the superintendent directed patrolmen to move far more aggressively toward the end of enforcement, ordering the force "to enter frequently on Sunday all places or rooms on their respective beats where they have good reason to believe that intoxicating drinks are sold."[89] But Washburn here encountered a barrier to his own authority: due to internal dissension among the police commissioners over the validity of Sunday closing, the command was never formally transmitted.[90] Still, mere news of the aims of the superintendent was enough to draw an intense reaction from those committed to the cause of "personal liberties"; his command, as the *Staats-Zeitung* reported, "caused a sensation."[91]

Immigrant political leaders, men who had already been agitating for months on the subject of Sunday closing, now could proceed with the project of creating a political party. *Illinois Staats-Zeitung* publisher Anton Hesing, the most prominent leader of the German Republicans, called upon all of the foreign-born voters of Chicago—the mass of the working people of the city—to stand together against those who demanded state regulation of their Sabbath-day habits. "Germans, Irish, and Scandinavians," he declared, "should consider it a duty of self-preservation to unite at the next election."[92] Moreover, the injury done to the "poor worker" by this blatant attempt to impose control over their precious leisure needed to be redressed: this fight for civic office, Hesing announced, was also the "cause of

DEVOTED TO REAL ESTATE INTERESTS, BUILDING, COMMERCIAL PROGRESS, MANUFACTURES AND IMPROVEMENT.

Entered according to Act of Congress in the year 1873, by J. M. Wing & Co., in the Office of the Librarian of Congress, at Washington.

VOL. V.—NO. 4. CHICAGO, APRIL, 1873.—SUPPLEMENT. $1.00 A YEAR, IN ADVANCE. SINGLE COPIES, TEN CENTS.

THE CHICAGO SITUATION—A HISTORICAL SKETCH OF OUR MUNICIPAL DIFFICULTIES.

MAYOR M—— *as King Henry IV.*—Now, Lords, if heaven doth give successful end to this (liquor) debate that bleedeth at our doors, we will our youth lead on to higher fields, and draw no swords but what are sanctified. * * * * * Only, we want a little *personal strength;* and pause us, till these REBELS now afoot, come underneath the yoke of government.—*King Henry IV., Act IV., Scene 4.*

Newspaper cover cartoon satirizing Sabbatarian initiatives of 1872–73. Mayor Medill sits on the throne at left, attended by temperance men, while a crowd of immigrants (led by a representative German and Irishman with their arms linked) make a boisterous entrance. The dog with a man's face (right bottom) represents Elmer B. Washburn, the controversial police commissioner appointed by Medill. Mark Sheridan, carrying the banner of the Police Board, tramples over the extra authority supposedly granted to Medill by the Mayor's Bill. Source: *The Land Owner,* April 1873. Courtesy of Chicago Historical Society.

the workingman."[93] To launch a fusion based upon class and ethnic identities, old partisan divisions had to fall. The question of Sunday closing thereby led straight to the creation of what even supporters of the new pan-ethnic coalition would describe as a "bastard child": an unlikely confederation of the mostly Democratic Irish with the mostly Republican Germans and Scandinavians.[94]

In an atmosphere where any sort of ethnicity seemed new grounds for solidarity, and appeals to a common class grievance resonated across other sorts of social divisions, the People's party would at least for the moment allow the immigrants of Chicago to set aside their more traditional partisan loyalties. Formally christened with its populist appellation at a May 21 mass meeting on the North Side, the party gained great momentum a week later, when Democrat Dan O'Hara, a Scots-Irish immigrant who served as the clerk of the County Court, publicly appeared with long-time Republican Hesing to announce his support for the new organization.[95] Further profiting from the mingled personal and political interests of brewers, distillers, and saloon and music hall owners—a group of immigrant entrepreneurs that gave especially generously of time, money, and meeting space—organizers held a whirlwind round of caucuses. Into mid-June, as journalist M. L. Ahern observed, "meetings in the wards followed fast and furious, awakening a perfect storm of feeling."[96] Taking their message straight to the neighborhoods of the city, working precinct by precinct in every ward with a sizable immigrant and working-class presence, the many experienced politicians who stood behind the ticket were well on the way to building a formidable party by the early summer.[97]

Sunday closing thus proved a potent springboard for an urban politics that openly revolved around the solidarities and interests born of particular group identities. In terms of how the People's party sought to construct its own legitimate claim to represent the best choice for the voters of the city, its rise ultimately owed much to a powerful irony. For even as the mechanics of party organization exploited ethnic divisions, the spokesmen for the avowed ticket of immigrants constantly reminded their followers that they fought not as Germans or Irishmen but as Americans: good citizens of the City of Chicago who were duty-bound to protect their civil rights. Immigrants, some further argued, had to seize the helm of civic stewardship from native-born Chicagoans, the Sabbatarianists who plainly had misunderstood or forgotten the original political purpose of their nation. Attorney Francis A. Hoffman Jr. spelled out this inversion of identity at the gathering that founded the party. Personal freedom, he declared, was *the* distinguishing mark of American citizenship; "[A]ll," he claimed, "here have a right to live according to their own ways." But for the moment, according to Hoffman, only immigrants seemed able to recall this American legacy and had to act, as immigrants, in its defense. "A man," he concluded, "was not worthy of the name *German* who would not now act to regain his rights." Paradoxically, ethnic unity and pride were deemed to reflect a truly "American" spirit; an assertion of "Germanness" here advanced a claim to good citizenship that was made more powerful by its very foundation in ethnic difference.

It would be naive to assume that such statements carried a deep ideological purity, given that these ethnic leaders were also experienced politicians who were highly skilled at the art of popular mobilization. Still, it is also wrong to dismiss these sentiments as mere rhetoric or empty manipulations. The immigrant claim to embody an American identity, an alternative vision of worthy citizenship that incorporated and refigured the class, ethnic, and cultural differences raised by the question of Sabbatarianism, plainly evidenced the growing sense of these people that they had a central place in the urban polity. These immigrants, as they made clear, not only deserved a place in a pluralistic urban polity—they were, as they argued, the primary guardians of all that was good and orderly in a representative democracy. To apply historian David Gerber's phrase, Francis Hoffman here presented an emerging form of social identity—the immigrant-American—that bespoke of the demand of this group for a more complete "civic integration."

As the summer wore on, People's party workers busied themselves behind the scenes; laboring precinct by precinct, the coalition quietly constructed a solid web of support throughout Chicago's immigrant neighborhoods.[98] Along with more overtly political activities, the German North Side was alive with reminders of the battle at hand: an amateur theater group mounted a wicked spoof of the temperance movement entitled *Die Wassersimpel* (The Water Morons), masquerade balls at local Turner Halls were decorated with caricatures of Mayor Medill and Police Superintendent Washburn, and the German Association of Brewers and Distillers formally and ceremoniously changed its name to the League of Free-Minded Citizens.[99] By the beginning of October, the movement spearheaded by the People's party had so saturated the cultural and political life of the city that both the Democrats and the Republicans effectively conceded the November election.[100] As in the case of the elite-led disruption of party politics carried off by the Union-Fireproof ticket two years before, neither organization saw the point of drawing up their own slate. Left alone to finish the fight, the Committee of Seventy finally turned its attention to the electoral arena in the last weeks of October, forming the Citizens' Union party—the coalition popularly known as the Law and Order ticket.

Founded at an October 19 mass meeting, the Law and Order ticket made no bones about its single-issue platform: only Sunday closing, they declared, could save the people of Chicago. Along with their very clear statement of what they felt to be an essential civic moralism, the leaders of the ticket, like the People's party, centered much of their campaign on an effort to seize the crown of true patriotism, to define the identity of the one and only good American citizen. In so doing, they proudly asserted their own status as the native-born "Yankees" of Chicago. Law and Order men indeed gloried in the favorite slander of their opponents, for were not Puritans the most original of Americans? "If it is Puritanical to seek the enforcement of laws promoting order and peace in society," proclaimed a party handbill, "then we should be Puritanical."[101] "Was it such a disgrace," asked a prominent attorney, "that our fathers fought at Yorktown and Saratoga?" (And not, of course, on the side of the Hessians.)[102] A speaker at a Law and Order rally put the point even more bluntly, in the process offering a similar censure of the immigrants who stood in the ranks of the opposition. "The People's Party," he announced, "is un-American in every way. This ticket should be put down by sensible, old-fashioned American men and citizens"—a group he defined as taxpayers, men of property, and native-born champions of Protestant values.[103] Much as David Gerber has described in his study of antebellum Buffalo, the need to acknowledge immigrants as actors in public life prompted a consolidation of a particular American identity that affirmed this group of Chicagoans. But such a dynamic, a sort of "ethnicization" of the Yankee Protestant, had an ironic consequence: simultaneously making it plain that this group was only one of many legitimate contenders for civic power.[104]

Yet for all the clarity and conviction of its platform, the party failed miserably in its execution of the practical steps necessary to realize its vision of governance. These men had no real sense of how to mount a campaign that would attract votes across the whole of Chicago; measured against the seasoned ward politicians of the People's party, the clergymen and their congregants who stood behind the Law and Order ticket were neophytes. The coalition did manage to slate many experienced officeholders, drafting attorney and alderman L. L. Bond—the man designated as "Acting Mayor" after the departure of Medill—to head their ticket. But the Committee of Seventy's relatively late turn to reconstituting itself as a political party meant they could not possibly match the organization of their opponents. Moreover, party leaders made a dramatic mistake in the process of slate-making, a serious blunder that is indicative of just how ill-equipped they were to win a citywide election. Law and Order men filled all of their highest slots with native-born Americans; only one Irish-American appeared far down the ticket as a candidate for an obscure county office. Such choices, in a contest revolving around ethnic divisions and identities, sent a strong symbolic message. By neglecting to construct a balanced slate—and their total exclusion of German-Americans—the party of Sunday closing dug itself into a very deep hole. Reporting on the Law and Order convention, the *Staats-Zeitung* offered the following assessment of the party's decisions: "Thanks to the stupidity of the mob which assembled last Saturday evening at the Pacific Hotel, the election . . . has been much simplified."[105] "A weaker ticket," seconded one local politician, "could hardly have been nominated."[106]

By contrast, the leaders of the People's party proved themselves to be expert players at the game of identity politics, at staking a claim to civic power based upon a coalition of interests rooted in more particular social groupings. Their slate—unveiled four days after the improvident nominations of the Law and Order ticket—was a model of ethnic and partisan balance. It was headed by native New Yorker Harvey D. Colvin, a wholesale grocer long active in the Democratic party who had been a member of Henry Greenebaum's Committee of Twenty Five; other executive slots were filled by protean Irishman/Scotsman Dan O'Hara and Saxony-born George Von Hoellen, an important German Republican. All the way down the ticket, the candidates for lesser offices reflected a similar concern for the proportional representation of the city's Democrats and Republicans—and the Irish, German, and native-born.[107] To insure that their message reached every segment of Chicago's increasingly diverse immigrant world, the party prepared and circulated campaign literature not only in German but in Norwegian, Dutch, Swedish, Bohemian, French, Polish, and Italian—a step that later became a common practice but at this point was unknown in the political history of the city. Moreover, in an extremely canny (if shady) move, the ticket made ironic use of a most American process: naturalization. Taking advantage of Dan O'Hara's position as clerk of the County Court, the People's party sent a steady stream of immigrants to the courthouse, all of whom claimed that their "first papers" had been lost in the Great Fire. Party loyalists, according to the outraged estimate of the *Tribune*, thereby added thousands of voters—both real and illegitmate—to the rolls.[108]

Powered by such a sure sense of politicking, the victory of the People's party seemed imminent—a prospect that so appalled the editors of the *Tribune* that the paper abandoned its earlier magnanimity toward the immigrant fight for "personal liberties." For tolerance of Sunday drink and the form of cultural pluralism this implied was one issue, but the acceptance of a mayor and a major contingent of aldermen who belonged to a ticket pledged to uphold the interests of the foreign-born and working people of Chicago was quite another.[109] Attorney Wirt Dexter, the head of the Executive Committee of the Relief and Aid Society, exemplified the dilemma that more secular native-born businessmen and professionals felt themselves to face at this moment. As he told a Law and Order rally, he could not support their demand for Sunday closing, since he personally believed in the rightfulness of "free sabbaths." But concern for the shape of city government—and hence for civic order—had drawn him to work for the Law and Order ticket. Chicago, he felt, could not risk the "abuses" that would surely follow from the elevation of the People's party.[110] For Dexter, long-time politicians like Hesing and O'Hara were typical "bummers"—dishonest, corrupt, and self-interested schemers who could never rise above their roots and bases of power in ethnic communities to render proper service to the "whole" of the city. Like ex-Mayor Medill, Dexter, as his work as the primary architect of Relief and Aid had so plainly shown, was given to reflexive equations of his particular sense of what Chicago required—a form of governance that somehow rose above "interests" and would safeguard the reputation of the city as a place to do business—with a universalized vision of what best served the "public interest."

After a string of nervous cautions to the Law and Order ticket about their poor preparations fell upon deaf ears, the *Tribune*, in the last days of the campaign, made its own last-ditch effort to bring out the vote against the People's party—seeking to alarm and galvanize its readership on several ideological fronts. Pages and pages of editorials slid well into the rhetoric of xenophobia and class antagonism, urging "every good citizen" to work "to repel the German conquest," to fight for the "security of life and property" in the face of "the incursion that the dangerous classes intend to make."[111] On election day, the paper damningly recalled the antifire limits rally of January 1872, offering a harsh account of the first post-Fire mobilization of an immigrant political coalition: "Less than two years ago a mob which displayed the Prussian flag . . . stoned the Council Chambers, and put the Council to flight." The point of this history lesson could not have been more clear: if the election was lost, the city could again fall under the disorderly influence of the same "piebald rabble."[112] Sounding like every anxious defender of the native-born as the rightful inheritors and custodians of their city, one piece declared that "American citizenship is the only kind of citizenship tolerated in Chicago."[113] Even "the power of the ladies" was enlisted, as the editors strove to win ballots for the Law and Order ticket by forging a connection between domestic harmony, a true national identity, and civic order: "Let every wife as she kisses her husband before going out in the morning call him back and give him another kiss, and remind him of his responsibility as an American citizen, and make him promise to vote for law and order."[114] Finally, the *Tribune* grimly warned that the People's party posed a sure risk to the order and stability that grew out of an urban economy devoted to the spirit and practice of enterprise, once again conflating the desires of the commercial class with those of the "public": "[B]usinessmen and employers must exert themselves in their own personal interests, as well as that of the city at large, to make sure of Hesing's defeat."[115]

But even such fierce rhetoric proved no match for the months of labor and sheer demographic realities that undergirded the People's party. At 6 A.M. on election day, precinct chairmen picked up their ballots. By 7 A.M., an army of ward heelers peddled Party tickets door-to-door. When the polls opened one hour later, long lines had already formed; on the heavily immigrant North Side, delays lasted throughout the afternoon.[116] While prosperous residence districts on the South and West Sides, the neighborhoods that were home to more elite, native-born Chicagoans, did elect six Law and Order aldermen, most of the ticket had a very bad day. Shocked and overwhelmed by the magnitude of their opposition—feeling, in the words of the *Tribune*, "as if they had been struck by lightning and didn't know where the lightning came from"—these Law and Order men retired early, "sadder and poorer."[117] But their rivals reveled in a late night: through the early morning hours, the North Side was alive with jubilant celebrations. As even the dignified Henry Greenebaum danced on a tabletop, Anton Hesing—eager to apply one last twist of the knife to an old enemy—gleefully dispatched a telegraph to the Paris sanctuary of Joseph Medill.[118] For the superior organization of the People's party and superior numbers of immigrants in the city had produced a landslide: the coalition of the foreign-born captured all of the executive offices of the city by 12,000-vote pluralities.[119] The majority, in Chicago, could indeed rule.

"The Committee of Seventy—born September 12, 1872; expired November 4, 1873. . . . Thus, it is ever: the good die young."[120] So went the *Tribune*'s biting postmortem of the election. An effort to realize the moral and civic vision of a group of evangelical Protestants had utterly backfired once the question moved into the realm of electoral politics; "[T]his condition," declared the paper, "never could have been brought about except by an attempt to make the Fourth Commandment a measure of city government."[121] As the Law and Order ticket learned quite painfully, the "intolerance of custom and tradition" dictated by a belief in state-enforced Sabbatarianism would never garner a majority vote "in a city so largely composed of the foreign-born."[122] The paper ended with a very bitter comment: "The election . . . proves that the ignorant and vicious classes, added to the entire German vote, are a majority of the population, and have the power to govern."[123] Such a statement was indicative of two tenets of the liberal values held by its editors: a frustration with an urban politics built out of "interests," and the mixture of condescension and fear sparked by the notion that the nonelite people of the city had in some measure won formal control of its highest offices. If this result was the legitimate end of representative democracy, the future did not look bright.

Yet for the immigrants of the city, particularly German-Americans, the municipal election of 1873 was a sweet and long-awaited triumph: a rebuff to what they perceived as an ever-lurking nativism and a clear signal that the foreign-born—as the foreign-born—had gained a central place in the urban community. Playing by the rules of representative democracy, one collection of voters had won a fair fight; the election, the *Staats-Zeitung* declared, was not "a subjugation of the Americans by a horde of foreigners"—it was a "victory of honorable and true American citizens over a smaller number of American citizens."[124] At the levels of social and civic identity, the ways that immigrants perceived themselves and their city, the results represented an important and highly symbolic mark of an ongoing transformation. Through the exercise of their American right of suffrage, the foreign-born had relied upon ethnic difference as a key to solidarity—and, as a consequence, to power and authority as citizens of the city of Chicago. Once and for all, the rise of an urban political and cultural pluralism seemed secure. For times had changed and the city had changed; "Chicago," proclaimed the

Staats-Zeitung "is no miserable Yankee village, but a cosmopolitan city."[125] And those who had the ability to determine what would be deemed a proper civic order had also changed: "[T]he citizens of the United States who were not born in America, but who have helped to make Chicago what it is *are here in the majority, and possess power.*"[126]

Did the ascension of this new coalition in fact transform the administration of the city? Like their immediate predecessors at the helm of the city, the leaders of the People's party had a relatively brief tenure, losing their offices by 1875. Moreover, it is necessary to recall here that politics functions on many levels, and that a win that had crucial symbolic meanings for particular communities certainly did not automatically translate into major shifts in the mode of governance—given the realities of institutional forms, the complex processes of policy making and the impact of a larger economic context. Once in power, the new Common Council quickly amended the Sunday closing ordinance to allow Sabbath-day business, asking only that all doors and windows that opened onto any public streets be kept closed or covered.[127] Yet little about the People's reign signaled any dramatic departures in the day-to-day workings of municipal governance, a turn of events that is not so surprising, given that most of the ordinary tasks of city governments of the time did not involve such sweeping issues. Moreover, Chicagoans would soon witness the plain limits of the power and abilities of this new administration to work for "the people": as 1873 ended, and Chicago sank steadily into the grip of a national depression, this administration proved sympathetic but ultimately helpless to respond to the increasingly dire needs of the immigrant, working-class constituency it had so ardently championed. What M. L. Ahern, the contemporary chronicler of the People's party, had deemed "The Great Revolution" was thus in a certain sense quite limited in its scope and impact.

Still, it would be wrong, based on these developments, to dismiss Chicago's post-Fire reckoning with Sabbatarianism as some sort of fluke, or the mere colorful product of an unusual moment. For it is clear that a calculation of the proper relation between morality, law, and civic authority was no trivial task. During their year-long battle over the issue of Sunday closing, Chicagoans struggled over issues that were key to their understanding of urban order. Ethnic identity, the rights and responsibilities of American citizenship, and the very nature of a civil state were among the potent questions that clamored for public discussion. The course of these debates is in turn indicative of how a dogged religious minority railed against a rising tide of secularism in public life, the growing place for immigrant Americans in urban politics, and the dilemmas and struggles of later nineteenth-century liberal reformers.

At its heart, moreover, the struggle in Chicago over Sunday closing turned on questions central to a democratic system. What, in the end, is the role of the state in civil society? Who makes laws, and how should they be applied? In the course of this episode, two understandings of law and civic order were irresolvably at odds. The immigrant cry of "personal liberty" rejected the claims of those who felt it was the duty of the state to uphold a form of religious morality. It stood, by contrast, for a system of rule that protected the rights of individuals—and, by extension, for an urban order that had embraced an array of traditions and cultures. "This must be a city," proclaimed the *Staats-Zeitung*, "in which the particular habits of life of all the nationalities from the blending of which the future American national existence is to be formed must be recognized in all of their full distinctiveness."[128] Yet for those who believed in a holy Sabbath, a government that failed to uphold their vision of what constituted an orderly city was not doing its duty. For them, the state could only safeguard the freedom and equality of all citizens if it functioned to protect the larger community against the threatening behavior of dangerous groups and individuals. Here lay an essential conflict: the exercise of state authority that many immigrants saw as an abject tyranny was, for the Sabbatarianists, simply the chastening hand of the law, the ultimate power behind the maintenance of their particular vision of civic order. As the *Law and Order Advocate* had bluntly proclaimed, "Few are not so ignorant to know that all government is founded on force."[129]

How the state should function, what its powers should be, how the law itself should operate, when and how "force" should become the duty of a civic body—these were not (and are not) eternal questions that could be answered with the abstract vocabulary of theories of government. For as these fifteen months made plain, the definition of precisely what constituted a "good" government or a "good" citizen was a dynamic process closely linked to particular historical constructions of identity and authority. At this moment in Chicago, the rise of the People's party thus signaled a majoritarian triumph by a coalition of groups self-identified by ethnicity and class. The very structure of ward politics—where representation by district mirrored the spatial concentrations of class and ethnic settlement—here allowed new sorts of claims to civic power, a forthright naming of the emergence of a pluralistic polity.

Yet other Chicagoans, particularly evangelical Protestant activists and certain native-born businessmen and professionals, clearly were not content with such an outcome—and its portent of an era in which they would have little chance to control the formal political system of their city. For the attorney Stephen A. Goodwin, a Law and Order stalwart, the system of a vote for every man in the city had its drawbacks; as he observed in the course of the campaign, "the problem of universal suffrage is not yet proven a success."[130] Charles C. Bonney, a lawyer and member of the Committee of Seventy, would draw an even more explicit connection between a proper urban order and an elevation of the interests and authority of his own class of the native-born. A suitable form of democracy, and the correct function of a civil state, he argued, was a natural consequence of the inherent talent, judgment, and moralism of such people: "The men who direct and control the immense business interests of Chicago are as a general thing, men in whose minds and hearts the principles of justice and fair dealings are so firmly entrenched that they need no restraints of civil law to compel them to deal correctly with their fellow man." "Such a people," Bonney continued, "govern themselves. . . . The restraints of civil law," he therefore concluded, "are required only for those who are unlike them."[131] One could hardly ask for a more plain example of how such beliefs were not merely drawn from ideal theories of democracy and governance, but also had deep roots within the web of social identities, differences, and relationships that are a part of every community of citizens.

EPILOGUE

OUR COMMUNISTS—this unusual headline appeared on the front page of the *Tribune* on Christmas Day 1873. The article underneath sent an odd mix of messages. At once proprietary and even boosterish (Chicago, like other world cities, now could lay claim to its own cast of social revolutionaries), slightly befuddled (just who was this "Carl Marx"?), and bluntly alarmist ("these men are wild and subversive of society"), the story aimed to explain the history, ideology, and structure of the expanding Socialist movement of the city.[1] Since the formal arrival of the International Workingman's Association (IWA) in North America in 1871, 400 Chicago workers committed to achieving a "more equal distribution of wealth" had organized themselves into six sections: three composed of Germans and one each of Polish, Scandinavian, and French immigrants.[2] For the first (though hardly the last) time in the history of the city, the *Tribune* now found it necessary to discuss how a revolutionary critique of the social relations of capitalism had taken root among a segment of its working class. The newspaper was careful to make plain its support for freedom of expression: "[S]o long as they are only debating," an editorial noted, "they are law-abiding citizens." Yet such a comment plainly hinted at deeper worries: what merely seemed "senseless" talk, the paper implied, might at any moment explode into action.

What had happened to vault the fledgling Socialist movement of Chicago to such sudden prominence? The answer to this question lay in the wider world of the national economy: the deflationary panic triggered some three months earlier by the failure of financier Jay Cooke.[3] Just as the hardships wrought by the Great Fire seemed to be abating, Chicago now faced an economic disaster—the first it had encountered as a modernizing industrial metropolis that was home to thousands of wage workers. In the city, as throughout the country, the rapid onset of hard times provided ample evidence of what social revolutionaries understood to be the evils inherent to capitalism. As cash flows withered, so too did opportunities for employment. Joblessness, always high during the winter, skyrocketed as scores of factories cut back production or closed entirely. According to the *Tribune*, 25,000 wage workers had lost their positions by the end of 1873.[4] The urban economy that had boomed so spectacularly in the year after the Great Fire now suffered a most painful contraction.

Economic crisis proved a bonanza for the small legion of Socialists in Chicago, a group that had already attempted to draw attention to what they saw as the dangers of capitalism for several years. For many who now searched in vain for work, their program had a sharp and compelling immediacy. Much like the hordes of writers and speakers who had argued that the ravages of the Great Fire in fact presented a singular moral and material opportunity, Mrs. M. D. Wynkoop—an English immigrant and Socialist who wrote a Sunday column on labor issues for the *Tribune*—managed to see the silver lining in this new emergency. For no one who lived through these hard times, she thought, could ignore its lessons: "The panic has already demonstrated itself to be a blessing in disguise to the laboring portion of the population. It has opened the eyes of citizens of this country to the fact that free labor was fast becoming slave labor."[5] Despite new legal guarantees of freedom and equality before the law for all Americans, she warned, wage workers were sure to shoulder evermore pressing burdens in the modern industrial age—unless they moved to act in their own defense.[6] And such a movement indeed appeared to be emerging: it seems plain that the *Tribune*'s Christmas Day article was largely a product of the fact that over 6000 men had chosen to affiliate with IWA sections in the few months since the beginning of the panic.[7]

A consideration of the public emergence of a Socialist movement offers one way to reflect upon the many debates and many results that emerged out of the extraordinary period that followed the Great Fire. In the space of slightly more than two years, Chicagoans had witnessed how a native-born elite acted to secure a disaster-ravaged urban community that many viewed as constantly on the verge of falling prey to its internal social divisions. Members of this same elite again and again equated their own particular vision of civic order with the "public interest"—and, in the form of one extremely important institution, the Relief and Aid Society, were granted the authority to act as arbiters of public policy. In so doing, the directors of the agency essentially created what might be deemed a "private state" determined to guard against any permanent dependence on the part of working-class victims of the Great Fire. In the realm of the economy, moreover, the uneasy position of construction trades unions made plain the power of the ideology of individualism and free markets among the commercial class. In all of these instances, a native-born urban elite presented their own beliefs and preferences as those that best served all of the people of their city.

Still, even as the striking power of such claims and their tight linkage of ideologies of economic individualism with a stable urban order became obvious, the post-Fire civic debates that engaged Chicagoans also revealed lively arenas of challenge to such forms of power—and, as a consequence, alternative justifications and realizations of social authority. Certain relief organizations rejected the "official," class-bound definitions of worthiness and want sent out by the Relief and Aid Society, instead holding to understandings of charity and need that privileged the ties of more particular communities within the city. In broad debates over property rights and the morality of Sunday drinking that eventually in large part turned on questions of ethnic identity, some Chicagoans successfully made use of representative institutions of municipal government to set out a defense of individual rights that presented ethnic difference as a key guarantor of American freedom. Such campaigns, through the vehicle of the People's party, eventually were potent enough nearly to sweep all of the offices at stake in the municipal election of 1873. This victory cemented a new legitimacy for political and cultural pluralism in a city full of immigrants. In addition, certain workers stood by an alternative understanding of "cooperation" that presented their unions as forces for urban order. Their leaders advanced a plan for a more cooperative economy that aimed to replace the norms of laissez faire with forms of state-run arbitration that would place labor and capital on more truly even footing, a plan that at its heart contested the elevation of the individual worker or employer in the marketplace. All of these claims, on some level and with varying degrees of success, sought to represent more particular "interests" as those that best served all of Chicago.

By the first days of 1874, the people of Chicago occupied a rebuilt metropolis. Though the physical losses caused by the Fire had been erased, there is no way to account for the emotional or financial scars that doubtless continued to mark the lives of thousands of individuals and families. Yet it seems clear that by this time the more regular patterns of urban life and politics had been restored. Tens of thousands of newer residents, moreover, had themselves *not* endured the Great Fire and its dislocations, a demographic fact that would become more and more common as Chicago entered into its greatest period of growth in the 1880s and 1890s. Within a decade, the overwhelming majority of Chicagoans indeed had no personal memory of the disaster and its sequel. Still, it is plain that the struggles of these months can be read as a blueprint for struggles yet to come. On the level of formal politics, a reckoning with the issues raised by Chicago's Socialists in the first months of 1874 laid the groundwork for a split between populist ward politicians, working-class radicals, and elite reformers, a trio of forces that would maintain a presence in the city through the turn of the century. In future contests over the shape of urban order, moreover, politics in all of its forms would remain inextricably wedded to the great urban fact of social difference, as an evermore diverse urban polity continued to draw upon particular social identities in order to construct their own claims to represent the "public interest."

As Chicagoans began to live with the effects of the Panic of 1873, they came to confront a set of very modern questions about what we now call social welfare. For in the days just before Christmas, radical leaders schooled in European theories of socialism had articulated the needs of the unemployed as political demands, as blunt calls for state action—a style of protest familiar to Paris or New York but new to Chicago.[8] A "Workingman's Committee," a body composed of representatives from all six Socialist sections, had petitioned municipal authorities, including those newly elected as part of the People's party, to draw upon the resources of the city to aid those in need. They asked, in short, for the governmental provision of "work or bread."

A new civic debate now rose to the fore. Was the larger urban community obligated to help those unable to support themselves? How could or should the government of Chicago address the hardships of a depression? Would the "public interest" be served by such a step? At this juncture, the novel demands of the Socialists led to a reprise of post–Great Fire struggles over understandings of want and "worthiness." Appeals for "work or bread" also led to the reappearance of some familiar players: casting about for a response to this appeal, city aldermen again saw fit to call upon the elite directors of the Chicago Relief and Aid Society. In the course of their dealings with the private agency, certain limits to the authority of elected officials were once again made clear. And as a broader civic debate took shape around the demands of the Socialists, what had seemed stark barriers born of class and ethnic difference quickly eroded. Groups that had been violently at odds over the rise of the People's party suddenly found a common ground in their commitment to what they defined as great American ideals: personal independence and the ultimate justice of a market economy largely free from state intervention.

On the evening of December 21, 1873, between 5000 and 7000 men assembled at Vorwaerts Turner Hall, filling this West Side German institution to its rafters. "Such a gathering," declared the *Times*, "has never before been witnessed in this city"; noting the international nature of the crowd and the strident tone of orators, the paper could not help but be "reminded . . . of the COMMUNISTIC UPRISINGS in Europe."[9] In the two years since the Paris Commune, the English-language press had seldom hesitated to raise the inflammatory specter of this event at the first sign of any sort of working-class or immigrant activism. For once, however, the comparison had some real validity: to the radical workers of Chicago, the Commune did represent a signal moment in the international history of their movement.[10] Organizers of the meeting, moreover, had drawn upon a body of European Socialist theory to present a challenge to the capitalist order in America, explicitly asking their followers to join together as a self-conscious and aggrieved class of workers.[11]

At the gathering, speakers from IWA sections again and again laid claim to "the right to live," a demand that was echoed in many northern cities during this winter of great misfortune.[12] America, they charged, had failed to deliver upon its fabled promise of liberty and equality for its workingmen and women. Along with their more abstract expositions on why this was so—their analysis of the social oppressions of "monopoly capitalism"—the orators had an immediate agenda: as a practical first step toward righting the wrongs of the market economy and society, they believed that the municipal government had to act to alleviate the effects of the late depression. "In this city," declared A. L. Thernaldt, a carpenter who held forth in his native French, "there are hundreds of starving families, and yet the city and the capitalists have done nothing to assist or relieve them in their hour of need."[13] The mass meeting therefore resolved to present the Common Council with four demands: employment for all those able to work, money or provisions for those unable to labor, and—in a pointed response to the post–Great Fire works of the Relief and Aid Society—working-class control over the administration of any such program. Finally, if cash on hand proved inadequate to fund these measures, the assembly asked that the city resort to its credit. Hard times, they argued, mandated radical steps; since the labor of working people had created the wealth that built Chicago, the very "bones and sinew" of the city most certainly deserved its aid.

The next night, a crowd estimated at 10,000 again gathered on the West Side, commencing a political event again unlike any other ever before seen in Chicago. Unprecedented in their demand that the city provide work or bread, that the state was obligated to provide a minimum level of security for all its people, the decorum of the marchers also struck even unfriendly observers as unique. Splitting into two bodies, columns of men—mostly German and Scandinavian immigrants—walked in silence to City Hall. Under the watch of a large police presence, the protestors wordlessly waited as a spokesman presented their petition to the alderman. In a remarkable passage, even the *Times* admitted the impropriety of the descriptions it so often had applied to incidents of working-class and immigrant protest. "The assembly was not a mob, for it was as quiet as a funeral procession," wrote a correspondent. "It was not a rabble, for in its long line was good order."[14] The report went on to note that the marchers were themselves an unusual cast of political actors, a group clearly unfamiliar with the more regular rituals (and routes) of partisan parades and rallies. "The men seemed to have little knowledge of the streets," observed the reporter. "Six, eight, ten sturdy fellows stood hand in hand, each fearing to let go, lest he should be lost in the great metropolis."[15] With their frank advocacy of state intervention into the lives of those most affected by the failing economy, the Workingman's Committee attracted a cadre of supporters who probably seldom strayed beyond their own neighborhoods and workplaces. But on this night, for this cause, they had made the journey to the center of Chicago that symbolized their connection to and claims upon the governance and resources of the larger city.

The new mayor and aldermen elected under the banner of the People's party were more than happy to listen to the demands of the Workingman's Committee—they, after all, owed their offices to the votes of precisely such citizens. But they were far less able to accommodate their requests: as Mayor Colvin explained, the coffers of the city were empty. Upward of 100,000 people had relocated to Chicago in the two years since the Great Fire, badly straining the ability of the municipality to provide regular services—an adequate number of schools and a decent standard of police and fire protection. Debts already totaled close to $2,000,000 dollars and a state-imposed limit on municipal borrowing had long since been exceeded.[16] Worse, auditors had just uncovered a major scandal: David Gage, the former city treasurer, had embezzled over $500,000 in municipal funds. Finally, the panic had cut deeply into tax revenues: little new money was coming in to pay for previous budgetary commitments.[17] Since the city was in no shape to spend or even to borrow new funds, the aldermen were spared from what likely would have been a contentious discussion of whether or not the municipality should commit itself to the task of providing jobs or other forms of aid.

Nevertheless, a few supportive council members kept the question alive by pointing to a civic institution that perhaps could afford such a program: the Relief and Aid Society. As Alderman Michael B. Bailey noted, the organization was rumored still to hold as much as $1,000,000 of the moneys sent to the city immediately after the Fire. Quick to grasp the significance of this observation, the council gladly, as it were, passed the buck. In an expression of sympathy for the suffering people of the city, two resolutions sponsored by Bailey won rapid approval. The first, remarking upon the city's "depleted" treasury, asked the Society to "distribute the funds in their hands liberally." And the second proposed to enforce this request, assigning five aldermen to secure the Society's "active cooperation with the Board of the Common Council."[18] Still smarting over the fact that the agency had not disbursed all of the municipal Fire relief fund, the aldermen of the city once again aimed to recapture the donations that had been entrusted to this private organization. Great hardship had again befallen the city, Bailey argued. Why not now spend these dollars in a manner that seemed to match the spirit in which they had first been given?

The initiative of the Common Council got off to a predictably poor start: citing prior business and holiday engagements, the Relief and Aid Society directors refused a request by Mayor Colvin for an immediate summit. Such a snub was no doubt intended to remind the aldermen that the agency formed its policies apart from the arena of electoral politics, a distance it had been careful to maintain. But on the day after Christmas, the mayor, the aldermanic delegation, and representatives of the Workingman's Committee all assembled at the downtown headquarters of the Society. After a round of introductions, a formality that demonstrated that the makeup of the Executive Committee had not changed in the two years since the Great Fire, the attorney Francis Hoffman Jr. spoke on behalf of the committee and the council.[19] Echoing the same arguments unsuccessfully advanced by Alderman Charles C. P. Holden and the Cook County Board in the winter that followed the Great Fire, Hoffman charged that the Society had no right to withhold the sum in question—a total now agreed to be a slightly less spectacular but still sizable $600,000. These funds were gifts to those who had suffered by the Great Fire, he claimed, and the failure of the agency to release all of these moneys ran directly contrary to "the interest of the givers."[20] But by recognizing the present state of great need in the city, by relinquishing their tight hold on what remained of the Fire fund—with these steps, he declared, the organization could yet erase its errors. Hoffman thus asked that the Society hand over the $600,000 to the city or county authorities—or, alternatively, agree to a reshuffled directorate of their own institution that accurately reflected the ethnic balance of the city. The policies of its elite, native-born leadership, he thereby implied, had never reflected the will and wishes of the mass of people that their agency claimed to serve.

It is no surprise that members of the Workingman's Committee and their supporters on the Council were answered with a quick and decisive rebuff. To begin with, those who had charge of the Relief and Aid Society, men confident in the opportunities that industrious individuals could find in the urban economy, were not at all sure that the workers of Chicago indeed faced any sort of crisis. As a skeptical Superintendent Charles Truesdell told the *Tribune* on December 23, he "remained convinced that a great many of the able-bodied men who are loafing about the streets could get something to do if they were not too lazy to look for it."[21] Moreover, the directors pointed to a range of technical obstacles to any reworking of the structure or powers of their institution. Executive Committee Chairman Wirt Dexter, for example, observed that the Society had no legal authority to transfer moneys to the city treasury. Finally, as they had done in the face of earlier charges of impropriety, the directors waved off the claim that the "world's charity" was in fact "the people's money." Once Mayor Mason had placed the task of municipal relief in their trust, declared Dexter, the Society had assumed sole responsibility for the disbursement of funds—and they fully intended to maintain the control that went hand in hand with their guardianship. Always suspicious of aldermen, men they viewed as beholden to a corrosive and corrupting set of "interests," the directors of the Society were hardly likely to cede what remained of the Fire fund to a council and administration dominated by the People's party. And a set of men who had flourished in the capitalist marketplace, a group that had thoroughly absorbed its attendant systems of value and definitions of good order, were most likely to reject the claims of Socialists.

In its response to the call for "work or bread," the Society further restated its own commitment to the precepts of "scientific charity," speaking of the aid it already delivered to those they considered to be among the "worthy poor." Dexter reminded his visitors that the Society still assisted significant numbers of Chicagoans; a staff of ten, as he noted, daily processed the claims of some fifty families and gave away $1200 in food, dry goods, and fuel. According to the attorney, the truly deserving ought not to hesitate to visit the offices of the Society, where their applications for aid would be processed and investigated in due course and with practiced care. Anyone that met their standards, he promised, would be helped. Leveling a parting shot at the popular protest organized by the Socialists and the aldermen sympathetic to their cause, Dexter ended with a ringing defense of his organization: "Who are the real friends of the poor? The men trying to beguile them with talk, or those who silently manage their suffering?"[22] For Dexter, "politics" had no place in the world of social welfare; echoing the sentiments that had justified the Society's initial placement as the managers of Fire relief, he argued that those in need were best aided by the businessmen and trained professionals who had assumed the power to evaluate their want and make determinations of their worthiness. Based on the accumulated weight of all of these ideological and practical objections, the Society thus bluntly rejected the demands of the Workingman's Committee and their aldermanic supporters.

The demand for "work or bread" apparently had reached an impasse: the city government was too impoverished even to begin to consider the request, and the Relief and Aid Society was only willing to help on its own terms. But an unbowed Workingman's Committee did not let the matter rest: all of the poor who wished to ask for assistance were instructed to take Wirt Dexter at his word and call upon the Society. The committee thus sent a flood of applicants to the downtown offices of the agency, recruiting a corp of sympathetic aldermen and clergy to write the preliminary references and letters of introduction required of all claimants. Outside the LaSalle Street headquarters of the Society, the waning days of December and the commencement of 1874 soon seemed eerily reminiscent of the immediate aftermath of the Great Fire. The words of a self-proclaimed "Old Citizen" described the thousands who flocked to the central depot—and once again faced rigorous tests of their need. Just as a crowd had stood under the gaze of General Sheridan's soldiers and volunteers, "a multitude of men and women" guarded by a "large police force" now waited in long, ragged cordons. Well aware that mothers with virtuous stories to tell were most often deemed worthy, hundreds of "pale, wan, and thinly clothed" women surrounded themselves with their children. And, as in the first days after the Fire, the huge crowd, coupled with the bureaucratic procedures of the Society, meant that many were never seen. "To all appearances," observed the "Old Citizen," large numbers "would have to wait all day without help, and come tomorrow and try again."[23]

Much as these sights stirred memories of the Great Fire, so too did the management of this new crisis. Fueled by fears that dependency would lead straight to an erosion of urban order, close investigation and temporary aid continued to reign as practical and ideological guideposts. In reaction to the Socialist-prodded barrage of applications, the Society hired sixty additional visitors—a staff quickly trained in home visits and the verification of all stories of lost jobs. At the same time, however, the organization took steps that from the outset denied or seriously complicated any claimant's access to aid. On January 3, the Society declared that all men—the sex deemed both able and obligated to fend for themselves—were no longer eligible to apply.[24] Later in the month, to reduce the numbers who waited to present their requests in person, the superintendent announced that all initial appeals to the organization had to be made in writing—a difficult, if not impossible, task for many immigrants who knew little English and the illiterate.[25] As in the months after the Fire, the bureaucracy created to deliver relief also sharply limited its distribution.

Moreover, this second great wave of applications to the Relief and Aid Society again gave evidence of how their understandings of class differences figured into their charitable efforts. Working people were once more made to wend their way through a morass of tightly controlled procedures and rigid standards; the "worthiness" of applicants was in the end determined by their ability to match the definition of "honest" poverty put in place by a directorate of self-made businessmen. For the Society, the ideal client remained a pious mother, a woman whose ill fortune had resulted through no fault of her own. Yet this notion continued to involve a paradox: if a woman herself came forward to ask for relief, she was automatically considered suspect. The organization thus continued to heroize those too proud to beg: the shadowy and sorrowful men and women who had once prospered, but now had fallen from independence. The *Tribune*, for example, described an especially "pitiable case," spinning a tale that might have been drawn from the annals of Great Fire Special Relief. Alerted by a letter unique in its "manner of appeal," Superintendent Truesdell himself had immediately rushed out to discover that a lady who "once moved in the highest circles of Society" was now "but a skeleton covered with scanty rags," that her husband, a former business partner of "one of the most prominent men in the country," lay beside her in "the last stages of consumption." Such a respectable couple, of course, required no external references or further investigation. Within hours, a stove, furniture, bedding, clothing, and coal had arrived on the scene.[26]

Yet for all these parallels to the project of Fire relief, a critical difference marked these post-Panic applications. For even in the wary view of the Society, the victims of the Great Fire were vested with a certain degree of innocence. While ideas about social differences had shaped the "official" administration of fire relief into a set of procedures that maintained a particular elite vision of urban order, it is also true that most who asked for aid in the aftermath of the Great Fire did eventually receive some, even if limited, form of assistance. But for those who suffered from the panic of 1873, the question of any person's responsibility for his or her own plight had become more complex—and Relief and Aid disbursements in turn became far less common. Even as the Society acknowledged that the depression had brought "considerable poverty" to Chicago, they ultimately approved fewer than one in ten applications filed during the period.[27] For the erosion of the urban economy to the point where a widespread loss of jobs caused great distress, the idea of a systemic problem of unemployment linked to a downturn in the larger economy, ultimately could not be reconciled with the profound commitment to self-reliance held by its directors. Placing the onus of failure upon individuals, the institution saw no need to assist most of the Chicagoans who now came to their doors. Indeed, to do so would sharply contradict their cherished faith in American independence.

By the time of the panic of 1873, as more and more Chicagoans found themselves caught up in a collapsing urban economy where they could not be sure of their own economic security, the Relief and Aid Society chose to narrow its mission. Over the next years, the agency adopted a series of new rules meant to "economize": clients were now dropped from their rolls after receiving aid for a certain number of years, anyone once sent out of town at the Society's expense could never again receive assistance from the organization, and applications from able-bodied single men or women were no longer accepted. As the city and the numbers of the poor in Chicago both continued to grow, the Society moved to turn back the clock, returning to a definition of worthiness that matched the pre–Great Fire policies of the organization. By 1875, only the sick, the aged, the infirm, or widows with families could receive assistance.[28] Though the directors at the Relief and Aid Society never specifically commented on the Socialist demand for "work or bread," their refusal to release any funds, coupled with their own increasingly restrictive procedures, strongly suggests that they would have sharply opposed such a step for the city. In the face of the Panic, an event that some understood as a plain example of the growing complexity and perilousness of the urban economy, the Relief and Aid Society thus reaffirmed its long-held conviction that any provision of aid to anyone who might in theory support themselves remained a serious threat to the urban order.

Falling back upon older arguments and standards, the Relief and Aid Society, like the Common Council, avoided any direct engagement with the new question that both bodies had faced: Was the larger urban community, through the apparatus of the state, in fact responsible for providing some measure of security to those who could not support themselves? Should a civil society guarantee what the Socialists of Chicago termed "the right to live"? Radical working-class leaders saw no better way to relieve economic hardship, the state of widespread misery that they understood as a common problem that could be traced to the wrongs of the industrial economy. But other responses to their proposals quickly proved that few shared their vision. Indeed, the issue of "work or bread" led to a new and striking unanimity of opinion between what recently had been ferociously warring parties.

During these weeks, it became plain that even as certain aldermen were willing to fund some sort of emergency assistance by once again trying to claim the Fire donations entrusted to the Relief and Aid Society, the Socialists of the city largely stood alone in upholding their particular vision of civic responsibility and state power. Given the political history of the previous months, their isolation begs a question: What had happened to the People's party, to the much ballyhooed "takeover" of the city by immigrants and working people? The coalition had enjoyed wide support based upon its pledge to fight for the "interests" of just such people. Yet once the Workingman's Committee had advanced a class issue that seriously challenged the people of the city to evaluate whether or not their community was in some measure obligated to aid the unemployed, the leaders of the People's party were nowhere to be found. Carl Klings, a spokesman for the IWA, pointed to the irony of this abandonment (and his own scorn for what he viewed as the opportunistic and insincere men behind the slate) in an interview with the *Tribune* in late December. "Where," he asked, "are Hesing and O'Hara now? "Why do they not lead us now as they did before the election?"[29] The rhetoric of the People's party, he implied, did not match its true commitments—or, indeed, what Klings saw as its signal lack thereof.

The failure of the People's party fully to endorse the demands of the Workingman's Committee is telling of an important distinction: that such a populist urban coalition, a slate built out of appeals to particular class and (especially) ethnic identities, was not at all the same sort of animal as the emerging Socialist movement—a political body organized around a critique of the social order that had grown out of a free market economy. Riding high on the single issue of

Sabbatarian enforcement, a volatile subject tailor-made for the creation and exploitation of political fissures along the lines of class and ethnic difference, the coalition had won its landslide victory. But as Klings's comment suggests, what had seemed a monolithic immigrant and working-class coalition in early November by late December had already broken apart over the issue of "work or bread." A broad and relatively easily won unity over the question of the right to drink, a debate fully within the confines of more usual conflicts over state power, splintered over the much more difficult question of whether or not all Chicagoans could look to their city to guarantee their "right to live." For this was a notion that many, including the key figures behind the rise of the People's party, understood as a highly problematic challenge to the value Americans placed upon individualism—and their subsequent understandings of freedom, equality, and the proper role of government.

In the last weeks of December, in a stunning marker of a newfound consensus, the *Tribune* approvingly reprinted a series of *Staats-Zeitung* editorials on the subject of "work or bread." Here, a powerful shared commitment to the ultimate justice of the American market economy overrode their acrid split over the meaning of the People's party. For to the minds of the German American Republicans who produced and owned the *Staats-Zeitung*, a Socialist class analysis of the economic woe that now gripped Chicago was best dismissed as mere foolishness, as the worthless stuff of "demagogues and agitators."[30] Sounding not unlike the *Times* or *Tribune* on the subject of the People's party, Anton Hesing's paper branded the Workingman's Committee as a band of self-interested opportunists, an unscrupulous gang "trying to make capital for themselves out of a deviltry that threatens the whole community."[31] This, the editors declared, was a form of politics that could never make a legitimate claim to representing the "public interest." Their prime objection centered around the sanctity of private property: in the opinion of the *Staats-Zeitung*, the obligation of the urban community to secure the welfare of any individual most definitely did not extend to any sort of state-sanctioned redistribution of wealth.

In a complete rejection of the Socialist program, the paper joined with the *Times* and *Tribune* in observing that any choice to devote municipal funds to relief for the unemployed would burden taxpayers unfairly. It was simply wrong, argued the editors, to force the thrifty and hard-working to pay the way of those unable to support themselves. Thus sharply dissenting from the vision of communal responsibility and state power held by those they derisively termed the "Bebels and Leibknechts" of Chicago, the *Staats-Zeitung* counseled a course that exactly opposed the demands of the Workingman's Committee, expressing its confidence in the ability of the urban economy to right itself. Eventually, promised the paper, prospects were bound to improve. And in the meantime, the German Americans of the city would do best to handle this crisis with "calm, patience, and cooperation."[32] Faced with a demand that asked them to consider the justice and propriety of a new form of state power, of a practical application of some of the theories of European socialism, the *Staats-Zeitung* showed its true Republican colors: faith in the free market, faith in the individual, and faith in American opportunities.

Finally, the *Tribune*, voice of the native-born businessmen of the city, produced an even more emphatic rejection of "the right to live," detailing its many subversions of American elevations of the rights of the individual. The state, declared the paper, could not properly assume the task of providing citizens with security. Reversing the claims of Sabbatarianists—that the municipality's highest function was to protect the community by restricting the personal freedoms of those deemed dangerous to it—an editorial made the following declaration: "Governments were instituted to defend the individual against the many." But, the writer noted, supporters of the call for work or bread held to the exactly opposite intent. "The advocates of the right to employment," charged the paper, "set the many over the individual."[33] Worse, by mandating some sort of redistribution of wealth, the Socialists would empower the city to appropriate private property, thus making the state into nothing less than "an organized robber." And those who stood to gain the most were those least entitled to such benefit: "[T]he sweat and toil of the thrifty and self-denying" would unjustly accrue to the good of "the idle, the improvident, the spendthrifts, and the drones of society."[34] If the state cared for "the laboring classes," the editors concluded, "it takes from them all inducements to take care of themselves."[35] So the *Tribune* pinpointed what it viewed as the most offensive element of the Socialist program: its challenge, on the grounds of the responsibility of the city to guarantee the minimum security of its citizens, to the rules of any individual's rise or fall in the free market.

In these mid-winter days, it became plain that the Socialist critique of capitalist market relations for many seemed akin to an assault on the finest qualities of their nation. A range of commentators indeed agreed that a more un-American set of beliefs could hardly be imagined. The *Times*, for example, drew the conclusion that the "foreigners" who stood behind the call for "work or bread" knew "nothing about trade or the laws of supply and demand."[36] Even Andrew Cameron, the most prominent labor leader in the city and the editor of the *Workingmans' Advocate*, did not support state guarantees of employment. Holding to an older vision of republicanism that turned on the figure of the free artisan, he argued that such a policy would inevitably erode the independence of all citizens, and thereby eat away at the original source of all personal and civic virtue.[37] And so these journals of opinion reaffirmed the commitment of most Chicagoans, immigrant and native-born, to a central ground rule of American political economy. Socialist demands for the state provision of support to the unemployed were so far outside the pale of normal definitions of what seemed just and proper in the city and nation that they were dismissed as "wild" and "senseless," as the very opposite of what defined a republic. In the end, workers could not expect an American state to guarantee them any "right to live."

In the course of Chicagoans' responses to the Panic of 1873, the People's party—a coalition named to signal its ostensible devotion to the interests of the working class and immigrants—did not satisfy the demands of a small set of immigrant workers who bluntly pursued a politics of class. Though the mayor and most aldermen were not opposed to making use of an extraordinary pot of seemingly "public" funds to answer a pressing need, once again affirming the populist instincts that had brought them to office, they were stymied by the resistance of a private agency. Meanwhile, the Relief and Aid

Society once more exercised their nonelectoral (yet quite considerable) authority by holding fast to an elite vision of civic stewardship that sharply restricted access to charity—maintaining an understanding of want and "worthiness" shaped by unerring faith in the ability of individuals to control their own fate and the ultimate justice of the free market. And a growing cadre of social revolutionaries, a group of radical leaders who would build a major American working-class movement in the city over the next fifteen years, gained their first highly visible forum. So Chicagoans were presented with three distinct blueprints of the future of their formal political institutions. Already sharply defined in the early 1870s, elite "structural" reformers, radical workers committed to some form of socialism, and populist urban machines that relied on local ward support would again and again openly contend to define the shape of urban order during the rest of the century.[38]

On February 1, 1874, Gilbert Gurney, a Socialist sympathizer, wrote to the *Tribune* to detail his idea for solving the plight of the unemployed and impoverished people of Chicago—a bitter spoof that aimed to indict those who readily dehumanized the poor. Taking his inspiration from *A Modest Proposal,* Jonathan Swift's famous satire of 1730 on the problem of poverty in Ireland and England, Gurney set forth his own "modified version" of this notorious call for cannibalism. Extending Swift's insight that the poor could survive (and at the same time lessen their numbers) by eating their own children, he proposed that girls of Chicago be "taken first," thereby at once establishing a steady food supply and curtailing both the "present and future population." Boys, he continued, could later be "easily reduced" by sending them to work at particularly hazardous jobs; very few, for example, could hope to last long as brakemen on the railroads. Surviving children might wear the clothes of those previously "utilized," thus "increasing their comfort and health and giving them the chance to become useful citizens."[39] No taxpayer would see a dime of his or her money go to the undeserving or improvident; the state would not take any steps to impede what the *Tribune* had recently described as the "law of the progress of civilization": the growth of "individuality."[40] Gurney's parody made a very serious point: that what many understood as universal standards of justice and compassion did not necessarily apply in kind to the lower classes of the city.

No one, of course, was meant to think that his outrageous suggestion could ever be serious, or thought a reasonable step by reasonable citizens. Still, while the Socialist calls for "work or bread" may now seem relatively ordinary in the context of a modern welfare state, it is worth noting that for Chicagoans in the early 1870s, such demands, if less monstrous than Gurney's "modest proposal," would have been similarly hard to fathom, let alone accept. For most older and newer Americans in the city, virtue and order seemed the direct products of economic independence; their guiding theories of political economy were formed an ocean apart from the radical workers who now called upon the municipal government to provide security to all its people. As the unprecedented editorial solidarity that emerged among the newspapers of Chicago suggests, a European Socialist vision of a state that redistributed wealth was so far outside the regular parameters of American political discourse that nearly all in the city shared a sense of its wrongs—even if for varying reasons and with separate measures of virulence.

The story of the years following the Great Fire ultimately offers the following lessons. As the people of Chicago struggled to make sense of a range of common problems, the diversity of their community ensured that an array of voices were heard. Moreover, even as native-born business leaders repeatedly (and often successfully) promoted the interests of the commercial class as those of the larger city, the power to claim the "public interest" still resided at many levels and in many corners of the larger metropolis. Yet, for all of the other differences and divergences that emerged out of Chicago's crisis, the response to a Socialist vision suggests that the sense of urban order held by a majority of Chicagoans in part rested on a belief in the social merit and "public good" widely ascribed to the figure of the independent American individual. Relatedly, most resisted the notion that a state authorized to guarantee the "right to live" might in fact realize a civic interest. This set of ideas and values in turn carried a form of power that was not easily overturned or challenged: the power to draw the "normal" boundaries of political discourse. Then as now, these boundaries most often excluded such blunt considerations of economic inequality.

When the Panic of 1873 closed the door on Chicago's grand recovery from the Great Fire, the people of the city thus faced what remain critical and divisive problems for all Americans: What, if any, are the responsibilities of the larger community toward those who cannot support themselves? Do people have a "right to live" that must be guaranteed by the state? How to make determinations of just who "deserves" public assistance? A sharp turn for the worse in the economy of an industrializing city prompted Chicagoans to grapple with what may be a singularly uncomfortable set of issues. For as this episode made plain, there would be no quick or easy answer to the problem of the urban poor. The call for "work or bread" was a step toward a vision of social welfare that aimed to reshape the existing balance of responsibility and power between individuals and the state. And while some saw this project as perfectly just and proper, others found such a notion to be the antithesis of their sense of what made for good order. The people of Chicago here collided with a great national dilemma: What to do when the land of opportunity proved not always to be so? Could older traditions of hostility to an active state, faith in the free market, and the cultural elevation of the individual still hold such force in an increasingly complex and interdependent economy and society? As Chicagoans turned from the Great Fire to the world of modern America, they would never lack for new debates that forced them to confront these questions.

NOTES

Introduction

1. W.P.A. Interview with Morris Horowitz (pseudonym), reprinted in Ann Banks, ed., *First Person America* (New York: Alfred A. Knopf, 1980), 32. According to Fire Department records, firemen had already responded to over thirty calls in the first week of October.

2. Chicago Relief and Aid Society, *Report on Disbursements to Sufferers by the Great Fire* (Cambridge, MA: Riverside Press, 1874), 15.

3. *The Land Owner* (March 1872).

4. *The World's Fire! The Great Conflagration in the City of Chicago, October 8th and 9th, 1871* (Chicago: Republic Life Insurance Printing Office, 1871), 10.

5. *The Land Owner* (March 1872).

6. Letter of James Milner, October 14, 1871. Great Fire Personal Narratives Collection, Chicago Historical Society (hereafter Personal Narratives, CHS). For an analysis that explores the origins of the gendered aspects of such understandings of good character and virtue, see Linda K. Kerber, *Women of the Republic: Intellect and Ideology in Revolutionary America* (Chapel Hill: University of North Carolina Press, 1980).

7. Christine Meisner Rosen, *The Limits of Power: Great Fires and the Process of City Growth in America* (New York: Cambridge University Press, 1986). Rosen explores the question of how city government responded (or, as she concludes, failed to respond) to a ready-made opportunity to impose planning initiatives. Ross Miller, a literary scholar and critic, has examined the mythologies surrounding the Great Fire in *American Apocalypse: The Great Fire and the Myth of Chicago* (Chicago: University of Chicago Press, 1990). See also Carl Smith, *Urban Disorder and the Shape of Belief* (Chicago: University of Chicago Press, 1995).

8. Works that fall into the first category include Robert Cromie and Herman Kogan, *The Great Fire: Chicago 1871* (New York: G. P. Putnam's Sons, 1971); Robert Cromie, *The Great Chicago Fire* (New York: McGraw Hill, 1957); and David Lowe, ed., *The Great Chicago Fire* (New York: Dover, 1979). Works in the second category include most general histories of the city. Among these are

the two standard histories of the city: Alfred T. Andreas, *A History of Chicago*, 3 vols. (Chicago: A. T. Andreas Co., 1887); and Bessie Louise Pierce, *A History of Chicago*, vol. 3 (Chicago: University of Chicago Press, 1957). Pierce thus described the experience of visitors to the city some eighteen months after the Great Fire: "Within and without they beheld a city reconstructed, risen Phoenix-like from its ashes . . . Chicago had conquered disaster, and was on the march towards the enviable rank of the second city of the United States" (18–19). Giving explicit sanction to the idea of the Great Fire as a watershed, Pierce used the catastrophe to periodize her work: she dated her final volume from 1871, commencing with an account of the conflagration.

9. The actual import of the Fire in regard to land use has been well documented, most recently in Rosen, *The Limits of Power.* Architectural historians have often told the story of how the ravages of the Fire turned Chicago into a mecca for designers, contributing to the eventual emergence of the Chicago School (see Carl Condit, *The Chicago School of Architecture* [Chicago: University of Chicago Press, 1964], 11–25). Scholarship that documents the city's growth in terms of technology and the use of space includes Harold M. Mayer and Richard C. Wade, *Chicago: Growth of a Metropolis* (Chicago: University of Chicago Press, 1969).

10. Dexter's comments are found in an account of the dispute that appeared in the *Chicago Republican*, January 26, 1872. See also Dexter's letter to the editor, in ibid., February 19, 1872.

11. The Cincinnatian's defense of the soup kitchens, an article that originally appeared in the *Cincinnati Gazette*, is quoted at length in the *Chicago Republican*, February 5, 1872.

12. See, for example, the classic sociological description of the city in Louis Wirth, "Urbanism as a Way of Life," in Wirth, *On Cities and Social Life: Selected Papers* (Chicago: University of Chicago Press, 1964).

13. I have found the following works to be useful models for a study of one urban community that uses an extraordinary episode as a window into "ordinary" social and political relationships: Iver Bernstein, *The New York City Draft Riots: Their Significance for American Politics and Society in the Age of the Civil War* (New York: Oxford University Press, 1990); Charles E. Rosenberg, *The Cholera Years: The United States in 1832, 1849, and 1866* (Chicago: University of Chicago Press, 1962); and Paul E. Johnson *A Shopkeeper's Millennium: Society and Revivals in Rochester, New York, 1815–1837* (New York: Hill and Wang, 1978).

14. *The Land Owner* (October 1869).

15. *New York Tribune* (1868). Cited in John S. Wright, *Chicago: Past, Present, and Future* (Chicago: Western News Co., 1868), xi.

16. On boosterism in Chicago, see Carl Abbott, *Boosters and Businessmen* (Westport, CT: Greenwood Press, 1981); John J. Pauly, "The City Builders: Chicago Businessmen and Their Changing Ethos," Ph.D. diss., University of Illinois at Urbana, 1979; and Rima L. Schultz, "The Businessman's Role in Western Settlement: The Entrepreneurial Frontier, Chicago, 1833–1872," Ph.D. diss., Boston University, 1985.

17. On antiurban sentiments dating from the mid-nineteenth century, see Paul S. Boyer, *Urban Masses and Moral Order in America, 1820–1920* (Cambridge, MA: Harvard University Press, 1978).

18. The ultimate narrative of this story can be found in William Cronon, *Nature's Metropolis: Chicago and the Great West* (New York: W. W. Norton, 1990).

19. On Chicago's role as an entrepôt during the 1850s and 1860s, see Bessie Louise Pierce, *History of Chicago* (New York: Alfred A. Knopf, 1940), 2:35–149.

20. On the Civil War's impact on intercity rivalries in the Midwest, see ibid., 2:271–73; and Wyatt Winton Belcher, *The Economic Rivalry between Chicago and St. Louis, 1850–1880* (New York: Columbia University Press, 1947), 145–56.

21. It is worth noting that in 1870 Chicago was only at the beginning of its greatest growth spurt. Up to 1900, the city's population doubled every ten years. In the 1880s and early 1890s, Chicago was probably the fastest growing metropolis in the Western hemisphere.

22. Historical geographer David Ward offers an overview of the spatial, economic, and demographic changes common to nineteenth-century American cities in *Cities and Immigrants: A Geography of Change in Nineteenth Century America* (New York: Oxford University Press, 1971).

23. David Ward, *Poverty, Ethnicity, and the American City, 1840–1925* (Cambridge: Cambridge University Press, 1989). For a description of the location of various industries, see S. S. Schoff, *The Glory of Chicago* (Chicago: Knight and Leonard, 1873). On the evolution of residential neighborhoods, see Dominic Pacyga and Ellen Skerrett, *Chicago: City of Neighborhoods* (Chicago: Loyola University Press, 1986).

24. Jon C. Teaford, *The Unheralded Triumph: City Government in America, 1870–1900* (Baltimore: Johns Hopkins University Press, 1984). On municipal governance in Chicago, see Robin L. Einhorn, *Property Rules: Political Economy in Chicago, 1833–1872* (Chicago: University of Chicago Press, 1991); and Pierce, *History of Chicago*, 2:303–53.

25. For a highly nuanced description of the process "metropolitan industrialization" in antebellum New York City, see Sean Wilentz, *Chants Democratic: New York City and the Rise of the American*

Working Class, 1788–1850 (New York: Oxford University Press, 1984). For information on rates of working-class property ownership, see Einhorn, *Property Rules*, 247–67.

26. Olivier Zunz, *Making America Corporate, 1870–1920* (Chicago: University of Chicago Press, 1990); Stuart M. Blumin, *The Emergence of the Middle Class: Social Experience in the American City, 1760–1900* (New York: Cambridge University Press, 1989).

27. For a recent general overview of the process of American urbanization, see Eric H. Monkkonen, *America Becomes Urban: The Development of U.S. Cities and Towns, 1780–1980* (Berkeley: University of California Press, 1988).

28. I draw this distinction in accordance with scholarship that makes the point that ethnicity is a more flexible category than nativity, emerging out of reckonings with notions of what constitutes American identity. See, for example, the historical essays collected in Werner Sollers, ed., *The Invention of Ethnicity* (New York: Oxford University Press, 1989); and Philip Gleason, "American Identity and Americanization," in Stephen Thernstrom et al., eds, *The Harvard Encyclopedia of American Ethnic Groups* (Cambridge, MA: Harvard University Press, 1980), 31–58. As David A. Gerber has noted in a recent study, native-born Americans were themselves subject to a process of "ethnicization" in an increasingly pluralistic society by the mid-nineteenth century. Gerber, *The Making of an American Pluralism: Buffalo, New York, 1825–1860* (Urbana: University of Illinois Press, 1989).

29. Census totals and breakdowns by nativity appear in Pierce, *History of Chicago*, 2:481–82.

30. Ibid., 2:17; John B. Jentz, "Class and Politics in an Emerging Industrial City: Chicago in the 1860s and 1870s," *Journal of Urban History* 17 (May 1991): 227–63, esp. 231–35. An 1884 census based on "ethnicity" rather than "nativity" gives credence to such estimates. According to this survey, seventy-six percent of Chicagoans, according to this survey, belonged to some ethnic community. Census reproduced in Bruce C. Nelson, *Beyond the Martyrs: A Social History of Chicago's Anarchists, 1870–1900* (New Brunswick: Rutgers University Press, 1988), 16.

31. Cited in Nelson, *Beyond the Martyrs*, 16.

32. F. F. Cook, *Bygone Days in Chicago* (Chicago: A. C. McClurg, 1910), 279.

33. A general survey of the origins of Chicago's German community can be found in Rudolph Hofmeister, *The Germans of Chicago* (Urbana: University of Illinois Press, 1976). The work of the Munich Project, headquartered at the Newberry Library, has resulted in a wealth of materials regarding Chicago's nineteenth- and early twentieth-century German working class. See Hartmut Keil

and John B. Jentz, eds., *German Workers in Industrial Chicago, 1850–1910: A Comparative Perspective* (DeKalb: Northern Illinois University Press, 1983); and Keil and Jentz, eds., *German Workers in Chicago: A Documentary History of Working-Class Culture from 1850 to World War I* (Urbana: University of Illinois Press, 1988). A detailed statistical study of a Scandinavian immigrant community is Ulf Beijboom's *Swedes in Chicago: A Demographic and Social Study of the 1840–1880 Immigration* (Vaxjo: Scandinavian University Books, 1971).

34. On the city's Irish community, see Michael F. Funchion, "Irish Chicago: Church, Homeland, Politics, and Class—the Shaping of an Ethnic Group, 1870–1900," in Melvin G. Holli and Peter d'A. Jones, eds., *Ethnic Chicago* (Grand Rapids: W. B. Eerdsman Publishing Co., 1981), 9–39. Also see Lawrence J. McCaffrey et al., *The Irish in Chicago* (Urbana: University of Illinois Press, 1987).

35. On the preeminent native-born families of the city, see Schultz, "The Businessman's Role in Western Settlement"; and Kathleen D. McCarthy, *Noblesse Oblige: Charity and Cultural Philanthropy in Chicago, 1849–1929* (Chicago: University of Chicago Press, 1982).

36. Cook, *Bygone Days*, 99.

37. The term "upper strata" is Frederic Cople Jaher's. See Jaher, *The Urban Establishment: Upper Strata in Boston, New York, Charleston, Chicago, and Los Angeles* (Urbana: University of Illinois Press, 1982).

38. Ibid., 492–98.

39. Ibid., 498. See also Cook, *Bygone Days*, 280.

40. Edward Bubnys, "Nativity and the Distribution of Wealth: Chicago, 1870," *Explorations in Economic History* 19 (April 1982): 101–9. Total wealth, in Bubny's calculations, is derived from adding entries for real wealth and personal wealth on the 1870 manuscript census schedules. Findings on nativity and occupation appear in Bubnys, "Chicago, 1870 and 1900: Wealth, Occupation, and Education," Ph.D. diss., University of Illinois at Urbana, 1978, 72. Similar data on occupational structure and nativity in 1870 is presented in Eric L. Hirsch, *Urban Revolt: Ethnic Politics in the Nineteenth-Century Chicago Labor Movement* (Berkeley: University of California Press, 1990), 92.

41. Bubnys, "Nativity," 106.

42. Ibid.

43. A rich literature within the field of labor history has considered these questions in regard to Chicago in the nineteenth and early twentieth century. See, for example, Jentz, "Class and Politics in an Emerging Industrial City"; Keil and Jentz, eds., *German Workers in Industrial Chicago;* and Hirsch, *Urban Revolt*. For the

twentieth century, see especially James R. Barrett, *Work and Community in the Jungle: Chicago's Packinghouse Workers, 1894–1922* (Urbana: University of Illinois Press, 1987); and Lizabeth Cohen, *Making a New Deal: Industrial Workers in Chicago, 1919–1939* (New York: Cambridge University Press, 1990). On the interrelations of class and ethnicity in other industrializing cities, see Olivier Zunz, *The Changing Face of Inequality: Urbanization, Industrial Development, and Immigrants in Detroit, 1880–1920* (Chicago: University of Chicago Press, 1982); and Stephen J. Ross, *Workers on the Edge: Work, Leisure, and Politics in Industrializing Cincinnati, 1788–1890* (New York: Columbia University Press, 1985).

44. For a very useful summary and critique of the historiography of class formation, see Theodore Koditschek, *Class Formation and Urban Industrial Society: Bradford, 1750–1850* (New York, Cambridge University Press, 1990). As Koditschek notes, E. P. Thompson's famous definition of class as a relationship undergirds most present scholarship, but it has also become increasingly plain that the social relations that define class identity are not fixed or absolute. Factors such as mobility or personal aspirations or self-identifications seemingly at odds with material circumstances complicate any simple assignment of class position, or more sweeping determinations of "class consciousness." For an important critique of how scholars have handled theories of class (and gender) identity, see Carolyn Kay Steedman, *Landscape for a Good Woman* (New Brunswick: Rutgers University Press, 1987). Also see Patrick Joyce, *Visions of the People: Industrial England and the Questions of Class, 1848–1914* (New York: Cambridge University Press, 1991). For the United States, Stuart M. Blumin makes an argument for the "cultural" dimensions of class identity in *The Emergence of the Middle Class*. On questions of the link between ethnicity and class, community studies such as Stanley Nadel, *Little Germany: Ethnicity, Class and Religion in New York City, 1845–1880* (Urbana: University of Illinois Press, 1990); or David M. Emmons, *The Butte Irish: Class and Ethnicity in an American Mining Town* (Urbana: University of Illinois Press, 1989), pay close attention to class differences within ethnic enclaves.

45. See John F. Kasson, *Rudeness and Civility: Manners in Nineteenth-Century Urban America* (New York: Hill and Wang, 1990); Christine M. Stansell, *City of Women: Sex and Class in New York, 1789–1860* (New York: Alfred A. Knopf, 1987); Mary P. Ryan, *Cradle of the Middle Class: The Family in Oneida County, New York, 1790–1865* (New York: Cambridge University Press, 1981); and Blumin, *The Emergence of the Middle Class*.

46. Cook, *Bygone Days*, 279.

47. My working definition of the process of politics is taken from

Keith Michael Baker: "The activity through which individuals and groups in any society articulate, negotiate, implement, and enforce the competing claims they make upon one another and upon the whole" (*Inventing the French Revolution* [New York: Cambridge University Press, 1990]), 4.

48. Among the many innovative studies I refer to here are David A. Gerber, *The Making of an American Pluralism;* Elizabeth R. Blackmar, *Manhattan for Rent, 1785–1850* (Ithaca: Cornell University Press, 1989); Amy C. Bridges, *A City in the Republic: Antebellum New York and the Origins of Machine Politics* (New York: Cambridge University Press, 1984); David C. Hammack, *Power and Society: Greater New York at the Turn of the Century* (New York: Russell Sage Foundation, 1982); David Harvey, *Consciousness and the Urban Experience* (Baltimore: Johns Hopkins University Press, 1985); Terrence J. McDonald, *The Parameters of Urban Fiscal Policy: Socioeconomic Change and Political Culture in San Francisco, 1860–1906* (Berkeley: University of California Press, 1986); Roy Rosenzweig, *Eight Hours for What We Will: Workers and Leisure in an Industrial City* (New York: Cambridge University Press, 1983); David M. Scobey, "Empire City: Politics, Culture, and Urbanism in Gilded Age New York," Ph.D. diss., Yale University, 1989; Christine M. Stansell, *City of Women;* Allen Steinberg, *The Transformation of Criminal Justice, Philadelphia, 1800–1880* (Chapel Hill: University of North Carolina Press, 1989); and Sean Wilentz, *Chants Democratic.*

49. On the subject of connections between social history and politics, see Alice Kessler-Harris, "Social History," in Eric Foner, ed., *The New American History* (Philadelphia: Temple University Press, 1990); and Thomas Bender, "Wholes and Parts: The Need for Synthesis in American History," *Journal of American History* 73 (June 1986): 120–36.

50. For a survey of literature dealing with the historical problem of "power" in cities, see Hammack, *Power and Society in Greater New York*, 3–27.

51. For a theoretical statement of how such historical problems might be conceptualized, see Martha Minow, "Rights Theories and Contemporary Legal Debates," in Minow, *Making All the Difference: Inclusion, Exclusion, and American Law* (Ithaca: Cornell University Press, 1990), esp. 148–59. For an analysis of how liberal visions of the abstract individual worked to inscribe particular relations of power within American legal doctrines of contract, see Christopher L. Tomlins, *Law, Labor and Ideology in the Early American Republic* (New York: Cambridge University Press, 1993). On the dynamic between universalism and social difference in the historical formulation of the American commitment to "equality," see J. R. Pole, *The*

Pursuit of Equality in American History (Berkeley: University of California Press, 1978).

52. On American journalism in the nineteenth century, see Mark Wahlgren Summers, *The Press Gang: Newspapers and Politics, 1865–1878* (Chapel Hill: University of North Carolina Press, 1994); Hazel Dicken Garcia, *Journalistic Standards in Nineteenth-Century America* (Madison: University of Wisconsin Press, 1989); and Frank Luther Mott, *American Journalism: A History of Newspapers in the United States* (New York: Macmillan, 1941).

53. Cited in Lloyd Wendt, *The Chicago Tribune: The Rise of a Great American Newspaper* (Chicago: Rand McNally, 1979).

Chapter One

1. For a description of the Peshtigo Fire, see Stephen J. Pyne, *Fire in America: A Cultural History of Wildland Rural Fire* (Princeton: Princeton University Press, 1985). Also see the short descriptions in contemporary histories of the Chicago Fire, for example, that contained in Elias Colbert and Everett Chamberlin, *Chicago and the Great Conflagration* (Chicago: J. S. Goodman and Co., 1871), 475–94.

2. The same evening also witnessed a sizable forest fire in western Michigan that did not claim a large number of lives but left over 15,000 homeless. See Colbert and Chamberlin, *Chicago and the Great Conflagration*, 474. For another account, and the theory that the coincidence of all these fires can be explained by the notion that a comet hit the Upper Midwest on this day, see Mel Waskin, *Mrs. O'Leary's Comet! Cosmic Explanations for the Great Chicago Fire* (Chicago: Academy Chicago, 1984).

3. For an account of the lumbering industry in the nineteenth-century Midwest, see William Cronon, *Nature's Metropolis*, 148–206.

4. *Boston Advertiser,* October 10, 1871. This article is contained in the Charles P. Deane Scrapbook of Clippings Relating to the Great Fire, Chicago Historical Society (CHS). Also see John J. Pauly, "The Great Chicago Fire as a National Event," *American Quarterly* 36 (Fall 1985): 682, for an account of a similar scene in New York City. Pauly's article argues that the Great Fire can be deemed the first national "media event" of the post–Civil War era.

5. *Prairie Farmer,* October 16, 1871. For the script of one of these lectures, see letter of Lavinia Perkins Clark, Great Fire of 1871 Personal Narratives Collection, CHS.

6. Alfred L. Sewell, *The Great Calamity! Scenes, Incidents, and Lessons of the Great Chicago Fire* (Chicago: Alfred L. Sewell, 1872).

7. Joseph Kirkland, *The Story of Chicago* (Chicago: Dibble Publishing Co., 1892), 306. Fire histories include Alfred L. Sewell, *The Great Calamity!*; Colbert and Chamberlin, *Chicago and the Great*

Conflagration; James W. Sheahan and George P. Upton, *The Great Conflagration. Chicago: Its Past, Present, and Future* (Chicago: Union Publishing Co., 1871); Frank Luzerne, *The Lost City!* (New York: Wells and Co., 1872); E. J. Goodspeed, *Chicago's Holocaust* (Chicago: J. W. Goodspeed, 1871); E. J. Goodspeed, *Histories of the Great Fires in Chicago and in the West* (Chicago: J. W. Goodspeed, 1871); and *"The Ruined City," or The Horrors of Chicago* (New York: American News Co., 1871). Carl S. Smith has described the similar outpouring of "instant" histories that occurred in the wake of the San Francisco Earthquake and Fire of 1906, drolly comparing at least twelve book-length accounts of that disaster to modern-day "chronicles of the rescue at Entebbe or the murder of the Scarsdale diet doctor" (see his "Urban Disorder and the Shape of Belief: The San Francisco Earthquake and Fire," *Yale Review* 74 [1984]: 79–95).

8. William Cronon has recently discussed how people construct their understandings of the "natural" components of their environments. (*Nature's Metropolis*, esp. 16–19).

9. Examples of such scholarship include Henry Nash Smith, *Virgin Land: The American West as Symbol and Myth* (Cambridge, MA: Harvard University Press, 1950); Leo Marx, *The Machine in the Garden: Technology and the Pastoral Ideal in America* (New York: Oxford University Press, 1964); and Boyer, *Urban Masses and Moral Order.*

10. The most sustained treatment of these questions, including comparisons of American and European cities, can be found in Andrew Lees, *Cities Perceived* (Manchester: University of Manchester Press, 1985). On literary representations of the city, see Alan Trachtenberg, *The Incorporation of America: Culture and Society in the Gilded Age* (New York: Hill and Wang, 1982); Michael Denning, *Mechanic Accents* (New York: Verso, 1987), 84–117, Janis Stout, *Sodoms in Eden* (Westport, CT: Greenwood Press, 1976); and Stuart M. Blumin, "Explaining the New Metropolis: Perception, Depiction, and Analysis in Mid-Nineteenth-Century New York City," *Journal of Urban History* 11 (November 1984): 9–38. On sensationalism and urban reporting, see Dan Schiller, *Objectivity and the News* (Philadelphia: University of Pennsylvania Press, 1981); Michael Schudson, *Discovering the News* (New York: Basic Books, 1978); and Frank Luther Mott, *American Journalism*, rev. ed. (New York: Macmillan, 1962).

11. William O. Stoddard, *The Volcano under the City, by a Volunteer Special* (New York: Fords, Howard, and Hulbert, 1887); Josiah Strong, *Our Country* (New York: Baker and Taylor, 1891). An influential nineteenth-century account of urban disorder is Joel T. Headley, *The Great Riots of New York, 1742–1873* (New York: E. P.

Treat, 1873). For a sustained analysis of the idea of the permanence of urban disorder, see Carl S. Smith, *Urban Disorder and the Shape of Belief: The Great Chicago Fire, the Haymarket Bomb, and the Model Town of Pullman* (Chicago: University of Chicago Press, 1995). Working independently, Professor Smith and I arrived at many similar conclusions about the state of disorder brought to bear by the Great Fire.

12. Luzerne, *The Lost City!* 100. On the conflation of fiction and reportage, see Robert Darnton, "Writing News and Telling Stories," *Daedelus* 104 (Spring 1975): 175–94.

13. Goodspeed, *Histories*, 242.

14. Ibid., 131. This sentiment, however, did not stop the minister from authoring two book-length treatments of the Great Fire.

15. H. W. Thomas, reprinted in Andreas, *A History of Chicago* 2:54.

16. Sewell, *The Great Calamity!* 28.

17. Chamberlin and Colbert, *Chicago and the Great Conflagration*, 212.

18. Luzerne, *The Lost City!* 93.

19. For a detailed description of the physical conditions of the "patches" of the South Side, see the *Chicago Times*, August 7 and 8, 1865.

20. Report of Thomas Mosher, Jr., October 16, 1871. Excerpted in *Chicago History* 1 (Fall 1971): 213–14. On the mechanics of convection, see Pyne, *Fire in America*, 21–24.

21. Frances L. Roberts, letter of October 21, 1871, printed in *The Christian Register*. Deane Scrapbook, CHS. Another account of this phenomenon can be found in the *Illinois Staats-Zeitung* of October 30, 1871, CFLPS Reel #20. Many lithographs and engravings of the city in flames also record the convection effect. See, for example, Colbert and Chamberlin, *Chicago and the Great Conflagration*, 199.

22. Luzerne, *The Lost City!* 96.

23. John V. LeMoyne described in detail how shifting winds spared the Ogden home. John V. LeMoyne, undated letter. Newberry Library Special Collections. Gift of William B. McIlvaine.

24. On the South and West Sides, a force of civilians and soldiers under the command of General Philip Sheridan halted the progress of the blaze "eating against the wind" by blowing up the buildings in the fire's path. See Colbert and Chamberlin, *Chicago and the Great Conflagration*, 252.

25. Goodspeed, *Histories*, 210.

26. The Prints and Photographs division at the Chicago Historical Society has a large collection of photographs of the ruins. The photographs reproduced in David Lowe, ed., *The Great Chicago Fire*, are largely drawn from this collection.

27. Goodspeed, *Histories*, 208.

28. A. C. Stinson, letter of October 27, 1871. Personal Narratives, CHS.

29. The figures in this paragraph are taken from the most complete account of fire damage available in fire histories, the "Losses By the Fire" chapter in Colbert and Chamberlin, *Chicago and the Great Conflagration*, 285–303.

30. Aurelia King, letter of October 26, 1871. Personal Narratives, CHS.

31. Thomas Foster, letter of October 14, 1871. Personal Narratives, CHS.

32. Mary Fales to mother, October 10, 1871. Personal Narratives, CHS.

33. Anonymous fire narrative, reprinted in Colbert and Chamberlin, *Chicago and the Great Conflagration*, 217.

34. For a survivor's description of the scene at the lakefront, see Frank Loesch, "Personal Experiences during the Chicago Fire," *Chicago History* 1 (Fall 1971): 202–5.

35. For examples of such images, see engravings reproduced in Lowe, ed., *The Great Chicago Fire*.

36. Goodspeed, *Histories*, 17.

37. The great bulk of extant personal narratives are assembled in the Great Fire of 1871 Personal Narratives Collection at the Chicago Historical Society, though others are reprinted and excerpted in various fire histories. Curators built the collection by soliciting contributions of materials from the membership, and on occasion they encouraged Fire survivors to record their reminiscences. The texts in the collection accordingly to a large degree reflect the fact that the Society has traditionally drawn most of its support from Chicago's more prosperous, native-born population.

38. Colbert and Chamberlin, *Chicago and the Great Conflagration*, 252. Horace White was a prominent journalist and liberal reformer. On his career and political philosophy, see Joseph Logsdon, *Horace White: Nineteenth Century Liberal* (Westport, CT: Greenwood Press, 1971).

39. John V. Lemoyne, undated letter. Newberry Library Special Collections.

40. Harriet Rosa, "Autobiography," 65. Harriet Rosa Collection, CHS.

41. It seems very likely that accounts of the Great Fire can be found in European archives, among collections of the letters of emigrants.

42. Luzerne, *The Lost City!* 181–82.

43. Colbert and Chamberlin, *Chicago and the Great Conflagration*, 285.

44. All of the contemporary fire histories, with the exception of Frank Luzerne's *The Lost City!* report this total. Luzerne estimates that as many as 1200 perished in the Great Fire. See ibid., 199.

45. Colbert and Chamberlin, *Chicago and the Great Conflagration,* 271.

46. See, for example, the *Chicago Republican,* October 26, 1871.

47. Colbert and Chamberlin, *Chicago and the Great Conflagration,* 373.

48. See Homer Hoyt, *One Hundred Years of Land Values in Chicago* (Chicago: University of Chicago Press, 1933), for a description of land use patterns in poor neighborhoods. Rosen makes a similar point in *The Limits of Power,* 171–74.

49. A map in Rosen demonstrates how graded streets were largely a feature of the business district and wealthy residential neighborhoods (*The Limits of Power,* 173).

50. Ross Miller notes that Chicagoans scrapped plans to build a Fire memorial, instead concentrating their energies on preparing the 1873 Interstate Industrial Exposition (*American Apocalypse,* 23).

51. Edward Payson Roe, *Barriers Burned Away* (New York: AMS Press, 1972, reprint of 1898 edition). Roe's career and body of writing is discussed in Glenn O. Carey, *Edward Payson Roe* (Boston: G. K. Hall, 1985). According to Carey, *Barriers Burned Away,* in terms of sales, was the "*Gone with the Wind* of the 1870s" (74). For specific statistics on the sales of this novel, see Frank Luther Mott, *Golden Multitudes: The Story of Best Sellers in the United States* (New York: Macmillan, 1947).

52. Sandra Sizer, in *Gospel Hymns and Social Religion: The Rhetoric of Nineteenth-Century Revivalism* (Philadelphia: Temple University Press, 1978), indeed cites *Barriers Burned Away* as a classic example of the manifestation of evangelical domesticity in fiction (97–106). For further analysis of religious usages of fiction in this period, see David Reynolds, *Faith in Fiction: The Emergence of Religious Literature in America* (Cambridge, MA: Harvard University Press, 1981).

53. Roe, *Barriers Burned Away,* 471.

54. For a similar response, see Thomas Hoyne, "Reminiscence of the Great Fire," 1882. Personal Narratives, CHS.

55. Francis Test, letter of October 13, 1871. Personal Narratives, CHS.

56. On the relationship between evangelical Christianity and class relations in nineteenth-century cities, see Paul Boyer, *Urban Masses and Moral Order*; Johnson, *A Shopkeeper's Millennium*; and Carroll Smith-Rosenberg, *Religion and the Rise of the American City* (Ithaca: Cornell University Press, 1971).

57. William Furness, "Autobiography," undated. William Furness Collection, CHS.

58. Luzerne, *The Lost City!*, 121.

59. William Gallagher, letter of October 17, 1871. Personal Narratives, CHS.

60. Furness, "Autobiography." William Furness Collection, CHS.

61. Laura Rollins, letter of October 11, 1871. Reprinted in the *New York Sun*, October 12, 1871.

62. William Gallagher, letter of October 17, 1871. Personal Narratives, CHS.

63. Horace White narrative, reprinted in Colbert and Chamberlin, *Chicago and the Great Conflagration*, 247.

64. Ibid.

65. See, for example, Sewell, *The Great Calamity!* 53; Sheahan and Upton, *The Great Conflagration*,199; Goodspeed, *Histories*, 228.

66. Laura Rollins, letter of October 11, 1871. Reprinted in the *New York Sun*, October 12, 1871.

67. On working-class family economy in the nineteenth-century, see Jeanne Boydston, *Home and Work: Housework, Wages, and the Ideology of Labor in the Early Republic* (New York: Oxford University Press, 1990). For accounts of the work of Irish women, see Hasia R. Diner, *Erin's Daughters in America: Irish Immigrant Women in the Nineteenth Century* (Baltimore: Johns Hopkins University Press, 1983).

68. Catherine O'Leary, Testimony before Chicago Fire Commissioners' Investigative Board, CHS. Portions of these records are reprinted in *Chicago History* 1 (Fall 1971): 215–18.

69. The content of the fire commissioners' report is detailed in *The Prairie Farmer* of December 16, 1871.

70. Cromie and Kogan, *The Great Fire: Chicago 1871*.

71. A famous photograph captures how an opportunistic media used this story. A few days after the Fire, one enterprising photographer showed the standard easy willingness to manipulate the particulars of the purported origins of the blaze, posing a borrowed stockyard steer as the infamous milk cow on the site of the ruined barn. This photograph is reproduced in *Chicago History* 1 (Fall 1971): 217.

72. The term "dangerous classes" was first given wide public usage following the publication of Charles Loring Brace, *The Dangerous Classes of New York and Twenty Years' Work among Them* (New York: Wynkoop and Hollenbeck, 1872). On Brace, see Thomas Bender, *Towards an Urban Vision* (Lexington: University of Kentucky Press, 1975).

73. Mrs. O'Leary and her cow have long endured in popular memory, cemented into place by songs, visual representations, and even a

1938 Hollywood film, *In Old Chicago*. (Actress Alice Brady indeed won the Academy Award for Best Supporting Actress for her role as Mrs. O'Leary, portrayed in the movie as the long-suffering mother of a Cain- and Abel-like pair of sons, played by Tyrone Power and Don Ameche.) In Chicago, even descendants of the O'Leary cow have been called upon to serve as historical symbols; at ceremonies marking the opening of Soldier Field in 1924, for example, the *Tribune* noted that "among the 'actors' will be 'Bessie,' a Holstein cow from Iowa, which the owner solemnly avers is a direct descendant of Mrs. O'Leary's cow" (*Chicago Tribune*, October 5, 1924, in Deane Scrapbook, CHS).

74. On anti-Irish sentiments, see Ray Allen Billington, *The Origins of Nativism in the United States, 1800–1844* (New York: Arno Press, 1974).

75. Goodspeed, *Histories*, 156.

76. Ibid., 157.

77. Colbert and Chamberlin, *Chicago and the Great Conflagration*, 372.

78. On the *Times'* editorial policy, see Justin Walsh's biography of *Times* owner and editor Wilbur R. Storey, *To Print the News and Raise Hell!* (Chapel Hill: University of North Carolina Press, 1968). Also see David Paul Nord, "The Public Community: The Urbanization of Journalism in Chicago," *Journal of Urban History* 11 (August 1985): 411–41. As Nord comments, "No American newspaper before the Hearst papers of the 1890s or perhaps even the jazzy New York tabloids of the 1920s was as dedicated as the *Times* to sensationalism" (417).

79. *Chicago Times*, October 23, 1871. The confession is reprinted in Luzerne, *The Lost City!* 186–96. Citation taken from Luzerne, *The Lost City!* 190.

80. Luzerne, *The Lost City!* 195.

81. *Illinois Staats-Zeitung*, October 30, 1871. Chicago Foreign Language Press Survey (hereafter CFLPS), Reel #20.

82. *Illinois Staats-Zeitung*, October 24, 1871. CFLPS #20. On the German press and the need to keep up with current European news, see the Hermann Raster Papers, Special Collections, Newberry Library.

83. *Illinois Staats-Zeitung*, October 24, 1871, CFLPS Reel #20.

84. Ibid.

85. Colbert and Chamberlin, *Chicago and the Great Conflagration*, 372.

86. On the Paris Commune, see Frank Jellinek, *The Paris Commune of 1871* (New York: Grosset and Dunlap, 1965); and Robert Tombs, *The War against Paris* (Cambridge: Cambridge University Press, 1981). Harvey, in *Consciousness and the Urban Experience*,

63–219, examines the spatial and class configuration of Paris from 1850 to 1871 as a case study for his theory of the urbanization of capital. For an examination of the construction of the image of "la petroleuse," the female "incendiaries" who were marked as particularly dangerous figures during the Commune, see Gay Gullickson, "La petroleuse," *Feminist Studies* 17 (Summer 1990).

87. Robert Collyer, *Some Memories* (New York: Dodd, Mead, 1909), 218.

88. For a discussion of how the Paris Commune perhaps functioned as a point of origin for anticommunism in America, see Samuel Bernstein, "The Impact of the Paris Commune in the United States," *Massachusets Review* (Spring 1971).

89. On elite fears of secret worker conspiracies, see Carl S. Smith, "Cataclysm and Cultural Consciousness: Chicago and the Haymarket Trial," *Chicago History* 15 (Summer 1986): 36–53. Nelson, *Beyond the Martyrs*, describes how Chicago Socialists and anarchists regularly celebrated the anniversary of the Commune at massive gatherings that sometimes drew between 10,000 and 20,000.

90. Luzerne, *The Lost City!* 196. Though the politics of the Paris Commune had no real counterpart in 1871 Chicago, recent observations by Terry Eagleton point to some similarities between the Great Fire and the Commune: both events produced shattering disruptions of a particular urban space that no city resident could escape. Eagleton notes that "the Commune was a question of the rapid, dizzying transformation of everyday life, a dramatic upheaval in everyday understandings of time and space, identity and language, work and leisure. . . . What the various subordinate groups had in common was precisely the besieged bastion of Paris, of a space that belonged to them all; and there could consequently be a constant traffic across the class lines" ("Foreword," in Kristin Ross, *The Emergence of Social Space: Rimbaud and the Paris Commune* [Minneapolis: University of Minnesota Press, 1988], ix).

91. Lowe, ed., *The Great Chicago Fire*, 49.

92. For a recent survey of work on the sociology of disaster, see Beverly Raphael, *When Disaster Strikes: How Individuals and Communities Cope with Catastrophe* (New York: Basic Books, 1986).

93. On the notion of the democratizing possibilities of an "instant history," see Ross Miller, "Chicago's Secular Apocalypse: The Great Fire and the Emergence of the Democratic Hero," in *Chicago Architecture, 1872–1922* (Munich: Prestel-Verlag, 1987).

94. Lowe, ed., *The Great Chicago Fire*, 60.

95. Sheridan, since 1870, had commanded the army's military Division of the Missouri, which was headquartered in Chicago.

96. Sheridan's own account of this episode appears in Philip H. Sheridan and Michael V. Sheridan, *Personal Memoirs of Philip*

Henry Sheridan, General, United States Army (New York: D. Appleton and Co., 1904), 2:472. His most recent biographer offers a brief mention of his service after the Chicago Fire. See Paul Andrew Hutton, *Phil Sheridan and His Army* (Lincoln: University of Nebraska Press, 1985), 209.

97. Beverly Raphael has noted that "looting is commonly rumored to occur in the immediate post-disaster phase." But on the whole, sociological research "suggests looting is rare and more in rumor and the media than in fact" (*When Disaster Strikes*, 118).

98. William Gallagher, for example, wrote about his fear of the "roughs," who "swore that the West Side should be burned too." Gallagher, letter of October 16, 1871. Personal Narratives Collection, CHS.

99. Ebon Matthews, "Recollections of the Great Chicago Fire," undated. Chicago Fire of 1871 Scrapbook, CHS.

100. See, for example, Francis L. Roberts, letter to the *Christian Register*, October 21, 1871. Deane Scrapbook, CHS, and Francis Test, letter of October 13. Personal Narratives, CHS.

101. Sheahan and Upton, *The Great Conflagration*, 203.

102. James Shaw, *The Military Occupation of Chicago* (Springfield: Illinois State Journal Printing, 1872). Speech delivered in the Illinois House of Representatives, January 24, 1872.

103. John M. Palmer, *Message from the Governor to the Illinois General Assembly*, December 9, 1871 (Springfield: Illinois State Journal Printing, 1871) (hereafter Palmer Message). For a narrative account of the constitutional issues at stake in this episode, see Lowell Dean Larsen, "Constitutionalism in Crisis: The Case of the Great Chicago Fire," M.A. thesis, University of Chicago, 1962. On Palmer, see George Thomas Palmer, *A Conscientious Turncoat: The Story of John M. Palmer* (New Haven: Yale University Press, 1941).

104. Eric Foner has described the issues at stake at length in *Reconstruction: America's Unfinished Revolution, 1863–1877* (New York: Harper and Row, 1988), esp. 444–59. On Palmer's activity in the Liberal Republican movement in 1872 and his emergence as a potential presidential candidate on the basis of the popularity of his states' rights stance over post-Fire Chicago, see ibid., 500–501.

105. Sheridan to R. B. Mason, October 12, 1871. In P. H. Sheridan, *The Condition of Affairs in the City of Chicago Occasioned by the Great Fire of October 8 and 9, 1871* (Chicago: n.p., 1871) (hereafter Sheridan Report).

106. Adjutant General H. Dilger, "Report of the Adjutant General to Governor John M. Palmer," October 15, 1871. Reprinted in *Report of the Select Committee on Governor J. M. Palmer's Messages of November 15 and December 9, 1871* (Springfield: Illinois State Journal Printing, 1872). (hereafter Select Committee Report).

107. Testimony of Police Commissioner Thomas Brown, Select Committee Report, 20.

108. James Milner, letter of October 14, 1871. Personal Narratives, CHS.

109. Ibid.

110. The army chief, Gen. W. T. Sherman, predictably supported Sheridan, as did President Grant. Sherman wrote to Sheridan in December to affirm that he and his forces "probably saved the city." Cited in Paul Andrew Hutton, *Phil Sheridan and His Army* (Lincoln: University of Nebraska Press, 1985), 210. Palmer did win his lawsuit, but not until well after all troops had withdrawn from Chicago. The legislature's investigation ended with a watered-down endorsement of Palmer's states' rights stance. The committee applauded the governor's protest against a "violation of the Constitution" but, in view of "trying circumstances," absolved the military of any "willful trespass" and, in a move that must have deeply galled the governor, particularly congratulated Sheridan for his valiant service. The resolution passed by the Illinois House of Representatives on January 25, 1872, is reprinted in Andreas, *A History of Chicago*, 2:780.

111. Palmer Message. The enmity between Palmer, Sheridan, and Army Commander-in-Chief W. T. Sherman was not entirely limited to their different interpretations of constitutionalism. They all had attended West Point together, and Palmer had resigned from the army after a dispute with Sherman. Palmer's account of this episode appears in John M. Palmer, *Personal Recollections of John M. Palmer* (Cincinnati: Robert Clarke Co., 1901).

112. None of the accounts of the episode specifically name these men, which is perhaps indicative of Sheridan's later awareness of the legal problems involved in his assumption of power. It seems clear, however, that the Relief and Aid Society—the elite organization charged with the task of public relief—plainly supported Sheridan. The members of its board—extremely successful and prominent businessmen like George M. Pullman, Marshall Field, Thomas Harvey, and Henry King—were the sort of commercial leaders in the city who readily involved themselves in civic affairs. So while neither Sheridan, Palmer, nor Mason ever specifically identified the "leading citizens" who pressed Sheridan to take command, it seems quite likely that the men who approached the general were connected to this elite circle.

113. The first actions of the mayor are detailed in a broadside that was posted throughout the city on the tenth, "LET US ORGANIZE FOR SAFETY IN CHICAGO." Reprinted in the Sheridan Report, 11. The activities of the state militia are described in H. Dilger, "Report of the Adjutant General to Governor John M.

Palmer," October 15, 1871. Reprinted in the Select Committee Report. See also the testimony of Police Commissioner Thomas Brown, Select Committee Report, 18–19. On the service of the Norwegian Battalion, see their petition for payment for their services (denied) to the Common Council. Chicago City Council Proceedings File (CCPF), Box 399, Folder 1872/148.

114. Select Committee Report, 18.

115. The account of Sheridan's activities in this and the following two paragraphs is taken from the Sheridan Report. While it is important to note that the only detailed account of these events is Sheridan's own, his story was confirmed by the investigation of the House Special Committee. Palmer's messages also indicate his acceptance of Sheridan's account. On the presence of the 600 regular troops, see "Report of the Committee on Finance," May 2, 1872. CCPF Box 407, Folder 1872/356.

116. Along with other newspapers, the *Chicago Times* sharply criticized Mason's lack of leadership following the Great Fire: "He has qualified himself more emphatically and eminently than any other man in Chicago for the position of a private citizen or church deacon in a country village, well removed from all possible excitement of a metropolis" (October 19, 1871). On Mason's election at the head of a reformist "Citizens'" ticket, see Einhorn, *Property Rules*, 232.

117. Thomas Brown testimony, Select Committee Report, 21–22.

118. Ibid., 20–21. Sheridan, "Report to W. T. Sherman," December 21, 1871. Reprinted in Sheridan Report, 12. According to Brown, he proposed that the army troops occupy only the burned district of the city, while Mark Sheridan asked that the troops be kept outside the city limits, at the ready to assist the police and militia, if needed. Both suggestions were rejected by General Sheridan.

119. On "weak" mayors in the nineteenth century, see Teaford, *The Unheralded Triumph*.

120. The declaration of October 11 is reprinted in Colbert and Chamberlin, *Chicago and the Great Conflagration*, 498.

121. *New York Tribune*, October 14, 1871. Reprinted in *"The Ruined City," or The Horrors of Chicago*, 34.

122. Francis Test, letter of October 13, 1871. Personal Narratives, CHS. For a similarly approving account of Sheridan's market interventions, see F. L. Roberts, letter to the *Christian Register*, October 21, 1871. Deane Scrapbook, CHS.

123. Orders, rosters, and reports concerning the volunteer militiamen can be found in the Chicago Fire Guards Collection at the Chicago Historical Society.

124. Francis Test, letter of October 13, 1871. Personal Narratives, CHS.

125. *New York Tribune,* October 14, 1871.

126. "Report of Adjutant General to Governor Palmer," Select Committee Report. On the structure of nineteenth-century militia and the participation of workingmen in the armed forces, see David Montgomery, *Citizen Worker* (New York: Cambridge University Press, 1993). Also see Marcus Cunliffe, *Soldiers and Civilians: The Martial Spirit in America, 1775–1865* (Boston: Little, Brown and Company, 1968).

127. *New York Tribune,* October 14, 1871.

128. Select Committee Report, 10.

129. Ibid.

130. According to Hutton, Palmer unsuccessfully attempted to indict Sheridan, Mason, and Colonel Frank Sherman, head of the "fire guards," for Grosvenor's murder as well (*Phil Sheridan and His Army,* 211).

131. Palmer Message.

132. Letter of George Pullman to R. B. Mason, October 23, 1871. George M. Pullman Collection, CHS.

133. Relief and Aid Society to General Philip Sheridan, October 28, 1971. Reprinted in Select Committee Report.

134. The other signers were Board of Trade President J. W. Preston, grain merchant Edward Henderland; and newspaper publishers and editors Horace White and Charles L. Wilson.

135. Sheridan to Townsend, October 29, 1871. Reprinted in Select Committee Report.

136. Sheridan to Underwood, December 18, 1871. Sheridan Report.

137. The article discussed in this and the following paragraph appeared in the *Chicago Evening Journal* of November 2, 1871, and was reprinted in the Select Committee Report.

138. Robert Schall, "The History of Fort Sheridan, Illinois" (unpublished manuscript, Chicago Historical Society, 1944).

139. On Sheridan's particular status as a hero to businessmen in Chicago, see Pierce, *History of Chicago,* vol. 3 (1959).

140. Elijah Haines of Lake County, speech in the Illinois House of Representatives, February 1, 1872. Reprinted in Shaw, "The Military Occupation of Chicago."

141. Ibid.

142. Ibid.

143. On the high rates of homeownership in Chicago, particularly in the North Side immigrant neighborhoods devastated by the Fire, see Einhorn, *Property Rules.*

144. All quotations in this and the next paragraph are taken from Thomas Brown testimony, Select Committee Report, 22–23.

145. For a more detailed account of this incident, see Chapter 4.

146. Select Committee Report, 11.
147. Cited in Goodspeed, *Histories*, 126–27.

Chapter Two

1. Holden reminiscence. Reprinted in Andreas, *History of Chicago*, 2:762.
2. Sidney Gay, letter to *New York Tribune*, undated. Cited in Sheahan and Upton, *The Great Conflagration*, 431.
3. Another graphic description of this scene can be found in William Gallagher's letter of October 16, 1871. Personal Narratives, CHS.
4. Andreas, *History of Chicago*, 2:762.
5. *Chicago Tribune* journalists Colbert and Chamberlin apparently coined this phrase, which soon became a common shorthand for the entire project of post-Fire charity.
6. Colbert and Chamberlin, *Chicago and the Great Conflagration*, 402.
7. Monetary contributions, according to the Chicago Relief and Aid Society, totaled nearly $5,000,000. Donated goods were not valued, but forty-six pages were needed to list them in the Society's 1874 comprehensive report. See *Report of the Chicago Relief and Aid Society of Disbursements to the Sufferers by the Chicago Fire* (Cambridge, MA: Riverside Press, 1874), 295–440 (hereafter CRAS Fire Report).
8. Colbert and Chamberlin, *Chicago and the Great Conflagration*, 419.
9. Cited in Elisabeth Kimball, "We Could Not Do without the Chicago Fire," *Chicago History* 1 (Fall 1971): 89–101. John J. Pauly convincingly advances the argument that the response to the Great Fire served as a convenient departure point for rhetoric encouraging post–Civil War reunification in "The Great Chicago Fire As a National Event," 668–83. But such rhetoric did not meet with universal approval; as Pauly notes, Southerners tended to be far less sympathetic to Chicago's plight. One striking example of this sentiment appears in Lloyd Lewis and Henry Justin Smith, *Chicago: The History of Its Reputation* (New York: Harcourt Brace Jovanovitch, 1929); a Democratic Rushville, Indiana, newspaper advanced the interpretation that the Great Fire was in fact divine retribution for the Union's conquest and burning of southern cities. "God adjusts balances," stated the paper. "Maybe with Chicago the books are now squared" (135).
10. *The Galaxy* (December 1871).
11. Emma Hambleton, letter of September 15, 1872. Personal Narratives, CHS.
12. Martha Shorey, letter of November 22, 1871. Personal Narratives, CHS.

13. *Chicago Republican,* November 23, 1871. As with the physical disaster, historians have safeguarded the instant mythic legacy of the world's charity. See, for example, Pierce, *History of Chicago,* Vol. 3; Andreas, *History of Chicago,* vol. 2; and Kimball, "We Could Not Do without the Chicago Fire." One major exception to this conventional treatment does exist: Timothy J. Naylor's "Responding to the Fire: The Work of the Chicago Relief and Aid Society," *Science and Society* 34 (Fall 1976): 407–19. Naylor's examination of Relief and Aid Society quite properly emphasizes the organization's deep awareness of class division in the city. This piece usefully summarizes the Society's methodology but incorrectly asserts that its practices were universally lauded. Naylor neglects to note that the Society was in fact one of many—albeit the wealthiest and most influential—charitable organizations in Chicago, and additionally fails to offer any context for or history of the evolution of the Society's guiding principles.

14. Robert Collyer, letter of May 23, 1872, to Flesher Bland. Reprinted in John Haynes Holmes, *The Life and Letters of Robert Collyer* (New York: Dodd, Mead, 1917), 2:173.

15. On seasonability of employment in the late nineteenth century, see David Montgomery, *The Fall of the House of Labor* (New York: Cambridge University Press, 1987); and Alexander Keyssar, *Out of Work: The First Century of Unemployment in Massachusetts* (New York: Cambridge University Press, 1986).

16. John Linden, letter to Henry Martin, Esq., January 25, 1872. Folder 2/2, Box 1443, Chicago Relief and Aid Society, Special Relief Records. United Charities Collection, CHS (hereafter CRAS Records).

17. *Industrial Chicago: The Manufacturing Interests* (Chicago: Goodspeed Publications Co., 1894), 2:591.

18. Sewell, *The Great Calamity!* 91.

19. Figures taken from Colbert and Chamberlin, *Chicago and the Great Conflagration,* 289. Their "Losses by the Fire" chapter (285–303) contains the most complete analysis of the physical and financial damage done by the Great Fire.

20. Ibid., 285–303; Andreas, *History of Chicago,* 2:378. On the central importance of these industries for Chicago's economy, see Cronon, *Nature's Metropolis;* and Pierce, *History of Chicago,* 3:65–144.

21. Ransom Handbill, Chicago Fire, 1871. Broadsides Collection, Prints and Photographs, CHS.

22. Jared Bassett, letter of October 21, 1871. Personal Narratives, CHS.

23. Samuel Greely, "Reminiscence of the Great Fire," September 10, 1909. Personal Narratives, CHS. Greely managed to save a pri-

vate set of property records. The loss of records, while a less obvious form of destruction than physical property such as buildings, would prove crippling to many businesses and governmental functions. Banks, for example, had no records of accounts, loans, or mortgages. Insurance companies similarly lost the details of policies. The files, billings, and libraries of attorneys were likewise destroyed. Allan Pinkerton's private detective agency, as Frank Luzerne noted, lost files on cases and criminals, and the records of the Secret Service of the Army of the Potomac, a function coordinated by Pinkerton. Public records—voting registration, tax lists, naturalization papers, court proceedings, land titles—were all, in some measure, damaged or completely burned.

24. William Furness, "Autobiography." William Furness Collection, CHS.

25. Greely, "Reminiscence of the Great Fire."

26. Hermann Raster, letter of October 15, 1871. Personal Narratives, CHS.

27. *Illinois Staats-Zeitung*, April 1, 1872, CFLPS #20. *Nord Seite* was a phrase employed by American satirists. See Cook, *Bygone Days*.

28. *Illinois Staats-Zeitung*, October 13, 1871. C.F.L.P.S. Reel #13.

29. Colbert and Chamberlin, *Chicago and the Great Conflagration*, 345.

30. James Milner, letter of October 12, 1871. Personal Narratives, CHS.

31. Colbert and Chamberlin, *Chicago and the Great Conflagration*, 285.

32. On the McCormick Reaper Work's recovery from the Great Fire, see William T. Hutchinson, *Cyrus Hall McCormick: Harvest, 1856–1884* (New York: D. Appleton Co., 1925), 502–11.

33. Colbert and Chamberlin, *Chicago and the Great Conflagration*, 343.

34. Ibid.

35. Frank Maiwarus, Special Relief Application, February 20, 1872. Box 1443, Folder 2/4, CRAS Papers.

36. Colbert and Chamberlin, 335.

37. Robert S. Critchell, *Recollections of a Fire Insurance Man* (Chicago: n.p., 1909), 76.

38. According to Bessie Pierce, of the $196,000,000 property loss in the fire, only $95,553,720.94 was covered by insurance. (It should be noted that Pierce does not address the question of whether policies equaled property values, or how much property was uninsured.) Of the 201 insurance companies that did business in Illinois, 26 agencies in New York, 7 in Connecticut, 3 in Massachusetts, 5 in Ohio, and 17 in Illinois were forced out of business. Pierce, *History*

of Chicago, 3:12. Colbert and Chamberlin list the exact losses suffered by each company (*Chicago and the Great Conflagration*, 307–13). According to Colbert and Chamberlin, only two Chicago agencies—Great Western and Republic—weathered the fire intact and paid 100 percent of claims.

39. Mrs. William Blair, letter of November 20, 1871. Personal Narratives, CHS.

40. Hutchinson, *Cyrus Hall McCormack*, 507.

41. Dietrich Voelker, letter to Robert Laird Collier. April 18, 1872. CRAS Papers, Box 1443, Folder 2/1.

42. Gotfried Schneitmann, Special Relief Application, undated. CRAS Papers, Box 1443, Folder 2/2.

43. According to Colbert and Chamberlin, German Mutual, with net assets of $223,967, faced actual losses of $3,000,000 (*Chicago and the Great Conflagration*, 301). On financial, credit, and insurance institutions run within ethnic communities, see Victor Greene, *American Immigrant Leaders* (Baltimore: Johns Hopkins University Press, 1987); Kathleen Neils Conzen, *Immigrant Milwaukee, 1836–1860* (Cambridge, MA: Harvard University Press, 1976); and Kerby Miller, *Emigrants and Exiles* (New York: Oxford University Press, 1985).

44. *First Special Report of the Chicago Relief and Aid Society* (Chicago: Culver, Page, Hoyne, and Co., 1871), 49 (hereafter CRAS Special Report). According to the German Aid Association of Chicago, three quarters of all of the victims of the Great Fire were German-born. *Illinois Staats-Zeitung*, October 14, 1871.

45. *Workingman's Advocate*, October 28, 1871.

46. *New York Herald*, October 12, 1871

47. General Relief Committee Poster, October 11, 1871. Broadside Collection, Chicago Fire, 1871, Prints and Photographs, CHS.

48. Holden, an attorney, in 1868 was elected Tenth Ward alderman as part of a Labor Reform slate. He was a Democrat who was sympathetic to the cause of organized labor. See the *Workingman's Advocate*, April 11, 1868.

49. Letter of Charles Holden, reprinted in Goodspeed, *Histories*, 414. For a detailed account of the work of the General Relief Committee, see Holden's lengthy description of his role in the first days of relief. Alderman Charles Holden, "To the Mayor and Aldermen . . . , " November 12, 1871. Chicago City Council Proceedings File, Box 397, Folder 1871/1239.

50. Roswell B. Mason, proclamation of October 13, 1871. Reprinted in CRAS Fire Report, 121.

51. On the Chicago Relief and Aid Society, see McCarthy, *Noblesse Oblige*. McCarthy offers an excellent discussion of transformation of charitable organizations in Chicago, with particular attention

to questions of gender. She describes the CRAS as a haven for "Christian Gentlemen": self-made, Protestant, believers in corporate organization and close monitoring of gifts. On the origins and early history of the CRAS, see Otto M. Nelson, "The Chicago Relief and Aid Society, 1850–1874," *Journal of the Illinois State Historical Society* 59 (1966): 48–66. More complete descriptions of the Society and its work can be found in John Albert Mayer, "Private Charity in Chicago from 1871 to 1915," Ph.D. diss., University of Minnesota, 1978; and James B. Brown, *A History of Public Assistance in Chicago* (Chicago: University of Chicago, 1941). For an unfriendly assessment of the Society, see Alexander Johnson, *Adventures in Social Welfare, Being Reminiscent of all Things, Thoughts, and Folks during Forty Years of Social Work* (Fort Wayne: n.p., 1923).

52. Gay letter, in Sheahan and Upton, *The Great Conflagration*, 322.

53. Goodspeed, *Histories*, 414.

54. CRAS Fire Report, 120. Dexter, a railroad attorney and lumberman, was chairman of the Society's Executive Committee. Fairbank, an industrialist known as the city's "lard king," was one of the private citizens appointed to Holden's General Relief Committee. It is interesting that the same sort of private takeover of relief by an elite men's organization occurred in the aftermath of San Francisco's 1906 earthquake and fire. See Judd Kahn, *Imperial San Francisco* (Lincoln: University of Nebraska Press, 1983).

55. James B. Brown, in his *History of Public Assistance in Chicago*, documents the breakdown between public and private administration of welfare in Chicago at the time of the fire. See 75–81. As historian Michael Katz has noted, this admixture of public and private initiatives in relief work was a common nineteenth-century phenomenon; "Everywhere," he argues, "relief had a mixed economy. In practice, throughout most of America it was a public/private venture" (*In the Shadow of the Poorhouse* [New York: Basic Books, 1986], 46).

56. Cited in Goodspeed, *Histories*, 414.

57. Sheahan and Upton, *The Great Conflagration*, 322. For a similar explanation of the Society's motives, see Sidney Howard Gay, "Chicago and the Relief Committee," *Lakeside Monthly* 7 (February 1872): 168. On Tammany Hall and the politics of New York City in the 1860s and 1870s, see Seymour Mandelbaum, *Boss Tweed's New York* (New York: J. Wiley and Co., 1965).

58. For a description of pre-Fire charges of corruption against the council, see Einhorn, *Property Rules*, 232–33.

59. The most complete description and analysis of post–Civil War liberal reformism appears in John G. Sproat, *The Best Men: Liberal*

Reformers in the Gilded Age (New York: Oxford University Press, 1968).

60. To explain further how the Common Council could be excluded from any official civic efforts, Gay claimed that the incoming flood of relief had been sent to the people of Chicago—which was an entity distinct from the municipality. Since the government of the city had not been designated as the official recipient of any funds, Gay reasoned that these moneys "no more fell under the control of the Board of Aldermen than under the Board of Trade." No formal legal challenge was ever made concerning this question, and in the course of the next two years, the Relief and Aid Society continually refused to relinquish any of the Fire fund to the Common Council (Gay, "Chicago and the Relief Committee").

61. It is worth noting that the *Chicago Republican*, the Society's sole critic in the ranks of the English-language press, would have scoffed at such reasoning. According to the *Republican*, the Society's directors were simply looking for personal profit. As the paper charged on December 4, "[T]he entire city is beginning to understand that the Relief and Aid Society is composed of a lot of self-constituted and unscrupulous men—working only for their own interest and aggrandizement." The *Republican* accused the Society of a wide range of abuses, including many forms of fraud and theft. But since the Society kept its own books, such charges are impossible to verify. The *Republican*, a daily founded in 1867 by a disgruntled group of *Tribune* employees, occupied an avowedly nonpartisan editorial stance. A self-appointed watchdog of all municipal authorities, the *Republican* was always especially pleased to embarrass Joseph Medill and his prominent associates (*Chicago Republican*, December 4, 1871).

62. Sheahan and Upton, *The Great Conflagration*, 325.

63. Ibid.

64. Ibid.

65. Frances Roberts, letter of December 20, 1871. Frances Roberts Collection, CHS. Roberts, a single woman, worked before the Fire as the secretary at Robert Collyer's Unity Church. A sample of occupations from the Third District payroll suggests that most men employed by the Society were salesmen, clerks, bookkeepers, real estate or insurance agents. Women were most often teachers. Box 1443, Folder 4/2, CRAS Papers.

66. A standard form required every applicant's name, pre- and post-Fire address, estimated property loss, value of insurance, nationality, occupation, income per week, marital status, number of children, relief from other sources, and two references. References had to be obtained from some "respectable" citizen; surviving records indicate that applicants were most often referred by clergy,

employers, and ethnic leaders. Politicians, not surprisingly, seldom served as referees. After this initial paper work was complete, a Society visitor investigated each claimant through a home visit.

67. Frances Roberts, letter of October 20, 1871. Roberts Collection, CHS.

68. "Burnt Out," letter to the *Chicago Republican*, December 4, 1871.

69. In the few years prior to the Great Fire, the Relief and Aid Society operated on an annual budget in the neighborhood of $25,000 and served perhaps 3000 individuals (*Chicago Relief and Aid Society Annual Report for the Year Ending October 31, 1871* [Chicago: J. M. W. Jones, 1871]).

70. As of January 6, 1872, of 9895 aided families, 2378 were headed by widows and deserted women; 3707 fell into the category of sick, aged, and infirm; and a minority of 3810 were deemed able-bodied (*Report of the Chicago Relief and Aid Society for 1871–72* [Chicago: Horton and Leonard, 1872], 31). On how ideas about "worthiness" were affected by charity-givers' understanding of gender difference, see Stansell, *City of Women;* Lori D. Ginzberg, *Women and the Work of Benevolence: Morality, Politics, and Class in the Nineteenth-Century United States* (New Haven: Yale University Press, 1990); Nancy A. Hewitt, *Women's Activism and Social Change: Rochester, New York, 1822–1872* (Ithaca: Cornell University Press, 1984); McCarthy, *Noblesse Oblige;* and Nancy F. Cott, *The Bonds of Womanhood: "Woman's Sphere" in New England, 1780–1835* (New Haven: Yale University Press, 1977).

71. Rufus Blanchard, *History of the Discovery and Conquest of the Northwest* (Wheaton, IL: R. Blanchard, 1878), 543.

72. Twenty-seven separate relief, benevolent, and protective associations, apart from the CRAS, are listed in Edward's City Directory for 1870.

73. Undated newspaper clipping, Chicago Relief and Aid Society Minute Book, 1867–71. United Charities Collection, CHS.

74. Ibid.

75. Blanchard, *History of the Discovery,* 543.

76. On the AICP, see Carroll Smith-Rosenberg, *Religion and the Rise of the American City* (Ithaca: Cornell University Press, 1971); Stansell, *City of Women;* and Bernstein, *The New York City Draft Riots.*

77. Chicagoans Robert Collyer, N. K. Fairbank, and Ezra McCagg all played prominent roles in the Sanitary Commission and the pre- and post-Fire work of the CRAS. Collyer indeed moved to Washington, D.C., to serve as Sanitary Commissioner Reverend Henry Bellows's second-in-command. For Collyer's account of his call to "minister and administrate," see Collyer, *Some Memories*, 120–25.

Additionally, many wives and daughters of Society members worked for the commission's Northwestern Sanitary Fair. On the work of the commission in Chicago, see Cook, *Bygone Days*, 106; Mary Livermore, *The Story of My Life* (Hartford: A. D. Worthington and Co., 1899); and Sarah Edwards Henshaw, *Our Branch and Its Tributaries; Being a History of the Work of the Northwestern Sanitary Commission* (Chicago: Alfred L. Sewell, 1868).

78. On the conservative intellectual currents behind the structure of the commission, George M. Fredrickson, *The Inner Civil War* (New York: Harper and Row, 1965), is particularly useful. As Fredrickson argues, the Sanitary Commission experience gave elite conservatives "a strong sense that philanthropy and reform could be carried on for practical, non-utopian, and even profoundly conservative purposes. They were encouraged to greater social activity and given an expectation that the principles of order and stability, a greater reverence for institutions that they favored, could be instilled in the popular mind by an aristocratic elite operating in a private or semi-official capacity. They began to believe that the kind of democratic politics they detested was not the only path to power and influence" (112). In *Women and the Work of Benevolence*, Lori Ginzberg largely concurs with Fredrickson's analysis of the commission, and further offers a superb account of the agency's key role in transforming upper- and middle-class women's attitudes toward social class and charity and in the remaking of gender dynamics within the project of benevolence 133–73. For an institutional history of the commission, see William C. Maxwell, *Lincoln's Fifth Wheel: A Political History of the Sanitary Commission* (New York: Longmans, Green, 1956).

79. On the linkages between the work of charity and constructions of gender in this period, see Ginzberg, *Women and the Work of Benevolence*. By the 1870s, as Ginzberg argues, "the new administrators of charity denied that women were better suited for benevolent work: they demanded professional—not gender—standards" (200).

80. Blanchard, *History of the Discovery*, 71. For a perceptive analysis of how Americans connect the "dignity of labor" and the prerogatives of citizenship, see Judith Shklar, *American Citizenship: The Quest for Inclusion* (Cambridge, MA: Harvard University Press, 1991), esp. 63–101. See also Daniel T. Rodgers, *The Work Ethic in Industrial America, 1850–1920* (Chicago: University of Chicago Press, 1978).

81. The Relief and Aid Society's approach towards charity was part of an emergent trend towards the centralized management of charitable functions in cities. "Charity Organization," which sought to bring the multiple agencies of any city under one controlling body, was pioneered in London in 1869. The first American offshoot

of this system appeared in Buffalo in 1878; the best-known American advocates of the ideology were Josephine Shaw Lowell and Robert Gurteen. According to Alexander Johnson, an early administrator of the Cincinnati Charity Organization Society, the CRAS, despite a similar reliance on "scientific" methods, was not a true example of organized charity; the Relief and Aid directorate, in Johnson's view, was too autocratic. Society leaders, he claimed, expected too much control over all charitable institutions in the city. Historiographically, the dates of transition to the era of organized charity remain fuzzy but are usually located in the late 1870s. Clearly, however, corporate models based on "scientific" investigation, if not true "organized charity," existed prior to this date; the CRAS probably stood on some sort of middle ground, using the precepts of scientific charity without the apparatus of organized charity. Given the poor fit of standard labels and periodization, it seems plain that this era represents a period of rapid change in the ideology of benevolence that needs more study. For surveys of the history of philanthropy and social welfare in this period, see Katz, *In the Shadow of the Poorhouse;* Walter Trattner, *From Poor Laws to Welfare State* (New York: Free Press, 1984), 77–102; Robert Bremner, *From the Depths: The Discovery of Poverty in the United States* (New York: New York University Press, 1956); and Bremner, *The Public Good: Philanthropy and Welfare in the Civil War Era* (New York: Alfred A. Knopf, 1981); and Roy Lubove, *The Professional Altruist* (Cambridge, MA: Harvard University Press, 1965), 1–21.

82. Thomas Haskell, in *The Emergence of Professional Social Science* (Urbana: University of Illinois Press, 1977), identifies the "perhaps conflicting" impulses behind scientific charity as "vigourous humanitarianism" and "conservative paternalism." (90). Haskell argues that though men such as those in charge of the Society might seem "callous" or "insensitive" to twentieth-century eyes, any definition of humanitarianism must account for the differing moral systems of the mid-nineteenth century. He observes that "their reform instruments seem blunt and superficial today—not because they were hypocritical or stupid, but because they perceived the causes of social problems to lie close to the surface of events, and therefore to require no very elaborate instruments of reform" (95).

83. Blanchard, *History of the Discovery,* 543.

84. Haskell notes that "the curious blend of humane sympathy and haughty condescension" that marked the ideology of scientific charity was a reflection of "the persistence of the assumption that the individual is the primary, if not the entire, cause of his own place in life" (*The Emergency of Professional Social Science,* 96). Chicago's rising class of elite entrepreneurs, mostly themselves self-

made, were largely unsympathetic to the lot of the city's poor. Gareth Stedman-Jones, discussing the founders of British "scientific charity," notes in *Outcast London* (New York: Pantheon, 1971) that "as a group who had attained positions of eminent respectability not by the accident of birth, but through the practice of austere virtues and long years of unrelenting hard work, they were prone to view the poor . . . with a hard-headed severity born of strong aversion to all those who stood condemned of fecklessness, indolence, and lack of resilience. With this background, the equation between virtue and vice, success and failure, was relatively simple to make" (270).

85. Undated clipping, CRAS Minute Book, 1867–71, CHS.

86. CRAS Special Report, 30.

87. Ibid., 11.

88. Dollar amount given in CRAS Fire Report, 440.

89. CRAS Special Report, 30.

90. *Overland Monthly* (December 1871). Cited in Naylor, "Responding to the Fire," 456.

91. As many scholars of nineteenth-century culture and society have observed, the creation of bureaucratic structures and new reliance upon expertise was symptomatic of American's post–Civil War turn, in John Higham's words, from "boundlessness to consolidation." See John Higham, *From Boundlessness to Consolidation: The Transformation of American Culture, 1848–1860* (Ann Arbor: University of Michigan Press, 1969).

92. The following men sat on the CRAS Executive Committee: Dexter; dry-goods merchant Henry King; Charles Hammond, executive vice-president of the Pullman Palace Car Company; lumber merchants Thomas Harvey and Thomas Avery; "lard king" Nathaniel Fairbank; George M. Pullman; Dr. Hosmer A. Johnson; the attorney E. C. Larned; the iron manufacturer N. S. Bouton; and the railway supply dealer J. MacGregor Adams. The "General Plan" is reproduced and explained in CRAS Special Report, 6–13.

93. On management strategies of the day, see Alfred D. Chandler, *The Visible Hand* (Cambridge, MA: Harvard University Press, 1977).

94. CRAS Special Report, 21. The telegraphers, mostly women, were employed by the Society as clerks and received the standard clerical salary of $2.00 per day.

95. Goodspeed, *Histories*, 426.

96. *Chicago Tribune*, October 22, 1871.

97. CRAS Circular, October 24, 1871. Reprinted in CRAS Fire Report, 158.

98. Though the axiom of full employment was probably correct in the Fire's immediate aftermath, it clearly did not remain valid by the following spring. The shifting state of the city's post-Fire labor market is considered in more detail in Chapter 4.

99. People of all classes reacted to the Great Fire by departing from Chicago. So many of the city's wealthy went up to their summer homes on Wisconsin's Lake Geneva that the resort community virtually had a second season. Morris Horowitz (pseudonym), a peddler, like many of his very mobile working-class counterparts, headed to the country (WPA Interview with Morris Horowitz, reprinted in Banks, ed., *First Person America,* 31). According to Sidney Gay, of the 100,000 left homeless by the fire, "20,000 probably left the city in the course of a few days" (Sheahan and Upton, *The Great Conflagration,* 331).

100. CRAS Special Report, 20.

101. *New York Times,* October 15, 1871.

102. It is worth noting that this policy might have been inspired in part by a wish of Chicago's elite to maintain an adequate supply of labor in the city. Timothy Naylor makes this argument, suggesting that General Sheridan, in support of the Society, was willing to use force to keep able-bodied men in the city. Naylor reports that, on October 17, a company of soldiers broke up an attempt to commandeer a train bound for Pittsburgh ("Responding to the Fire," 412). I have not been able to verify this citation.

103. Anne McClure Hitchcock, letter to Mrs. Jewell, December 8, 1871. Anne McClure Hitchcock Collection, CHS.

104. CRAS Special Report, 8.

105. Ibid. In the 1870s, Chicago was one of few American cities with relatively high rates of working-class homeownership. The cultural, economic, and political meaning of property rights is the central theme of Chapter 3.

106. On nineteenth-century upper- and middle-class views of the cultural import of domesticity and the fact of homeownership, see Gwendolyn Wright, *Building the Dream* (New York: Pantheon, 1981); Clifford Clark, *The American Family Home, 1800–1960* (Chapel Hill: University of North Carolina Press, 1986); and Kathryn Kish Sklar, *Catherine Beecher: A Study in American Domesticity* (New York: W. W. Norton, 1976).

107. CRAS Special Report, 8.

108. CRAS Fire Report, 189. One of the barracks went up in Washington Park, directly across from the single surviving home on the north side, the Mahlon Ogden mansion. Anna Shelton Ogden West, Mahlon Ogden's niece, took special note of the tension borne of the close proximity of these two very different types of shelter: "I can remember the men going out with their guns to help keep watch . . . this being the more necessary as it seemed that their were ill feelings about our house not being burned. This was especially the case after we achieved many new neighbors in the hastily run up barracks with which Washington Park was soon filled" West reminis-

cence, Personal Narratives, CHS. Hermann Raster, editor of the *Staats-Zeitung*, called upon General Sheridan to defuse the symbolic import of this ironic conjunction. "This house," wrote Raster, "must be confiscated for the shelterless, or the condition will become general that the rich Yankeedom wants to reconstruct Chicago as a Yankee city, at the cost of poor Germans and Scandinavians. Also for another reason—hundreds of those who have lost everything have become half insane, and have only one thought that all should be equal in misfortune. How if one of these unfortunates, with the idea of compensating an injustice of fate, were to put the burning torch to the millionaire Ogden's house?" *Illinois Staats-Zeitung*, October 17, 1871. CFLPS #20, 108.

109. CRAS Special Report, 8.

110. *Chicago Tribune*, November 3, 1871. Construction of Relief Society shelters proceeded quickly; over 300 16-feet x 20-feet homes went up by the end of October. Temporary housing of this sort apparently made for a very uncomfortable winter. As P. C. Conway, a recipient of a Society shanty, complained in March 1872, "[I]t defends neither *Frost*, *Wind*, or *Rain*." The visitor dispatched to investigate Conway's request for funds for repairs came back with this sobering report: "in as good a condition as the other Shelter Houses." P. C. Conway Special Relief Application, March 26, 1872. Box 1443, Folder 2/1, CRAS Papers.

111. The antebellum ideology of free labor is analyzed with great clarity in Eric Foner, *Free Soil, Free Labor, Free Men: The Ideology of the Republican Party before the Civil War* (New York: Oxford University Press, 1970). Post–Civil War modifications of this ideology are considered in David Montgomery, *Beyond Equality: Labor and the Radical Republicans* (New York: Alfred A. Knopf, 1967).

112. CRAS Special Report, 22. The Society, for example, gave E. D. Place, a carpenter, chisels, saws, planes, and other tools worth $18.00. Box 1443, Folder 2/1, CRAS Papers.

113. The Society supplied these makeshift factories with piece goods and fully funded their payrolls. Women's societies engaged in this work included the Ladies' Relief and Aid Society, the Ladies' Industrial Aid Society of St. John's Church, the Ladies' Christian Union, the Ladies' Society of the Park Avenue Church, and the Ladies' Society of the Home of the Friendless. CRAS Fire Report, 152; CRAS Special Report, 18. Approximately 200 women were employed in this manner. Judging from payroll records, most were immigrants (predominantly Irish), many of whom were unable to write (marking their "X" instead of a signature roughly one-third of the time). Box 1443, Folder 4/3. CRAS Papers.

114. CRAS Special Report, 22.

115. CRAS Memo, October 27, 1871. Broadsides Collection, Chicago Fire, 1871. Prints and Photographs, CHS.

116. CRAS Special Report, 22–24.

117. *Chicago Tribune*, November 14, 1871.

118. *Chicago Times*, November 30, 1871. Reports of extreme belligerence and incompetence indeed prompted O. C. Gibbs, in early December, to issue a special circular inviting "all persons who think they have been treated with incivility, rudeness, or neglect" to point out particular offenders to the subdistrict superintendents (*Chicago Republican*, December 4, 1871).

119. Frances Roberts, letter of January 11, 1872. Frances Roberts Collection, CHS.

120. *Chicago Republican*, November 23, 1871.

121. The sole Relief and Aid director born abroad was Julius Rosenthal, a prominent German-Jewish merchant.

122. Since the bridges leading to the North Side had all burned, victims could only reach depots after a long, dark trip through the very congested Clark Street tunnel.

123. *Illinois Staats-Zeitung*, December 10, 1871. CFLPS #20.

124. From the first days after the Fire, Germans had organized to make sure that their community would be well-treated; as a meeting on October 13 stated the following purpose: "To take protective measures for the relief of German sufferers, and to take necessary steps to take up the side of German representation in the general relief organization" *Illinois Staats-Zeitung*, October 13, 1871). The German Aid Association, a group that existed before the Fire, did distribute close to $65,000 in fire relief to German sufferers. But since an estimated 50,000 German Chicagoans were left homeless by the fire, the burden of relief was far beyond what this smaller organization could handle. On the post-Fire activities of the German Aid Association, see the *Chicago Times*, October 2, 1872.

125. *Illinois Staats-Zeitung*, December 25, 1871. CFLPS, #20.

126. Sidney Gay, quoted in Sheahan and Upton, *The Great Conflagration*, 322.

127. CRAS Circular, October 24, 1871. Reprinted in Fire Report, 158.

128. Terrence Mulhern, Shelter Committee application, undated. Box 1443, Folder 4/4, CRAS Papers, CHS.

129. Kate Moran, Shelter Committee Application, undated. Box 1443, Folder 4/4, CRAS Papers, CHS. As the language of these files suggests, preexisting anti-Irish prejudice clearly figured into Society workers' accounts of this particular community's response to the Great Fire. But it also seems plain that such hostilities had some due cause: Irish families did collect Fire relief in numbers out of propor-

tion to their percentages of either the population at large or among those who lived in the conflagration's path.

Anecdotal evidence indicates that some of Chicago's Irish were quick to apply for a share of the Society's cash and goods. On October 20, for example, according to relief worker Frances Roberts, "the applicants were mostly Irish, and the population of the North Side—which is the chief section of the burnt district—had but few Irish but were largely German." Frances Roberts, letter of October 20, 1871. Frances Roberts Collection, CHS. A conversation reportedly overheard at the Ottawa, Illinois train depot was reprinted in the *Chicago Tribune* in late November:

> "Well, Tim, and what is it you are doin' here!"
>
> "Faith, ans it's to Chicago I'm going; and what are ye askin' for?"
>
> "Sure, it's there I'm goin' meself; and what are ye goin' for?"
>
> "Sure an' ain't the Relief Society there?"
>
> (*Chicago Tribune*, November 29, 1871)

As this piece of reportage suggests, post-Fire attitudes toward the Irish poor were rooted in older cultural stereotypes attached to this community; it is difficult to know just what is "true" here. Numbers do offer some indications, though, that Chicago's Irish poor, reflecting their own differing definitions of charity, did not hesitate to file claims with the Society. According to the 1870 Census, approximately twenty percent of Chicago's population was of Irish origin. As a group, the Irish made up the poorest segment of the city; before the Fire, they comprised close to one-third of the Society's clientele. In the first months of Fire relief, the great bulk of aided families (in keeping with the geography of destruction) were of German or Scandinavian origins—Society records show that 7280 German families and 2102 Scandinavian families were assisted; 5612 Irish families also received aid. CRAS Special Report, 25. While the preexisting poverty of this group would have definitely increased their overall economic vulnerability and hence made them candidates for Fire relief, the heaviest concentrations of Irish settlement in the city remained outside the burned district, rendering this high number somewhat anomalous.

130. CRAS Fire Report, 272.

131. Colbert and Chamberlin, *Chicago and the Great Conflagration*, 403.

132. "to the Pastors . . . , " Committee on Special Relief broadside, undated. Chicago Fire, 1871, Broadside Collection, Prints and Photographs, CHS. This bureau was headed by Robert Laird Collier, a minister, and E. C. Larned, an attorney. Three women also served on this committee's directorate, making Special Relief the

only branch of post-Fire relief to incorporate women in executive positions. All of the three—Mrs. Joseph Medill, Mrs. David Gage, and Mrs. J. Tyler—had previously worked with the Sanitary Commission.

133. Jeremiah Healey, letter to the Committee on Special Relief, April 13, 1872. Folder 2/1, Box 1443. CRAS Papers.

134. A. Poncelet, letter to the Committee on Special Relief, February 5, 1872. Box 1443, Folder 2/1, CRAS Papers.

135. According to CRAS records, the Bureau of Special Relief aided 1525 families—less than five percent of the total 39,000 families who received relief. CRAS Fire Report, 428.

136. Ibid., 197.

137. Successful applicants seemed to employ a stylized language that stressed their own shock at their destitution and horror at having to ask for aid. Like stories of the Fire, this pattern might have sprung from Chicagoans' sense of literalized melodrama. On the other hand, it was perhaps just good politics to sound deferential. For a comparative perspective on the nexus between fact and fiction in self-presentation to higher authorities, see Natalie Zemon Davis's analysis of sixteenth-century French pardon tales, *Fiction in the Archives* (Stanford: Stanford University Press, 1987).

138. These and other markers of mid-nineteenth-century middle-class mores and values are discussed in Karen Halttunen, *Confidence Men and Painted Women: A Study of Middle-Class Culture in America, 1830–1870* (New Haven: Yale University Press, 1982); Ryan, *Cradle of the Middle Class;* Stuart M. Blumin, *The Emergence of the Middle Class;* John Kasson, *Rudeness and Civility;* and Sklar, *Catherine Beecher.*

139. Goodspeed, *Histories*, 428; CRAS Special Report, 17.

140. Colbert and Chamberlin, *Chicago and the Great Conflagration*, 432.

141. Anne McClure Hitchcock to Mrs. Jewell, letter of December 8, 1871. Hitchcock Collection, CHS.

142. CRAS Fire Report, 196.

143. Goodspeed, *Histories*, 428.

144. *Chicago Republican*, November 11, 1871.

145. According to Robert Laird Collier, the Special Relief chairman, nine of ten requests endorsed by a clergyman were immediately approved by his committee (*Chicago Tribune*, November 22, 1871).

146. C. C. Phillips, Special Relief application, April 14, 1872. Box 1443, Folder 2/5, CRAS Papers.

147. CRAS Fire Report, 281. This portion of the budget, which totaled $95,000, was called the A. T. Stewart Fund. Stewart, a New York City department store magnate, had sent the Society its largest

gift from a single donor: $50,000 specifically earmarked for the care of single women and widows.

148. On the gender-segregated economy and employment opportunities available to women at this time, see Alice Kessler-Harris, *Out to Work: A History of Wage-Earning Women in the United States* (New York: Oxford University Press, 1982).

149. CRAS Special Report, 18. It seems clear that the 132 women who received machines from Special Relief by December were not engaged in mass production or piecework but, rather, were skilled seamstresses who relied on custom jobs.

150. *Chicago Republican*, March 4, 1872. Sewing machines represented a substantial investment of capital at this time, retailing for around $60. Special discounts provided by major manufacturers such as the Singer Sewing Company allowed the Society to make this equipment available at this lower cost. On women's often uncertain ability to support themselves through home sewing in the mid-nineteenth century, see Stansell, *City of Women;* Boydston, *Home and Work;* and Mary H. Blewett, *Men, Women, and Work* (Urbana: University of Illinois Press, 1988).

151. Forty of forty-two Special Relief applications from February 1872 are for housing repair or construction. Box 1443, Folder 4/3. CRAS Papers.

152. Forty-two applications from this month are found in the CRAS papers. Among the applicants, 11 identified themselves as laborers, 9 as construction tradesmen, 5 as tailors. Other occupations listed included wagonmaker, cigarmaker, shoemaker, ship's cook, liveryman, railroad porter, teamster, night watchman. The application of one woman, Barbara Guillaume, can be found in this sample; Guillaume identified herself as a housekeeper. Box 1443, Folder 2/4, CRAS Papers.

153. Frances Roberts, letter of December 18, 1871. Roberts Collection, CHS.

154. Nicholas Kalter, Special Relief Application, February 12, 1872. Box 1443, Folder 2/4, CRAS Papers.

155. Augusta Sansbach, Special Relief application, May 18, 1872. Box 1443, Folder 2/2, CRAS Papers.

156. Mary Johnson, Special Relief application, April 10, 1872. Box 1443, Folder 2/3, CRAS Papers.

157. "A Chicago Lady," *Relief: A Humorous Drama* (Chicago: Lakeside Press, 1872). This play satirizes the work of the Ladies' Relief and Aid, a society largely composed of the wives and other female relatives of the elite men who belonged to the Relief and Aid Society. Though officially an independent organization, the Ladies' Relief and Aid worked closely with the Society, handling the investigation of families headed by women and, further, in connection with

the Employment Bureau, hiring single women who had lost their positions as "sewing women" in a makeshift factory. In the mid-nineteenth century, middle-class men and women commonly wrote and performed "parlor theatricals." For a fascinating interpretation of the importance of "artifice" and theatricality in sentimental culture, see Halttunen, *Confidence Men and Painted Women,* 153–90.

158. On the idea of working-class role playing, see Stansell, *City of Women;* and Peter Bailey, "Will the Real Bill Banks Please Stand Up? Towards a Role Analysis of Mid-Victorian Working Class Respectability," *Journal of Social History* 12 (Spring 1979): 336–53.

159. According to Rev. Robert Patterson of the Chicago YMCA, over thirty "orders and fraternities" worked to assist their members. This number probably includes organizations such as the Masons, Oddfellows, and the major ethnic societies; it probably excludes union benevolent associations and women's groups. Robert Patterson, *Relief Work of the Chicago YMCA,* October 25, 1871. In Chicago Fire, 1871, Broadsides Collection, Prints and Photographs, CHS. For a more detailed summary of alternative relief agencies, see the *Chicago Times,* October 3, 1872.

160. Anne McClure Hitchcock to Mrs. Jewell, December 8, 1871. Anne McClure Hitchcock Collection, CHS.

161. Earlier historians of the post-Fire relief effort have made this error. John Albert Mayer, for example, asserts that "in spite of its Protestant characteristics, the society was not accused during the period of fire relief of exhibiting any type of prejudice in dispensing relief" ("Private Charity in Chicago," 27). Timothy Naylor, while pointing to scattered evidence of what he terms "resistance" to the Society, similarly concludes that the "dissent from Relief and Aid Society policy was minimal." "Responding to the Fire," 462.

162. Anne McClure Hitchcock to Mrs. Jewell, December 8, 1871. Hitchcock Collection, CHS.

163. Aurelia R. King, letter of October 21, 1871. Personal Narratives, CHS.

164. The term "sisterhood" is used here in its nineteenth-century sense. On the idea of middle-class sisterhood, see Cott, *The Bonds of Womanhood.*

165. Sarah Bigelow, letter of October 11, 1871. Personal Narratives, CHS.

166. Anne McClure Hitchcock, letter of December 8, 1871. Hitchcock Collection, CHS.

167. Ibid.

168. Letter of Miss Locke, undated. Box 1442, Folder 1/1, CRAS Papers, CHS.

169. Letter of Mrs. William Dickinson, October 31, 1871. Box 1442, Folder 1/1, CRAS Papers, CHS.

170. On the ways in which benevolence granted power and authority to antebellum women and structured their own sense of their distinctive social roles, see Ginzberg, *Women and the Work of Benevolence*, 11–35. For a discussion of the role of "personalism" in shaping women's charities, see Suzanne Lebsock, *The Free Women of Petersburg: Status and Culture in a Southern Town, 1784–1860,* (New York: W. W. Norton, 1984), chap. 7.

171. This dispute is detailed in a letter that appeared in the *Missouri Republican* from Phoebe W. Couzins to the "Citizens of St. Louis." Couzins, a St. Louis woman who supported the claims of the Ladies' Relief and Aid Society, broke sharply with Dickinson over her conduct. This undated newspaper clipping is located in Box 1442, Folder 1/1, CRAS Papers, CHS.

172. Mrs. E. C. Dickinson to Mrs. H. L. Hammond, December 24, 1871. Box 1442, Folder 1/1, CRAS Papers, CHS.

173. After the Civil War, according to Lori D. Ginzberg, benevolent women began to elevate class allegiance over any sensibility of what was conceived in antebellum times as the special moral power of their sex. As Ginzberg writes, "They severed their own benevolent work from its traditional moorings in the ideology of gender difference . . . ; indeed, they seemed to free themselves entirely from awareness of their sex, demonstrating instead a newly explicit loyalty to their class" (*Women and the Work of Benevolence*, 190). Following this argument, it seems that women's post-Fire relief stands as a marker of a transitional moment in nineteenth-century definitions of the connections between class, gender, and cultural authority. Some Chicago women functioned quite comfortably within the Relief and Aid system, apparently content (in support of Ginzberg's argument) to adopt the interests of their class and labor, in the words of the "Chicago Lady," "as men work," and show their "ability to do things in a business-like way." Others accepted the propriety of a bureaucratized system for Chicago's workers but, eager to aid women of their own class, still clung to an older language of women's benevolence as a way of legitimating their semi-renegade activities. But still others held fast to the ideal of "doing a charity," understanding benevolence as both a source and special marker of women's cultural authority—and hanging on to their hopes that a charity rooted in sympathy could rescue both individuals and their larger community. For a more sustained analysis of these issues, see Karen Sawislak, "Relief, Aid, and Order: Class, Gender, and the Definition of Community in the Aftermath of Chicago's Great Fire," *Journal of Urban History* 20 (November 1993): 3–18.

174. Patterson, *The Relief Work of the Chicago YMCA*, 2.

175. Ibid.

176. Ibid. On America's 1858 revival and its roots in the financial crisis of 1857, see William McLoughlin, *Modern Revivalism* (New York: Ronald Press Co., 1959). On the activities of the YMCA in Chicago, see James Findlay, *Dwight Moody* (Chicago: University of Chicago Press, 1969). The Christian currents represented by the YMCA of this time are explored in George Marsden, *Fundamentalism and American Culture* (New York: Oxford University Press, 1980).

177. *Chicago Tribune*, October 14, 1871.

178. Ibid., November 2, 1871. As yet another marker of the tremendous national impact of the Great Fire, the dollar amounts collected for union relief efforts far exceeded those normally mustered for out-of-town strike support. On the finances of expressions of trade solidarities at this time, see Montgomery, *Beyond Equality,* 183–85.

179. *Illinois Staats-Zeitung,* November 1, 1871. On Chicago butchers and their traditions, see James R. Barrett, *Work and Community in the Jungle* (Urbana: University of Illinois Press, 1987); and Louise Carroll Wade, *Chicago's Pride: The Stockyards, Packingtown, and Environs in the Nineteenth Century* (Urbana: University of Illinois Press, 1986).

180. *Illinois Staats-Zeitung,* November 1, 1871.

181. Ibid., October 13, 1871. CFLPS #20.

182. CRAS Fire Report, 439. This outpouring of international aid—going from the old country to the United States—stands in contrast to the common tendency of historians of immigration to portray capital flows as purely one-directional: from new immigrants back to their families. See John Bodnar, *The Transplanted.*

183. *Illinois Staats-Zeitung,* October 13, 1871. CFLPS #20.

184. Ibid. On Chicago's Jewish community, see Hyman L. Meites, ed., *History of the Jews of Chicago* (Chicago: Jewish Historical Society of Illinois, 1924); and Edward Mazur, "Jewish Chicago: From Diversity to Community," in Holli and Jones, eds., *The Ethnic Frontier,* 263–92.

185. *Illinois Staats-Zeitung,* October 13, 1871. CFLPS #20.

186. *Proceedings*, Cook County Board of Commissioners, March 7, 1872.

187. *Chicago Republican,* March 12, 1872.

188. Ibid., March 21, 1872; CRAS Report for 1872, 20.

189. According to James B. Brown, the Relief and Aid Society's decision not to spend all of the Fire fund on Fire victims allowed the organization to cease all fund-raising until 1885. Yearly expenditures —which steadily diminished through the 1870s—came out of the Fire fund, which was never relinquished to the city council. Brown, *History of Public Assistance in Chicago,* 75.

Chapter Three

1. *Chicago Tribune*, November 25, 1871.

2. According to Colbert and Chamberlin, noteworthy fires had stricken New York in 1835, Charleston in 1838, Pittsburgh in 1845, St. Louis in 1849, Philadelphia in 1850 and 1865, San Francisco in 1851, and Portland, Maine, in 1866. Prior to the Great Fire, Chicago had experienced sizable conflagrations in 1857, 1859, 1866, and 1868 (*Chicago and the Great Conflagration*, 468–74).

3. Ibid.

4. *Chicago Tribune*, November 1, 1871.

5. "Fire zones" often were limited to central business districts, though variations existed from city to city. See the *Chicago Republican*, May 27, 1867, for a survey of regulations in New York, Brooklyn, Cincinnati, Pittsburgh, and other cities. See also Rosen, *The Limits of Power*, 95; and Andrew J. King, *A Pre-History of Zoning in Chicago* (New York: Garland Publishing, 1986).

6. Rosen, *The Limits of Power*, 95.

7. *Chicago Tribune*, October 15, 1871.

8. *Chicago Republican*, November 13, 1871.

9. *Chicago Tribune*, October 15, 1871.

10. Ibid.

11. Ibid., November 15, 1871.

12. Chicago businessmen had departed the city soon after the Fire to promote investment. For example, city booster William Bross immediately traveled to New York, and German National Bank representative Franz Arnold set sail for Europe (*Illinois Staats-Zeitung*, November 1, 1871).

13. The twenty seats at stake represented one-half of the city council. The twenty city wards, at this time, were each represented by two aldermen elected to two-year terms, with one seat contested yearly. Mayors served for two years, with a consequent biennial election. For an account of Chicago's municipal structure in 1871, see Samuel Sparling, *Municipal History and Present Organization of the City of Chicago*, bulletin no. 23 (Madison: University of Wisconsin, 1898).

14. *Chicago Times*, October 19, 1871.

15. *Illinois Staats-Zeitung*, October 27, 1871. CFLPS #15.

16. Richard Schneirov, in "Class Conflict, Municipal Politics and Governmental Reform in Gilded Age Chicago, 1871–1875," in Keil and Jentz, eds., *German Workers in Industrial Chicago, 1850–1910*, 183–206, places the Fireproof ticket in the same reform tradition that fueled the election of Roswell Mason on 1869's Citizen's Reform Ticket. I would argue that while the "antibummer" rhetoric of both elections were very similar, the sanctioned bipartisanship of the Fireproof ticket was truly exceptional and representative of a

unique, disaster-borne impetus toward a new competence in municipal officers, particularly the office of the mayor.

17. *Chicago Tribune*, November 3, 1871.

18. *Illinois Staats-Zeitung*, November 6, 1871. CFLPS #15.

19. *Chicago Times*, October 19, 1871.

20. The general currents of cultural consolidation that marked this period are explored in Higham, *From Boundlessness to Consolidation;* Trachtenberg, *The Incorporation of America;* and Robert H. Wiebe, *The Search for Order, 1877–1920* (New York: Hill and Wang, 1967). Fredrickson describes the turn by elites to more conservative forms of governance and administration in *The Inner Civil War.* More specific studies of political process that consider the call for a "businesslike" style of politics in this period include Sproat, *The Best Men;* and Morton Keller, *Affairs of State: Public Life in Late Nineteenth-Century America* (Cambridge, MA: Harvard University Press, 1977). For accounts of how such reformers operated in the Progressive Era, see Martin J. Schiesl, *The Politics of Efficiency: Municipal Administration and Reform in America, 1880–1920* (Berkeley: University of California Press, 1977); and Samuel P. Hays, "The Politics of Reform in Municipal Government in the Progressive Era," *Pacific Northwest Quarterly* 55 (1964): 157–69.

21. Einhorn, *Property Rules.*

22. On the origins of Tammany Hall and the rise of the Tweed Ring, see James Bryce's classic, condemnatory account in *The American Commonwealth* (London: Macmillan, 1888), 377–403. Mandelbaum, *Boss Tweed's New York,* offers a fine analysis of the shape and function of machine politics in that city. For a reinterpretation of municipal politics and class relations in New York City during this period, see Bernstein, *The New York City Draft Riots,* 195–236. On "antiparty" currents in American politics, see Richard Hofstadter, *The Idea of a Party System* (Berkeley: University of California Press, 1969). On Thomas Nast, see Morton Keller, *The Art and Politics of Thomas Nast* (New York: Oxford University Press, 1968).

23. *Chicago Tribune*, November 7, 1871.

24. Medill, a native of New York, had owned the *Tribune* since 1860. In earlier days, he acted as one of the founders of the Republican party and played a critical role in securing Lincoln's nomination in 1860. Medill kept a hand in *Tribune* editorial matters, though day-to-day supervision fell to editor Horace White. Unfortunately, there is no scholarly biography of this important figure in the history of United States politics and journalism. Medill's papers, owned by the *Tribune,* are sealed to the public, pending publication of an authorized biography of Medill's grandson, Colonel Robert McCormick. For more on Medill see David Protess, "Joseph Medill: Chi-

cago's First Modern Mayor," in Melvin Holli and Paul Green, eds., *The Mayors: The Chicago Political Tradition* (Carbondale: Southern Illinois University Press, 1986). His part in the creation of a Republican party in Illinois is discussed in William E. Gienapp, *The Origins of the Republican Party, 1852–1856* (New York: Oxford University Press, 1987).

25. According to historian Wayne Andrews, "Medill valued his time too much to waste a second chatting with a friend. One result of this was that he had no friends at all" (*The Battle for Chicago* [New York: Harcourt Brace Jovanovitch, 1946], 49). Medill had repeatedly tried, without success, to secure a congressional nomination from his party. He did serve as an elected delegate to the 1869 Illinois Constitutional Convention.

26. In putting forward Greenebaum's name, the *Tribune*, on October 23, 1871, argued that his international financial connections could prove fruitful for a city in dire need of creditors. "He could be the means," noted the paper, "of obtaining or causing to be obtained, many millions of foreign capital to be loaned to the mechanics, manufacturers, and others of the laboring and productive classes who truly stand in need of such help to get on their feet again." Greenebaum himself indeed moved immediately to bring capital to Chicago, dispatching information on investment opportunities to agents in London, Paris, Amsterdam, Berlin, Leipzig, Geneva, Stuttgart, Basel, and Zurich. Information on Greenebaum's varied commercial ventures is located in the Henry Greenebaum Collection, Chicago Historical Society. On Greenebaum's religious and philanthropic activism, see Meites, *History of the Jews of Chicago*.

27. *Illinois Staats-Zeitung*, October 31, 1871. CFLPS #13.

28. *Chicago Times*, November 6, 1871. On the Storey/Medill enmity, see Walsh, *To Print the News and Raise Hell*.

29. *Chicago Republican*, October 31, 1871.

30. Ibid., October 30, 1871.

31. Ibid., October 28, 1871.

32. Ibid., October 30, 1871; October 28, 1871.

33. On the political significance of journalism, see Nord, "The Public Community."

34. Like Medill, most of the Union Fireproofers were nonoffice holders but no strangers to party politics. For example, two incumbent aldermen, Arthur Dixon and John McAvoy, held spots on the Union Fireproof slate.

35. The *Chicago Tribune*, *Chicago Times*, and *Illinois Staats-Zeitung* all carried versions of this story on November 5 and 6, the two days before the election.

36. *Chicago Tribune*, November 8, 1871. The *Tribune*'s apology was at best half-hearted. While conceding the error of its charges,

the paper refused to assume responsibility for any sort of improper libel. As the editors mysteriously declared, "If Mr. Holden has suffered in reputation, . . . he has nobody but himself to blame for it."

37. Ibid., November 2, 1871.

38. *Illinois Staats-Zeitung*, November 6, 1871. CFLPS #15.

39. *Chicago Times*, November 3, 1871.

40. *Chicago Tribune*, November 7, 1871.

41. Ibid., November 6. 1871.

42. Ibid., November 7, 1871.

43. The final tally was as follows: Medill 16,125, Holden 5988. Most Fireproof candidates won similarly easy victories, but not all emerged victorious. Incumbent aldermen Thomas Carney, J. J. McGrath, William Tracy, and George Powell held on to their seats, and two newcomers, Edward Cullerton and Jacob Lengacher, also defeated the Fireproof candidates.

44. Special election procedures are discussed by Rev. Robert Collyer in his letter to the *Tribune* of November 7, 1871.

45. On election day practices, see Jean H. Baker, *Affairs of Party: The Political Culture of Northern Democrats in the Mid-Nineteenth Century* (Ithaca: Cornell University Press, 1983).

46. *Chicago Tribune*, November 8, 1871; *Chicago Times*, November 8, 1871.

47. *Chicago Times*, November 8, 1871.

48. *Chicago Tribune*, November 8, 1871.

49. Medill won in every ward. For precinct-by-precinct election totals, see the ibid., November 9, 1871.

50. On the institutional structure of late-nineteenth-century urban governments, see Teaford, *The Unheralded Triumph*, esp. 15–82. Powerful, independently elected commissions in Chicago included the Board of Public Works and the fire and police commissions.

51. *Chicago Republican*, November 21, 1871.

52. Ibid.

53. Ibid.

54. Ibid., November 21, 1871.

55. *Journal of the Proceedings of the Common Council of the City of Chicago*, December 4, 1871 (hereafter *Proceedings*).

56. Medill had been reluctant to run for mayor because he felt the powers of the municipal executive were so limited. As he complained to John D. Caton soon after his election, only "a shadow of authority with all the responsibility falls on the office." (Medill to John D. Caton, December 8, 1871. John D. Caton Papers, Library of Congress. Cited in Pierce, *History of Chicago*, 3:541. The "Mayor's Bill" was drafted in advance of the November 7 election by Judge Murray F. Tuley, a Cook County jurist who became Medill's corporation counsel. The new mayoral powers were as follows: boards

such as police, fire, and public works to be appointed rather than elected, and the mayor could fire his appointees; the mayor now presides over the council and appoints all standing council committees. The bill, which was passed by the Illinois legislature on February 9, 1872, with an effective date of July 1, marked a new departure in the relations between state and local governments in Illinois, becoming the basis of a general city-charter bill that was passed and enacted in 1874. State of Illinois, "An Act concerning the appointment and removal of city officers . . . , conferring additional powers upon Mayors," passed February 9, 1872, implemented July 1, 1872. See also Elias Colbert, "Address on Joseph Medill," February 26, 1903. Joseph Medill Collection, Chicago Historical Society.

57. Medill was also very concerned that Chicago take steps to ward off fire by improving water supply mechanisms, but he felt that fire limits were the far more critical step. As he argued, "[N]o supply is adequate to quench a fire, with twenty minutes start, among thousands of timber box structures." But Medill did note particularly the insufficiency of a pumping system that relied upon waterworks and proposed to construct a water system of linked artesian wells (*Proceedings*, December 4, 1871). For a discussion of the city's eventual failure to improve its water supply method, see Rosen, *The Limits of Power*, 120–24.

58. *Proceedings*, December 4, 1871.

59. Ibid.

60. Ibid.

61. Olivier Zunz, in his study of late-nineteenth-century Detroit, observes that working-class home ownership was common at this time (*The Changing Face of Inequality*, esp. 152–76). Gregory R. Zeiren has similarly noted that a high degree of working-class home ownership was a common feature of nineteenth-century western American cities. See Zeiren, "The Propertied Worker: Working-Class Formation in Toledo, Ohio, 1870–1900," Ph.D. diss., University of Delaware, 1981, 146–47.

62. As journalist James Parton wrote in the *Atlantic Monthly:* "In all Chicago there is not one tenement house. Thrifty workmen own the homes they live in, and the rest can still comfortably hire a house" (March 1867, 338–39). For maps detailing immigrant populations and levels of property ownership in 1870, see Einhorn, *Property Rules*, 264–65. On American's fear that European-style tenements would be replicated in their cities, see Ward, *Poverty, Ethnicity and the American City*, esp. 13–45; and Wright, *Building the Dream*.

63. Wright, *Building the Dream*. The definition of citizenship is of course the subject of much political philosophy and theory. Two

useful works that trace the historical development of this concept are Shklar, *American Citizenship;* and James Kettner, *The Development of American Citizenship, 1608–1870* (Chapel Hill: University of North Carolina Press, 1978).

64. *Chicago Tribune*, December 4, 1871.

65. Sidney Myers, *Labor: Extracts, Magazine Articles, and Observations Relating to Social Science and Political Economy as Bearing upon the Subject of Labor* (Chicago: n.p., 1867).

66. *Proceedings*, November 27, 1871.

67. Ibid. A copy of Bailey's communication to the Council also can be found in the Chicago City Council Proceedings File (CCPF), Box 400, File 1872/181 B #5.

68. *Proceedings*, November 27, 1871.

69. Such readiness to identify anti-German sentiment virtually constituted an editorial position for the *Illinois Staats-Zeitung.* An aggressive political defense of German ethnicity in America was a common stance of educated immigrants such as owner Anton C. Hesing and editor Hermann Raster. On the political culture of mid-nineteenth-century German Americans, see Bruce C. Levine, *The Spirit of 1848: German Immigrants, Labor Conflict, and the Coming of the Civil War* (Urbana: University of Illinois Press, 1992). On the political dynamics of German communities in New York City and Buffalo, see Nadel, *Little Germany;* and Gerber, *The Making of an American Pluralism.*

70. *Illinois Staats-Zeitung*, October 20, 1871. CFLPS #15.

71. Ibid. Jentz puts forth a similar interpretation of German immigrant resistance to the idea of a Fireproof city in "Class and Politics in an Emerging Industrial City," 240.

72. On the process of post-Fire physical realignments, see Rosen, *The Limits of Power,* 109–20, 127–76.

73. *Illinois Staats-Zeitung*, October 20, 1871. CFLPS #15.

74. Ibid., October 18, 1871. CFLPS #15.

75. *Chicago Tribune*, November 11, 1871.

76. Ibid., November 27, 1871.

77. About fifteen of these petitions and remonstrances remain extant in the Chicago City Council Proceedings File (CCPF), Illinois Regional Archive Depository, Northeastern Illinois University, Chicago.

78. The few women who signed these petitions, according to a check of city directories, seem to have been widows who owned property.

79. Petition of "Northsiders," CCPF 400 1872/181 B #2.

80. CCPF 400 1872/181 B #3.

81. Petition of December 21, 1871. CCPF 400 1872/181 B #4.

82. Petition of West Side Property Holders, undated. CCPF 400 1872/181 B #1.

83. Remonstrance of Property Holders and Tax Payers South of 22nd Street and West of State Street, undated. CCPF 400 1872/181B #4; Remonstrance of South Side Property Holders, CCPF 400 1872/181 B #2.

84. Einhorn, *Property Rules*, 104–43.

85. CCPF 400 1872/181 B #2.

86. Petition of Property Owners South of Douglas Place, undated. CCPF 400 1872/181 B #3.

87. For an example of the thinking of some prominent business leaders who did not support coextensive limits but instead favored limits that only encircled the downtown, see the *Chicago Tribune*, December 18, 1871.

88. Unidentifed Field, Leiter manager to Joseph Medill, January 15, 1872. CCPF 400 1872/181 B #3.

89. Ibid.

90. *Illinois Staats-Zeitung*, January 15, 1872. CFLPS #15.

91. *Chicago Times*, January 14, 1872. The *Times* account of this meeting, as with all of their coverage of the fire limits protest, was exceptionally hostile toward city Germans. For a more neutral account, see the *Chicago Republican*, January 15, 1872. Hesing, born in 1823 near Bremen, emigrated in 1839 to Cincinnati. He moved to Chicago in 1854, where he went into business as a brick manufacturer. Entering politics through the Republican party in the late 1850s, he served as deputy sheriff and sheriff of Cook County from 1858 to 1862. During the Civil War, he organized and funded an infantry regiment known as the "Hesing Sharpshooters." He became sole owner of the *Staats-Zeitung* in 1867. For more on Hesing, see Rudolph Hofmeister, *The Germans of Chicago*.

92. On Hesing's support for Medill's candidacy, see the *Illinois Staats-Zeitung*, November 7, 1871. CFLPS #15.

93. Ibid., January 16, 1872. CFLPS #15.

94. For an example of German immigrant usage of such language, see ibid., January 17 and 29, 1872. CFPLS #15.

95. Ibid., January 15, 1872. CFLPS #15.

96. *Chicago Republican*, January 15, 1872. Jentz suggests that this appeal to working-class identity was part of an effort by established immigrant leaders such as Hesing to attract the support of German workers sympathetic to the radical message of the international Left, which was beginning to gain more influence in the city ("Class and Politics in an Emerging Industrial City," 240).

97. Though question of home protection seemingly would involve women, this protest was organized strictly within the realm of the male world of ward politics. The procession apparently was no place for wives, daughters, or even women who themselves owned homes. For a discussion of the political and social function of parades

in this period, see Michael E. McGerr, *The Decline of Popular Politics* (New York: Oxford University Press, 1986). On women's exclusion from the public space claimed by such ritual enactments of politics in the mid-nineteenth century, see Mary P. Ryan, *Women in Public: Between Banners and Ballots, 1825–1880* (Baltimore: Johns Hopkins University Press, 1990).

98. Detailed accounts of the march are found in the *Illinois Staats-Zeitung, Chicago Tribune, Chicago Republican,* and *Chicago Times* of January 16, 1872.

99. *Chicago Tribune,* January 16, 1872.

100. *Illinois Staats-Zeitung,* January 16, 1872. CFLPS #15.

101. Ibid., January 17, 1872. CFLPS #15.

102. *Proceedings,* January 17, 1872.

103. *Chicago Times,* January 17, 1872.

104. *Chicago Tribune,* January 17, 1872.

105. *Chicago Times,* January 16, 1872.

106. On the Lager Beer protest, see Richard Wilson Renner, "In a Perfect Ferment: Chicago, the Know-Nothings, and the Riot for Lager Beer," *Chicago History* 5 (Fall 1976): 161–70. One protestor was shot and killed in the course of this event. On the political nativism of the 1850s, see David Bennett, *The Party of Fear* (Chapel Hill: University of North Carolina Press, 1988); Ray Allen Billington, *The Protestant Crusade* (New York: Rinehart and Co., 1938); and Bridges, *A City in the Republic.* On post–Civil War nativism, see John Higham, *Strangers in the Land,* 2d ed. (New Brunswick: Rutgers University Press, 1988). The historiography of nativism generally suggests that the era of Reconstruction represented a lull in nativist sentiment. While the rise of the Republican party may have spelled the end of political nativism, it seems plain that nativist sentiments remained deeply ingrained (and occasionally expressed) throughout the late 1860s and 1870s. As historians become more acquainted with sources drawn from immigrant communities, this accepted periodization will likely be rethought.

107. *Chicago Times,* January 21, 1872.

108. Ibid.

109. *Chicago Republican,* January 18, 1872.

110. *Illinois Staats-Zeitung,* January 24, 1872. CFLPS #15.

111. *Chicago Republican,* January 22, 1872.

112. The Collyer-Hesing exchange, originally drafted, respectively, on January 18 and 19, 1872, was widely reprinted in Chicago's press. This account is taken from a side-by-side reprinting of the letters that appeared in the January 22, 1872, issue of the *Republican.*

113. It is interesting to note that, as a German free thinker, the

often anticlerical Hesing was sympathetic to the kind of then-radical Christianity practiced by the Unitarian minister. Other commentators noted what they saw as the extreme and illogical divergence between Collyer's religious and social views. As "Don Carlos" wrote to the *Republican*, "This doctrine comes with ill grace from a man whose liberalism is so positive and well-defined, as to be often charged with bordering on infidelity. It is difficult to conceive how Mr. Collyer can be so very liberal in religion, and so very illiberal in politics, unless it be true that extremes always meet" (*Chicago Republican*, January 25, 1872). For an account of the Unitarian movement, see William R. Hutchinson, *The Modernist Impulse in American Protestantism* (New York: Oxford University Press, 1976).

114. A record of the complex legislative processes leading up to final passage of the fire limits ordinance can be found in CCPF 399 1872/177 B.

115. For a map of the new limits, see Rosen, *The Limits of Power*, 106.

116. Ibid., 102. As Rosen further observed, the fire limits bill also contained too many exceptions and provisions that allowed inflammable construction practices—such as wooden cornices or tar roofs on stone buildings—to be truly effective.

117. See the *Chicago Tribune*, January 19, 1872, for a lengthy explanation of the proposal that became the fire limits ordinance.

118. Ibid., January 19, 1872.

119. *Chicago Times*, January 20, 1872.

120. *Illinois Staats-Zeitung*, January 29, 1872. CFLPS #15. John Jentz suggests that German Chicagoans used "cosmopolitanism" as a negative description linked to their fears of proletarianization. I would argue, to the contrary, that German immigrants viewed the "cosmopolitan" city as their ultimate desideratum, viewing this term as a marker of diversity and tolerance (Jentz, "Class and Politics in an Emerging Industrial City," 241).

121. *Illinois Staats-Zeitung*, February 14, 1872.

122. Ibid., January 29, 1872.

123. Ibid., February 14, 1872. CFLPS #15.

124. *Chicago Republican*, January 17, 1872.

Chapter Four

1. *The Land Owner*, (October 1872).

2. For an example of the usage of this epithet, see the *Chicago Tribune*, October 6, 1872.

3. Ibid., September 8, 1872. The paper based its calculations on an eight-hour day, concluding that over 1600 commercial class buildings would be finished in this period.

4. *The Land Owner* (July 1872).
5. Ibid.
6. For broad considerations of the cultural and political implications of the question, see Trachtenberg, *The Incorporation of America;* David Montgomery, *Beyond Equality;* and Eric Foner, *Reconstruction.*
7. *Chicago Tribune,* October 11, 1872.
8. For an account of this dispute, see the *Chicago Times,* October 11, 1872.
9. For an exceptionally thorough survey of the ideological meanings attached to the notion of free labor prior to the Civil War, see Jonathan A. Glickstein, *Concepts of Free Labor in Antebellum America* (New Haven: Yale University Press, 1991).
10. *New York Tribune,* October 17, 1871.
11. Ibid.
12. *Chicago Tribune,* October 27, 1871. Other early reports of the need for skilled workers in the building trades can be found in ibid., October 28, 1871; the *Workingman's Advocate,* November 4, 1871; and the *New York Tribune,* October 17, 1871.
13. Samuel Greely, "Reminiscence of the Great Fire," September 10, 1909. Great Fire Personal Narratives Collection, Chicago Historical Society. It is important to note that these figures are an approximate count of those who permanently settled in the city. The number of migrants who did not settle permanently in Chicago is impossible to determine. But given the city's traditional status as a supply point for migratory labor, it seems likely that these numbers were quite substantial. Throughout the last four decades of the nineteenth century, Chicago's population grew at an extremely fast pace. Still, the post-Fire influx was reckoned, by contemporaries, to be extraordinary. Estimates of the numbers participating in the post-Fire migration to Chicago appear in the October 1872 issues of the *Lakeside Monthly* and the *Land Owner.* One account by a participant is L. Morton's letter of October 9, 1872, to the *Wigan (U.K.) Observer,* Personal Narratives Collection, CHS.
14. On the seasonality of construction work, see Thomas J. Suhrbuhr and Richard Schneirov, *Union Brotherhood, Union Town: The History of the Carpenters' Union of Chicago, 1863–1987* (Carbondale: Southern Illinois University Press, 1988); and Royal E. Montgomery, *Industrial Relations in the Chicago Building Trades* (Chicago: University of Chicago Press, 1927).
15. *Lakeside Monthly* (October 1872).
16. *New York Times,* October 21, 1871; Dr. Jared Bassett, letter of October 21, 1871. Personal Narratives Collection, CHS.
17. Dr. Jared Bassett, letter of October 21, 1871. Personal Narratives, CHS.

18. *Illinois Staats-Zeitung*, October 10, 1893. Chicago Foreign Language Press Survey, Reel #23.

19. This dumping process created five acres of downtown landfill that is now part of Chicago's Grant Park. The Great Fire proved a bonanza for scrap iron scavengers, who sold their findings to city foundries located within the untouched West Side. On the activities of such entrepreneurs, see the *Chicago Republican*, October 25, 1871.

20. Ibid.

21. *New York Times*, October 21, 1871; *New York Tribune*, October 21, 1871.

22. Frank A. Randell, *The Development of Chicago Building Construction* (Urbana: University of Illinois Press, 1949), 8. This seemingly substantial number would be dwarfed by the over 1600 commercial-class structures erected during the coming construction season. For a report on this out-of-season activity, see the *Chicago Tribune*, November 25, 1871.

23. For a detailed survey of the problems presented by out-of-season work in these particular trades, see the *Chicago Tribune*, December 5, 1871.

24. John McKenna, *Reminiscences of the Great Fire* (Chicago: n.p., 1920).

25. I am indebted to historian/apprentice mason Bruce O'Brien for my understanding of the mechanics of brick construction. For more detail about the hardships of out-of-season construction, see the *Chicago Tribune*, December 5, 1871.

26. *Workingman's Advocate*, December 30, 1871.

27. John Jentz has chronicled the rising and falling fortunes of Chicago unions in the period in "Class and Politics in an Emerging Industrial City." Jentz describes the existence of relatively separate German-language and English-language labor movements in the city, noting that English speakers primarily controlled the building trades. On the general structure and function of trades unions in this period, see Montgomery, *Beyond Equality*, 139–51. Montgomery reports that the Chicago Trades Assembly directed the activities of thirty-three different unions in 1869. City directories list twenty-six unions in the city at the time of the Great Fire.

28. *Workingman's Advocate*, December 30, 1871.

29. Just before the Great Fire, unionized bricklayers earned between \$3.00 and \$3.25 for a day's labor. (*Chicago Tribune*, October 20, 1871; *New York Times*, October 21, 1871).

30. The *Chicago Times* claimed that bricklayers and other skilled workmen were prepared to strike unless they received wages of \$7–\$10 per day—highly inflated rates that seem to have no basis in fact. The editors also implied that workers who were not satisfied

with these rates of pay would willingly go idle, and "be subsisted upon public charity"—an echo of the suspicions of working-class dependency formalized in the rules of the CRAS (October 26, 1871).

31. *Chicago Tribune*, October 26, 1871.

32. *Workingman's Advocate*, November 11, 1871.

33. *Chicago Times*, October 28, 1871.

34. *Chicago Tribune*, October 30, 1871. It is interesting that the newspaper failed to acknowledge the fact that the Bricklayers' Union had imposed an artificial *ceiling* on wages—thereby not operating within the "laws" of the markets that these tradesmen, according to the editors, had so rightfully upheld.

35. *Workingman's Advocate*, November 4, 1871.

36. For examples of such thinking in liberal economic discourse in the latter decades of the nineteenth century, see Sproat, *The Best Men*, esp. 158–65 and 204–42. For a comparative perspective on the development of a "market culture" in nineteenth-century France, an exploration of how the "laws" of the market came to be constructed and imposed upon French workers, see William Reddy, *The Rise of Market Culture: The Textile Trades and French Society* (New York: Cambridge University Press, 1984).

37. *Workingman's Advocate*, November 4, 1871. On the unionists' fears that employers would encourage the migration of skilled tradesmen to Chicago, see ibid., February 17, 1872.

38. Ibid., November 4, 1871.

39. On the carpenters' unions of Chicago, see Suhrbuhr and Schneirov, *Union Brotherhood, Union Town*.

40. On the carpenter's organizing drive, see the *Workingman's Advocate*, January 27, 1872; February 17, 1872; March 23, 1872.

41. Ibid., March 23 and 30, 1872.

42. For a more detailed description of the issues at hand in 1867, see Karen Sawislak, "Smoldering City: Class, Ethnicity, and Politics in Chicago At the Time of the Great Fire, 1867–1874," Ph.D. diss., Yale University, 1990, esp. 1–25. Also see Montgomery, *Beyond Equality*, 307–11. The activities and functions of local trades assemblies are described in Montgomery, *Beyond Equality*, 160–62.

The fight for the Eight Hour Day was one of the most critical and enduring labor movement issue of the latter part of the nineteenth century. For an explanation of the ideology of Eight Hour advocates, see Montgomery, *Beyond Equality*, 230–60. Efforts to secure a legal eight-hour day are explored in Montgomery, *Beyond Equality*, 296–334. A sustained discussion of the meaning of strikes for eight hours in New York City in 1872 is found in Bernstein, *The New York City Draft Riots*, 237–57. A very useful contemporary explanation of these issues is George E. McNeill, "The Hours of Labor," in McNeill, ed., *The Labor Movement: The Problem of To-Day* (Boston: A. M. Bridgeman and Co., 1887), 470–82. For a more general survey of worker movements organized around the hours of labor, see David R. Roediger and Philip S. Foner, *Our Own Time: A History of American Labor and the Working Day* (Westport, CT: Greenwood Press, 1989).

43. *Workingman's Advocate*, March 23, 1872.

44. On antebellum general strikes in New York City, see Wilentz, *Chants Democratic*. On strikes in Philadelphia, see Bruce Laurie, *The Working People of Philadelphia, 1800–1850* (Philadelphia: Temple University Press, 1980).

45. On antistrike beliefs of liberal theorists centering around what was perceived as infringements upon the individual's right to work, see Sproat, *The Best Men*, 227–28.

46. As John G. Sproat notes, "No issue in late nineteenth-century America more vividly exposed the ambivalence in the liberal attitude toward laissez-faire than the labor problem. The most coercive power of any government is its military arm, and the liberal reformers approved and often demanded the full use of power against American workers. . . . strikes were matters for the U.S. Army, for strikes threatened property rights rather than human rights" (*The Best Men*, 235).

47. *Chicago Tribune*, May 4, 1867.

48. For an important counterview of the strikes, see the reports provided by the *Chicago Republican*, especially May 4, 1867. The mayoral proclamation is reprinted in the *Chicago Tribune*, May 5, 1867.

49. On the Civil War years in the city, see Robin Einhorn, "The Civil War and Municipal Government in Chicago," in Maris Vinovskis, ed., *Towards a Social History of the American Civil War: Exploratory Essays* (New York: Cambridge University Press, 1990). See also Pierce, *A History of Chicago*, vol. 2.

50. *Workingman's Advocate*, February 17, 1872.

51. Ibid., March 23, 1867.

52. As Sproat notes in his study of elite postwar reformers, "According to liberal theory, the owners of capital had a natural right to use their capital as they saw fit, free from governmental or other limitations. Workingmen had a right to offer their services freely, and to make the best terms possible with anyone who would bid for their services. . . . Left to themselves, labor and capital would adjust to each other's requirements in any given situation. . . . Every artificial limitation, however slight, on the free interplay of capital and labor altered the natural relations of the various elements in the economy, and weakened the moral foundations of society" (*The Best Men*, 206).

53. *Chicago Times*, October 28, 1871.

54. *Chicago Tribune*, May 14, 1871.

55. Such a position was consistent with the philosophy of the National Labor Union (NLU), the loose federation of trade unions that was the labor movement's first post–Civil War attempt at national organization. Chicago was a critical center of NLU activity; the *Workingman's Advocate*, in addition to its coverage of local events, was also the national organ of the NLU, and the country's most influential labor paper of the 1860s and 1870s. On the NLU, see David Montgomery, *Beyond Equality*, 176–85; and David Montgomery "William H. Sylvis and the Search for Working-Class Citizenship," in Melvyn Dubofsky and Warren Van Tine, eds., *Labor Leaders in America* (Urbana: University of Illinois Press, 1987). See as well John R. Commons, *History of Labour in the United States*, vol. 2 (New York: Macmillan, 1919). Two important nineteenth-century accounts of the work of the NLU are found in Friedrich A. Sorge, *The Labor Movement in the United States* (Westport, CT: Greenwood Press, 1977); and McNeill, ed., *The Labor Movement, The Problem of To-Day.*

56. *Workingman's Advocate*, March 2, 1872. The analysis of such gendered constructions have become the subject of much recent work in labor history. For many fine examples of this scholarship, see the essays collected in Ava Baron, ed., *Work Engendered: Toward a New History of American Labor* (Ithaca: Cornell University Press, 1991).

57. James C. Sylvis, *The Life, Speeches, Labors, and Essays of William H. Sylvis* (Philadelphia: Green, Remsen, and Haffelfinger, 1872), 168.

58. Ibid., 390.

59. Ibid., 197.

60. According to Steven Bernard Leikin, attempts at the practice of cooperation led to the establishment of 500 producer cooperatives and at least 500 consumer cooperatives in the United States between 1865 and 1890. As Leikin details it, the theory of cooperation went on to assume a preeminent role in the efforts of the Knights of Labor, the largest American labor organization of the nineteenth century. For a fine survey of the meaning and practice of cooperation in this period, see Leikin, "The Practical Utopians: Cooperation and the American Labor Movement, 1860–1890," Ph.D. diss., University of California at Berkeley, 1992. A contemporary account of the movement is Franklin H. Giddings, "Co-operation," in George E. McNeill, ed., *The Labor Movement: The Problem of To-Day.*

As Leikin observes, American cooperators, many of whom were born in England, drew much inspiration from the British example, particularly in the case of consumer cooperatives such as those established by the well-known Rochdale Plan (Leikin, 79). For more on this subject, see Clifton K. Yearley, *Britons in American Labor: A History of the Influence of United Kingdom Immigrants on American Labor, 1820–1914* (Baltimore: Johns Hopkins University Press, 1957).

61. *Chicago Tribune,* December 5, 1871.

62. Relief and Aid Society circular, January 12, 1872. Reprinted in the *Workingman's Advocate,* January 27, 1872. The circular was in part directed specifically against the newspaper's advertisement of supposed job opportunities; as the Society declared, "The journals which are urging these people to come here at this season are unintentionally doing them a cruel wrong; and adding to a city already overburdened with the destitute."

63. On working-class migration in the nineteenth century, see Jonathan Prude, *The Coming of Industrial Order* (New York: Oxford University Press, 1983). For a detailed study of how workers secured employment in one particular city, see Walter F. Licht, *Getting Work* (Cambridge, MA: Harvard University Press, 1992).

64. *Chicago Tribune,* November 18, 1871.

65. For an example of some of the advertisements that appeared in London, see the *Workingman's Advocate,* April 6, 1872.

66. For example, the *Moulder's Journal* of March 1872 specifically warned against traveling to Chicago: "Good union men are not those who, knowing the condition of affairs in Chicago, rush there for work." Reprinted in the *Workingman's Advocate,* April 20, 1872. The bricklayers also circulated a letting asking brother masons to stay away in late March. (*Workingman's Advocate,* March 30, 1872). One grim letter from a British migrant to Chicago appeared in the *Manchester Courier* in late March. Noting that "money is scarce here," the writer reported that 100 bricklayers had left the city, "finding it impossible to support themselves and families, board and everything else being so high" (reprinted in the *Workingman's Advocate,* April 6, 1872).

67. *Workingman's Advocate,* March 9, 1872.

68. Ibid., April 27, 1872.

69. For a more detailed account of the geographic elements of this migration, see Karen Sawislak, "Smoldering City," *Chicago History* 17 (Fall/Winter 1988–89): 70–101, esp. 85.

70. *Workingman's Advocate,* April 6, 1872.

71. Ibid., April 27, 1872.

72. *Chicago Tribune,* May 11, 1872.

73. *The Land Owner* (April 1872).

74. *Chicago Tribune,* May 5, 1872.

75. *Workingman's Advocate,* March 30, 1872.

76. Tulloch's letter appears in the *Chicago Tribune,* May 7, 1872.

77. *Chicago Republican,* March 14, 1872; *Workingman's Advocate,* May 25, 1871. To combat the housing crunch, the bricklayer's union organized a worker-owned housing cooperative that planned

to build cottages and flats to be let at half of what they would bring on the open market. But the organization apparently never enrolled enough members—perhaps due to the hefty $3.00 weekly payment required of potential owners—to build or lease anything. See the *Workingman's Advocate*, July 6, 1872.

78. *Chicago Times*, September 24, 1872.

79. According to a table compiled by Eric L. Hirsch based on an 1898 Department of Labor bulletin, the average daily wage paid to all trades in Chicago jumped to higher levels in 1872, with bricklayers, stonecutters, and stonemasons receiving the greatest boost. All wages again declined by 1874, the next year surveyed. It is difficult to assess the reliability of these figures, but contemporary accounts of the situation seem to validate the general pattern that they reveal. See Eric L. Hirsch, "Revolution or Reform: An Analytical History of an Urban Labor Movement," Ph.D. diss., University of Chicago, 1981, 271. A revision of this study has subsequently appeared as Hirsch, *Urban Revolt*.

80. For information on the employment of women and standard wages for domestic help in the year of the Great Rebuilding, see the *Chicago Tribune*, October 20, 1872. A possible exception can be found in the case of boardinghouse keepers, a major employment for women, who probably did very well in light of the housing shortage and influx of out-of-town workers.

81. Ibid., May 7, 1872.

82. Ibid., May 8, 1872.

83. Christopher L. Tomlins has recently explored how this dynamic was replicated and advanced by evolving legal doctrines of the nineteenth century. As he notes, "From the early years of the republic, the equalitarian discourse of civil society existed side-by-side with significant and growing disparities of power in the social relations of production and employment. . . . Working people were thereby doubly disadvantaged. For them, symmetry promised in the republic's revolutionary claim of civic equality outside the employment relation always became asymmetry within" (*Law, Labor, and Ideology in the Early American Republic*, 383–84).

84. The rally was formally conceived and organized by a federation of building trades unions, with the assistance of the *Workingman's Advocate*. Editor Andrew Cameron apparently played a major role in the planning process. On preparations for the rally, see the *Workingman's Advocate*, May 11, 1872.

85. *Illinois Staats-Zeitung*, May 14, 1872.

86. I borrow this term from Montgomery's *Citizen Worker*, a series of essays in which he explicates the many ways that working people understood and acted to maintain their place in American polities.

87. *Chicago Tribune*, May 7, 1872. One of the commissioners, Mark Sheridan—an ex-alderman with strong ties to the city's labor movement, attended despite the three-man board's official denial of this request.

88. *Workingman's Advocate*, May 11, 1872.

89. Due to a linkage of drunkenness with the disorderly image of working people, union leaders especially cautioned their members to avoid strong drink on the day of the march, asking their members to "resolve, if you never did so before, that on the 15th of May, at least, you will not enter a saloon" (*Workingman's Advocate*, May 11, 1872). The cause of temperance had wide support among NLU leaders (see Montgomery, *Beyond Equality*, 201–2).

90. *Chicago Tribune*, May 11, 1872.

91. *Workingman's Advocate*, May 11, 1872.

92. *Chicago Tribune*, May 1, 1872. The *Tribune* again invoked May of 1867 on the day before the rally, noting that despite the "strenuous efforts" made "to bring capitalists to their terms," the Eight Hour demonstrations "were not anywhere attended with success" (*Chicago Tribune*, May 14, 1872). It is worth noting that both the *Times* and *Tribune* argued that the ultimate issue at hand in May of 1872 was also eight hours as opposed to the more obvious question of wages. It is true that major strikes for the eight-hour day would take place that same summer of 1872 in New York City, and publicity over these events may have kept the issue alive in Chicago. Yet the evidence published by these papers on the status of the building trades indicates that no union, with the exception of the stonecutters (who had won such a general rule prior to the Fire), had sought or planned to push for the eight-hour day as part of their post-Fire contracts. It seems likely that such frequent revisitation of arguments against the eight-hour day served to deflect discussions of the difficulties faced by local construction workers *and* as a way to again conjure up a specter of disorder and fear. For a discussion of the rally centering on the supposed aim to secure an eight-hour day, see the *Chicago Tribune*, May 2, 1872. For a detailed account of the 1872 eight-hour strikes in New York City, see Bernstein, *The New York City Draft Riots*, 237–57.

93. *Chicago Tribune*, May 1, 2, 8 and 14. The *Chicago Times* set out even more inflammatory accounts of the planned rally; many examples can be found in the run between May 1 and May 15. For another account of the status of separate trades, see the *Illinois Staats-Zeitung*, May 15, 1872. It is worth noting that the *Staats-Zeitung* offered much more limited coverage of the planned rally; material on the demonstration appeared only on May 14, 15, and 16. This relative lack of interest on the part of a paper that served so many workers and Fire victims suggests that the sort of "strike

fears" spawned by the rally did have a particular rooting in the native-born, more prosperous readership of the major English-language dailies.

94. *Chicago Tribune*, May 2, 1872.

95. Ibid., May 14, 1872. In the same article, the paper also made plain its awareness of the practical difficulties of worker organization among a very large, ethnically diverse labor force. Their report noted that "there is no doubt that Unions have received large accessions during the last months." But the members "don't all pull the same way, and there being so many nationalities being represented, it is an exceedingly difficult undertaking to harmonize with them."

96. As Sproat observes, "Liberals had mixed feelings about trade unionism in America. They saw nothing basically wrong in the idea of workers banding together for mutual benefits or for resisting the practices of unscrupulous employers. Yet they viewed the typical trade union as a device tending to the destruction or weakening of traditional American individualism" (*The Best Men*, 218).

97. *Chicago Tribune*, May 15, 1872.

98. Ibid.

99. Ibid.

100. The labor movement answer to this precise problem under the theory of cooperation was to approach the market from the point of consumption through the organization of cooperative stores and even some cooperative housing associations. On nineteenth-century consumer cooperatives in the United States, see Helen Laura Sorenson, *The Consumer Movement* (New York: Arno Press, 1978).

101. For examples of letters to the editor on this subject, see the *Chicago Tribune*, May 7, 8, 10, and 11, 1972.

102. Ibid., May 7, 1872.

103. Ibid., May 11, 1872.

104. Horseshoers were closely involved in the work of reconstruction, caring for animals at building sites and at suppliers' and freighters' stables. Some unions, such as the ship caulkers, had apparently from the first declined to participate (see the *Workingman's Advocate*, May 18, 1872). Also, though some women obviously attended the rally as guests and spectators, this was an event very much geared to the exclusive participation of the all-male unions.

105. On labor processions as expressions of artisanal republicanism, see Wilentz, *Chants Democratic*, 87–92; and Wilentz, "Artisanal Republican Festivals and the Rise of Class Conflict in New York City, 1788–1837," in Michael H. Frisch and Daniel J. Walkowitz, eds., *Working-Class America* (Urbana: University of Illinois Press, 1983), 37–77. For a more general discussion of the function and meaning of processions and parades in the nineteenth century, see

Mary P. Ryan, "The American Parade: Representations of the Nineteenth-Century Social Order," in *The New Cultural History*, ed. Lynn Hunt (Berkeley: University of California Press, 1989); and Susan G. Davis, *Parades and Power* (Philadelphia: Temple University Press, 1986).

106. *Illinois Staats-Zeitung*, May 16, 1872. The *Chicago Times* offered a typically hostile reading of the deliberate decorum, announcing, "The whole procession would have passed for a first class funeral, so sober-looking and harassed did the men appear" (May 16, 1872). This general account of the procession is taken from descriptions of the morning's activities contained in the *Chicago Tribune*, May 16, 1872; the *Workingman's Advocate*, May 18, 1872; and the *Illinois-Staats-Zeitung*, May 16, 1872.

107. Medill, concerned that all in the large assembly would not be within range of his unamplified voice, provided copies of his text to city newspapers. The account quoted here is taken from the *Workingman's Advocate*, May 18, 1872.

108. For a detailed explanation of the Republican ideology of free labor, see Foner, *Free Soil, Free Labor, Free Men*, esp. 29–39.

109. Medill laid out the essential dependency of workers upon their employers in the following manner: "What labor needs is plenty of steady employment at fair wages, which cannot be had without employers with abundance of capital, who believe they can realize a satisfactory profit at particular business" (*Workingman's Advocate*, May 18, 1872).

110. In *The Pursuit of Equality in American History*, Pole examines how American equality has most often come to be defined as equality of opportunity. He notes, "[T]he national belief in opportunity, and in the rhetoric of equality, . . . bestowed an exceptional touch of moral authority on the force of liberated individuality at first deplored but later exalted as individualism" (147).

111. Tomlins has recently observed that "the ideology of freedom in contractualist discourse was really quite deceptive. [E]ven in its formal garb the freedom of self-creation that the contractualist vision celebrated was not reflected in the essential constitutive relations of everyday productive and reproductive life—of parent and child, husband and wife, employer and employee" (*Law, Labor, and Ideology in the Early American Republic*, 218–19). In formulating this analysis, I have been assisted by the philosopher G. A. Cohen's concept of "proletarian unfreedom," or how and why "free labor" is not so "free" ("The Structure of Proletarian Unfreedom," *Philosophy and Public Affairs* 12 [Winter 1983]). My thanks to Debra Satz for this reference.

112. Pole offers a useful description of the labor movement's new drive to achieve what he terms "equality of condition" in his discus-

sion of the post–Civil War period (*The Pursuit of Equality*, 200–213). An exploration of how Radical Republicans, despite their devotion to political equality, were unable to imagine how a free market economy might be regulated to serve the aim of achieving greater economic equality is a central theme of Montgomery's *Beyond Equality*. As Montgomery notes, "Radicalism was admirably suited for the task of erecting the equality of all citizens before the law, but beyond equality lay the insistence of labor's spokesmen that as the propertyless, as factors of production, wage earners were effectively denied participation in the Republic" (446).

113. The literature on the formation of American middle-class ideology in the nineteenth century is substantial and varied. Two particularly useful recent works are Charles S. Sellers, *The Market Revolution: Jacksonian America, 1815–1846* (New York: Oxford University Press, 1991); and Blumin, *The Emergence of the Middle Class*.

114. The establishment of Boards of Arbitration was an idea then popular in Britain as a feature of so-called new model unionism. See Montgomery, *Beyond Equality*, 154–56. For a more detailed contemporary exposition on the idea of arbitration, see John J. O'Neill, "Arbitration," in McNeill, ed., *The Labor Movement: The Problem of To-Day*, 497–507.

115. *Workingman's Advocate*, May 18, 1872.

116. *Chicago Tribune*, May 16, 1872.

117. The *Chicago Times* and the *Chicago Tribune* offered almost no specific commentary on the proposed Board of Arbitration, an absence that suggests that the notion that employers might concede some of their own freedom of action was simply seen as impossible or even absurd. On the other hand, Medill himself had indicated his sympathy for the idea of arbitration—at least in theory. Given the behavior of Chicago's largest builders and contractors in the strikes that marked the end of the Great Rebuilding, it seems likely that the stiffest resistance to the formation of a civic board came from this quarter.

118. According to the *Chicago Times*, one-half of the city's carpenters were among the thousands of skilled workers who did not attend the demonstration (May 16, 1872). The May 16 *Tribune* noted that the march's organizers had expected over 20,000 participants in their procession and actually drew less than a third of the number they had hoped to attract. The *Advocate*, of course, gives no hint of any disappointment with the turn-out.

119. As the *Chicago Times* commented, "The results have proved that a labor strike at present is impossible in Chicago. There are too many new men in the city, anxious to earn something, and who cannot be relied upon in the event of a general strike" (*Chicago Times*, May 16, 1872).

120. Henry S. Jaffray to George M. Pullman, May 15, 1872. George M. Pullman Collection, CHS.

121. For an account of an early stage of out-migration in the spring, see the *Workingman's Advocate*, April 4, 1872.

122. For an account of boss stonecutters who "have only been in business since the lamentable 9th of October" and other tradesmen who formed their own firms, see the *Workingman's Advocate*, November 16, 1872.

123. Ibid., June 23, 1872.

124. Ibid., April 4, 1872.

125. *Chicago Republican*, March 14, 1872. On the brick-making business, see McKenna, *Reminiscences of the Great Fire*.

126. *Workingman's Advocate*, April 6, 1872; *Chicago Tribune*, July 28, 1872.

127. *Chicago Republican*, March 14, 1872.

128. On falling walls and the technical explanation of masons for these failures, see the *Workingman's Advocate*, April 13, 1872. For two specific accounts of such accidents, see the *Chicago Republican*, November 21, 1871.

129. *Chicago Tribune*, June 23, 1872. See ibid., July 28, 1872, for an extensive description of the new technology employed in Chicago's rebuilding. William Haber's *Industrial Relations in the Building Trades* (Cambridge, MA: Harvard University Press, 1930), 32–33, contains a discussion of how technological innovations transformed the nature of construction work at this time. Also see Condit, *The Chicago School of Architecture*.

130. On the origins of workman's compensation, see E. H. Dorney, *Workmen's Compensation* (New York: Macmillan, 1924). For an incisive account of the legal evolution of employer immunity from prosecution in workplace accidents in the nineteenth century, see Tomlins, *Law, Labor, and Ideology in the Early American Republic*, 318–84.

131. *Workingman's Advocate*, June 15, 1872.

132. *Chicago Tribune*, June 23, 1872. Approximately 300 lives were thought to have been lost in the Great Fire.

133. Ibid., July 28, 1872.

134. Funeral benefits were a prime reason to join a union or a mutual benefit society in the nineteenth century. To date, I am unaware of any scholarly investigations of these working-class rituals of the union funeral.

135. *Chicago Tribune*, May 29, 1872.

136. *Workingman's Advocate*, July 27, 1872. Chicago's early carpenters' unions were apparently prone to internal dissent. As the *Advocate* rather snidely remarked three months after the fire, "The Carpenters and Joiners have succeeded in raising another organization. How long this one will last time must determine" (Decem-

ber 30, 1871). On the early history of the organized carpenters, see Thomas J. Suhrbuhr, "Ethnicity in the Formation of the Chicago Carpenters' Union: 1855–1890," in Keil and Jentz, eds., *German Workers In Industrial Chicago, 1850–1910*.

137. An explanation of the carpenters' grievances can be found in the *Chicago Times*, September 19, 1872.

138. According to standard building practices of the day, carpenters went to work on a structure only after construction was fairly advanced. The *Tribune* explained that "the mason, the carpenter, the plasterer, and the painter accede each other in order" (September 29, 1872).

139. Ibid., September 15, 1872.

140. *Chicago Times*, September 24, 1872.

141. *Chicago Tribune*, September 24, 1872.

142. *Chicago Times*, September 17, 1872.

143. Ibid., September 22, 1872.

144. *Chicago Tribune*, September 24, 1872. The paper, with some apparent surprise, also made note of the lack of "violence or even indecorous demonstrating" accompanying the carpenters' action.

145. *Chicago Times*, September 24, 1872.

146. Ibid. The *Workingman's Advocate* provided a slightly more upbeat account of the strike and its outcome, reporting that several large contractors eager to avoid any delays had granted the $4.00 rate and that carpenters on other jobs had won raises of between twenty and fifty cents (September 28, 1872; October 5, 1872).

147. The *Tribune*, for example, noted the "extraordinarily earnest and aggressive" nature of the bricklayer's union on May 14, 1872. On the national history of the bricklayers, see George E. McNeill, "The Building Trades," in McNeill, ed., *The Labor Movement: The Problem of To-Day*, 331–60.

148. *Illinois Staats-Zeitung*, October 5, 1872.

149. *Workingman's Advocate*, October 5, 1872.

150. *Chicago Times*, October 11, 1872.

151. *Chicago Tribune*, October 8, 1872. At a meeting on the evening of October 10, the Master Masons and Builders' Association resolved to hire private detectives to track down any union men who attacked or harassed scab labor, promising to "ferrit [sic] out the assailants, and upon arrest, prosecute them to the fullest extent of the law" (*Chicago Times*, October 11. 1872).

152. For accounts of this incident, see the *Chicago Tribune* and the *Chicago Times* of October 10, 1872.

153. *Chicago Tribune*, October 8, 1872. Another, similar resolution and a list of forty-five signatory members of the Master Masons and Builders' Association can be found in the *Chicago Times*, October 11, 1872.

154. *Chicago Tribune*, October 11, 1872.
155. *New York Times*, October 14, 1872.
156. *Chicago Tribune*, October 11, 1872.
157. William O'Brien, "To an Unprejudiced Public," October 9, 1872. Reprinted in the *Chicago Times*, October 11, 1872.

Chapter Five

1. As John J. Pauly suggests, the Great Fire's destructive scope made it a natural focus for apocalyptic analogies ("The Great Chicago Fire as a National Event"). For an examination of how a Norwegian immigrant freethinker used the Great Fire, by contrast, to disabuse explanations of a religious nature, see Terje Leiren, "Propaganda as Entertainment: Marcus Thrane and the Chicago Fire," *Scandinavian Journal of History* 14 (Fall 1989): 239–244. My thanks to Susan Johnson for this reference.
2. All quotations from this sermon are taken from W. W. Everts, "The Lessons of Disaster," *Chicago Pulpit*, October 19, 1872.
3. For descriptions of such Protestant theology, see Sidney E. Ahlstrom, *A Religious History of the American People* (New Haven: Yale University Press, 1972); McLoughlin, *Modern Revivalism;* and Boyer, *Urban Masses and Moral Order in America.*
4. Everts, "The Lessons of Disaster."
5. Ibid. On the moral rationale behind Sabbatarian crusades, see Robert T. Handy, *A Christian America: Protestant Hopes and Historical Realities*, 2d ed. (New York: Oxford University Press, 1984), 73–77.
6. Ethnocultural political historians argue that voter's behavior is conditioned more by cultural identifications than economic motivations, and therefore have looked to issues such as temperance and sabbatarianism as key markers of such allegiances. Two influential treatments of temperance as an ethnocultural factor in late-nineteenth-century Midwestern politics are Paul Kleppner, *The Cross of Culture: A Social Analysis of Midwestern Politics, 1850–1900* (New York: Free Press, 1970); and Richard Jensen, *The Winning of the Midwest* (Chicago: University of Chicago Press, 1971).

For an important critique of how ethnocultural studies, with their sharp focus on voting behavior, perhaps limit the interpretive scope of such political histories, see Richard L. McCormick, "Ethnocultural Interpretations of Voting Behavior," in McCormick, *The Party Period and Public Policy* (New York: Oxford University Press, 1986), 29–63. More recently, Ronald P. Formisano has asserted that the concept of an ethnocultural school is largely illusory and based on historiographic misreadings. See Formisano, "The Invention of the Ethnocultural Interpretation," *American Historical Review* 99 (April 1994): 453–77.

7. Frances L. Roberts, letter of March 18, 1873. Frances Roberts Collection, CHS.

8. The Aurora Turner Hall was probably the largest beer hall in Chicago, with the capacity to serve close to a thousand customers. Most beer halls were of course not nearly so large. For a description of smaller neighborhood saloons, see Perry Duis, *The Saloon: Public Drinking in Chicago and Boston, 1880–1920* (Urbana: University of Illinois Press, 1983). On music halls as a nineteenth-century urban institution, see Gunther Barth, *City People: The Rise of Modern City Culture in Nineteenth-Century America* (New York: Oxford University Press, 1980); and Robert Snyder, *The Voice of the City: Vaudeville and Popular Culture in New York* (New York: Oxford University Press, 1989).

9. On the place of the beer garden in German-American culture and communal life, see Nadel, *Little Germany,* 104–21.

10. *Chicago Tribune*, October 11, 1872.

11. John J. Flinn, *History of the Chicago Police* (Chicago: Police Book Fund, 1887), 136.

12. *Chicago Tribune*, January 14, 1872.

13. Since most patrolmen walked a regular beat, the city's physical devastation completely transformed the force's tasks. Ordinary police practices of this day are described in Robert M. Fogelson, *Big City Police* (Cambridge, MA: Harvard University Press, 1977).

14. Flinn, *History of the Chicago Police*, 137.

15. *Chicago Times*, October 10, 1872.

16. Ibid., September 10, 1872. On the composition and operations of the police force in Chicago prior to the Great Fire, see Flinn, *History of the Chicago Police*. Robin Einhorn points to the fact that few Chicagoans saw any need for a large force prior to the Civil War to support her argument about the "segmented" nature of pre-Fire city governance. On the commonality of the use of private police known as "specials," see Einhorn, *Property Rules*, 147–48.

17. For a list of the members of the Committee of Twenty Five, see the *Chicago Tribune*, October 28, 1872.

18. *Chicago Times*, September 12, 1872.

19. *Chicago Tribune*, September 10, 1872.

20. *Chicago Times*, September 13, 1872.

21. *Chicago Tribune*, September 13, 1872.

22. *Chicago Times*, September 13, 1872.

23. On the colonial origins of Sunday laws, see A. H. Lewis, *A Critical History of Sunday Legislation* (New York: D. Appleton & Co., 1888); and David N. Laband and Deborah Henry Heinbuch, *Blue Laws* (Lexington, MA: D. C. Heath, 1987), esp. 7–43.

24. Robert T. Handy describes the antebellum preference among temperance and Sabbatarian reformers for "volantaryism" in *A*

Christian America, 37–39. On the Maine Law movement, a sometimes successful campaign for state prohibition statutes, and a portrait of guiding force Neil Dow, see Norman H. Clark, *Deliver Us from Evil* (New York: W. W. Norton, 1976), 35–43.

25. Such an approach to temperance work mirrored the nationwide antebellum preference for voluntary measures. Jack S. Blocker usefully describes the "spectrum between persuasion and coercion" characteristic of the American temperance efforts in *American Temperance Movements: Cycles of Reform* (Boston: G. K. Hall and Co., 1989). For general accounts of pre–Civil War temperance work, see John Krout, *The Origins of Prohibition* (New York: Alfred A. Knopf, 1925); Alice Felt Tyler, *Freedom's Ferment* (Minneapolis: University of Minnesota Press, 1946), 308–50; and Ian Tyrrell, *Sobering Up* (Westport, CT: Greenwood Press, 1979). On temperance activities in Chicago in the 1830s and 1840s, see Pierce, *A History of Chicago*, 1:256–63.

26. On the Lager Beer Riot, see Renner, "In a Perfect Ferment."

27. Robin Einhorn treats this episode as an exception to what she has termed the "segmented" system of municipal rule, a process where the city government basically functioned in the service of the well-demarcated aims and needs of individual owners of property. (*Property Rules*, 159–64, 186).

28. On the role of city government during the Civil War, see ibid., 188–204; and Cook, *Bygone Days*. Also see Pierce, *A History of Chicago*, 2:435–40.

29. *City Council Proceedings*, December 5, 1870. *Illinois Staats-Zeitung*, October 25, 1869. Reprinted in the *Chicago Republican*, October 27, 1869.

30. The resolution, which stalled in committee, was retracted after eight weeks. *Illinois Staats-Zeitung*, June 14, 1872. CFLPS #13.

31. For a description of the debate surrounding the "Ohio Law," see ibid., January 12, 1872. CFLPS #15.

32. On the idea of a "Christian America," and for an explanation of how Protestant churches made forays into the realm of "civil religion" in this period, see Handy, *A Christian America*, 82–100.

33. *Illinois Staats-Zeitung*, June 26, 1873. CFLPS #15.

34. Scandinavian-Americans and some German-Americans were likely supporters of temperance legislation. The antitemperance *Staats-Zeitung* conceded on June 10, 1871, that "there is a considerable number of highly respected German citizens, mostly Methodists and Lutherans, who prefer the stricter American conception. If one estimates this number at 200, one is likely to put it rather too low than too high." Little work has been done on church-backed temperance societies within the immigrant communities of American cities. Such organizations are briefly mentioned in Jay Dolan, *The Immigrant Church* (Baltimore: Johns Hopkins University Press, 1975), 128–29.

35. *Illinois Staats-Zeitung,* April 26, 1873. CFLPS #15.

36. On the notion of the "ethnicization" of native-born Americans, see Gerber, *The Making of an American Pluralism,* esp. 386–95. The dynamic between "ethnic" and "American" identity—and the question of how ethnicity can shape a new sort of American identity—has begun to receive much attention from historians of immigration. See, for example, April Schultz, "'The Pride of the Race Has Been Touched': The 1925 Norse-American Immigration Centennial and Ethnic Identity," *Journal of American History* 77 (March 1991): 1265–95; Kerby Miller, "Class, Culture, and Immigrant Group Identity in the United States," in Virginia Yans-McLaughlin, ed., *Immigration Reconsidered: History, Sociology, and Politics* (New York: Oxford University Press, 1990), 96–129; and Kathleen Neils Conzen, "Ethnicity as Festive Culture," in Werner Sollers, ed., *The Invention of Ethnicity* (New York: Oxford University Press, 1989), 44–76.

37. David Swing, "Chicago's Creed," *Lakeside Monthly* (October 1873).

38. *Chicago Tribune,* May 24, 1873.

39. Many historians have made the argument that control over leisure, especially the consumption of alcohol, constituted a primary means by which more elite Americans attempted to control and discipline working people and immigrants. In regard to temperance, and the shift to legal forms of regulation, see Joseph R. Gusfield, *Symbolic Crusade: Status Politics and the American Temperance Movement* (Urbana: University of Illinois Press, 1963). On contests over working-class leisure, including class-based struggles over saloons, see Roy Rosenzweig, *Eight Hours for What We Will* (New York: Cambridge University Press, 1983), esp. 93–126. On the "Saloon Question," also see Sidney L. Haring, *Policing a Class Society* (New Brunswick: Rutgers University Press, 1983), 149–82. In *Profits, Power, and Prohibition* (Albany: State University of New York Press, 1989), John J. Rumbarger argues that temperance efforts in America have largely been animated by employers' desire to create a malleable industrial workforce. Brian C. Harrison makes similar argument about British temperance work in *Drink and the Victorians: The Temperance Question in England, 1815–1872* (Pittsburgh: University of Pittsburgh Press, 1971).

40. *Chicago Times,* September 18, 1872.

41. Ibid., September 25, 1872.

42. Most of the signers were members of Baptist, Methodist, and Presbyterian congregations. On the city's Protestant churches and ministers, see George Searle, *Chicago and Her Churches* (Chicago: Lakeside Press, 1867); and Swing, "Chicago's Creed." In his article, Swing attempted to describe the overall religious tenor of the time.

According to the minister, if a place like Philadelphia could be described as the product of a primarily Quaker influence, Chicago Christianity as a whole was dominated by a broad spirit of Evangelicalism that crossed the usual sectarian boundaries. A "practical gospel," he argued, lay behind the particular religious culture of the city: "being the halting place of a great army of businessmen, . . . the local gospel was compelled to become a mode of virtue, rather than a jumble of doctrines" (337).

43. *Chicago Times*, September 25, 1872.

44. The account of this meeting in the paragraphs that follow is taken from ibid., September 27, 1872.

45. Medill's office distributed copies of this document to all city newspapers. The quotations here are taken from the reprint that appeared in the *Tribune*, October 3, 1872.

46. The 2500 saloons cited by Medill were, as he pointed out, only the duly licensed establishments in the city. An unknown number of entrepreneurs supplied alcohol illegally. Further, liquor was readily available at hotels, restaurants, many boardinghouses, retail stores, and pharmacies—none of which were regulated under the city's Sunday closing ordinances.

47. Handy, *A Christian America*, 22–23.

48. Like Medill's statement on Sunday closing, the committee's response was circulated to all city newspapers. This account is taken from the *Chicago Times*, October 6, 1872.

49. On the Washingtonians, see Tyrrell, *Sobering Up*, 159–83; and Wilentz, *Chants Democratic*, 306–14.

50. Medill's message to the police commissioners was reprinted in the *Chicago Tribune*, October 11, 1872.

51. Elmer Washburn, a veteran of the Civil War Secret Service, had been installed by Medill—an unprecedented act of executive power allowed by the "Mayor's Bill" passed by the state legislature in the aftermath of the Fire. Looking to upgrade the standards of the police force by putting a law enforcement "professional" at its head, Medill selected Washburn, who was then the highly regarded chief of the state prison at Joliet. A highly competent and organized administrator, Washburn had little tolerance for the decentralized, precinct-by-precinct style of police management that had evolved in the city. His tenure, which was primarily marked by an attempt to consolidate authority in the superintendent's office, was deeply resented by the force. For an account of Washburn's superintendency, see Flinn, *History of the Chicago Police*, 135–43. His clashes with the popularly elected Board of Police Commissioners are detailed in Fremont O. Bennett, *Politics and Politicians of Chicago, Cook County, and Illinois 1787–1886* (Chicago: Blakely Printing Company, 1886), 140–42.

52. *Chicago Tribune*, October 15, 1872.

53. The policemen were specifically instructed *not* to arrest saloon keepers or attempt to close down sales, since such steps were felt by Medill to be too provocative and risky. For the mayor's justification of this policy, see ibid., October 22, 1872.

54. Ibid., October 15, 1872.

55. Ibid.

56. For details on the resignations of Greenebaum and Hesing, see ibid., October 25, 1872.

57. *Illinois Staats-Zeitung*, October 20, 1872. CFLPS #20.

58. *Chicago Tribune*, October 21, 1872.

59. On police court activities, see the *Chicago Times*, October 25, 1872. In 1865, a state law established police courts in each of the city's three divisions. Magistrates were either popularly elected, or appointed by the City Council. For a fuller description of the municipal courts, see Pierce, *A History of Chicago*, 2:308. Peter Eckstrom has done fine work in reconstructing the patterns of ethnic allegiance behind the dispensation of cases by the police courts (see "Ethnic Community and the American Legal System: German-American Opposition to Chicago Temperance Ordinances," unpublished seminar paper, University of Chicago, 1992).

60. *Illinois Staats-Zeitung*, November 15, 1872. CFLPS #13.

61. *Chicago Tribune*, October 21, 1872.

62. Ibid., October 25, 1872.

63. *Illinois Staats-Zeitung*, October 20, 1872. CFLPS #13.

64. German-Americans were themselves a highly diverse group, encompassing Catholics and Protestants, and many particular regional identities. In many ways, their status as immigrants in America worked to create a more homogenous German-American identity that to some degree effaced these differences. For a description and analysis of this dynamic, see Kathleen Neils Conzen, "German-Americans and the Invention of Ethnicity," in Frank Trommler and Joseph McVeigh, eds., *America and the Germans* (Philadelphia: University of Pennsylvania Press, 1985), 1:131–47.

65. *Chicago Tribune*, October 23, 1872.

66. Ibid.

67. Ibid., November 2, 1872.

68. As Kwame Anthony Appiah has noted in his work, which concerns how African-Americans invented the notion of a unified "Africa," the diverse immigration from the German states was easily described by hostile and even friendly Americans as a unified nation—a collectivity that effaced the real complexities and differences of its many peoples (see Appiah, *In My Father's House: Africa in the Philosophy of Culture* [New York: Oxford University Press, 1992]).

69. *Chicago Tribune,* October 25, 1872.

70. Ibid.

71. Ibid., November 1, 1872.

72. Ibid., October 27, 1872.

73. Medill to Common Council, July 15, 1872. CCPF 406 1872/564.

74. Ibid., July 18, 1872. CCPF 406 1872/580.

75. Medill's brief letter of resignation was reprinted in the *Chicago Tribune,* August 12, 1872. The Common Council elected L. L. Bond, the alderman of the Tenth Ward, to the position of acting mayor.

76. *Chicago Tribune,* May 29, 1873. The paper's account of the circulation of this joke describes a mass meeting in the heavily immigrant Eight Ward, where one orator spoke of Medill as "at one time a very good man," until he "lent his ear to the temperance men."

77. On Medill and the Republican party of Illinois, see Gienapp, *The Origins of the Republican Party;* and Jay Monaghan, *The Man Who Elected Lincoln* (Indianapolis: Bobbs-Merrill, 1956).

78. *Illinois Staats-Zeitung,* May 2, 1873.

79. Medill's decision to leave office is sensitively discussed by David Protess in "Joseph Medill," in *The Mayors: The Chicago Political Tradition,* ed. Holli and Green (Carbondale: Southern Illinois University Press, 1987), 11–13.

80. *Chicago Tribune,* July 16, 1873.

81. See Sproat, *The Best Men,* 244–71.

82. On urban progressivism, see Bradley Rice, *Progressive Cities: The Commission Government Movement in America, 1901–1920* (Austin: University of Texas Press, 1977).

83. Given the problems presented by ward-based politics, it seems no accident that Progressives directed much of their energy to reshaping the institutions that were premised on more local representation, often moving to replace voting by district with commission systems, at-large elections, and handing much of the power traditionally in the hands of aldermen to a professional "city manager" (see Rice, *Progressive Cities*).

84. Einhorn describes the emergence of the concept of a "new public" by the time of the Great Fire, a transition to an urban politics that included a "more integrated public household" (*Property Rules,* 241–43).

85. See, for example, the weekly edition of the *Illinois Staats-Zeitung,* September 1, 1869, reprinted in the *Chicago Republican,* September 2, 1869; and the *Illinois Staats-Zeitung,* June 10, 1871, CFLPS #13.

86. On the idea of "civic integration," the incorporation of groups explicitly organized on the basis of ethnicity, into the American ur-

ban polity, see Gerber, *The Making of an American Pluralism*, esp. 117, 359–61.

87. *Chicago Tribune*, May 27, 1873.

88. According to ibid., November 7, 1873, the Committee of Seventy was "dormant" during this season.

89. The text of this directive, General Order #20, appears in journalist M. L. Ahern's account of the rise of the People's party (*The Great Revolution* [Chicago: Lakeside Publishing and Printing Co., 1874], 25).

90. Commissioner Mark Sheridan, one of the city's most influential Irish politicians, strongly objected to Washburn's order on the grounds that such a directive violated constitutional guarantees against illegal searches. Sheridan's battle with Washburn quickly escalated into a months-long struggle. For full accounts of the Police Board troubles, see Ahern, *The Great Revolution;* and Fremont O. Bennett, *Politics and Politicians of Chicago, Cook County, and Illinois* (Chicago: Blakely Printing Company, 1886), 140–42. As Einhorn notes, the organized labor movement of the city had worked to secure the election of sympathetic police commissioners in the wake of the 1867 Eight Hours Strikes (*Property Rules*, 234).

91. *Illinois Staats-Zeitung*, May 3, 1873. CFLPS #14.

92. Ibid.

93. *Chicago Tribune*, May 16, 1873. On Hesing's role in the formation of the party, and an analysis of his appeals to class and ethnic solidarities, see Jentz, "Class and Politics in an Emerging Industrial City."

94. Flinn, *History of the Chicago Police*, 143.

95. O'Hara, himself a Scottish immigrant, was an extremely adept ethnic politician, "a rare combination," as journalist F. F. Cook observed, "of Yankee shrewdness, German *Gemutlichkeit*, and Hibernian wit and humor" (*Bygone Days*, 264). For further information on O'Hara's career, see his biographical sketch in Ahern, *The Great Revolution*. The German community had witnessed an equivalent symbolic joining of forces a week earlier, when German Democratic leader Francis Hoffman clasped hands with Hesing at a May 14 mass meeting in the Seventeenth Ward (*Chicago Tribune*, May 15, 1873).

96. Ahern, *The Great Revolution*, 70.

97. The People's party had a coordinating committee and further maintained an organizing committee in almost every ward. At least 100 men served the party by enlisting new members, securing donations, and otherwise husbanding the creation of a new political organization. While prominent immigrant politicians like Hesing, O'Hara, and Hoffman dominated the central committee, ward committees were a mix of small businessmen, professionals, and trades-

men. A grocer, a saloon keeper, a dry goods wholesaler, and a stonecutter, for example, were among the fourteen members of the Eighteenth Ward Committee. For sample lists of ward committee membership, see the *Chicago Tribune*, May 29, 1873.

98. During the height of summer, the public presence of the People's party diminished, leading the *Illinois Staats-Zeitung* to issue the following reassurance to its readers: "It has been asked why nothing is heard any longer from the German-American organization. No one has need to be worried. The German-American organization is doing well, and will appear at the political arena at the right moment" (July 26, 1873).

99. Ibid., April 22, 1873. CFLPS #18; *Chicago Tribune*, May 30, 1873; *Illinois Staats-Zeitung*, February 3, 1873.

100. Ahern, *The Great Revolution.*

101. *Law and Order Advocate*, October 30, 1873.

102. *Chicago Tribune*, November 2, 1873.

103. Ibid.

104. Gerber, *The Making of an American Pluralism*, 117.

105. *Illinois Staats-Zeitung*, October 21, 1873. CFLPS #13.

106. *Chicago Times*, October 20, 1873.

107. The People's party's full slate and brief biographies of all candidates can be found in Ahern, *The Great Revolution*, 97–130.

108. The activities of O'Hara's "naturalization mill" are described in the *Chicago Tribune* of October 31, 1873. Many of the applicants, the paper charged, were applying for citizenship under assumed names, thereby vesting themselves with a privilege not uncommon in Chicago politics: the right to vote twice. A county judge shuttered this operation a few days after its opening.

109. One measure of backlash against immigrants can be found in the fact that all of Chicago's thirteen English-language papers, regardless of their stance on Sunday closing, united to condemn the People's party.

110. *Chicago Tribune*, November 2, 1873. As Dexter argued, in a comment that should be instructive for all students of local politics in the years prior to the explosion of federal functions, "[T]he aldermen of the city were more important to Chicagoans as individuals than the President."

111. Ibid., October 31, 1872; November 2, 1872.

112. Ibid., November 4, 1873.

113. Ibid.

114. Ibid., November 2, 1873.

115. Ibid., November 3, 1873.

116. For detailed accounts of the election and its results, see ibid., November 5, 1873; and the *Chicago Times*, November 5, 1873.

117. *Chicago Tribune*, November 5, 1873.

118. The text of the telegraph, which was signed by Hesing and Jacob Rehm, another major German Republican, ran as follows: "Your policy has been defeated by a 10,000 vote majority" (*Illinois Staats-Zeitung*, November 5, 1873. CFLPS #15).

119. As Richard Schneirov points out, one measure of the People's party success at mobilizing Chicago's immigrants can be found in the fact that voter turnout doubled that of the 1871 mayoral election. It is also important, however, to recall that the 1871 election took place about five weeks after the Great Fire, which had a major impact on the conduct of the campaigns for office and the numbers who made their ways to the polls ("Class Conflict, Municipal Politics, and Governmental Reform in Gilded Age Chicago, 1871–1875," in *German Workers in Industrial Chicago, 1850–1910*, ed. Keil and Jentz).

120. *Chicago Tribune*, November 8, 1873.

121. Ibid., November 5, 1873.

122. Ibid.

123. Ibid.

124. *Illinois Staats-Zeitung*, November 6, 1873.

125. Ibid., November 5, 1873.

126. Ibid.

127. The Council took this action on March 16, 1874 (*Proceedings of the Common Council*, 1873–74, 130).

128. *Illinois Staats-Zeitung*, November 5, 1873. Quoted in translation in the *Chicago Tribune*, November 6, 1873.

129. *Law and Order Advocate*, October 30, 1873.

130. *Chicago Tribune*, November 2, 1873.

131. Charles C. Bonney, "The Chicago of the Publicist," *Lakeside Monthly* (October 1873).

Epilogue

1. *Chicago Tribune*, December 25, 1873. It is important to note that despite the present-day connotations of these terms, "Socialist," "Communist," and "social revolutionary" were all used more or less interchangeably by the press at this point in the nineteenth century to describe members of the International Workingman's Association (IWA). Founded by Marx in 1864, the International's North American Federation was organized in New York City in 1871. At this assembly, Chicago's German Sozialpolitikal Arbeiterverein received designation as Sections 4 and 5 (of a total of six) of the North American Federation (*Report of the North American Central Committee of the IWA*, April 2, 1871. Reprinted in John R. Commons et al., *A Documentary History of American Industrial Society*, vol. 9 (Cleveland: Arthur H. Clarke Co., 1910). On the activities of organized Socialists in Chicago, see Henry David, *History of the Haymarket Affair* (New York: Farrar and Rinehart, 1936).

2. On the activities of the IWA in America, see John R. Commons et al., *History of Labour in the United States*, (New York: Macmillan, 1918), 2:203–22; and Montgomery, *Beyond Equality*. For a general account of the First International, see G. M. Stekloff, *History of the First International* (London: M. Lawrence, Ltd., 1928).

3. The causes of the Panic of 1873 are closely examined in Irwin Unger, *The Greenback Era: A Social and Political History of American Finance, 1865–1879* (Princeton: Princeton University Press, 1964), 213–48. For a more sweeping account of the impact of this economic crisis, see Eric Foner, *Reconstruction*, 512–19.

4. *Chicago Tribune*, December 25, 1873.

5. Ibid., January 18, 1874. Beginning in 1873, Wynkoop, an English-born ex-Chartist, wrote regularly on labor issues in the Sunday *Tribune*.

6. On rhetorical usage of "slave labor" by worker activists, see David R. Roediger, *The Wages of Whiteness: Race and the Making of the American Working Class* (New York: Verso, 1991).

7. *Chicago Tribune*, December 25, 1873.

8. For an analysis of the new ideological underpinnings of the demand for "work or bread," see Richard Schneirov's important article on the essentially different understandings of the state held by labor activists committed to American "republicanism" and those who subscribed to Socialist theories devised in Europe ("Political Cultures and the Role of the State in Labor's Republic: The View from Chicago, 1848–1877," *Labor History* 32 [Summer 1991]: 376–400).

9. *Chicago Times*, December 22, 1871.

10. On commemorations of the Paris Commune, a yearly ritual for the Socialists and the anarchists of the city in the 1870s and 1880s, see Nelson, *Beyond the Martyrs*.

11. On the intellectual genealogies of Chicago socialists, see David, *History of the Haymarket Affair*.

12. Chicago workers' demands for "work or bread" was part of a national outburst of such activism in many industrial cities during the winter following the Panic of 1873. Municipal authorities in New York, Philadelphia, Patterson, Newark, Boston, Detroit, Pittsburgh, Louisville, Cincinnati, and Indianapolis all came under some pressure to fund public works programs or step up relief measures. None of the movements met with any substantial success. The leadership of these protests varied from city to city; a Socialist-led protest was unique to Chicago. For an account of these activities, see Herbert G. Gutman, "The Failure of the Movement by the Unemployed for Public Works in 1873," *Political Science Quarterly* 80 (June 1965): 254–76. More detail on the New York City movement can be found in Gutman, "The Tompkins Square 'Riot' in New York City on Janu-

ary 13, 1874: A Reexamination of its Causes and Its Aftermath," *Labor History* 6 (Winter 1965), 44–70.

13. *Chicago Times*, December 23, 1873. The *Times* report offered translations of all foreign-language speeches. A striking measure of Chicago's increasingly cosmopolitan population can be found in the fact that speakers addressed this meeting in English, German, French, Italian, Polish, Norwegian, and Dutch.

14. Ibid.

15. Ibid.

16. City assets totaled $754,707, while debts added up to $1,861,704 (*Chicago Tribune*, December 2, 1873).

17. David Gage, as was the custom of the day, had provided his personal bond to guarantee the city's funds. With his loss to Dan O'Hara in the November 1873 election, Gage's appropriation of over $500,000 in city funds came to light. For the details of this episode, see Ahern, *The Great Revolution*, 45–64.

18. *Workingman's Advocate*, December 27, 1873.

19. Henry King still presided over the Society, and Wirt Dexter still held the powerful position of Executive Committee Chair. Others present at this meeting, all of whom had worked on fire relief, included E. C. Larned, Thomas Avery, N. S. Bouton, Murray Nelson, J. T. Ryerson, N. K. Fairbank, Julius Rosenthal, J. MacGregor Adams, and C. L. Hammond. (*Chicago Times*, December 27, 1873).

Francis Hoffman Jr. was the son of a prominent German-American Democratic who had served as the lieutenant governor of Illinois. Some observers charged that his allegiance to socialism was simply a product of political expediency, and that he planned to ride his newfound prominence to a spot in the state legislature. The German press was particularly virulent toward Hoffman; see, for example, the *Illinois Staats-Zeitung* of December 22, 1873.

20. *Chicago Times*, December 27, 1873.

21. *Chicago Tribune*, December 23, 1873.

22. *Chicago Times*, December 27, 1873.

23. *Chicago Tribune*, January 3, 1874.

24. *Chicago Times*, January 4, 1874.

25. *Chicago Tribune*, January 18, 1874.

26. Ibid., January 4, 1874.

27. Ibid., January 20, 1874.

28. Chicago Relief and Aid Society, *Report to Common Council for 1875* (Chicago: Horton and Leonard, 1876).

29. *Chicago Tribune*, December 23, 1873.

30. *Illinois Staats-Zeitung*, December 22, 1873. Printed in translation in the *Tribune*, December 23, 1873.

31. Ibid.

32. Ibid.
33. *Chicago Tribune*, January 2, 1874.
34. Ibid.
35. Ibid.
36. *Chicago Times*, January 2, 1874.
37. *Workingmans' Advocate*, January 24, 1874. For an analysis of Cameron's thinking on this subject, see Richard Schneirov, "Political Cultures and the Role of the State in Labor's Republic."
38. On late-nineteenth-century Chicago politics, see Richard Schneirov, "The Knights of Labor in the Chicago Labor Movement and in Municipal Politics, 1877–1887," Ph.D. diss., Northern Illinois University, 1984; and Nelson, *Beyond the Martyrs*. On the organizations of business leaders that formed in part to influence urban politics, institutions such as the Citizen's Association, the Municipal Voters' League, the Union League and the Civic Federation, see Pierce, *A History of Chicago*, 3:340–80; and Donald David Marks, "Polishing the Gem of the Prairie: The Evolution of Civic Reform Consciousness in Chicago," Ph.D. diss., University of Wisconsin, 1974.
39. *Chicago Tribune*, February 1, 1874.
40. Ibid., January 2, 1874.

BIBLIOGRAPHY

I. PRIMARY SOURCES

A. Manuscript Collections

MANUSCRIPTS AND ARCHIVES, CHICAGO HISTORICAL SOCIETY, CHICAGO

Chicago Fire Guards Collection
Chicago Relief and Aid Society Papers, United Charities Collection
Charles S. Deane Scrapbook of the Great Fire
William Furness Collection
Great Fire of 1871 Personal Narratives Collection
Henry Greenebaum Collection
Anne McClure Hitchcock Collection
George M. Pullman Collection
Frances L. Roberts Collection
Harriet Rosa Collection

PRINTS AND PHOTOGRAPHS, CHICAGO HISTORICAL SOCIETY, CHICAGO

Chicago Fire of 1871 Broadsides Collection.

SPECIAL COLLECTIONS, NEWBERRY LIBRARY, CHICAGO

Hermann Raster Papers.
Lambert Tree Papers.

ILLINOIS STATE ARCHIVES REGIONAL DEPOSITORY, NORTHEASTERN ILLINOIS UNIVERSITY, CHICAGO

Chicago Common Council Proceedings, 1871–74.

B. Newspapers and Periodicals

Chicago Evening Journal, 1871.
Chicago Pulpit, 1872–74.
Chicago Republican, 1867–72.
Chicago Times, 1867–74.

Chicago Tribune, 1867–74.
Illinois Staats-Zeitung, 1867–74.
Lakeside Monthly, 1871–74.
The Land Owner, 1869–74.
Law and Order Advocate, 1873.
New York Herald, 1871.
New York Sun, 1871.
New York Times, 1871–72.
New York Tribune, 1871.
Prairie Farmer, 1871.
Workingman's Advocate, 1867–74.

C. Reports and Pamphlets

Chicago. Common Council. *Journal of the Proceedings*, 1871–74.

Chicago Relief and Aid Society. *Report to the Common Council for 1875*. Chicago: Horton and Leonard, 1876.

———. *Report on Disbursements to Sufferers by the Great Fire*. Cambridge, MA: Riverside Press, 1874.

———. *Report of the Chicago Relief and Aid Society for 1871–72*. Chicago: Horton and Leonard, 1872.

———. *Annual Report for the Year Ending October 31, 1871. Chicago: J. M. Jones, 1871.*

———. *First Special Report of the Chicago Relief and Aid Society*. Chicago: Culver, Page, Hoyne, and Co., 1871.

Cook County. Board of Commissioners. *Journal of the Proceedings*, 1871–1872.

Illinois. General Assembly. *Report of the Select Committee on Governor John M. Palmer's Messages of November 15 and December 9*. Springfield: Illinois State Journal Printing, 1872.

Shaw, James. *The Military Occupation of Chicago*. Springfield: Illinois State Journal Printing, 1872. Speech delivered in the Illinois House of Representatives, January 24, 1872.

United Hebrew Relief Association of Chicago. *Annual Report for 1870–71 and 1871–72*. Chicago: Max Stern, 1872.

United States Army. *The Condition of Affairs in the City of Chicago Occasioned by the Great Fire of October 8 and 9, 1871*. By Lieut. Gen. Phillip H. Sheridan. Chicago: n.p., 1871.

D. Books and Articles

Ahern, M. L. *The Great Revolution*. Chicago: Lakeside Publishing and Printing Co., 1874.

Andreas, Alfred T. *A History of Chicago*. 3 vols. Chicago: A. T. Andreas Co., 1887.

Bennett, Fremont O. *Politics and Politicians of Chicago, Cook County, and Illinois, 1787–1886*. Chicago: Blakely Printing Co., 1886.

Blanchard, Rufus. *History of the Discovery and Conquest of the Northwest*. Wheaton, IL: R. Blanchard, 1878.

Bonney, Charles C. "The Chicago of the Publicist." *Lakeside Monthly* (October 1873).

"A Chicago Lady." *Relief: A Humorous Drama*. Chicago: Lakeside Press, 1872.

Colbert, Elias, and Everett Chamberlin. *Chicago and the Great Conflagration*. Chicago: J. S. Goodman and Co., 1871.

Collyer, Robert. *Some Memories*. New York: Dodd, Mead, 1909.

Cook, F. F. *Bygone Days in Chicago*. Chicago: A. C. McClurg, 1910.

Critchell, Robert S. *Recollections of a Fire Insurance Man*. Chicago: n.p., 1909.

Everts, W. W. "The Lessons of Disaster." *Chicago Pulpit*, October 19, 1872.

Flinn, John J. *History of the Chicago Police*. Chicago: Police Book Fund, 1887.

Gay, Sidney Howard. "Chicago and the Relief Committee." *Lakeside Monthly* 7 (February 1872): 168.

Goodspeed, E. J. *Chicago's Holocaust*. Chicago: J. W. Goodspeed, 1871.

———. *Histories of the Great Fires in Chicago and in the West*. Chicago: J. W. Goodspeed, 1871.

Henshaw, Sarah Edwards. *Our Branch and Its Tributaries; Being a History of the Work of the Northwestern Sanitary Commission*. Chicago: Alfred L. Sewell, 1868.

Holmes, John Haynes. *The Life and Letters of Robert Collyer*. 2 vols. New York: Dodd, Mead, 1917.

Industrial Chicago: The Manufacturing Interests. Vol. 2. Chicago: Goodspeed Publications Co., 1894.

Johnson, Alexander. *Adventures in Social Welfare: Being Reminiscent of All Things, Thoughts, and Folks during Forty Years of Social Work*. Fort Wayne: n.p., 1923.

Kirkland, Joseph. *The Story of Chicago*. Chicago: Dibble Publishing Co., 1892.

Luzerne, Frank. *The Lost City!*. New York: Wells and Co., 1872.

McKenna, John. *Reminiscences of the Great Fire*. Chicago: n.p., 1920.

Myers, Sidney. *Labor: Extracts, Magazine Articles, and Observations Relating to Social Science and Political Economy as Bearing upon the Subject of Labor*. Chicago: n.p., 1867.

Palmer, John M. *Personal Recollections of John M. Palmer*. Cincinnati: Robert Clarke Co., 1901.

Roe, Edward Payson. *Barriers Burned Away*. New York: AMS Press, 1972.

"The Ruined City," or The Horrors of Chicago. New York: American News Co., 1871.

Schoff, S. S. *The Glory of Chicago*. Chicago: Knight and Leonard, 1873.

Sewell, Alfred L. *The Great Calamity! Scenes, Incidents, and Lessons of the Great Chicago Fire*. Chicago: Alfred L. Sewell, 1872.

Sheahan, James W., and George P. Upton. *The Great Conflagration. Chicago: Its Past, Present, and Future*. Chicago: Union Publishing Co., 1871.

Sheridan, Philip H., and Michael V. Sheridan. *Personal Memoirs of Philip Henry Sheridan, General, United States Army*. 2 vols. New York: D. Appleton and Co., 1904.

Swing, David. "Chicago's Creed." *Lakeside Monthly* (October 1873).

The World's Fire! The Great Conflagration in the City of Chicago, October 8th and 9th, 1871. Chicago: Republic Life Insurance Printing Office, 1871.

Wright, John S. *Chicago: Past, Present, and Future*. Chicago: Western News Co., 1868.

II. SECONDARY SOURCES

A. Books and Articles

Abbott, Carl. *Boosters and Businessmen: Popular Economic Thought and Urban Growth in the Antebellum Middle West*. Westport, CT: Greenwood Press, 1981.

Ahlstrom, Sydney. *A Religious History of the American People*. New Haven: Yale University Press, 1972.

Andrews, Wayne. *The Battle for Chicago*. New York: Harcourt Brace Jovanovitch, 1946.

Appiah, Kwame Anthony. *In My Father's House: Africa in the Philosophy of Culture*. New York: Oxford University Press, 1992.

Appleby, Joyce. *Capitalism and a New Social Order: The Republican Vision of the 1790s*. New York: Oxford, 1984.

Bailey, Peter. "Will the Real Bill Banks Please Stand Up? Towards a Role Analysis of Mid-Victorian Working Class Respectability." *Journal of Social History* 12 (Spring 1979): 336–53.

Baker, Jean H. *Affairs of Party: The Political Culture of Northern Democrats in the Mid-Nineteenth Century*. Ithaca: Cornell University Press, 1983.

Baker, Keith Michael. *Inventing the French Revolution*. New York: Cambridge University Press, 1990.

Banks, Anne, ed. *First-Person America*. New York: Alfred A. Knopf, 1980.

Baron, Ava, ed. *Work Engendered: Toward a New History of American Labor.* Ithaca: Cornell University Press, 1991.

Barrett, James R. *Work and Community in the Jungle: Chicago's Packinghouse Workers, 1894–1922.* Urbana: University of Illinois Press, 1987.

Barth, Gunther. *City People: The Rise of Modern City Culture in Nineteenth-Century America.* New York: Oxford University Press, 1980.

Beijboom, Ulf. *Swedes in Chicago: A Demographic and Social Study of the 1840–1880 Immigration.* Vaxjo: Scandinavian University Books, 1971.

Belcher, Wyatt Winton. *The Economic Rivalry between Chicago and St. Louis, 1850–1880.* New York: Columbia University Press, 1947.

Bender, Thomas. "Wholes and Parts: The Need for Synthesis in American History." *Journal of American History* 73 (June 1986): 120–36.

———. *Towards an Urban Vision.* Lexington: University of Kentucky Press, 1975.

Bennett, David. *The Party of Fear: From Nativist Movements to the New Right In American History.* Chapel Hill: University of North Carolina Press, 1988.

Bernstein, Iver. *The New York City Draft Riots: Their Significance for American Politics and Society in the Age of the Civil War.* New York: Oxford University Press, 1990.

Bernstein, Samuel. "The Impact of the Paris Commune in the United States." *Massachusetts Review* (Spring 1971).

Billington, Ray Allen. *The Origins of Nativism in the United States, 1800–1844.* New York: Arno Press, 1974.

———. *The Protestant Crusade.* New York: Rinehart and Co., 1938.

Blackmar, Elizabeth R. *Manhattan for Rent, 1785–1850.* Ithaca: Cornell University Press, 1989.

Blewett, Mary H. *Men, Women, and Work: Class, Gender, and Protest in the New England Shoe Industry, 1780–1910.* Urbana: University of Illinois Press, 1988.

Blocker, Jack S. *American Temperance Movements: Cycles of Reform.* Boston: G. K. Hall and Co., 1989.

Blumin, Stewart M. *The Emergence of the Middle Class: Social Experience in the American City, 1760–1900.* New York: Cambridge University Press, 1989.

———. "Explaining the New Metropolis: Perception, Depiction, and Analysis in Mid-Nineteenth-Century New York City." *Journal of Urban History* 11 (November 1984): 9–38.

Bodnar, John. *The Transplanted: A History of Immigrants in Urban America.* Bloomington: University of Indiana Press, 1985.

Boydston, Jeanne. *Home and Work: Housework, Wages, and the Ideology of Labor in the Early Republic*. New York: Oxford University Press, 1990.

Boyer, Paul S. *Urban Masses and Moral Order in America, 1820–1920*. Cambridge, MA: Harvard University Press, 1978.

Brace, Charles Loring. *The Dangerous Classes of New York and Twenty Years' Work among Them*. New York: Wynkoop and Hollenbeck, 1872.

Bradley, Donald S. and Mayer N. Zald. "From Commercial Elite to Political Administrators: The Recruitment of the Mayors of Chicago." *American Journal of Sociology* 70 (1965): 153–67.

Bremner, Robert H. *The Public Good: Philanthropy and Benevolence in the Civil War Era*. New York: Alfred A. Knopf, 1981.

———. *American Philanthropy*. Chicago: University of Chicago Press, 1960.

———. *From the Depths: The Discovery of Poverty in the United States*. New York: New York University Press, 1956.

Bridges, Amy C. *A City in the Republic: Antebellum New York and the Origins of Machine Politics*. New York: Cambridge University Press, 1984.

Brown, James B. *A History of Public Assistance in Chicago*. Chicago: University of Chicago, 1941.

Bryce, James. *The American Commonwealth*. New York: Macmillan, 1888.

Bubnys, Edward L. "Nativity and the Distribution of Wealth: Chicago, 1870." *Explorations in Economic History* 19 (April 1982): 101–9.

Carey, Glenn O. *Edward Payson Roe*. Boston: G. K. Hall, 1985.

Chandler, Alfred D. *The Visible Hand: The Managerial Revolution in American Business*. Cambridge, MA: Harvard University Press, 1977.

Clark, Clifford. *The American Family Home, 1800–1960*. Chapel Hill: University of North Carolina Press, 1986.

Clark, Norman H. *Deliver Us from Evil: An Interpretation of American Prohibition*. New York: W. W. Norton, 1976.

Cohen, G. A. "The Structure of Proletarian Unfreedom." *Philosophy and Public Affairs* 12 (Winter 1983).

Cohen, Lizabeth. *Making a New Deal: Industrial Workers in Chicago, 1919–1939*. New York: Cambridge University Press, 1990.

Commons, John R. *History of Labour in the United States*. Vol. 2. New York: Macmillam, 1919.

Commons, John R., et al., eds. *A Documentary History of American Industrial Society*. Vol. 9. Cleveland: Arthur H. Clark, 1910.

Condit, Carl. *The Chicago School of Architecture*. Chicago: University of Chicago Press, 1964.

Conzen, Kathleen Neils. "Ethnicity as Festive Culture." In *The Invention of Ethnicity,* edited by Sollers, 1989.

———. "German-Americans and the Invention of Ethnicity." In *America and the Germans.* Vol. 1. *Immigration, Language, and Ethnicity.* edited by Frank Trommler and Joseph McVeigh. Philadelphia: University of Pennsylvania Press, 1985.

———. *Immigrant Milwaukee, 1836–1860: Accommodation and Community in a Frontier City.* Cambridge, MA: Harvard University Press, 1976.

Cott, Nancy F. *The Bonds of Womanhood: "Woman's Sphere" in New England, 1780–1835.* New Haven: Yale University Press, 1977.

Cromie, Robert. *The Great Chicago Fire.* New York: McGraw-Hill, 1958.

Cromie, Robert, and Herman Kogan. *The Great Fire: Chicago 1871.* New York: G. P. Putnam's Sons, 1971.

Cronon, William. *Nature's Metropolis: Chicago and the Great West.* New York: W. W. Norton, 1991.

Cumbler, John T. "The Politics of Charity: Gender and Class in Late Nineteenth-Century Charity Policy." *Journal of Social History* 14 (1980): 99–111.

Cunliffe, Marcus. *Soldiers and Civilians: The Martial Spirit in America, 1775–1865.* Boston: Little, Brown, 1968.

Darnton, Robert. "Writing News and Telling Stories." *Daedelus* 104 (Spring 1975): 175–94.

David, Henry. *History of the Haymarket Affair.* New York: Farrar and Rinehart, 1936.

Davis, Natalie Zemon. *Fiction in the Archives.* Stanford: Stanford University Press, 1987.

Davis, Susan G. *Parades and Power: Street Theatre in Nineteenth-Century Philadelphia.* Philadelphia: Temple University Press, 1986.

Denning, Michael. *Mechanic Accents: Dime Novels and Working-Class Culture in America.* New York: Verso, 1987.

Diner, Hasia R. *Erin's Daughters in America: Irish Immigrant Women in the Nineteenth Century.* Baltimore: Johns Hopkins University Press, 1983.

Dolan, Jay. *The Immigrant Church: New York's Irish and German Catholics, 1815–1865.* Baltimore: Johns Hopkins University Press, 1975.

Dorney, E. H. *Workmen's Compensation.* New York: Macmillan, 1924.

Duis, Perry. *The Saloon: Public Drinking in Chicago and Boston, 1880–1920.* Urbana: University of Illinois Press, 1983.

Eagleton, Terry. "Foreword." In Kristin Ross, *The Emergence of Social Space: Rimbaud and the Paris Commune.* Minneapolis: University of Minnesota Press, 1988.

Einhorn, Robin L. *Property Rules: Political Economy in Chicago, 1833–1872*. Chicago: University of Chicago Press, 1991.

———. "The Civil War and Municipal Government in Chicago." In *Towards a Social History of the American Civil War*, edited by Vinovskis, 1990.

Emmons, David M. *The Butte Irish: Class and Ethnicity in an American Mining Town, 1875–1925*. Urbana: University of Illinois Press, 1989.

Erie, Stephen P. *Rainbow's End: Irish Americans and the Dilemmas of Machine Politics*. Berkeley: University of California Press, 1988.

Findlay, James. *Dwight Moody*. Chicago: University of Chicago Press, 1969.

Fisher-Fishkin, Shelley. *From Fact to Fiction: Journalism and Imaginative Writing in America*. Baltimore: Johns Hopkins University Press, 1985.

Fogelson, Robert M. *Big City Police*. Cambridge, MA: Harvard University Press, 1977.

Foner, Eric. ed. *The New American History*. Philadelphia: Temple University Press, 1990.

———. *Reconstruction: America's Unfinished Revolution, 1863–1877*. New York: Harper and Row, 1988.

———. *Free Soil, Free Labor, Free Men: The Ideology of the Republican Party before the Civil War*. New York: Oxford University Press, 1970.

Formisano, Ronald P. "The Invention of the Ethnocultural Interpretation." *American Historical Review* 99 (April 1994): 453–77.

Fredrickson, George M. *The Inner Civil War*. New York: Harper and Row, 1965.

Funchion, Michael F. "Irish Chicago: Church, Homeland, Politics, and Class—the Shaping of an Ethnic Group, 1870–1900." In *Ethnic Chicago*, edited by Holli and Jones, 1981.

Garcia, Hazel Dicken. *Journalistic Standards in Nineteenth-Century America*. Madison: University of Wisconsin Press, 1989.

Gerber, David A. *The Making of an American Pluralism: Buffalo, New York, 1825–1860*. Urbana: University of Illinois Press, 1989.

Giddings, Franklin H. "Co-operation." In *The Labor Movement: The Problem of To-Day*, edited by McNeill, 1887.

Gienapp, William E. *The Origins of the Republican Party, 1852–1856*. New York: Oxford University Press, 1987.

Ginzberg, Lori D. *Women and the Work of Benevolence: Morality, Politics, and Class in the Nineteenth-Century United States*. New Haven: Yale University Press, 1990.

Gleason, Philip. "American Identity and Americanization." In Stephen Thernstrom et al., eds., *The Harvard Encyclopedia of*

American Ethnic Groups. Cambridge, MA: Harvard University Press, 1980.

Glickstein, Jonathan A. *Concepts of Free Labor in Antebellum America*. New Haven: Yale University Press, 1991.

Greene, Victor. *American Immigrant Leaders: Marginality and Identity*. Baltimore: Johns Hopkins University Press, 1987.

Gullickson, Gay. "La petroleuse." *Feminist Studies* 17 (Summer 1990).

Gusfield, Joseph R. *Symbolic Crusade: Status Politics and the American Temperance Movement*. Urbana: University of Illinois Press, 1963.

Gutman, Herbert G. "The Failure of the Movement by the Unemployed for Public Works in 1873." *Political Science Quarterly* 80 (June 1965): 254–76.

———. "The Tompkins Square 'Riot' in New York City on January 13, 1874: A Reexamination of Its Causes and Its Aftermath." *Labor History* 6 (Winter 1965): 46–70.

Haber, William. *Industrial Relations in the Building Trades*. Cambridge, MA: Harvard University Press, 1930.

Halttunen, Karen. *Confidence Men and Painted Women: A Study of Middle-Class Culture in America, 1830–1870*. New Haven: Yale University Press, 1982.

Hammack, David C. *Power and Society: Greater New York at the Turn of the Century*. New York: Russell Sage Foundation, 1982.

Handy, Robert T. *A Christian America: Protestant Hopes and Historical Realities*. 2d ed. New York: Oxford University Press, 1984.

Haring, Sidney L. *Policing a Class Society*. New Brunswick: Rutgers University Press, 1983.

Harris, Carl V. *Political Power in Birmingham, 1871–1921*. Knoxville: University of Tennessee Press, 1977.

Harrison, Brian C. *Drink and the Victorians: The Temperance Question in England, 1815–1872*. Pittsburgh: University of Pittsburgh Press, 1971.

Hartog, Hendrick. *Public Property and Private Power: The Corporation of the City of New York in American Law, 1730–1870*. Chapel Hill: University of North Carolina Press, 1983.

Harvey, David. *Consciousness and the Urban Experience*. Baltimore: Johns Hopkins University Press, 1985.

Haskell, Thomas. *The Emergence of Professional Social Science*. Urbana: University of Illinois Press, 1977.

Hays, Samuel P. "The Politics of Reform in Municipal Government in the Progressive Era." *Pacific Northwest Quarterly* 55 (1964): 157–69.

Headley, Joel T. *The Great Riots of New York, 1742–1873*. New York: E. P. Treat, 1873.

Hewitt, Nancy A. *Women's Activism and Social Change: Rochester, New York, 1822–1872*. Ithaca: Cornell University Press, 1984.

Higham, John. *Strangers in the Land: Patterns of American Nativism, 1860–1925*. 2d ed. New Brunswick: Rutgers University Press, 1988.

———. *From Boundlessness to Consolidation: The Transformation of American Culture, 1848–1860*. Ann Arbor: University of Michigan Press, 1969.

Hirsch, Eric L. *Urban Revolt: Ethnic Politics in the Nineteenth-Century Chicago Labor Movement*. Berkeley: University of California Press, 1990.

Hofmeister, Rudolph. *The Germans of Chicago*. Urbana: University of Illinois Press, 1976.

Hofstadter, Richard. *The Idea of a Party System*. Berkeley: University of California Press, 1969.

Holli, Melvin G. *Reform in Detroit: Hazen F. Pingree and Urban Politics*. New York: Oxford University Press, 1969.

Holli, Melvin G., and Paul R. Green, eds. *The Mayors: The Chicago Political Tradition*. Carbondale: Southern Illinois University Press, 1986.

Holli, Melvin G., and Peter d'A. Jones, eds. *Ethnic Chicago*. Grand Rapids: W. B. Eerdsman Publishing Co., 1981.

———. *The Ethnic Frontier*. Grand Rapids: W. B. Eerdsman, 1974.

Hoyt, Homer. *One Hundred Years of Land Values in Chicago*. Chicago: University of Chicago Press, 1933.

Hutchinson, William R. *The Modernist Impulse in American Protestantism*. New York: Oxford University Press, 1976.

Hutchinson, William T. *Cyrus Hall McCormick: Harvest, 1856–1884*. New York: D. Appleton and Co., 1925.

Hutton, Paul Andrew. *Phil Sheridan and His Army*. Lincoln: University of Nebraska Press, 1985.

Jaher, Frederick Cople. *The Urban Establishment: Upper Strata in Boston, New York, Charleston, Chicago, and Los Angeles*. Urbana: University of Illinois Press, 1982.

Jellinek, Frank. *The Paris Commune of 1871*. New York: Grosset and Dunlap, 1965.

Jensen, Richard. *The Winning of the Midwest*. Chicago: University of Chicago Press, 1971.

Jentz, John B. "Class and Politics in an Emerging Industrial City: Chicago in the 1860s and 1870s." *Journal of Urban History* 17 (May 1991): 227–63.

———. "Artisan Culture and the Organization of Chicago's German Workers in the Gilded Age, 1860–1900." *Amerikastudien* 29 (1984): 133–48.

Johnson, Paul E. *A Shopkeeper's Millennium: Society and Revivals in Rochester, New York, 1815–1837*. New York: Hill and Wang, 1978.

Joyce, Patrick. *Visions of the People: Industrial England and the Questions of Class, 1848–1914*. New York: Cambridge University Press, 1991.

Kahn, Judd. *Imperial San Francisco: Politics and Planning in an American City, 1897–1906*. Lincoln: University of Nebraska Press, 1983.

Kasson, John F. *Rudeness and Civility: Manners in Nineteenth-Century Urban America*. New York: Hill and Wang, 1990.

Katz, Michael B. *In the Shadow of the Poorhouse*. New York: Basic Books, 1986.

Katznelson, Ira. *City Trenches: Urban Politics and the Patterning of Class in the United States*. New York: Pantheon, 1981.

Keil, Hartmut, and John B. Jentz, eds. *German Workers in Chicago: A Documentary History of Working-Class Culture from 1850 to World War I*. Urbana: University of Illinois Press, 1988.

———. *German Workers in Industrial Chicago, 1850–1910: A Comparative Perspective*. DeKalb: Northern Illinois University Press, 1983.

Keller, Morton. *Affairs of State: Public Life in Late Nineteenth-Century America*. Cambridge, MA: Harvard University Press, 1977.

———. *The Art and Politics of Thomas Nast*. New York: Oxford University Press, 1968.

Kerber, Linda K. *Women of the Republic: Intellect and Ideology in Revolutionary America*. Chapel Hill: University of North Carolina Press, 1980.

Kessler-Harris, Alice. "Social History." In *The New American History*, edited by Foner, 1990.

———. *Out to Work: A History of Wage-Earning Women in the United States*. New York: Oxford University Press, 1982.

Kettner, James. *The Development of American Citizenship, 1608–1870*. Chapel Hill: University of North Carolina Press, 1978.

Keyssar, Alexander. *Out of Work: The First Century of Unemployment in Massachusetts*. New York: Cambridge University Press, 1986.

Kimball, Elisabeth. "We Could Not Do without the Chicago Fire." *Chicago History* 1 (Fall 1971): 89–101.

King, Andrew J. *A Pre-History of Zoning in Chicago*. New York: Garland Publishing, 1986.

Kinsley, Philip. *The Chicago Tribune: Its First Hundred Years*. Vol. 2. *1865–1880*. Chicago: Chicago Tribune Co., 1945.

Kleppner, Paul. *The Third Electoral System, 1853–1892: Parties,*

Voters, and Political Cultures. Chapel Hill: University of North Carolina Press, 1979.

———. *The Cross of Culture: A Social Analysis of Midwestern Politics, 1850–1900.* New York: Free Press, 1970.

Koditschek, Theodore. *Class Formation and Urban Industrial Society: Bradford, 1750–1850.* New York: Cambridge University Press, 1990.

Krout, John. *The Origins of Prohibition.* New York: Alfred A. Knopf, 1925.

Laband, David N., and Deborah Henry Heinbuch. *Blue Laws: The History, Economics, and Politics of Sunday Closing Laws.* Lexington, MA: D. C. Heath, 1987.

Laurie, Bruce. *From Artisan to Worker: Labor in Nineteenth-Century America.* New York: Noonday Press, 1989.

———. *The Working People of Philadelphia, 1800–1850.* Philadelphia: Temple University Press, 1980.

Lebsock, Suzanne. *The Free Women of Petersburg: Status and Culture in a Southern Town, 1784–1860.* New York: W. W. Norton, 1984.

Lees, Andrew. *Cities Perceived.* Manchester: University of Manchester Press, 1985.

Leiren, Terje. "Propaganda as Entertainment: Marcus Thrane and the Chicago Fire." *Scandinavian Journal of History* 14 (Fall 1989): 239–44.

Levine, Bruce C. *The Spirit of 1848: German Immigrants, Labor Conflict, and the Coming of the Civil War.* Urbana: University of Illinois Press, 1992.

Lewis, A. H. *A Critical History of Sunday Legislation.* New York: D. Appleton and Co., 1888.

Lewis, Lloyd, and Henry Justin Smith. *Chicago: The History of Its Reputation.* New York: Harcourt Brace Jovanovitch, 1929.

Licht, Walter F. *Getting Work: Philadelphia, 1840–1950.* Cambridge, MA: Harvard University Press, 1992.

Lipin, Lawrence M. *Producers, Proletarians, and Politicians: Workers and Party Politics in Evansville and New Albany, Indiana, 1850–87.* Urbana: University of Illinois Press, 1994.

Livermore, Mary. *The Story of My Life.* Hartford: A. D. Worthington and Co., 1899.

Loesch, Frank. "Personal Experiences during the Chicago Fire." *Chicago History* 1 (Fall 1971): 202–5.

Logsdon, Joseph. *Horace White: Nineteenth Century Liberal.* Westport, CT: Greenwood Press, 1971.

Lowe, David, ed. *The Great Chicago Fire.* New York: Dover, 1979.

Lubove, Roy. *The Professional Altruist: The Emergence of Social Work as a Career, 1880–1930.* Cambridge, MA: Harvard University Press, 1965.

Luria, Daniel D. "Wealth, Capital, and Power: The Social Meaning of Home Ownership." *Journal of Interdisciplinary History* 2 (1976): 261–82.

McCaffrey, Lawrence J., et al. *The Irish in Chicago*. Urbana: University of Illinois Press, 1987.

McCarthy, Kathleen D. *Noblesse Oblige: Charity and Cultural Philanthropy in Chicago, 1849–1929*. Chicago: University of Chicago Press, 1982.

McCormick, Richard L. "Ethnocultural Interpretations of Voting Behavior." In *The Party Period and Public Policy: American Politics from the Age of Jackson to the Progressive Era*, by Richard L. McCormick. New York: Oxford University Press, 1986.

McDonald, Terrence J. *The Parameters of Urban Fiscal Policy: Socioeconomic Change and Political Culture in San Francisco, 1860–1906*. Berkeley: University of California Press, 1986.

McGerr, Michael E. *The Decline of Popular Politics: The American North, 1865–1928*. New York: Oxford University Press, 1986.

McLoughlin, William G. *Modern Revivalism: Charles Grandison Finney to Billy Graham*. New York: Ronald Press Co., 1959.

McNeill, George E. "The Building Trades." In *The Labor Movement: The Problem of To-Day*, edited by McNeill, 1887.

———. "The Hours of Labor." In *The Labor Movement: The Problem of To-Day*, edited by McNeill, 1887.

———. *The Labor Movement: The Problem of To-Day*. Boston: A. M. Bridgman and Co., 1887.

Mandelbaum, Seymour. *Boss Tweed's New York*. New York: J. Wiley and Co., 1965.

Marsden, George M. *Fundamentalism and American Culture*. New York: Oxford University Press, 1980.

Marx, Leo. *The Machine in the Garden: Technology and the Pastoral Ideal in America*. New York: Oxford University Press, 1964.

Maxwell, William C. *Lincoln's Fifth Wheel: A Political History of the Sanitary Commission*. New York: Longmans, Green, 1956.

Mayer, Harold M., and Richard C. Wade. *Chicago: Growth of a Metropolis*. Chicago: University of Chicago Press, 1969.

Mazur, Edward. "Jewish Chicago: From Diversity to Community." In *The Ethnic Frontier*, edited by Holli and Jones, 1974.

Meites, Hyman L., ed. *A History of the Jews of Chicago*. Chicago: Jewish Historical Society of Illinois, 1924.

Miller, Kerby. "Class, Culture, and Immigrant Group Identity in the United States." In *Immigration Reconsidered*, edited by Yans-McLaughlin, 1990.

———. *Emigrants and Exiles: Ireland and the Irish Exodus to North America*. New York: Oxford University Press, 1985.

Miller, Ross. *American Apocalypse: The Great Fire and the Myth of Chicago*. Chicago: University of Chicago Press, 1990.

———. "Chicago's Secular Apocalypse: The Great Fire and the Emergence of the Democratic Hero." In *Chicago Architecture, 1872–1922: Birth of a Metropolis*, edited by John Zukowsky. Munich: Prestel-Verlag, 1987.

Minow, Martha. "Rights Theories and Contemporary Legal Debates." In *Making All the Difference: Inclusion, Exclusion, and American Law*, by Martha Minow. Ithaca: Cornell University Press, 1990.

Monaghan, Jay. *The Man Who Elected Lincoln*. Indianapolis: Bobbs, Merrill, 1956.

Monkkonen, Eric H. *America Becomes Urban: The Development of U.S. Cities and Towns, 1780–1980*. Berkeley: University of California Press, 1988.

Montgomery, David. *Citizen Worker*. New York: Cambridge University Press, 1993.

———. *The Fall of the House of Labor: The Workplace, the State, and American Labor Activism, 1865–1925*. New York: Cambridge University Press, 1987.

———. "William H. Sylvis and the Search for Working-Class Citizenship." In *Labor Leaders in America*, edited by Melvyn Dubofsky and Warren Van Tine. Urbana: University of Illinois Press, 1987.

———. "The Shuttle and the Cross: Weavers and Artisans in the Kensington Riots of 1844." *Journal of Social History* 5 (1972): 411–46.

———. *Beyond Equality: Labor and the Radical Republicans, 1862–1872*. New York: Random House, 1967.

Montgomery, Royal E. *Industrial Relations in the Chicago Building Trades*. Chicago: University of Chicago Press, 1927.

Morgan, Edmund S. *Inventing the People: The Rise of Popular Sovereignty in England and America*. New York: W. W. Norton, 1987.

Mott, Frank Luther. *American Journalism: A History of Newspapers in the United States through 260 Years, 1690–1950*. Rev. ed. New York: Macmillan, 1950.

———. *Golden Multitudes: The Story of Best Sellers in the United States*. New York: Macmillan, 1947.

Nadel, Stanley. *Little Germany: Ethnicity, Religion and Class in New York City, 1845–1880*. Urbana: University of Illinois Press, 1990.

Naylor, Timothy J. "Responding to the Fire: The Work of the Chicago Relief and Aid Society." *Science and Society* 34 (Fall 1976): 407–19.

Nelson, Bruce C. *Beyond the Martyrs: A Social History of Chicago's Anarchists, 1870–1900*. New Brunswick: Rutgers University Press, 1988.

Nelson, Otto M. "The Chicago Relief and Aid Society, 1850–1874." *Journal of the Illinois State Historical Society* 59 (1966): 48–66.

Nord, David Paul. "The Public Community: The Urbanization of Journalism in Chicago." *Journal of Urban History* 11 (August 1985): 411–41.

Oestricher, Richard. "Urban Working Class Political Behavior and Theories of American Electoral Politics, 1870–1940." *Journal of American History* 74 (March 1988): 1257–86.

O'Neill, John J. "Arbitration." In *The Labor Movement: The Problem of To-Day,* edited by George E. McNeill, 1887.

Pacyga, Dominic, and Ellen Skerrett. *Chicago: City of Neighborhoods*. Chicago: Loyola University Press, 1986.

Palladino, Grace. *Another Civil War: Labor, Capital, and the State in the Anthracite Regions of Pennsylvania*. Urbana: University of Illinois Press, 1990.

Palmer, George Thomas. *A Conscientious Turncoat: The Story of John M. Palmer.* New Haven: Yale University Press, 1941.

Pauly, John J. "The Great Chicago Fire as a National Event." *American Quarterly* 36 (Fall 1985): 668–83.

Pierce, Bessie Louise. *A History of Chicago*. 3 vols. Chicago: University of Chicago Press, 1937–57.

Pole, J. R. *The Pursuit of Equality in American History.* Berkeley: University of California Press, 1978.

Protess, David. "Joseph Medill: Chicago's First Modern Mayor." In *The Mayors: The Chicago Political Tradition*, edited by Holli and Green. Carbondale: Southern Illinois University Press, 1986.

Prude, Jonathan. *The Coming of Industrial Order: Town and Factory Life in Rural Massachusetts, 1810–1860*. New York: Oxford University Press, 1983.

Pyne, Stephen J. *Fire in America: A Cultural History of Wildland Rural Fire*. Princeton: Princeton University Press, 1985.

Randell, Frank A. *The Development of Chicago Building Construction*. Urbana: University of Illinois Press, 1949.

Raphael, Beverly. *When Disaster Strikes: How Individuals and Communities Cope with Catastrophe*. New York: Basic Books, 1986.

Reddy, William. *The Rise of Market Culture: The Textile Trades and French Society, 1750–1900*. New York: Cambridge University Press, 1984.

Renner, Richard Wilson. "In a Perfect Ferment: Chicago, the Know-Nothings, and the Riot for Lager Beer." *Chicago History* 5 (Fall 1976): 161–70.

Reynolds, David. *Faith in Fiction: The Emergency of Religious Literature in America*. Cambridge, MA: Harvard University Press, 1981.

Rice, Bradley. *Progressive Cities: The Commission Government Movement in America, 1901–1920*. Austin: University of Texas Press, 1977.

Rodgers, Daniel. *The Work Ethic in Industrial America, 1850–1920*. Chicago: University of Chicago Press, 1978.

Roediger, David R. *The Wages of Whiteness: Race and the Making of the American Working Class*. New York: Verso, 1991.

Roediger, David R., and Philip S. Foner. *Our Own Time: A History of American Labor and the Working Day*. Westport, CT: Greenwood Press, 1989.

Rosen, Christine Meisner. *The Limits of Power: Great Fires and the Process of City Growth in America*. New York: Cambridge University Press, 1986.

Rosenberg, Charles E. *The Cholera Years: The United States in 1832, 1849, and 1866*. Chicago: University of Chicago Press, 1962.

Rosenzweig, Roy. *Eight Hours for What We Will: Workers and Leisure in an Industrial City, 1870–1920*. New York: Cambridge University Press, 1983.

Ross, Stephen J. *Workers on the Edge: Work, Leisure, and Politics in Industrializing Cincinnati, 1788–1890*. New York: Columbia University Press, 1985.

Rumbarger, John S. *Profits, Power, and Prohibition: Alcohol Reform and the Industrializing of America, 1800–1930*. Albany: State University of New York Press, 1989.

Ryan, Mary P. *Women in Public: Between Banners and Bullets, 1825–1880*. Baltimore: Johns Hopkins University Press, 1990.

———. "The American Parade: Representations of the Nineteenth-Century Social Order." In *The New Cultural History*, edited by Lynn Hunt. Berkeley: University of California Press, 1989.

———. *Cradle of the Middle Class: The Family in Oneida County, New York, 1790–1865*. New York: Cambridge University Press, 1981.

Sawislak, Karen. "Relief, Aid, and Order: Class, Gender, and the Definition of Community in the Aftermath of Chicago's Great Fire." *Journal of Urban History* 20 (November 1993): 3–18.

———. "Smoldering City." *Chicago History* 17 (Fall/Winter 1988–89): 70–101.

Schiesl, Martin J. *The Politics of Efficiency: Municipal Administration and Reform in America, 1880–1920*. Berkeley: University of California Press, 1977.

Schiller, Dan. *Objectivity and the News: The Public and the Rise of*

Commercial Journalism. Philadelphia: University of Pennsylvania Press, 1981.

Schneirov, Richard. "Political Cultures and the Role of the State in Labor's Republic: The View from Chicago, 1848–1877." *Labor History* 32 (Summer 1991): 376–400.

———. "Class Conflict, Municipal Politics, and Governmental Reform in Gilded Age Chicago, 1871–1875." In *German Workers in Industrial Chicago, 1850–1910*, edited by Hartmut Keil and John B. Jentz. DeKalb: Northern Illinois University Press, 1983.

Schudson, Michael P. *Discovering the News: A Social History of American Newspapers*. New York: Basic Books, 1978.

Schultz, April. "'The Pride of the Race Has Been Touched': The 1925 Norse-American Immigration Centennial and Ethnic Identity." *Journal of American History* 77 (March 1991): 1265–95.

Searle, George. *Chicago and Her Churches*. Chicago: Lakeside Press, 1867.

Sellers, Charles S. *The Market Revolution: Jacksonian America, 1815–1846*. New York: Oxford University Press, 1991.

Shklar, Judith. *American Citizenship: The Quest for Inclusion*. Cambridge, MA: Harvard University Press, 1991.

Sizer, Sandra. *Gospel Hymns and Social Religion: The Rhetoric of Nineteenth-Century Revivalism*. Philadelphia: Temple University Press, 1978.

Sklar, Katherine Kish. *Catherine Beecher: A Study in American Domesticity*. New York: W. W. Norton, 1976.

Smith, Carl S. *Urban Disorder and the Shape of Belief: The Great Chicago Fire, the Haymarket Bomb, and the Model Town of Pullman*. Chicago: University of Chicago Press, 1995.

———. "Cataclysm and Cultural Consciousness: Chicago and the Haymarket Trial." *Chicago History* 15 (Summer 1986): 36–53.

———. "Urban Disorder and the Shape of Belief: The San Francisco Earthquake and Fire." *Yale Review* 74 (1984): 79–95.

Smith, Henry Nash. *Virgin Land: The American West as Symbol and Myth*. Cambridge, MA: Harvard University Press, 1950.

Smith-Rosenberg, Carroll. *Religion and the Rise of the American City*. Ithaca: Cornell University Press, 1971.

Snyder, Robert. *The Voice of the City: Vaudeville and Popular Culture in New York*. New York: Oxford University Press, 1989.

Sollors, Werner, ed. *The Invention of Ethnicity*. New York: Oxford University Press, 1989.

Sorenson, Helen Laura. *The Consumer Movement*. New York: Arno Press, 1978.

Sorge, Friedrich A. *The Labor Movement in the United States: A History of the American Working Class from Colonial Times to*

1890. Edited by Philip S. Foner and Brewster Chamberlin. Westport, CT: Greenwood Press, 1977.

Sparling, Samuel. *Municipal History and Present Organization of the City of Chicago*. Bulletin 23. Madison: University of Wisconsin, 1898.

Sproat, John G. *The Best Men: Liberal Reformers in the Gilded Age*. New York: Oxford University Press, 1968.

Stanley, Amy Dru. "Beggars Can't Be Choosers: Compulsion and Contract in Antebellum America." *Journal of American History* 78 (March 1992).

Stansell, Christine M. *City of Women: Sex and Class in New York, 1789–1860*. New York: Alfred A. Knopf, 1987.

Stedman-Jones, Gareth. *Outcast London: A Study in the Relationship between Classes in Victorian Society*. New York: Pantheon, 1971.

Steedman, Carolyn Kay. *Landscape for a Good Woman*. New Brunswick: Rutgers University Press, 1987.

Steinberg, Allen. *The Transformation of American Criminal Justice: Philadelphia, 1800–1880*. Chapel Hill: University of North Carolina Press, 1989.

Steinfeld, Robert. *The Invention of Free Labor: Employment Relations in English and American Law and Culture, 1350–1870*. Chapel Hill: University of North Carolina Press, 1991.

Stekloff, G. M. *History of the First International*. London: M. Lawrence, Ltd., 1928.

Stoddard, William O. *The Volcano under the City, by a Volunteer Special*. New York: Fords, Howard, and Hulbert, 1887.

Stout, Janis. *Sodoms in Eden*. Westport, CT: Greenwood Press, 1976.

Strong, Josiah. *Our Country*. New York: Baker and Taylor, 1891.

Suhrbuhr, Thomas J., and Richard Schneirov. *Union Brotherhood, Union Town: The History of the Carpenters' Union of Chicago, 1863–1987*. Carbondale: Southern Illinois University Press, 1988.

Summers, Mark Wahlgren. *The Press Gang: Newspapers and Politics, 1865–1878*. Chapel Hill: University of North Carolina Press, 1994.

Sylvis, James C. *The Life, Speeches, Labors, and Essays of William H. Sylvis*. Philadelphia: Green, Remsen, and Haffelfinger, 1872.

Teaford, Jon C. *The Unheralded Triumph: City Government in America, 1870–1900*. Baltimore: Johns Hopkins University Press, 1984.

Tombs, Robert. *The War against Paris*. Cambridge: Cambridge University Press, 1981.

Tomlins, Christopher L. *Law, Labor, and Ideology in the Early American Republic*. New York: Cambridge University Press, 1993.

Trachtenberg, Alan. *The Incorporation of America: Culture and Society in the Gilded Age*. New York: Hill and Wang, 1982.

Trattner, Walter. *From Poor Laws to Welfare State: A History of Social Welfare in America*. New York: Free Press, 1984.

Tyler, Alice Felt. *Freedom's Ferment*. Minneapolis: University of Minnesota Press, 1946.

Tyrrell, Ian. *Sobering Up: From Temperance to Prohibition in Antebellum America*. Westport, CT: Greenwood Press, 1979.

Unger, Irwin. *The Greenback Era: A Social and Political History of American Finance, 1865–1879*. Princeton: Princeton University Press, 1964.

Vinovskis, Maris, ed. *Towards a Social History of the American Civil War: Exploratory Essays*. New York: Cambridge University Press, 1990.

Wade, Louise Carroll. *Chicago's Pride: The Stockyards, Packingtown, and Environs in the Nineteenth Century*. Urbana: University of Illinois Press, 1986.

Walker, Mack. *Germany and the Emigration, 1816–1885*. Cambridge, MA: Harvard University Press, 1964.

Walsh, Justin. *To Print the News and Raise Hell! A Biography of Wilbur F. Storey*. Chapel Hill: University of North Carolina Press, 1968.

Ward, David. *Poverty, Ethnicity, and the American City, 1840–1925: Changing Conceptions of the Slum and the Ghetto*. Cambridge: Cambridge University Press, 1989.

———. *Cities and Immigrants: A Geography of Change in Nineteenth-Century America*. New York: Oxford University Press, 1971.

Waskin, Mel. *Mrs. O'Leary's Comet! Cosmic Explanations for the Great Chicago Fire*. Chicago: Academy Chicago, 1984.

Wendt, Lloyd. *The Chicago Tribune: The Rise of a Great American Newspaper*. Chicago: Rand McNally, 1979.

Wiebe, Robert H. *The Search for Order, 1877–1920*. New York: Hill and Wang, 1967.

Wilentz, Sean. *Chants Democratic: New York City and the Rise of the American Working Class, 1788–1850*. New York: Oxford University Press, 1984.

———. "Artisanal Republican Festivals and the Rise of Class Conflict in New York City, 1788–1837." In *Working-Class America*, edited by Michael H. Frisch and Daniel J. Walkowitz, Urbana: University of Illinois Press, 1983.

Wirth, Louis B. "Urbanism as a Way of Life." In Wirth, *On Cities and Social Life: Selected Papers*. Chicago: University of Chicago Press, 1964.

Wright, Gwendolyn. *Building the Dream: A Social History of Housing in America*. New York: Pantheon, 1981.

Yans-McLaughlin, Virginia, ed. *Immigration Reconsidered: History, Sociology, and Politics*. New York: Oxford University Press, 1990.

Yearley, Clifton K. *Britons in American Labor: A History of the Influence of United Kingdom Immigrants on American Labor, 1820–1914*. Baltimore: Johns Hopkins University Press, 1957.

Zunz, Olivier. *Making America Corporate, 1870–1920*. Chicago: University of Chicago Press, 1990.

———. *The Changing Face of Inequality: Urbanization, Industrial Development, and Immigrants in Detroit, 1880–1920*. Chicago: University of Chicago Press, 1982.

B. Unpublished Materials

Albares, Richard P. "The Structural Ambivalence of German Ethnicity in Chicago." Ph.D. diss., University of Chicago, 1981.

Ballard, Thomas. "Distribution of Chicago's Germans, 1850–1914." M.A. thesis, University of Chicago, 1969.

Bubnys, Edward Leo. "Chicago, 1870 and 1900: Wealth, Occupation, and Education." Ph.D. diss., University of Illinois at Urbana, 1978.

Buettinger, Craig. "The Concept of Jacksonian Aristocracy: Chicago as a Test Case, 1833–57." Ph.D. diss, Northwestern University, 1982.

Eckstrom, Peter. "Ethnic Community and the American Legal System: German-American Opposition to Chicago Temperance Ordinances." Unpublished seminar paper, University of Chicago, 1992.

Hirsch, Eric L. "Revolution or Reform: An Analytic History of an Urban Labor Movement." Ph.D. diss., University of Chicago, 1981.

Larsen, Lowell Dean. "Constitutionalism in Crisis: The Case of the Great Chicago Fire." M.A. thesis, University of Chicago, 1962.

Leiken, Stephen Bernard. "The Practical Utopians: Cooperation and the American Labor Movement, 1860–1890." Ph.D. diss., University of California, Berkeley, 1992.

Marks, Donald David. "Polishing the Gem of the Prairie: The Evolution of Civic Reform Consciousness in Chicago, 1874–1900." Ph.D. diss., University of Wisconsin, 1974.

Mayer, John Albert. "Private Charity in Chicago from 1871 to 1915." Ph.D. diss., University of Minnesota, 1978.

Pauly, John J. "The City Builders: Chicago Businessmen and Their Changing Ethos." Ph.D. diss., University of Illinois at Urbana, 1979.

Sawislak, Karen Lynn. "Smoldering City: Class, Ethnicity, and Politics in Chicago at the Time of the Great Fire, 1867–1874." Ph.D. diss., Yale University, 1990.

Schall, Robert. "The History of Fort Sheridan, Illinois." Unpublished manuscript, Chicago Historical Society, 1944.

Schneirov, Richard. "The Knights of Labor in the Chicago Labor Movement and in Municipal Politics, 1877–1887." Ph.D. diss., Northern Illinois University, 1984.

Schultz, Rima L. "The Businessman's Role in Western Settlement: The Entrepreneurial Frontier, Chicago, 1833–1872." Ph.D. diss., Boston University, 1985.

Scobey, David M. "Empire City: Politics, Culture, and Urbanism in Gilded Age New York." Ph.D. diss., Yale University, 1989.

Zeiren, Gregory R. "The Propertied Worker: Working-Class Formation in Toledo, Ohio, 1870–1900." Ph.D. diss., University of Delaware, 1981.

INDEX

Note: Italic page numbers indicate locations of illustrations.